MW01040550

Students,

If your instructor is using CourseBank, the code below will allow you to register for free. To register, use the URL and directions provided by your instructor

Scratch here for your access code

This code is only valid for a single user. This code may be invalid if the protective scratch-off coating covering the code has been removed and redeemed by the book's previous owner.

Instructors,

CourseBank is a pre-built online course for your LMS, with learning assets and auto-graded assignments. CourseBank easily integrates with Blackboard, Canvas, D2L, Moodle, and any other LMS for a single sign-on and single grade book experience.

support@chicagobusinesspress.com

Professional
SELLING

Dawn R. Deeter
Kansas State University

Gary K. Hunter
Clemson University

Terry W. Loe
Kennesaw State University

Gregory A. Rich
Bowling Green State University

Ryan Mullins
Clemson University

Lisa Beeler
Ohio University

Wyatt Schrock
Michigan State University

CHICAGO
BUSINESS PRESS

PROFESSIONAL STAFFING

For product information or assistance, please visit
www.chicagobusinesspress.com

ISBN: 978-1-948426-17-6

Brief Table of Contents

Table of Contents

4 Lead Generation and Prospecting 65

14 Role-Play   263

About The Authors

Dawn Deeter – Kansas State University   Dr. Deeter is an experienced sales leader. She built and leads the National Strategic Selling Institute at Kansas State University. After earning her Ph.D. from the University of South Florida in 1998, Deeter has served on the faculties of Monmouth University, Ohio University, and Kansas State University.   During that time, she has earned numerous teaching awards, including the Hormel Teaching Excellence Award, the Kansas State Bank Outstanding Teaching Award, and the 2016 K-State Professor of the Year.

Gary Hunter – Clemson University   Dr. Hunter is Associate Professor of Marketing at Clemson University. His primary research centers on sales technology, strategic account management, and negotiations and includes three award-winning "best paper" publications. It appears in the Journal of Marketing, International Journal of Research in Marketing, Journal of Business Research, Industrial Marketing Management, and the Journal of Personal Selling & Sales Management, among other outlets. Gary has taught courses in sales and marketing in undergraduate, graduate, and executive education programs. His academic career followed more than 10 years of leadership, management, sales, and marketing experiences with the US Army, PepsiCo, and Procter & Gamble.

Terry Loe – Kennesaw State University   Dr. Loe is currently the Co-Director of the Center for Professional Selling and Professor of marketing and sales at Kennesaw State University. Prior to entering academia, Dr. Loe spent eleven years in industry in sales and marketing. He received his PhD from the University of Memphis in 1996. Dr. Loe taught at Baylor University for 7 years serving as the Assistant Director of the Center for Professional Selling where he founded the National Collegiate Sales Competition (NCSC) and continues to serve as the Executive Director. Since its inception in 1999 the NCSC has contributed more than $6.5 million to the university sales community. Dr. Loe has published more than 50 articles in the areas of sales, sales management and ethics, and received several excellence in teaching and research awards.

Greg Rich – Bowling Green State University   Dr. Rich is a marketing professor at Bowling Green State University, where he focuses his teaching and research on professional selling and sales management issues. His other publications include the textbook Sales Force Management and a number of articles in leading marketing journals, such as the Journal of the Academy of Marketing Science and Journal of Personal Selling and Sales Management. Greg regularly coaches undergraduate students for the National Collegiate Sales Competition and other case competitions, and is co-developer of a sales force simulation game called Cantopia. Greg has a Ph.D. in Business from Indiana University (1995). He enjoys golfing, jogging, playing guitar and spending time with his wife Linda and their three sons.

Ryan Mullins – Clemson University   Dr. Mullins is an award-winning author, professor, and consultant, focused on helping leaders improve sales force performance. He has authored 16 academic articles, with 7 of those appearing in the Financial Times Top 50 business journals in the world. In the classroom, Ryan teaches courses focused on personal selling, sales management, and sales leadership while also serving as the director for the Sales Innovation Program. Ryan greatly enjoys industry collaborations and has conducted research projects with Fortune 500 companies, providing data analysis, insight, and training interventions when needed.

Lisa Beeler - Ohio University   Dr. Beeler took her first sales role in 2005, with a B2B home décor company. She didn't know at the time that this job would alter the course of her life. Lisa fell in love with all things sales over the next eight years as she worked her way up to becoming the National Marketing & Sales Director of a B2B services firm in Atlanta, GA. A passion for teaching and mentorship lead Lisa to attain a PhD from the University of Tennessee in 2017. Since then, she has been a teacher and researcher of all things sales and marketing.

Wyatt Schrock – Michigan State University Dr. Schrock is an Assistant Professor of Marketing at Michigan State University. Dr. Schrock holds a Ph.D. (Marketing) from Michigan State University, an M.B.A. (Finance) from the University of Miami, and a B.B.A. (Marketing) from the University of Michigan. Dr. Schrock's research interests include salesperson motivation and sales manager leadership. His research has received the annual James M. Comer Award for "Best Contribution to Selling and Sales Management Theory." He serves on the Editorial Review Board at the Journal of Personal Selling & Sales Management. Dr. Schrock also has ten years of corporate experience in sales-related roles, working for companies such as Procter & Gamble and Gannett.

Acknowledgements

With deep gratitude, we acknowledge the reviewers who gave us ideas and advice. Professional Selling is a better book because of their willingness to share their insightful input.

Nicolo Alaimo, Florida International University
Aaron Arndt, Old Dominion University
Carolyn Curasi, Georgia State University
Steve Dahlquist, Grand Valley State University
Rebecca Dingus, Central Michigan University
Diane Edmondson, Middle Tennessee State University
Aaron Gleiberman, Louisiana State University
Rich Gooner, University of Georgia
Charles Howlett, Northern Illinois University
Alicia Lupinacci, Tarrant County Community College
Robert Nadeau, Plymouth State University
Steve Tufts, University of Florida
Vicki West, Texas State University

And special thanks to Abbey Woodward of Salesforce, who's expertise with the platform and experience in higher education made her uniquely qualified to relate the specific features and functionality of Salesforce to the concepts in the book.

Instructor Supplements

Adopters will be supported by an instructor's manual, test bank, and lecture PowerPoints. The book is also available with *CourseBank*, a pre-built online course of assets and auto-graded assignments that easily integrates with Blackboard, Canvas, D2L, or any other LMS.

CHAPTER 1

Sales and Today's Sales Role

Learning Objectives

- Define and describe sales as a position in an organization
- Understand the benefits associated with a sales role
- Explain the skills and traits that lead to sales success
- Summarize how the sales role has transformed
- Compare and contrast the different types of sales roles
- Evaluate the eight different sales myths

hat do the following people have in common?

- A retail associate who works at the local Apple store
- A car dealership salesperson
- A consultant who helps companies improve their internal communications
- A political candidate who seeks election to local office
- A warehouse expert who creates innovative solutions for manufacturing clients
- An entrepreneur trying to secure funding for a startup
- A job candidate interviewing with a new potential employer
- A community activist trying to change a local ordinance or policy
- An attorney attempting to convince a new client to retain their law firm

If you guessed that all of these people are in sales, you are right. Although a retail or car salesperson might represent a more commonly held view of someone working in sales, in today's environment almost everyone engages in sales behavior in some form or another. A consultant has to sell a company on the benefits of her services before she can help them improve internal communications. A political candidate has to sell his ideas in exchange for votes. A warehouse expert is working as a consultative seller to improve customers' businesses. In fact, according to Daniel Pink, author of *To Sell Is Human*, over 10% of the American workforce is employed in a sales role, and those in non-sales roles engage in what would typically be considered sales activities, such as persuasion and influence, approximately 40% of the time.[1] If you learn how to sell effectively, you are much more likely to be successful in your professional life.

In this chapter, we define the sales process and examine the benefits associated with understanding the sales process. We then review the traits and skills associated with sales, briefly describe the transformation of the sales process, and compare and contrast the different types of roles in sales. Finally, we end the chapter with a critique of the eight great myths associated with a sales role.

What Is Sales?

According to most dictionaries, the term *sales* refers to an exchange of a product or service for money. A career in sales, however, involves much more than this definition reflects. Although the ultimate goal of the selling process may be to exchange a product for money, that activity reflects a simple transaction. In reality, sales includes all the activities related to selling a product or service to a buyer. These activities include, but are not limited to, understanding industries, markets, and products; finding potential customers; learning about customers and their various problems and needs; determining solutions; communicating benefits; monitoring the order process and shipping; ensuring customer satisfaction; and much, much more. It might take a salesperson hours, months, or even years to achieve the result of an exchange of money for a product, depending on the type of product sold and the needs of the customer. And, it is worth noting that the exchange does not always involve a product in exchange for money. Non-profits "sell" potential customers on the value of donations, and consultants "sell" potential customers their ideas and opinions. Regardless of the product or service sold, most salespeople today act as consultants, helping customers solve problems and become more successful. When the customer is successful, the salesperson and the salesperson's company are also successful.

The Benefits of Sales Experience and Understanding the Sales Process

The opportunities available to students interested in a sales career are immense. Why? Because nothing happens in a business until somebody makes a sale. That sale sets into motion all other business functions, from accounting to shipping to hiring and recruiting. Every industry and every company, from small business-to-consumer retail stores to massive manufacturers, needs someone to start the sales process for the company to stay in business. There are several reasons why understanding the sales process is beneficial.

Take Advantage of the Global Sales Talent Shortage

Because every company and industry seeks to hire highly qualified sales talent, a sales talent shortage has developed globally. Manpower Group has routinely identified the role of the sales representative as one of the most difficult to fill, with the sales role included in the top five most difficult positions to fill for each of the last ten years.[2] Further, CSO Insights has reported in their 2018 Sales Talent Study that only 16% of sales executives believe they have the necessary sales talent in place in their organizations to ensure ongoing success.[3] What does this mean for an undergraduate student in a sales class? Job opportunities in sales are plentiful. Table 1-1 illustrates employment projections for sales and sales-related occupations through 2026, as reported by the Bureau of Labor Statistics, United States Department of Labor. Total sales-related jobs are expected to rise 7.1% over the next ten years, with an average median annual wage of almost $71,000. Demand is expected to increase in all roles reported except for advertising sales.

Given this demand for sales talent, it is not surprising that approximately 30% of business graduates and 80% of marketing majors accept a sales position immediately after graduation.[4,5] Not all of these graduates, however, have taken a sales class and understand what it means to be a sales professional. Those who develop a strong set of sales skills and a professional attitude can make the most of this important career opportunity.

Make a Meaningful Contribution Quickly

For people wishing to make a quick and meaningful impact on a company, sales could be the right career choice. Salespeople who put forth a great deal of effort and succeed early on are likely to be noticed by superiors and may receive an early promotion. Evaluation of the sales role is performance-based; performing well is rewarded with commissions, bonuses, and/or promotions. Such salespeople would have the opportunity to take on important company roles at a young age.

Furthermore, because salespeople bring in revenues for the firm, the sales role can be a spotlight career for top performers. As figure 1-1 illustrates, many well-known, successful business people got their start in sales. Howard Schultz, CEO of Starbucks, began his career as a sales representative at Xerox. One of the world's richest men, Warren Buffett, started his career selling securities (after a stint as a paperboy). Billionaire Mark Cuban (Dallas Mavericks, Shark Tank) started his path to fame and fortune selling software. William C. Weldon, retired CEO of Johnson & Johnson, started his career at the same firm as a pharmaceutical representative.[6] Success as a salesperson can drive your career into many exciting directions if you take advantage of the opportunities created.

Table 1-1 Employment Projections through 2026, Sales and Sales-Related Occupations

Occupation Title	Employment 2016 (thousands)	Projected Employment 2026 (thousands)	Projected Employment change, 2016-2026 (thousands)	Projected Employment change, 2016-2026 (percent)	Projected Occupational openings, 2016-2026 annual average (thousands)	2018 median annual wage
Advertising sales agents	149.9	144.5	-5.4	-3.6	17.7	$51,740
Insurance sales agents	501.4	551.2	49.8	9.9	54.7	$50,600
Personal financial advisors	271.9	312.3	40.4	14.9	25.5	$88,890
Real estate brokers	95.3	100	4.7	4.9	9.3	$58,210
Real estate sales agents	348.8	369	20.2	5.8	34.4	$48,690
Sales engineers	74.9	80.1	5.2	6.9	8.3	$101,420
Sales managers	385.5	414.4	28.9	7.5	36.3	$124,220
Sales representatives, services, all other	983	1,077.90	94.9	9.7	131	$54,550
Sales representatives, wholesale and manufacturing, except technical and scientific products	1,469.90	1,546.30	76.4	5.2	158.4	$58,510
Sales representatives, wholesale and manufacturing, technical and scientific products	343.6	361.3	17.6	5.1	37	$79,680
Securities, commodities, and financial services sales agents	375.7	398.9	23.3	6.2	38	$64,120
TOTAL SALES-RELATED JOBS	4999.9	5355.9	356	7.1	550.6	$70,966.36

Source: Bureau of Labor Statistics, United States Department of Labor, https://data.bls.gov/projections/occupationProj. Accessed 5.25.2019.

Figure 1-1 Business Giants Who Started in Sales

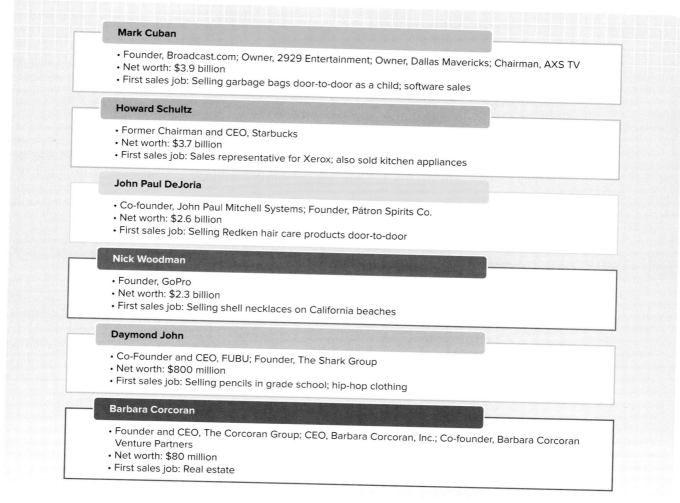

Mark Cuban
- Founder, Broadcast.com; Owner, 2929 Entertainment; Owner, Dallas Mavericks; Chairman, AXS TV
- Net worth: $3.9 billion
- First sales job: Selling garbage bags door-to-door as a child; software sales

Howard Schultz
- Former Chairman and CEO, Starbucks
- Net worth: $3.7 billion
- First sales job: Sales representative for Xerox; also sold kitchen appliances

John Paul DeJoria
- Co-founder, John Paul Mitchell Systems; Founder, Pátron Spirits Co.
- Net worth: $2.6 billion
- First sales job: Selling Redken hair care products door-to-door

Nick Woodman
- Founder, GoPro
- Net worth: $2.3 billion
- First sales job: Selling shell necklaces on California beaches

Daymond John
- Co-Founder and CEO, FUBU; Founder, The Shark Group
- Net worth: $800 million
- First sales job: Selling pencils in grade school; hip-hop clothing

Barbara Corcoran
- Founder and CEO, The Corcoran Group; CEO, Barbara Corcoran, Inc.; Co-founder, Barbara Corcoran Venture Partners
- Net worth: $80 million
- First sales job: Real estate

Sources: Efti, Steli. https://blog.close.com/5-mega-successful-entrepreneurs-who-launched-their-careers-in-sales. https://money.cnn.com/interactive/economy/my-american-success-story-daymond-john/index.html. https://wealthygorilla.com/barbara-corcoran-net-worth/.

Build a Powerful Network

In the book *Endless Referrals*, author Bob Burg defines a network as "an arrangement of people crossed at regular intervals by other people, all of whom are cultivating mutually beneficial, give-and-take, win-win relationships with each other." In the highly acclaimed book *The Go-Giver*, authors Bob Burg and John David Mann expand on this idea by discussing the value of having your own "army of personal walking ambassadors."[7] In other words, the more people we know and are in our corner, the more people who can help us, and whom we can help. With a strong network, you can communicate with colleagues to further develop sales skills, get feedback on how to deal with a customer problem, find a mentor, or find a new job, among other things.

Importantly, a strong network can result in **referrals**. A referral occurs when someone provides a recommendation for a potential customer or gives an endorsement when speaking to others. Referrals are very powerful and can help in a variety of ways. In sales, referrals are an excellent way to expand your customer base. Referrals are also extremely helpful when trying to find a first job or switch jobs mid-career. A powerful network means you have more influence, and more influence means you can add more value to more people.

referrals

when someone provides a recommendation for a potential customer or gives an endorsement when speaking to others

Build a Flexible Career

A career in sales offers flexibility that can be beneficial as your life and priorities change over time. If in outside sales, you may work from a home office. Even with an inside sales job, working out of an office, a flexible schedule is likely. Companies care most about the ability to meet and exceed sales goals and deliver value to customers and the employer. If a salesperson is delivering on these expectations, then there is more flexibility. For example, get all your calls in for the day, and you might be able to take off early to see your child's soccer game.

Keep in mind, of course, that with this flexibility comes responsibility. Good time management skills and internal motivation are crucial to being successful in this type of environment. The salesperson must deliver on your performance goals. Moreover, the flexibility will need to be extended to customers; if a customer has a problem after 5:00 p.m., for example, it will likely be important to take that call. Ultimately, a flexible career is very beneficial if you have the organizational skills and drive to make it work for yourself, the company, and the customers.

Be in Charge of Your Destiny

Many people who are in sales say they enjoy being in charge of their destiny. This benefit ties to sales compensation plans. Although some straight-salary sales jobs exist, most sales roles include a base salary plus some form of bonus and commission structure (see Table 1-2 for examples). The harder you work, and the better the performance, the higher the compensation. Because there is a direct correlation between effort and performance, the salesperson is responsible for the outcomes. For someone who wants to create his or her own success, a sales role can be a good fit.

Get the Desired Job or Promotion

Even if we don't end up in a sales role, the selling skills are invaluable. How? On every job interview, we are selling our skills and value. Need a raise? We can use our selling skills to negotiate a positive outcome with our boss. Heading into an accounting position at a top accounting firm? Accountants who make partner bring clients to the business; whether the accountants realize it or not, that is a sales role. Starting our own business? We will need to sell our idea to investors as well as to customers. The list goes on and on.

Table 1-2 Examples of Sales Compensation Plans

Compensation Plan	Definition
Salary Only	The sales representative is paid a salary without a bonus or commission; the salary is not tied to productivity.
Straight-Line Commission	The sales representative is paid based on how much that representative sells; 100% of the compensation paid is from commission earned on sales. The commission paid is usually somewhere between 5% and 45% of sales.
Base Salary Plus Commission	The sales representative earns a fixed annual salary plus commission, providing the safety of a salary plus a motivational incentive. The industry standard is 60% salary, 40% commission.
Base Salary Plus Bonus	Similar to *Base Salary Plus Commission*, in that the sales representative earns a fixed salary. However, instead of earning a commission, the representative earns a fixed bonus amount for achieving set goals.

Source: Baker, Kristen. "The Ultimate Guide to Sales Compensation." Hubspot. https://blog.hubspot.com/sales/sales-compensation?_ga=2.152612479.736291923.1556077506-54427254.1534474280.

Perhaps Daniel Pink sums it up best in *To Sell Is Human*: "The ability to move others to exchange what they have for what we have is crucial to our survival and our happiness."[8] Regardless of the career path, if working in a business, you will need to understand customers. Having a sales role early in a career supplies the opportunity to develop intuition about customer behavior. Most product and marketing managers begin their careers in sales because it gives them experience applying marketing concepts one customer at a time. Further, because salespeople drive business growth, successful salespeople often are rewarded with additional leadership opportunities. As a consequence, everyone can benefit from understanding how to sell.

Sales and Entrepreneurs

Related to the previous discussion, aspiring entrepreneurs also benefit from starting their careers in a sales role. Experts have noted that how one sells can be more important than what one sells. When early-stage entrepreneurs fail, it is usually because they do a poor job at selling their ideas, not because the product or business idea is bad. Understanding how to sell is especially important to entrepreneurs, who must sell their products or business idea not only to potential customers but also to potential investors and other sources of capital.

One author offers five reasons that entrepreneurs should start in sales prior to starting a business: (1) build tenacity and the ability to deal with failure and rejection, (2) improve networking skills, (3) improve the ability to make persuasive arguments, (4) learn how to set and achieve realistic goals, and (5) understand what customers and markets are seeking.[9] Others suggest entrepreneurs can benefit from understanding how to identify customer problems, becoming comfortable with approaching qualified prospects and asking for referrals, recognizing the need to focus on the problems solved by a product rather than the product itself, and understanding how to sell the company.[10] Entrepreneurs can improve their chances of success tremendously by learning how to sell.

The Sales Professional: What Leads to Sales Success?

Now that it is clear that knowing and being able to apply the sales process is a benefit, perhaps we should consider what skills and traits lead to sales success. When we ask students what they think are the top traits of successful salespeople, they usually say things like "good speaking skills" and "extrovert." Although extroverts with good speaking skills can be successful salespeople, these traits don't necessarily lead to sales success. Students are often surprised to learn that introverts can be very successful in sales. So, what traits and skills do lead to sales success?

Strong Communication Skills

Certainly, the ability to speak and present can contribute to sales success. But other communication skills are equally, and in some cases even more, important. The communication skill routinely identified as most important to sales success is *listening*. Surprised? Yes, successful salespeople spend most of their time asking good questions and subsequently listening to the answers, not talking endlessly about their products. Of particular importance is **active listening**, a distinct type of listening in which the person listening receives a message from an individual, internally evaluates that message and then responds to the message sender to confirm the message was received as intended.[11] Active listening is the best way to uncover what customers need and want. Active listening and asking good questions may also help uncover problems in the customer's company they may not have recognized. Not surprisingly, research

active listening
hearing what an individual says, internally evaluating the message and then responding to confirm the message was received as intended

has found that a customer's perceptions of a salesperson's listening behavior affect the relationship between that customer and salesperson, including trust development and anticipation of future interactions.[12] The good news is that it is possible to develop your active listening and questioning skills. And, a quick note to the introverts reading this textbook—research by Adam Grant on introverts, extroverts, and ambiverts (individuals in the middle of the extrovert scale who display traits of both introverts and extroverts) indicates that you can be very successful in sales by taking advantage of your natural tendency to listen rather than speak.[13]

Writing skills are also important to salespeople. Much communication will take place via email and text. Emailing and texting with a client, however, are much different than with friends. Your writing—even when using more informal modes of communication—sends a message about your level of competence and professionalism. The person who possesses or develops strong writing skills will surpass many peers and competitors.

Negotiation Skills

negotiation
a bargaining process focused on reaching an agreement or compromise

Negotiation is a bargaining process focused on reaching an agreement or compromise. Or, as stated by negotiation expert G. Richard Shell, a "negotiation is an interactive communication process that may take place whenever we want something from someone else or another person wants something from us."[14] Not surprisingly, buyers and sellers frequently find themselves in a position to negotiate something, whether it be a purchase price, contract terms, or some other detail. As such, salespeople need to possess good negotiation skills.

Everyone engages in negotiation at some point. A child may have negotiated bedtime or allowance. An adult will likely negotiate a car or house purchase. Still, not everyone has the strong negotiation skills needed in a sales role. Fortunately, negotiation skills can be learned, practiced, and improved.

Business Acumen

business acumen
the ability to understand and address business situations quickly and effectively

In the past, salespeople sold products and took orders. Although this remains true for some sales roles (largely in the retail sector), it is not accurate for the bulk of business-to-business sales positions. Today's seller is a consultant for clients, helping those customers improve their businesses and make their lives easier. Thus, **business acumen**—the ability to understand and address business situations quickly and effectively—is a crucial skill to possess.

As noted by author Bob Rickert in the book *Profit Heroes*, sales today is about contributing to the customer's documented profitability and earnings.[15] As a consequence, a successful salesperson needs to be familiar with all aspects of a business: not only sales and marketing, but also accounting and finance. The salesperson who understands how the product or service can help improve the customer's revenue stream and cost structures, and who can articulate that solution effectively, will be a tremendous asset for the client.

fizkes

Other-Focused

Contrary to popular belief, sales is not about the salesperson and how much the person can sell. It is about how much value can be brought to customers and how to help improve their lives. By staying focused on delivering value to others rather than turning inward, the sales results will follow. One of the classic books on this topic is the previously mentioned *The Go-Giver*.[16] Through the use of a parable, authors Bob Burg and John David Mann relay a series of "laws" that will help enable tremendous success.

One of the most important messages in this book is to stay focused on others and provide more value than we receive. This philosophy, more than anything else, is the underpinning of sales success.

One sales program alumnus provides an example of how staying focused on others can lead to success. A recent graduate of a university sales program once called his professor to tell her he had been named top salesperson for the quarter. He had graduated eight months earlier and earned this honor over colleagues who had been selling 20 years or more. When asked what he was doing to be successful, he said he woke up each day and thought about how he could make his customers' lives better. He focused on adding value daily, and the rest fell into place. Everyone won—the customer, the salesperson's company, and the salesperson.

Resilient with a Will to Win

Resilience is an important trait for salespeople, largely because salespeople deal with rejection on a routine basis. Rejection is a normal part of sales. Not every sales call will be successful, and most won't. To handle this rejection successfully, one must be resilient and be able to remove emotion from the equation. The customer is not rejecting you; rather, your product is not the right fit, or it is not clear to the customer how your product will provide a solution to the problem. After recognizing that the rejection is not personal, the ability to deal with it becomes much easier.

A "will to win" goes hand-in-hand with resilience. Competitiveness can lead to sales success. Some employers call this trait "fire in the belly." Scholar and author Angela Duckworth identifies this trait as **grit**, a never-give-up attitude based on both passion and perseverance. According to Duckworth, grit relies heavily on effort: effort builds skill, and effort makes skill productive.[17] When you possess grit, you will be able to deal with the rejection more easily, be driven to beat your goals, and also handle the freedom that can come with the sales role because you are willing to work as hard as it takes to achieve your goals. What it does NOT mean is a desire to win at all costs. Rather, you have a desire to win *and* help your clients win, too.

grit
a never-give-up attitude based on both passion and perseverance

Self-Motivated and Willingness to Accept Challenge

Business speaker and author David McNally states that "motivation is completely and entirely an inside job."[18] In other words, only we can motivate ourselves to do something; no one else can do that for us. Extrinsic rewards such as compensation and bonuses *can* encourage certain activities. However, without internal motivation, the effects of external rewards will be short-lived. Self-motivation will keep us driving toward goals in the face of rejection and other obstacles.

A willingness to challenge yourself is another important trait. Are you willing to push the boundaries of your comfort zone to get on the phone and call someone you have never met? Will you push past your fear of leading a presentation or asking for the sale? Getting comfortable with being uncomfortable can help you grow both personally and professionally. Internship training at one organization, for example, includes phone calls to potential customers who have been difficult to approach. These calls can be tough, and the interns experience not only rejection but rudeness. Successful interns are the ones who push past their fears to start making these calls and learn from each effort. Over time, the calls get easier as the interns learn what works well and what to avoid. They also continue to build their resilience.

Dedicated to Lifelong Learning

Good salespeople dedicate time to their craft. They read sales books and attend training sessions. They do role-plays at work, and they discuss their sales approach with their colleagues, sales managers, and mentors or coaches. Their goal is continuous improvement because improving selling skills improves performance.

If you've been an athlete or musician at some point in your past, you know that the only way to stay performance-ready is through continued practice and learning. The same is true for sales.

Ability to Constantly Learn and Use New Technology

Companies have more access to sales technology than ever before. As a consequence, today's salespeople are very likely to be using one or more types of technology. The good news is that members of the younger generation are very comfortable with technology. Success, however, requires that one be not only comfortable with technology but also devoted to constantly learning about new technologies and learning how to use them effectively to grow sales and serve the clients.

In this textbook, we'll discuss many new forms of technology that directly affect sales, but the most common type of sales technology in use today is a **Customer Relationship Management (CRM)** system. Many companies use cloud-based systems such as Salesforce.com or Microsoft Dynamics, to name a few, to manage customer interaction, manage information, and track the **sales pipeline**, a comprehensive view of where customers are in the sales process. Many of these systems now use artificial intelligence (AI) to provide more comprehensive information on potential customers and customers. The more strategically you can use your company CRM system, the better you can keep your sales process moving toward closing and better serve the customers.

Customer relationship management systems represent just one form of technology. Salespeople commonly use LinkedIn to search for potential customers and companies such as HubSpot for social selling. Software exists to help map sales territory or improve sales conversation skills. The variety of sales enablement tools is mind-boggling. Importantly, the key is to understand how to use these tools efficiently to leverage them in order to exceed goals and serve customers more effectively.

Good Time Management Skills

Because the sales role is so flexible, good time management skills are a must. If working from a home office, your commute might be 10 yards down the hallway. The temptation to sleep in or to work on personal projects will be great, without planning the day and organizing the time effectively. Successful salespeople use the previously discussed technology, as well as a calendar system, to keep themselves organized. Important calls need to be scheduled, and deadlines noted. There will be paperwork that needs to be completed for the company, in addition to sales calls to complete and shipments to verify. The abilities to be organized and create a structure for the workday are of critical importance in a job that can, at times, be hectic.

It is also important to protect your calendar and make time for important activities. Mike Weinberg, author of several influential sales books, including *New Sales. Simplified.* and *#SalesTruth*, notes that salespeople responsible for **new business development**, the activities associated with adding new customers, must block time on their calendars for **prospecting**, which is identifying individuals or companies who may need the selling firm's products or services.[19] A salesperson to whose role prospecting is important should block time each day to make sure to complete the activity. If another activity is important, you should reserve time on the calendar for that activity. An activity that is put on your calendar is more likely to be completed.

Professional with High Integrity

Throughout history, society has often had a negative impression of salespeople. This reputation stems, in part, from experiences people have had with unprofessional salespeople. Think about your own experiences. Have you ever

Customer Relationship Management (CRM)
a system for managing a company's interaction with current and potential customers

sales pipeline
a comprehensive view of where customers are in the sales process

new business development
the activities associated with adding new customers

prospecting
identifying individuals or companies who may need the selling firm's products or services

Figure 1-2 What Is Professional Dress?

Commercial Construction Sales
- Scenario: A sales rep meets with a customer at the customer's building site to demonstrate construction materials.
- Appropriate clothing: Shirt with a collar, khaki slacks, steel-toed shoes, hard hat

Medical Device Sales
- Scenario: The sales rep attends a surgery to ensure product performs as intended and serve as a resource for the doctor.
- Appropriate clothing: Scrubs and white athletic shoes.

Agricultural Sales
- Scenario: A sales rep meets with a farmer to discuss farming equipment needs.
- Appropriate clothing: Shirt with a collar, jeans or khaki slacks, sensible shoes for walking in fields and barnyards.

Technology Sales
- Scenario: A sales rep meets with the managing partner of a law firm to review case management software alternatives.
- Appropriate clothing: Business professioinal suit in a conservative color and dress shoes.

Apparel Sales
- Scenario: A sales rep meets with a retail buyer to review a line of women's fashion clothing.
- Appropriate clothing: Dressy business casual, i.e., sportscoat or shirt with slacks or a skirt. Less conservative colors are acceptable.

encountered a salesperson who behaved less than professionally? How did that make you feel? Salespeople who lack professionalism, or who tend to demonstrate manipulative sales tactics, make a very bad impression. The best way to change this negative perception is to behave as a true professional.

What does it mean to be a professional? It means keeping your word, being reliable, and dependable. You maintain open lines of communication, and that communication has a professional tone. You dress appropriately for the industry and customers (see Figure 1-2 for examples). You care about the job and clients, and always behaves with integrity. Salespeople are often perceived to be unethical because they are attempting to persuade. To counter this perception, the salesperson should keep clients' best interests in mind and concentrate on doing the right thing at all times. In the long run, this will increase the likelihood of success. Customers and potential customers are more likely to do business with a salesperson they know, like, and trust.[20]

Are Good Salespeople Born or Made?

Some people will argue that good salespeople are born, not made. In other words, if you are born an extrovert with a gift for conversation and interpersonal skills, you are likely to be successful at sales. Although those skills can be helpful in a sales career, the career demands much more than a sparkling personality. Sales is a process requiring listening, excellent questioning, great attention to detail, and empathy for others. These skills can be learned; in fact, research has shown that regardless of personality type, salespeople can be successful if they learn the ability to influence decisions, one component of the sales process.[21] Like any skill, repetitive practice is critical to developing proficiency. The more one practices, the better the sales skill set, and the greater the success. Remember: effort equals results.

The Transformation of the Sales Process: The Sales Timeline

Selling as a profession has been around for hundreds of years since peddlers sold their wares via horse-drawn wagons. However, the transformation of the sales role from a peddler to a modern professional salesperson has taken place more recently. Still, events that occurred many years ago set the stage for what is happening today.

In an interesting blog post, author Matt Smith notes that sales role specialization began in 1870 with insurance sales, as insurance companies developed sales producer and sales collector roles that quickly caught on in other industries. Next, in 1924, International Business Machines (IBM) founder Thomas J. Watson, Sr., focused on creating and implementing sales training programs and recruiting college-educated sales representatives. Shortly after that, in 1925, E.K. Strong published *The Psychology of Selling*, a book featuring sales principles still taught today. Around this same time, entrepreneur and sales trainer Dale Carnegie began sales training that delineated sales as a repeatable process that could be learned.[22]

Through the 1950s and 1960s, door-to-door selling was the norm. Another big change occurred in the late 1960s and 1970s, as sales began to move toward a customer-oriented model. In the 1970s, legendary sales trainers and consultants like Zig Ziglar, Brian Tracy, and Tom Hopkins began to build what are now world-renowned organizations for sales training and coaching. Importantly, their sales training methods focused on consultative selling are still in use today. In the 21st century, salespeople are strategic business partners who help their customers grow and become more successful. The sales role has truly transformed from one focused on selling a given product to one focused on helping customers achieve success.

Variety in Sales Roles

Not all sales roles are the same, and some roles are a better fit for some than others. More comfortable managing customer relationships? Then perhaps **account management** might be appropriate. Competitive and like the thrill of winning the deal? Then perhaps business development. The following list describes a few of the sales roles found in companies, along with a brief description of what the role entails. Understanding your own strengths and the responsibilities of the position will help with an effective career search.

Account Management

An **account manager** takes care of existing clients. Sometimes known as "**farmers**," salespeople in this role are nurturing relationships and working with clients to improve business. They meet with their clients regularly to discuss current sales and opportunities with new products. They track the customer's orders to ensure on-time delivery and problem-solve as needed. If the client needs a new product, they bring in other members of their team to help in the design process. Account managers focus on developing customer satisfaction and selling more to current clients. Account

account management
managing customer relationships

account manager
focusing on developing customer satisfaction and selling more to current clients

farmers
another term for salespeople responsible for nurturing relationships with existing customers

management is an important role in selling firms because selling products to existing clients tends to be more profitable than trying to attract new clients.

New Business Development

Whereas account managers are "farmers," new business development representatives are sometimes called **"hunters"** because they are hunting for new business. In other words, new business development representatives are responsible for the activities involved in identifying and pursuing new business opportunities. Salespeople charged with bringing new business into the firm are focused on prospecting. They develop a strong network and work with the members of their network to identify prospective customers and obtain referrals. They also engage in **cold calling**, which is attempting to meet or speak with someone they have never met or contacted before. Once they get an appointment, they work with the prospect to determine whether their solution is a good fit for that company. If the fit is good and the customer sees the value, they will close the business.

Some readers may be familiar with *Top Hat* education and learning platform. *Top Hat* divides its sales force into distinct new business development and account management roles. The new business development representative finds new prospects, demonstrates the product, answers any questions, and secures the sale. Once an instructor agrees to use *Top Hat,* that instructor is turned over to an account manager who helps set up the class and provides ongoing support.

Alternatively, sometimes the account management and new business development roles are merged into one role. This dual role is more challenging because one must assume both aspects of the sale: hunting and farming. If responsibilities do include taking care of existing customers and finding new customers, one will need to build time into the day for prospecting. People more comfortable with the farming role sometimes find the new business development role difficult. But with planning and preparation, it is manageable.

Strategic Account Management

Strategic account management (SAM) is "the selection, establishment, and maintenance of close institutional relationships with a firm's most important customers."[23] Thus, **strategic account managers** are responsible for overseeing several of the firm's most important accounts. For example, someone serving as a strategic account manager for a major athletics manufacturer might be in charge of five accounts ranging from a small group of department stores to a nationwide chain of sporting goods retailers. These accounts generate a substantial amount of revenue for the selling firm and thus are worth dedicating an individual to ensure the appropriate solutions provided. In our athletic manufacturer example, the strategic account manager would work with the customer to plan out purchases over the year, develop specialized promotion campaigns, and follow up with the client frequently to ensure the selling firm has met all of the client's needs.

A salesperson interested in becoming a strategic account manager should make sure to perform well early in his or her sales career: experienced sales representatives or account managers who also demonstrate their abilities to perform at top levels are most likely to be placed in SAM roles. Only the best sales representatives get to work with the top clients. Ryan Knight is a Field Enterprise Specialist for Dell EMC. He began his career with Dell in inside commercial sales and then moved to inside commercial specialty management before his current role. Today, Ryan works with the 15 largest accounts headquartered in his Midwest territory. His SAM role is focused on relationship building and maintenance and involves working with his clients on strategic planning, financial models, and proposal development.

hunters
another term for salespeople responsible for new business development

cold-calling
attempting to meet or speak with someone they have never met or contacted before

strategic account management
the selection, establishment, and maintenance of close institutional relationships with a firm's most important customers

strategic account managers
responsible for overseeing several of the firms most important accounts

Missionary Selling

Missionary salespeople do not close sales in the traditional sense. The main focus of **missionary selling** is education. In other words, they educate customers about their product and then encourage them to use it. The customer does not order directly from the missionary sales representative. A classic example of a missionary salesperson is a pharmaceutical sales representative who calls on doctors to inform them about the medications the salesperson represents. This representative would teach the doctor about the drug, including how it works and how it can help patients. The "sale" is not completed, however, until the doctor prescribes the medication for a patient.

Missionary salespeople exist in other industries and roles. Athletic-maker Nike, for example, used to employ missionary salespeople to educate retail sellers on the different products offered and set up displays in stores. These missionary salespeople worked in conjunction with account executives responsible for selling the product. The missionary seller helps create goodwill, improve the customer experience, and increase the value provided by the selling organization.

Sales Engineers

Sales engineers use their technical and scientific expertise to help develop appropriate solutions for customers and prospective customers. Often working with an account manager or selling team, the value added by the sales engineer is the ability to work with the customer's technical experts or engineers and ensure that the solution under consideration will resolve the customer's issue, perhaps even designing new products for the situation. Consider, for example, the design and building of a New York City skyscraper. A seller of piping and pipe couplings might involve a sales engineer in the process to ensure that the products selected will meet building requirements and perform as expected. After the sale, the sales engineer may continue to work with the customer to ensure implementation goes as planned and troubleshoot any problems that arise on-site.

Sales engineers have many opportunities. As noted in Table 1-1, jobs for sales engineers are expected to grow by 7% between 2016 and 2026. Further, sales engineering roles commanded one of the highest median salaries among all sales roles in 2018.

Outside Sales Representative

Also referred to as **field sales, outside sales representatives** visit customers in their place of business and work a defined territory. The size and definition of that territory will vary widely by company and location. If selling the technology in Manhattan, NY, your territory may be a few city blocks, given a large number of businesses located in those city blocks. Alternatively, your territory might consist of a few adjacent states or even the eastern United States. In some cases, you can drive to visit customers and potential customers. If the territory is larger, you may need to fly. With a large territory, you would expect to do a great deal of overnight travel.

Many people involved in outside sales enjoy the freedom and flexibility associated with the role. They work with their clients to set their schedules and may work out of a home office. Their company may provide them with a car and an expense account. Visiting with a potential customer face-to-face has many advantages, such as the ability to read body language and receive immediate feedback. They can also learn a great deal by visiting a client's place of business.

Inside Sales Representative

Inside sales representatives use the telephone or voice over internet protocol (VoIP) to approach and sell to customers and potential buyers rather than visiting face-to-face. Although often confused with the inconvenient telemarketing calls received at dinnertime, inside sales activities in a business-to-business setting provide value for customers as well as selling firms. Inside salespeople might serve in sales support, account management, or new business development, among other roles. Further, inside sales positions often serve as a training position for outside sales; in other words, if you want to be in outside sales, there is a high likelihood you will need to start in inside sales. Although many people do want to move to outside sales, others enjoy the benefits of being in a sales role without the travel associated with outside sales.

In some cases, inside sales representatives are responsible for helping outside sales representatives provide services to clients. Security Benefit Corporation, a leading retirement solutions provider, headquartered in Topeka, Kansas, maintains both inside and outside sales forces. The inside sales force helps the outside sales representatives set appointments and service clients, and it also has direct responsibility for smaller accounts. In other cases, the company maintains an inside sales force to handle all selling functions. Shamrock Trading Corporation, a rapidly growing firm with headquarters in the Midwest and operating in the transportation industry, uses an inside sales force for all of its services, from transportation logistics to international trade finance to discount programs for trucking companies.

inside sales representative role involving the use of phone and technology to interact with potential buyers rather than visiting face-to-face

Other Roles

Table 1-3 provides a review of the previously described roles. Notably, this review is just a glimpse of the most common job titles and sales roles in organizations. Different organizations may use different titles for similar jobs or may have completely different roles. Some firms may use the title "account executive" for "account managers," or "key account managers" for "strategic account managers," for example. Sales organizations use the titles and roles that make the most sense for their companies and industries.

As individuals learn more about sales, they tend to find themselves more attracted to certain roles. Some people may prefer account management and tending existing relationships, whereas others might prefer hunting for new business, for instance. Once starting your career and beginning to learn more about the other roles available, you may develop skills further to take on new roles. A sales career is often an evolution.

Eight Myths about Sales

We have talked throughout this chapter about the importance of the sales role and how it has transformed from essentially an order-taker role to that of a strategic partner. Still, many people continue to misperceive what it means to be in sales. Some of these erroneous notions are a result of the way salespeople are portrayed in movies and on television. In the following paragraphs, we debunk the eight great myths about sales to demonstrate the differences between those negative misconceived images and the reality of professional selling.

Only Salespeople Need to Understand How to Sell

We hope it is obvious by now that this statement is a myth. As suggested by Daniel Pink,[24] we are all in a position to persuade and influence in our jobs,

Table 1-3 A Sample of the Different Sales Roles in Organizations

Sales Role	Examples of Related Job Titles	Definition	Example Job Descriptions
Account Manager	Account Executive, Sales Executive & Account Manager, Renewal Sales Account Manager	Work with existing accounts to grow business and ensure customer satisfaction.	Responsible for connecting customers, sales, and all business units. Manage customer relationships to make certain that precise and well-timed program implementation occurs. Increase sales and retain current accounts. Accountable for customer management, growth, profitability, sales, and inventory control.
New Business Development Representative	Sales Development Representative, New Business Account Executive	Focus on identifying and pursuing new accounts.	Responsible for prospecting, qualifying, and closing new accounts. Source and develop new business opportunities. Successfully present and describe products and explain the value proposition to prospective customers. Develop a strong pipeline of prospective customers to achieve monthly sales goals.
Strategic Account Manager	Key Account Manager, Key Account Representative, National Account Manager	Selects, manages, and maintains relationships with the company's most important accounts.	Responsible for driving organization-wide sales programs into a defined territory while achieving goals and creating satisfied customers. Be the key contact for information gathering sessions with executives, developing strategic solutions, organizing the appropriate technical specialists and internal company resources, and ensuring successful implementation with our top customers.
Missionary Salesperson	Pharmaceutical Detailer, Sales Consultant	Educate customers about the product and encourage them to use the product.	Responsible for developing contacts with established and prospective clients within a geographical territory. Manage and grow territory, which includes identifying potential clients and coordinating client visits. Maintain detailed knowledge of each client and potential client, which includes competing products, company and market information, and key employees. Visit clients to promote and educate on products.
Sales Engineer	Technical Specialist, Technical Sales Engineer, Sales Specialist	Provide technical and scientific expertise to help create appropriate solutions for customers.	Responsible for technology sales & presales. Work with the sales team to identify and sell large opportunities. Use market and scientific knowledge in identifying opportunities across markets. Understand the key business challenges of senior executives and be capable of developing a proposed solution & strategy. Should be revenue-driven.
Outside Sales Representative	Outside Sales Account Manager, Field Sales Representative	Work with customers at the customer's place of business and manages a geographical territory. Can include account management or new business development roles, among others.	Work independently to sell products to customers in a geographically defined territory. Responsible for achieving sales goals using a consultative selling approach. Focus on relationship development with key organization contacts. Listen to customer needs and provide product solutions and customer service that results in customer satisfaction.
Inside Sales Representative	Inside Sales Account Manager, Senior Account Executive—Inside Sales	Work with customers via telephone or Webinar. Can include account management or new business development roles.	Book orders from assigned customers via telephone. Follow-up on order processing and respond to customer inquiries about deliveries. Inform customers of company promotions and upgrades, and sell related products, services, and supplies—coordinate sales activities with outside sales reps as necessary.

and as a consequence, we are all in sales. Entrepreneurs sell investors on their business ideas. CEOs sell board members and shareholders on company strategy. A salesperson sells the warehouse supervisor on the idea to ship his customer's products out first. An employee sells her boss on the idea that she needs a raise or promotion. Everyone benefits by understanding how to sell.

Only Extroverts Succeed in Sales

Although commonly believed, this myth is not accurate. Extreme extroverts may struggle in sales if they don't take the time to ask good questions and listen. As Adam Grant has demonstrated, ambiverts—those who display tendencies of both introverts and extroverts—tend to be more successful in sales because they can listen well.[25] Introverts can also be successful, given their tendency to listen instead of talk. In reality, anyone possessing any personality type can be successful in selling as long as they can adapt their behavior, ask good questions, and listen.

Successful Salespeople Are Fast-Talking and Manipulative

The opposite is true: salespeople who are fast-talking and manipulative are NOT successful in today's business environment. Successful salespeople engage in active listening and ask good questions to understand and solve the customer's problems. As the adage goes, you have two ears and one mouth for a reason; you should be listening twice as much as you talk.

Salespeople Are Unethical

The myth about salespeople being unethical arises from our previous point, namely that sometimes salespeople are perceived as fast-talking and manipulative. Both assumptions are incorrect. Research has shown that when it comes to ethical behavior, salespeople are no different from other marketing professionals[26] and that salespeople are more likely to be satisfied with their jobs when their employers are deemed ethical.[27] Why, then, are salespeople seen as unethical by some people? Often, it is because they are in a position to persuade. The portrayal of salespeople in television and the movies also has an impact. Further, when unethical business practices occur that involve salespeople, others assume that the behavior is typical. Take, for example, the recent case of ethical misconduct involving approximately 5,000 Wells Fargo salespeople who were creating fraudulent accounts in customers' names as a way to address the pressure from Wells Fargo managers to meet sales goals.[28] To fight these misperceptions and impressions based on the misconduct of others, salespeople must behave ethically.

All Sales Jobs Are Alike

As demonstrated in Table 1-3, sales roles vary widely. There is hunting new business, or focusing on long-term relationship development with existing accounts. There is working from an office using the phone, or traveling a defined territory. You might work with consumers, business customers, or strategic accounts. Sales roles vary so widely that some companies give assessments to determine the best sales role for each individual. Within sales, a person can explore an assortment of job options to find the best particular one.

No Need for a College Degree to Go into Sales

Although this statement may have been true in the 1950s and 1960s, it is no longer true today. Most sales roles DO require a college degree, largely because one needs to have the business acumen and knowledge to do the job well. In fact, in response to organizational demand for college-educated sales talent, more universities than ever are offering certificates, minors, and majors in sales. According to the *Sales Education Foundation* (https://www.salesfoundation.org), more than 100 universities with sales programs exist across the United States, Canada, and Europe. The *University Sales Center Alliance* (https://www.universitysalescenteralliance.org), a consortium of universities with sales programs dedicated to enhancing the quality of sales education, boasts over 52 members and continues to grow rapidly. As the sales role has become more strategic and professional, the need for a college degree has increased substantially.

Salespeople Don't Need to Understand Accounting and Finance

As mentioned earlier, salespeople today are strategic business partners for their customers. The goal is to help customers be successful. As argued by author Bob Rickert, that means helping them—and the company—be profitable.[29] Understanding profitability means you need to understand accounting and finance, as well as the impact that purchasing the product will have on the customer's bottom line. The ability to quantify the value of your solution in terms of the profit impact will greatly increase the likelihood of winning a customer's business.

A Sales Career Lacks Security

Job security is an important issue for many people, and some students worry that this security is lacking in a sales career. Fortunately, this concern is not realistic! Salespeople enjoy great job security, for several reasons. First, a salesperson who is bringing in revenues for the firm is extremely valuable to the company. Companies have a vested interest in retaining employees who add directly to the bottom line. Second, sales skills are highly transferable. Sales is a process, and someone who understands that process well can apply it to different products. Someone who has had success with one company and product is likely to experience similar success at other companies selling other products. Those skills will always be in demand by employers.

Applying this Chapter to Salesforce   salesforce

A customer relationship management (CRM) system or platform enables a salesperson to track the entire sales process, including every interaction with prospects, potential buyers, and current customers. CRM enables the salesperson to see in one place the details of every interaction a buyer, prospect, buyer, or customer has had with them or their company, improving the ability to respond to their needs and improve the relationship.

In the office, on the way to a sales call, or while with a buyer, CRM provides access to all the relevant information necessary to earn the sale. CRM helps put buyers in the center of everything, providing a 360-degree view of them, their organization, processes, needs, and history of interaction. CRM also improves sales performance by enabling salespeople to connect with buyers at exactly the right time with just the right message.

Although there are dozens of CRM options, **Salesforce** is the dominant provider, with twice the market share as the next largest provider of a CRM system. Given its popularity, we've chosen Salesforce to demonstrate how the concepts of each chapter can be enhanced by CRM. Although the features described in each chapter are specific to Salesforce, other CRM products may offer similar features or functions.

Source: https://www.gartner.com/en/newsroom/press-releases/2019-06-17-gartner-says-worldwide-customer-experience-and-relati

Chapter Summary

- Sales includes all the activities related to selling a product or service to a buyer.
- The benefits of the sales role as a career include the opportunity to take advantage of the global sales talent shortage, to make a meaningful contribution quickly, to build a powerful network, to build a flexible career, to be in charge of your destiny, and to get the job or promotion you are pursuing.
- Entrepreneurs who understand how to sell are more effective at selling their business ideas and building successful organizations.
- The skills and traits required by successful salespeople include communication and active listening skills, negotiation skills, business acumen, other-focused, resilient, self-motivated, a dedication to lifelong learning, technology skills, time management skills, and integrity.
- Sales skills can be learned and improved with practice.
- Sales has transformed over the years, with the sales role moving from more of an order taker to a strategic consultant focused on helping customers achieve success.
- Sales roles vary widely and include account managers, new business development representatives, strategic account managers, missionary sellers, sales engineers, outside sales representatives, and inside sales representatives.
- Because many people misunderstand the sales role, there is a need to set people straight regarding the eight myths about sales. Everyone benefits from understanding how to sell. All personality types can be good at sales. Successful salespeople ask good questions, listen, and have high integrity. Sales jobs vary widely. Salespeople benefit from having a college degree, and it is often a requirement of the job. Salespeople do need a good understanding of accounting and finance. A sales career has good job security.

Key Terms

account management (p. 12)
account manager (p. 12)
active listening (p. 7)
business acumen (p. 8)
cold-calling (p. 13)
Customer Relationship Management
   (CRM) (p. 10)
farmers (p. 12)
field sales (p. 14)
grit (p. 9)
hunters (p. 13)

inside sales representative (p. 15)
missionary selling (p. 14)
negotiation (p. 8)
new business development (p. 10)
outside sales representative (p. 14)
prospecting (p. 10)
referrals (p. 5)
sales engineers (p. 14)
sales pipeline (p. 10)
strategic account management (p. 13)
strategic account managers (p. 13)

Application 1-1

Taylor Smallwood recently graduated from college with a degree in marketing. She had taken a sales class her senior year and found she liked learning more about customer problems and creating solutions that might add value. As she searched for job openings online, she began to gravitate toward sales roles. She was surprised by the wide variety of job titles listed. Which role would be best for her?

(Continued)

(Continued)

After hours of searching, Taylor settled on three that seemed most interesting. All three jobs were in Chicago, her top choice for relocating. All three were entry-level positions. She printed off the three postings to review them.

Job 1:

In this job, the successful applicant would perform the administrative functions needed to ensure customer needs are being met; support the outside sales force by ensuring the delivery of timely price quotes and accurate order processing; and update customer contracts, coordinate warehouse deliveries, and answer phone calls from customers requesting sales information.

Job 2:

Responsibilities for this job include conduct research and lead generation daily to identify and qualify potential customers; record all information on potential customers in the CRM system; participate in team planning sessions to make sure quality opportunities are identified; participate in industry events such as trade shows.

Job 3:

The successful applicant will meet with existing customers, develop product knowledge, and deliver sales presentations. Emphasis is placed on creating a positive experience for customers to ensure customer satisfaction.

Taylor studied the job postings carefully, trying to figure out what she should do. Each job was slightly different. What would be the best job for her skill set? She decided to call her former sales professor to gather some information on these different types of sales roles.

1. What sales role is best reflected by Job 1?
2. What sales role is best reflected by Job 2?
3. What sales role is best reflected by Job 3?

Application 1-2

Sales manager Robert Lindsey was meeting with Heather McDonald, head of Human Resources at Smith Pipe Fittings. Robert had a sales role he needed to fill, and Heather was helping him write the job description.

"How would you describe the role?" asked Heather. Robert replied, "I've always called them hunters, but the actual job title is Business Development Representative."

Heather jotted down the title and asked Robert to tell her the activities associated with the role. Robert outlined the job of the business development representative as follows:

- Proactively pursue sales leads via phone, email, social media, and on-site.
- Generate and qualify new business leads before passing on to the sales team.
- Meet with senior executives at prospective accounts to identify business needs.
- Coordinate activities with the sales team and schedule calls, webinars, and appointments with qualified leads for the team.
- Work with the sales team to develop appropriate strategies.

"Great!" said Heather. "Based on these job requirements, what traits or skills would you prefer in an applicant?" Robert thought for a second. As a business development representative, the successful applicant would face a lot of rejection. This person would need to understand business problems to identify needs. And, because the successful individual would be coordinating with a team, there would be a need to utilize technology effectively and organize activities with multiple other people. "Good question, Heather," Robert replied. "Can we brainstorm a list of traits and skills?" Robert and Heather thought for a minute and then started jotting down traits for the job advertisement.

1. Robert indicated that the business development salesperson would face a lot of rejection when trying to identify potential customers. What trait of successful salespeople would be important for someone experiencing rejection?
2. The applicant who accepts the business development role will need to understand and address business situations quickly and effectively. What sales skill does this definition describe?
3. The business development representative will need to coordinate activities with the sales team. What skills will be most useful for this task?

CHAPTER 2

The Buying Process

Learning Objectives

- Explain the buying role and why sellers need to understand it
- Compare and contrast the different types of buyers
- Identify different buyer motivations
- Recognize and demonstrate features and benefits important to buyers
- Discuss buying decision criteria and the buying process
- Summarize the factors influencing the buying decision process
- Express the role of the salesperson in reducing the risk associated with a purchase decision
- Illustrate how the salesperson can become a trustworthy consultant to the buyer

business-to-business (B2B)
a business interaction, such as a purchase, between two organizations

business-to-consumer (B2C)
an interaction between a consumer and a business

buyer
the person responsible for making a personal or organizational purchase

buying organization
the organization making a purchase

salesperson
the individual responsible for selling the product to the buyer

supplier / vendor
the selling organization

retail buyer
purchase already manufactured products and services and subsequently resell them in retail stores

efore something is sold, organizational processes from the buyer's side are triggered. At its core, the buying process includes all the considerations, evaluations, and decisions involved in choosing whether to purchase a product or service. We all engage in this process in our personal lives, whether it is to buy a car, rent an apartment, or buy a pair of shoes. The complexity of the process may change depending on the product and the reason for purchase, but the process itself is present each time someone chooses to make a purchase. The buying process is sometimes referred to as the *buyer's journey*, in that it represents the buyer's movement through the purchase process, from recognizing a need to researching possible solutions, determining important decision criteria, evaluating options, and finally making a decision and evaluating results.

In this chapter, we discuss this important process and the people involved and review the sellers' need to understand this process. Before we begin this discussion, however, it is necessary to understand some key terminology: **Business-to-business (B2B)** is a business interaction, such as a purchase, between two organizations. **Business-to-consumer (B2C)** is an interaction between a consumer and a business, such as a consumer making a purchase from a retailer or service provider. A **buyer** is the person responsible for making a personal or organizational purchase. A **buying organization** is the organization making a purchase (B2B purchases only). A **salesperson** is the individual responsible for selling the product to the buyer; also referred to as the seller. And a **supplier** is the selling organization; also known as a **vendor**.

What Is the Buying Role?

The decision to make a purchase occurs at many levels and in many situations. Table 2-1 offers a simple categorization of the different types of buyers. Consumers represent the biggest group of buyers, buying products and services to fulfill personal and family needs. In your role as a consumer, you might work with a salesperson when purchasing products such as insurance, financial planning, or automobiles, to name a few examples. Although your needs as a buyer might be different from those of professional buyers working in an organization, you still go through a process to make a purchase decision and still encounter some of the same influences and issues experienced by buyers in an organization. The products bought by consumers are available, in part, as a result of the retail buying process. **Retail buyers** purchase already manufactured products and services and subsequently resell them in retail stores. Retail buyers often have job titles like Buyer or Associate Buyer. Every retailer, from Walmart to Macy's, from supermarket chains to small clothing boutiques, has at least one person, and sometimes many people, serving as buyers to determine the product assortment available in the store. In addition to being responsible for product assortments in the store, retail buyers manage inventory levels, analyze sales patterns, create sales forecasts, and manage budgets.

Similar to retail buyers, organizational buyers purchase products for an organization. These buyers, however, purchase products and services used in the creation of the products sold by the organization. Organizational buyers may have job titles such as Purchasing Manager or Purchaser, and they are responsible for purchasing a wide variety of products, ranging from materials needed to create the company's products to products and services needed to facilitate product sales and run the company (e.g., advertising services, janitorial services, paper, paper towels, computers). Author and professional buyer Hubert Lachance distinguishes these different types of products as part of direct procurement or indirect procurement.[1] **Direct procurement** involves the purchase of products and services used to create the product or service provided to end-users, such as a piece of equipment used in the manufacturing line or a part built into a product. **Indirect procurement** refers to the purchase of products or services used in company operations, such as a copy machine used in the organization's accounting office or the paper towels used in the office kitchen.

Institutional and Government Buyers are the last category presented in Table 2-1. People in these roles may have the job titles of procurement officer or procurement manager, among others. Buyers in this category purchase items for schools, universities, hospitals, and local, state, or federal governments. In fact, in the United States, the federal government is the largest purchaser in the country. Buyers for institutions and governments sometimes face unique issues, including the need to follow policies and laws regarding purchasing. State universities, for example, must follow state laws when choosing suppliers. In these instances, the buying process tends to be very formal and rule-bound, and a committee may determine the final result.

direct procurement
the purchase of products and services used to create the product or service provided to end-users

indirect procurement
the purchase of products or services used in company operations

Table 2-1 Types of Buyers Engaged in the Buying Process

Type of Buyer	Examples of Job Titles	Examples of Buying Organizations	Primary Purchase Motivation	Examples of Products Purchased from Professional Salespeople
Consumer	—	—	Fulfill personal or family needs	• Automobiles • Insurance • Financial Services
Retail Buyer	Buyer, Associate Buyer, Buying Assistant	Department stores, supermarkets, big box stores, boutiques, etc.	Create a product assortment consumers will want to purchase	• Clothing • Food products • Furniture • Household goods • Office products
Organizational Buyer	Purchasing Manager, Purchaser	Manufacturers, distributors, etc.	Purchase products used in creating the products sold by the organization (e.g., raw materials, parts, equipment) and products needed to keep the business running (maintenance, repair, operations)	• Steel • Automobile parts • Plastic parts • Machinery • Capital equipment • Advertising services • Copy machines • Paper • Computers
Institutional/ Government Buyer	Procurement Officer, Procurement Manager	Schools, universities, hospitals, local/state/ federal governments	Purchase products used to serve clients (e.g., food, equipment) and keep the institution or government entity running (maintenance, repair, operations)	• Food • Cooking equipment • Copy machines • Paper • Computers • Insurance • Scientific equipment • Military equipment

Shutterstock/BR Photo Addicted

Further, the variety of products purchased ranges widely. Consider all the products the federal government must purchase! The products range from pens to toilet paper to military jets, and everything in between.

It is worth noting that sometimes people in an organization end up in a purchasing role, even when they do not possess the title of "buyer" or "purchaser." Your professor, for example, decided to adopt this textbook for this course, and as a consequence, made a purchase decision for your class and university. Administrative associates often make decisions about purchasing office supplies, and a company president might make the purchase decision about which insurance policy to choose for the organization's employees. A wide variety of people can take on the function of the buying role in an organization or institution, depending on how the organization is structured. These people may include decision-makers who have budget authority (such as the company president) but do not fall within the purchasing department, as well as product users, operators, IT directors, human resource specialists, or mechanics who use or interact with the product on a daily basis and thus have a great deal of influence in the final decision.

Why Do Sellers Need to Understand the Buying Role?

value
the perceived importance, worth, or usefulness of a product or service

Value is the perceived importance, worth, or usefulness of a product or service. To create value for customers, sellers must understand the buying process and the various issues facing the buyer. The salesperson who can be put in the customer's shoes, so to speak, has a better chance of recognizing key issues and opportunities. That salesperson also has a better chance of making the buyer's life easier, which increases the chance of sales success.

As author Kim Ward notes in his book *The New Selling IQ*, buyers want sellers to understand their business, design applications to fit their needs, treat them fairly, be accessible to solve problems, and be creative in responding to needs.[2] To be successful as a seller, the salesperson needs to understand the buyer and the buying firm's process for making decisions.

Buying in Organizations and the Transformation of the Buying Role

Like salespeople, buyers working for an organization's purchasing department are professionals in their field. The Institute for Supply Management recommends aspiring purchasing professionals obtain a four-year college degree in business or purchasing along with continuing education and credentials such as the Certified Professional in Supply Management.[3] The main difference between salespeople and buyers relates to how the buying role complements the selling role. Buyers and sellers work together to negotiation decisions that result in exchange. Sellers bring in revenues from selling products or services; buyers control costs when purchasing products from the sellers.

Professional buyers create value for their firms by bringing in the products and services offering the most value, thereby allowing the firm to deliver high-quality products with a good profit margin for the firm. Ideally, buyers accomplish these outcomes efficiently and effectively so that internal organizational processes flow smoothly. Buyers need to develop relationships with personnel internal to the firm to identify needs and facilitate the buying process. Buyers spend a great deal of time gathering information from paid and unpaid sources, as well as from salespeople, to make the best decisions.

Like many people in the workforce today, buyers are asked to do more with fewer resources and less time. In her influential book *Snap Selling*, author Jill Konrath discusses what she terms "frazzled customer syndrome." Buyers are extremely busy and overwhelmed, attempting to complete work amid a deluge of daily disruptions. As a consequence, they avoid change (which is difficult) and meetings with salespeople. They are slow to respond but demanding when they need an answer. Author Konrath suggests salespeople must change their approach to add value to these "crazy-busy" buyers.[4]

Of course, as noted previously, not all buyers reside in the purchasing department. Users, operators, human resource professionals, information technology (IT) professionals, mechanics, and members of the top management team, among others, can all be potential buyers or influencers in the buying process. The individuals involved may depend on how the company is structured, and the product or service purchased.

Buyer Motivation

At its most basic level, buyer motivation includes all the factors that drive a buyer to move from a current state, such as having a problem, to a desired state, such as having the problem solved.

According to Kim Ward, buyers are motivated to move from their actual state to their desired state for one of three reasons: **situation repair**, when something is broken and requires repair or replacement; **situation improvement**, when an opportunity resulting in business improvements exists; or **situation continuance**, when the buyer does not see the value in changing and elects to remain with the status quo.[5]

When something needs to be fixed to avoid negative consequences (situation repair), the buyer can be highly motivated to make a decision. This situation may arise when a piece of important machinery breaks down, or when the buyer's firm needs to upgrade its products to continue to appeal to its customer base and remain competitive in the marketplace.

Opportunities available to a firm can be related to a wide variety of issues, ranging from improving internal processes to productivity to profitability and more. When an opportunity arises, the need to make a change is less obvious (situation improvement). If the buyer does not find the reason to buy compelling and does not recognize the negative consequences that might arise from maintaining the current state, that buyer is more likely to elect to remain with the existing situation (situation continuance). The seller can help the buyer understand the opportunities available. An example might be a salesperson selling a customer relationship management system that is superior to a competitor's system in use at a buyer's firm. By asking good discovery questions and clarifying the buyer's implicit and explicit needs, the seller can demonstrate how this opportunity can be of value for the buyer. Trust plays a critical role in this example. Only when the salesperson is trusted and has done the work to establish a strong buyer-seller relationship will the buyer be open to new ways of looking at the problem. In consultative or solutions selling, one of the most important reasons to establish a relationship with the buyer is for precisely this purpose—to help customers identify those areas of opportunity and guide them to an optimal solution to the problem.

situation repair
when something is broken and requires repair or replacement

situation improvement
when an opportunity resulting in business improvements exists

situation continuance
when the buyer does not see the value in changing and elects to remain with the status quo

The previously described motivations suggest buyers respond rationally to buying situations. Although the application of a rational process can be accurate, emotions can also play a role in the buying process, especially in B2C situations but even in B2B contexts. Researchers have found, for example, that buying team members experience a wide range of emotions when choosing a supplier. These emotions can include contentment, discontentment, confidence, surprise, worry, and shame.[6] Salespeople capable of reading others' emotions can recognize rational versus emotional behaviors and adjust their messages accordingly.

Understanding Features and Benefits

Ultimately, buyers purchase products, not just to own them, but because of what those products will do for the buyer. A **feature** of a product or service is just one of its characteristics or attributes. The **benefit** is the value of the feature that the buyer perceives or experiences. This idea is critical to the sales role because, in order to help motivate the buyer to move from the current state to the desired state, the salesperson must be able to translate product features into meaningful benefits and the value created for customers.

There is an adage in sales: "Features tell, benefits sell." Even though in today's complex environment the salesperson must move beyond product benefits to sell solution benefits and value, the phrase still applies. The salesperson needs to be able to translate a solution attribute into the benefit the buyer cares about, namely how this attribute will address the problem at hand and add value to the buyer's firm. If the benefits associated with the solution outweigh the perceived costs, the buyer is more likely to make a purchase.

Value is a comparison of benefits to costs, where costs include not only monetary cost but also any time, effort, and mental focus associated with the purchase. For example, when purchasing a car, a person might read online reviews, visit car lots, and take some test drives before purchasing. The time and effort associated with those activities are part of the total cost. The buyer receives value when the benefits received exceed this bundle of monetary and non-monetary costs.

Value is in the eye of the beholder; what constitutes value for one person or organization may not reflect value to a different person or organization. Some buyers may equate value with low price. Other buyers will associate value with quality, and still others consider value achieved when they get what they want to solve a particular problem or fill a certain need.[7] The successful salesperson uncovers what value means to each buyer and buying organization and presents the relevant features and benefits accordingly.

Benefits can create value for customers in several ways, including saving time, monetary gain, adding value for the customers' customer, or reducing psychological pain. The first two benefits are obvious. If the solution can save the buyer time, for example, by reducing time in production processes or the time it takes to make a decision, that solution is saving resources and thus has a positive impact on the customer's bottom line. If the solution is saving the customer money or increasing sales, there is the same positive impact on the bottom line.

In direct procurement situations, value is also created when the product purchased

feature
a characteristic or attribute of a product or service

benefit
the value of a product or service feature that the buyer perceives or experiences

Shutterstock/fizkes

Table 2-2. Features and Benefits—Huhtamaki Example

Feature	Benefit	Benefit Category
Food and packaging expertise	Peace of mind	Reduce psychological pain
Sustainable packaging	Important to the customers; increase sales	Value-add for customer's customers
Customizable products	Increase sales by improving brand image	Monetary gain
Global corporation A wide variety of products	Create efficiency through "one-stop shopping"	Save time

adds value for the customer's customer. Let's go back to the car example. If a car manufacturer purchases bumpers rated the safest on the market for use in its automobiles, those bumpers would add value to car buyers who place a priority on the safety of the vehicle. Thus, the buyers for the car manufacturer will consider their customers' needs when purchasing products for use in the products they build.

The other type of benefit mentioned above is reducing psychological pain. This type of pain sounds dramatic, but it's pretty simple: this benefit is about making the customer's life easier and more comfortable. With the right solution, you can reduce the fear associated with making a mistake and increase customer satisfaction.

Let's work through an example. Huhtamaki is a global specialist in packaging for food and drink. The North American division sells, among other products, insulated paper cups, ice cream containers, molded fiber food packaging (e.g., egg cartons, food trays, clamshell containers). Their packaging is sustainable and can be customized and embossed to highlight a brand. Huhtamaki is a technical expert in the food packaging industry.

Based on this example, what possible benefits might the salesperson stress to an organizational buyer? Consider the following example.

Huhtamaki's expertise in the food packaging can give you peace of mind, knowing that you are making the right decision. All our food packaging is sustainable, making it an added value for your customers. We can customize our packaging for your brand, thereby building your brand image, which can lead to increased sales. Because we are a global corporation providing a wide variety of food packaging options, we can serve as your vendor for all your food packaging needs across the globe, creating efficiency for you and your organization.

Table 2-2 illustrates how the features offered by Huhtamaki translate into benefits, thereby creating value for the customer. A salesperson who can translate features into meaningful buyer benefits and communicate the value associated with those benefits will be well on the way to a successful sales career.

Buying Decision Criteria

Buyers use a wide variety of attributes when deliberating a purchase decision, and the importance of those criteria will vary by buying organization as well as by buying decision. One model used to describe the process for evaluating criteria is the **multi-attribute model**. Multi-attribute models can be defined as the weighted sum of buyers' preferences for product or brand attributes.[8] In other words, the

multi-attribute model
the weighted sum of buyers' preferences for product or brand attributes

multi-attribute model mirrors the multiple decision criteria used by buyers when making a purchase decision. The weights assigned to the different attributes signal the importance of some criteria over others.[9]

Common criteria used by buyers in the decision process include price, quality, satisfaction, and ability to deliver on time. This brief list, however, is not at all comprehensive; the criteria used can be wide and varied. Further, the multi-attribute model does not take into account the total solution that can be offered by a selling organization. Today's buyers often have complex problems that must be solved; these problems are not always solved by a single product but rather by a set of product and service offerings that are sometimes customized for a particular customer. The salesperson can play a large role in developing and delivering this solution. The ease of working with a supplier and a supplier's salesperson can be an important part of that solution. Adding value to the buying firm, making the buyer's life easier, and solving the buyer's problems will substantially increase the chances of making a sale.

The Buying Decision Process

buying decision process
the buyer's journey from recognition of a need through the evaluation of the performance of the supplier

The **buying decision process** reflects the buyer's journey that begins with the recognition of a need for a product or service and ends with an evaluation of the performance of the supplier. This process is illustrated in Figure 2-1.

1. Recognize a Need

   At this point in the process, the buyer becomes aware of a need. For a consumer, this could be as simple as the recognition that the family is out of toothpaste, or as complex as the recognition that the family is growing in size and the current house is not big enough. For a buyer within an organization, the recognition of a need can come from anyone within the

Figure 2-1 The Buying Decision Process

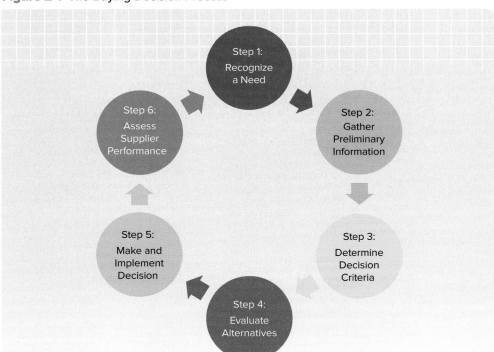

organization. A supervisor managing a production line may come across broken machinery that needs a new part. An IT manager might recognize that current software programs are outdated. An office administrator might notice that paper supplies are running low. The CEO could alert purchasing about a need to evaluate health care providers. Sometimes a salesperson can trigger the need recognition step by uncovering a problem unrecognized by the buyer, especially when the buying motivation is situation improvement. Regardless of the need, it is the recognition of the need that triggers the buying decision process.

2. Gather Preliminary Information

   Step 2 in the buying decision process is about conducting preliminary research to determine whether a purchase is warranted and, if so, what options are available to solve this problem. Kim Ward, author of *The New Selling IQ*[10], states that the buyer is thinking about three things when acquiring information: the importance of the decision to the buyer and the organization, sources of trustworthy information that can improve the quality of the decision, and the costs associated with making or not making a decision. Keep in mind that the status quo is always easier than change for an organization. If the buyer does not believe that the value of a purchase will outweigh the costs associated with the purchase, the decision will be to do nothing. The consultative salesperson may be one source of information used during this stage.

3. Determine Decision Criteria

   During this stage, buyers will determine the decision criteria important to making a decision. Some buyers may use the previously discussed multi-attribute model to determine important decision criteria such as product quality, delivery, and desired cost, whereas others will use specifications established by the individual or department with the need. Still others may use a value-based or solution-based model. Regardless of the approach, the decision criteria set at this step will be useful later when evaluating the various options available.

   It is worth noting that this process tends to be much more formalized in B2B settings. Although some consumers determine purchase criteria ahead of time, this is not always the case.

4. Evaluate Alternatives

   Once the decision criteria have been determined, buyers will begin to search for specific options to consider. For organizational, institutional, and government buyers, this stage may include sending an RFP (request for proposal) or RFQ (request for quote) to the supplier. Buyers will then evaluate the suppliers that submit the RFP or RFQ. Consultative sellers will be involved in this process as buyers contact suppliers about specific solutions. Salespeople who have a well-established relationship with the buyer and buying organization are more likely to be included as an option for evaluation.

   As buyers evaluate alternatives, they will consider the decision criteria as well as the input of others involved in the decision process. In some cases, especially with institutional and government buyers, the evaluation may be handled by a committee assigned to this task.

5. Make and Implement the Decision

   Once buyers have evaluated all alternatives, a choice will be made. Three possible choices are available: purchase from a supplier, fill the need internally, or do nothing. For example, some buying organizations might have the capability to make a particular part in-house and will do so if that option offers more value than purchasing a ready-made part from a supplier. In other situations, buyers may decide it makes more sense to continue with the current situation rather than make a change. Suppliers must show sufficient value to buyers to encourage a purchase.[11]

If the choice is made to purchase from a supplier, details will be negotiated as appropriate and purchase orders generated. Once products are received from the supplier, they will be put to use. If the buyer is a retail buyer, products will be shipped to retail stores and stocked on shelves for consumers to purchase. If the buyer is an organizational buyer, the product may be put into a piece of machinery or added to a manufacturing production line.

6. Assess Supplier Performance

After the decision has been made and implemented, the buyers will evaluate the performance of the solution implemented and determine satisfaction. Satisfaction is achieved when the buyers' expectations regarding solution performance are met or exceeded. If expectations are not met, the buyer will not be satisfied. Outcomes that might be evaluated include performance relative to decision criteria, return on investment (ROI), and satisfaction with the sales representative, among other things. The knowledge gained from this experience will be retained for use in future decisions.

Notice in Figure 2-1 that this process is circular. The last step of the process, achieving satisfaction, provides information for the first step of subsequent buying decision processes. If the buyer has a positive experience and is satisfied, the seller becomes more trusted and is more likely to be invited to participate in the next purchase decision. If the buyer is not satisfied, the trust with the seller either does not develop or is diminished.

The Buying Decision Process in Action: An Example

Let's work through a hypothetical example to illustrate how the buying decision process might work. Todd is the sales manager at a medium-sized company called Strength Saw Blades that produces steel saw blades of all sizes. His firm sells these saw blades to power-tool makers, furniture manufacturers, and other select manufacturers. Todd oversees a sales force that consists of five field sales representatives who travel to visit customers and potential customers on-site, and an additional three inside sales representatives who provide after-sales service and sell to smaller customers.

To date, the sales force of Strength Saw Blades has used spreadsheets to track clients and sales. Todd believes a customer relationship management (CRM) system would help the sales force be more productive and close more sales. Thus, sales manager Todd has recognized a need (Step 1).

Todd goes to company president Sarah with his idea to purchase a CRM system for the sales force. After listening to his rationale, Sarah instructs the buyer, Chris, to gather information on the options available (Step 2). Chris begins her search online by exploring the different CRM systems available. She is particularly interested in reviewing third-party critiques of the different systems. She also contacts a colleague at another organization who recently implemented a CRM system to learn what they chose and why. Finally, she contacts the sales representatives for a handful of companies to understand the capabilities of the system offered by each. She pulls all this information together and creates a report for Sarah and Todd.

Meanwhile, Sarah is working with Todd to determine the most important criteria for the new CRM system (Step 3). Todd is interested in several things, including sales pipeline management and forecasting, as well as consistent use by the sales force. Sarah wants to ensure the new system can be integrated with current accounting systems and is concerned about the overall cost. Both Sarah and Todd agree that ongoing training and service after the sale are of critical importance. They rank their criteria in order of importance.

Chris schedules a meeting with Todd and Sarah to review the report based on the information she has gathered about alternatives. Based on this review, they decide jointly to consider three companies. They also agree that a member of the sales force should be involved in the selection of the system, as well as the IT manager. Chris contacts the sales representative for each of the three firms to schedule a meeting and presentation for what is now an informal decision-making group.

After a presentation by each firm, the group gets together to review the options. They use the previously established criteria when making the final decision (Step 4), following the importance rankings set by Todd and Sarah. Ultimately, they decide to purchase the product that fits their criteria most closely. Chris contacts the sales representative for the chosen company to set the purchase into motion. A purchase order is generated, and the sales representative arranges installation and training.

At the end of the year, Sarah and Todd meet to evaluate the performance of the new CRM system. The system has had the desired effect on productivity, with sales up 10%. The implementation was a bit rocky as salespeople struggled somewhat with the transition from spreadsheets to a new CRM system. However, the supplier provided outstanding training, and the supplier's salesperson was on-site frequently to help users gain experience with the system and resolve problems. As a result, salespeople are using the system. Further, it has integrated well with the existing accounting system and provided realistic sales forecasts easily. Overall, Sarah and Todd agreed that the system was a good purchase, and they were satisfied with the results (Step 5).

Why Salespeople Need to Understand the Buying Decision Process

The salesperson must understand each step of the buyer's process for several reasons. First, the salesperson should make sure to maintain communication with the buyer and the buying organization in order to be present and in the buyer's choice set when alternatives are being considered and when decisions are being made. The salesperson might miss being considered for a sale by being unaware of the decision process as the buyer works through the early stages.

Second, the seller needs to recognize the various ways to add value in the stages of the buying decision process. Early in the process, the seller can add value by providing information on how the seller and firm can potentially solve the buyer's problem. Later, it may become necessary to submit an RFP or RFQ and demonstrate the competitive advantage of the salesperson's solution relative to this problem. If the salesperson's product is selected for purchase, add value by ensuring the product is delivered on time and implemented properly.

Third, to solve the buyer's problem, the seller must have a clear understanding of the issues involved. The seller can even help clarify issues for the buyer, thereby adding more value. Accomplishing this value-add necessitates being present early in the process to ask the right questions and highlight important implications.

Finally, the salesperson needs to recognize the importance of the final step, assessing performance. The salesperson's activities before and after the sale play a huge role in the development of customer satisfaction.

Factors That Influence the Buying Decision Process

The previous section described how the process is influenced by a wide variety of issues, ranging from the organization and the people involved to the product being purchased. Figure 2-2 and the following section highlight a few of the more important influencing factors.

Product Complexity

Not surprisingly, the buying decision process becomes more complex as the product itself becomes more complex. Additionally, the buyer's familiarity with the product or service influences the process. Consider a situation in which the buyer needs to source a sensitive piece of equipment for medical testing and has no prior experience purchasing such equipment. In this case, the buyer is likely to spend more time acquiring information and considering alternative solutions. The buyer may search online to learn more about the product type and possible suppliers and consult with product users to learn more about specifications. Third-party sources are also a good information source; for example, Gartner is a consulting firm that specializes in providing business insights, advice, and reports to people making decisions about technology. Finally, salespeople provide useful information.

Now consider a purchase of paper for the office copy machines and printers. The product is not complex, and the buyer has likely purchased the product before. Little time will be spent acquiring information or considering alternatives. Once the desired paper quality is identified, the buyer will likely buy based on criteria such as price or supplier relationship. The same is true for products seen as

Figure 2-2 Factors Influencing the Buying Decision Process

commodities. When few differences exist between the quality of supplier offerings, the price and the level of value provided by the supplier and supplier's salesperson can be the primary points of consideration.

Commoditization of Products

If a product or service is considered a commodity, that perception can influence the buying decision process. A **commodity** product or service has no unique features in the eyes of customers and potential customers. **Commoditization** is a term used to describe buyer perception when there little to no meaningful differentiation among the available options. In other words, regardless of the brand or manufacturer, all products are seen as the same. When all other features are considered equal, buyers will then purchase on price alone. This situation is bad for selling organizations because competing on price is a weak strategic position. Another organization can always undercut a low price. It is much better to offer unique features that make a product different from other offerings and thereby more attractive to buyers.

commoditization
buyers perceive little to no meaningful differentiation among the available options

Experts have noted that even when a product is a commodity, ways exist to differentiate, including innovation, product bundling, and market segmentation.[12] Innovation includes adding features and benefits not available from similar products. Bundling refers to combining a commodity product with another product or service, thereby making the offering unique. Through market segmentation, sales organizations can broaden their targeted markets to include other groups.

Consider, for example, gasoline. Gasoline is often identified as a commodity product. To make its product unique, Chevron has developed a strong brand name and made its gasoline unique by adding Techron, which improves vehicle mileage and acceleration, reduces emissions, and protects the vehicle engine.[13] Consequently, Chevron has made its commodity product unique to consumers.

Salespeople need to understand how buyers perceive the seller's offerings, and salespeople need to be capable of identifying the unique features and benefits associated with their proposed solutions. The salesperson can be one of the unique benefits for the buyer. Research has shown that customer satisfaction is affected by both functional attributes of the proposed solution (e.g., performance, features, reliability, durability, service, aesthetics) as well as psychological attributes (e.g., competence, courtesy, empathy, communication, reliability, trustworthiness, reputation). Further, while functional attributes were responsible for 37% of the customers' satisfaction, the interpersonal skills of the salesperson (i.e., the psychological attributes) accounted for 63% of customers' satisfaction![14] This finding shows the important role the salesperson can play in differentiating product or service solutions, even when those products or services are considered commodities.

Process Complexity

Product complexity is related to process complexity. The more important the purchase is to the organization, the more likely that other people will get involved. The people within the organization who get involved with a given buying process are sometimes referred to as the **buying center**. The size of the buying center grows and shrinks based on the significance of the decision to the organization, with members moving in and out depending on the nature of the purchase decision. **Buying teams** represent a more formal version of buying centers, in that membership in the team is permanent regardless of the decision, with members possessing complementary skills. Buying teams tend to be responsible for ongoing supplier relationships, along with purchase transactions and strategy.[15]

buying center
the people within the organization who get involved with a given buying process

buying teams
a more formal version of buying centers. Team members are permanent regardless of the decision, with members possessing complementary skills

An example of a buying center might be one's family members and friends who provide input and suggestions as one looks for a car, or the people who provide input to an organizational buyer considering the purchase of a copy machine. Their provision of input automatically places these individuals in a buying center role for that particular decision. Alternatively, a buying team would be formally recognized within an organization as a team and be responsible for ongoing decisions, relationships, purchases, and processes. Sometimes when a buying team is in place, the buying decision process might be broken into two phases. In Phase I, a technical qualification evaluation is conducted by the buying team. If the supplier is deemed qualified in Phase I, that firm moves to Phase II and the purchasing department, which handles the remainder of the buying decision process.

Within the buying center or team, individuals hold certain roles (Figure 2-3). In addition to the buyer, who places the order, buying center members can include various influencers, users, gatekeepers, and decision-makers. **Influencers** provide information or opinions that affect, or influence, the outcome of the purchase decision process. Depending on the nature of the purchase, influencers can range from top executives to technical experts to supplier salespeople.

Those individuals who will use the product, **users,** can also play an essential role in the process. Users can provide information on needed product specifications and needed delivery dates, among other things. If included in the decision process, users can also become influencers. The critical role of users cannot be understated, particularly under certain conditions. For example, a radiologist in an orthopedic clinic or a facilities technician in a manufacturing plant would have more knowledge of the product types and solution needs than the buyer and consequently would play a very influential role in the buying center. In these types of cases, users are product experts and need to be included in the decision process.

Gatekeepers represent anyone who controls the flow of information. Typical examples of gatekeepers in organizations include administrative assistants who guard their bosses' calendars, making it difficult for salespeople to gain appointments. However, anyone within the buying center can take on the gatekeeper role if the flow of information stops for some reason. For example, if the COO has a favorite vendor, that person might withhold information on other suppliers to ensure the favorite supplier is selected.

Traditionally, salespeople have focused their efforts on trying to identify the **decision-maker**, the person with the final say on whether to purchase or not. The thinking was that if the seller could gain the approval of the decision-maker, the sale would go through. Certainly, finding the decision-maker is important,

influencer
a person providing information or opinions that affect or influence the outcome of the purchase decision process

user
individuals who will use the product

gatekeeper
anyone who controls the flow of information

decision-maker
the person with the final say on whether to purchase or not

Figure 2-3 Buying Center Roles

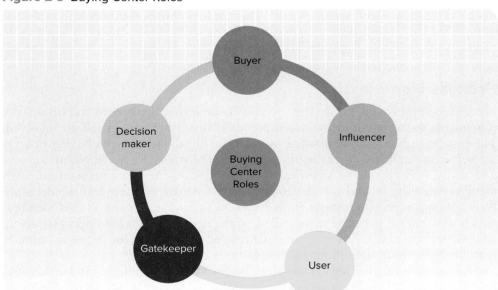

and unfortunately, that person does not have "Decision Maker" stamped on business cards. The salesperson has to gather much information to figure out who is responsible for the final decision. Importantly, though, the decision-maker is not the only buying center member who must be satisfied. Each member of the buying center has different goals and objectives and different information needs; consequently, each member of the buying center may be interested in a different solution benefit. The salesperson needs to determine how to help buying center members so that they, in turn, see the value of the solution.

Let's go back to our previous hypothetical buying decision, with the informal group from Strength Saw Blades considering the purchase of a CRM system. In this case, the committee is the buying center. Chris is the buyer, and the member of the sales force and IT manager serving in the group are both influencers. Sales manager Todd and company president Sarah are also influencers and likely the main decision-makers. Todd and the sales force member are the most likely users, although everyone in the company is likely to use the system at some level. As you can see, individual members of the buying center can take on several roles, and more than one person can fill the same role.

Decision Level

Most organizations have different levels in which decision-making takes place. Members of the buying center can exist at each of these levels. As shown in Figure 2-4, these organizational levels are often illustrated in the form of a pyramid, with the top-level representing the top leaders in the organization, or C-Suite, the middle level representing middle managers, and the bottom level representing users and front-line employees. Sometimes this pyramid is flipped to show that the users and front-line employees are the most important people in the firm. Regardless of how the organization portrays the levels, each of these levels has different information needs and may be interested in different solution features and benefits.

C-Suite   The term **C-suite** reflects the top executives leading the firm, such as the chief executive officer (CEO), chief operating officer (COO), and chief financial officer (CFO). These leaders are responsible for setting the vision and mission, growing the organization to meet goals, and delivering desired results, and they are interested in how a particular solution could help achieve profitability, revenue growth, company goals, competitive advantage, and increased market share.

C-suite
the top leaders in the organization

Figure 2-4 Decision Levels in Organizations

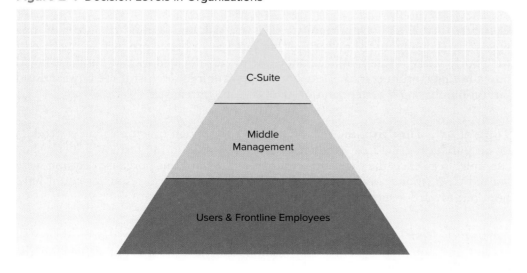

middle managers
managers responsible for core processes within an organization

Middle Managers

Middle managers are responsible for core processes within an organization, with core processes defined as "activities or tasks, which, if not properly or consistently performed, will cause the company to fail in its primary mission."[16] Human resources, IT, sales, and purchasing all represent core processes. Buyers and purchasing managers are part of this level and are interested in achieving objectives, improving the buying decision process, improving purchase outcomes, benefits for users or their organization's customers, and affecting the budget positively.

front-line employees
employees who directly interact with customers

Users and Front-line Employees

Users and **front-line employees** represent those workers who either interact directly with the product or service purchased or deal directly with the buying organization's customers to deliver products or services. These employees possess valuable knowledge useful to the buying decision process, given their close proximity to products and customers. Users and front-line employees are often interested in how the solution purchased helps them improve job performance, achieve better results, and make their work processes easier and more convenient.

Risk

The reason companies employ professional buyers, follow a decision process, and gather information from a variety of sources is singular: to reduce the risk associated with making a bad purchase decision. Consider, for example, a retail buyer responsible for purchasing athletic footwear for a large chain of department stores. If that buyer makes a bad decision to purchase a large quantity of fashion athletic shoes that end up not selling well, several bad outcomes occur. First, retail sales are lower than expected, thereby reducing profits. Second, the dollars used to purchase that inventory are now tied up in that purchase and cannot be used to purchase something else. Third, the buyer may have missed out on purchasing a style that would have sold well because the budget was devoted to this poorly selling style. This same buyer could have chosen to purchase a well-selling shoe, but not purchase enough. In this case, sales and profits could have been higher if the inventory included enough products. When buyers make the right decision, sales and profits are good, and customers are satisfied. It's not surprising, then, that organizations devote critical time and resources to the buying decision process.

The previous example highlighted several different types of risk facing buyers. Additionally, other forms of risk can influence how buyers behave, including the following (see also Table 2-3).

opportunity risk
the risk of spending resources on one product and giving up the opportunity to purchase a better product

Opportunity Risk

Opportunity risk is the risk of spending resources on one product and giving up the opportunity to purchase a better product. In the case of the poorly selling fashion athletic shoe, the money devoted to that purchase could buy a hot new product in that category. Opportunities are lost if the buyer missed out on purchasing a better solution than the one purchased.

time risk
the risk of spending too much time on the new product or on purchasing the new product

Time Risk

Time risk, the risk of spending too much time on the new product or on purchasing the new product, is also illustrated in the fashion athletic shoe example. In essence, the time and resources put toward this purchase decision were wasted when money was lost. Further, that time and those resources could have been put toward a successful decision.

financial risk
the risk that the costs of the product will exceed any potential benefits

Financial Risk

Financial risk is the risk that the costs of the product will exceed any potential benefits. The fashion athletic shoe did not deliver on the expected benefit of high sales, and the result was a financial loss. Because this is a

Table 2-3 Types of Buying Risk

Risk Type	Definition	Example
Opportunity Risk	The risk of spending resources on a product and giving up the opportunity to purchase a better product	A retail buyer uses a significant portion of the budget to add one consumer product to the store's assortment. Because of the budget implications of that purchase, the buyer decides to pass on another consumer product expected to sell well and misses an opportunity.
Time Risk	The risk of spending too much time on the new product or purchasing the new product	An IT manager purchases a new software system for organization employees, only to discover it is taking six months longer than expected for employees to learn how to use the new system effectively.
Financial Risk	The risk that the cost of the product will exceed potential benefits or result in a financial loss	A manufacturer purchases a new piece of equipment expected to save time and money, only to find out that the equipment costs exceed the realized return on investment.
Social/Psychological Risk	The risk of embarrassment or psychological pain	A buyer makes a poor decision that results in budget losses for the firm and a lost promotion for the buyer.
Functional Risk	The risk the product will not perform as intended	A purchasing manager makes a bulk buy of replacement parts at a good price, only to discover those parts are not compatible with the company's equipment.
Physical Risk	The risk that the product will be unsafe or cause harm	A well-known rental car firm purchases a fleet of vehicles from an automobile manufacturer, and then after the vehicles are delivered it discovers the vehicles contain faulty airbags that could harm rental car customers.

retail sales example, the buyer likely had to mark the product down below cost to sell the inventory, thereby losing money on each sale. Using a different example, if a machine part does not perform as expected, the manufacturing process could slow down or be more costly.

Social/Psychological Risk **Social/psychological risk** is the risk of embarrassment. If you are a professional buyer and you make a major mistake with a purchase decision, you might be embarrassed by the failure. Your boss may give you a hard time and make you feel bad. You might take these bad feelings home with you, as job satisfaction affects life satisfaction.[17] If you make bad decisions over time, you might even lose your job. Do you remember our earlier discussion about psychological pain? These psychological risks are very real for organizational buyers.

social/psychological risk
the risk of embarrassment

Functional Risk **Functional risk** is the risk that the product will not perform as intended. Sometimes called *performance risk*, this type of risk is based on the uncertainty that the product or solution purchased will not meet expectations.[18] This risk is very real when purchasing equipment parts, food products, software products, etc., and it is commonly experienced in B2B buying situations. This risk might arise if a product is faulty or fails. Additionally, it's possible the product purchased is not the right solution to the problem.

functional risk / performance risk
the risk that the product will not perform as intended

When functional risk is realized, the buyer is likely to be dissatisfied. Fortunately, this type of risk can be mitigated by the selling organization. Strategies to reduce functional risk include ensuring the solution sold is the best fit for the buyer's needs, providing training for customers after the sale, and ensuring clear use directions are provided. Buyers and sellers need to work together closely to avoid functional risk.

physical risk
the risk that the product will be
unsafe and cause harm

Physical Risk   Related to functional risk is **physical risk**, meaning that the product might be unsafe and cause harm. Unfortunately, history provides several examples of catastrophic results arising from physical risk. In January 1986, the Space Shuttle Challenger explosion, which resulted in the death of the entire crew, was triggered by defective O-rings, i.e., circular gaskets sealing the rocket boosters.[19] More recently, faulty airbags installed in tens of millions of automobiles ran the risk of exploding under extreme exposure to hot and humid weather conditions. When the airbags exploded, metal shards rocketed into the vehicle and its passengers. This defective product resulted in a major recall of affected automobiles and caused at least 180 injuries and 20 deaths.[20] Although these examples are extreme, they demonstrate the risks associated with a bad product purchase. The physical risk of products is a serious issue for buyers.

Timeline for Purchase

The timeline available to make a decision also affects the buying process. A long timeline suggests the members of the buying center have ample time to make a decision and can adopt a more complex buying process aimed at reaching the best decision. If the timeline is short, a rushed process results.

In an attempt to mitigate all the previously described risks and uncertainty associated with the purchase process, buyers are inclined to purchase from current suppliers because those suppliers have a proven track record for delivering on expectations. This reality is important for a selling organization to recognize and respond accordingly. If a firm is a proven or current supplier, the selling and buying processes will be affected as it will be more likely to be invited to participate in the buying decision process. If not a current or proven supplier, a firm will have to adjust its strategies to gain access to the purchase decision process. This situation highlights the importance of the salesperson's understanding of the buying decision process and the actions needed to become one of the alternatives considered for purchase.

Adding Value to the Buyer's Process

As we have discussed throughout this chapter, the key to sales success is figuring out how to add value to buyers' processes and businesses. Determining the most effective way to add value necessitates understanding the buyer's processes and needs, as well as how the buyer defines value. Three ways to add value are reducing risk and complexity, aligning processes, and becoming a trustworthy consultant.

Reduce Risk and Complexity

As we discussed earlier, buyers face many different types of risk when making purchase decisions—the greater the risk associated with the purchase, the greater the uncertainty associated with the outcomes. Further, complexity in processes and products can add more risk. A highly complex buying process involving many people and several layers of management, for example, faces substantial time and opportunity risk that can result in a less-than-optimal decision. Fortunately, research has suggested an inverse relationship between risk and value; as perceived risk is reduced, perceived value increases.[21] The salesperson should focus on various ways to reduce the risk and complexity associated with the buyer decision process.

Align Processes

Author and sales expert Kim Ward recommends aligning a solution to the buyer's decision criteria directly by using what he calls "one-to-one solution to criteria alignment."[22] By addressing each buying decision criterion, the salesperson demonstrates the ability to deliver on the best solution for the buyer's issue or problem. The ability to align the buying and selling processes, of course, depends in part on the ability to understand the buyer's process and decision criteria. It also depends on the salesperson's knowledge of the products, services, and solutions and how they can resolve the buyer's problems, as well as the salesperson's skill in asking deep and thoughtful questions to uncover the buyer's real issues.

Become a Trustworthy Consultant

Ultimately, the salesperson should strive to become a trustworthy consultant for the buyer and the buyer's firms. Buyers are interested in working with sellers who can add value to their process and their work lives. A seller who can reduce the risk and complexity associated with the buyer's decision will add significant value. Further, aligning a solution directly with the buyer's criteria will make the added value obvious to the buyer. Over time, as the buyer experiences success with these solutions, the salesperson can become a trusted resource, to whom the buyer will turn for additional business. The key to all selling (B2B or B2C) is not to make one sale, but to create a value-based relationship in which the buyer trusts the seller with current and future needs. Creating and managing well-developed buyer-seller relationships is the most efficient and effective way to achieve sales success.

Applying this Chapter to Salesforce

Customer Relationship Management (CRM) systems like Salesforce are used in both B2B and B2C companies, as well as in government agencies, and non-profit organizations. Car companies use CRM to track interactions with potential new partners, manage inventory, and analyze trends in relationships with current business partners. A popular athletic apparel company utilizes CRM to track individual consumer website visits, email opens, link clicks, and purchasing habits. They use the same system to track orders and support service inquiries. Government agencies have started implementing CRMs for recruiting, retention, advancement, communication, and community engagement. And non-profit organizations use CRM to manage their fundraising, outreach, and volunteer efforts more effectively.

This chapter covered the importance of knowing your customer and what affects their likelihood of buying. Learning the roles and decision-makers for each consumer is critical to influencing the purchasing decision. But most salespeople find it difficult to remember so many details when balancing several clients. At a minimum, Salesforce allows the salesperson to collect the title of each contact, who they report to, and whether their approval is critical to closing the sale. Over time, Salesforce will organize this data into a virtual organizational chart the salesperson can use to ensure they are engaging with the correct decision-makers and influencers.

As the salesperson learns more about their buyers, their organizations, and needs, the discipline of adding information to Salesforce can payoff for several reasons. The first, and most important, is that all the information about the buying decision process will be in one place to review any time within the sales cycle. Second, Salesfoce data can provide transparency to management or anyone else helping with the sale. Lastly, it can reveal trends in the buying process by customer, across the territory, and the entire firm.

Salesforce can also improve the outcome for a salesperson against a specific competitor. The salesperson can review details about their own prior experience against the competitor, as well as information about the competitor from other salespeople, their marketing department, or anyone else in the salesperson's firm. This information can help the salesperson better position their offering against the competitor's known strengths and weaknesses.

Salesforce can also automatically add up the data to produce a *pipeline* and other easy-to-read reports, sometimes called *dashboards*, showing the percentage of times the salesperson's company wins when in a competitive situation, and providing estimates for the timeline to purchase based on similar sales situations.

Chapter Summary

- The buying process includes the considerations, evaluations, and decisions involved in choosing whether to purchase a product or service solution.
- The buying role includes consumers, retail buyers, organizational buyers, and institutional/government buyers.
- To create value for customers and achieve success, salespeople need to understand the buying process and the various issues facing buyers.
- Buyer motivations include situation repair, situation improvement, and situation continuance, and they can be rational or emotional in nature.
- Buyers purchase products for the benefits they provide; adept salespeople can translate features into benefits of interest to the buyer.
- Buyers use a wide variety of decision-making criteria when making a purchase decision, and the salesperson can play an important role in identifying and delivering on those criteria.
- The buying decision process includes six steps: (1) recognize a need; (2) gather preliminary information; (3) determine decision criteria; (4) evaluate alternatives; (5) make and implement decision; and (6) assess supplier performance.
- The factors influencing the buying decision process include product complexity, commoditization of products, process complexity, decision level, risk, and the timeline for purchase.
- The buying center consists of anyone involved in the purchase decision process, including the buyer, influencer, user, gatekeeper, and decision-maker roles.
- The salesperson can become a trustworthy consultant by reducing risk and complexity and aligning the selling process with the buying decision process.

Key Terms

B2B (p. 24)
B2C (p. 24)
benefits (p. 28)
buyer (p. 24)
buying center (p. 35)
buying decision process (p. 30)
buying organization (p. 24)
buying teams (p. 35)
C-Suite (p. 37)
commodity/commoditization (p. 35)
decision maker (p. 36)
direct procurement (p. 25)
features (p. 28)
financial risk (p. 38)
front-line employees (p. 38)
functional risk (p. 39)
gatekeeper (p. 36)

indirect procurement (p. 25)
influencer (p. 36)
middle managers (p. 38)
multi-attribute model (p. 29)
opportunity risk (p. 38)
physical risk (p. 40)
retail buyer (p. 24)
salesperson (p. 24)
situation continuance (p. 27)
situation improvement (p. 27)
situation repair (p. 27)
social/psychological risk (p. 39)
supplier (p. 24)
time risk (p. 38)
user (p. 36)
value (p. 26)

Application 2-1

Megan Townsend is a purchasing director for a private regional hospital located in the Midwest. A few weeks ago, Megan was approached by CFO Bill Mitchell about replacing the hospital's antiquated accounting software. Bill mentioned that the reports from the current software are not user-friendly, and the system itself is inefficient. Bill asked Megan to work directly with the head of the accounting department Roger Stales to learn more what the department would need the software to accomplish, as he had already approached Roger about his desire for a change. He also mentioned that CEO Brenda Everly would like to be kept in the loop regarding the decision process, as well as IT Director Chris Rowe. Chris would have specific ideas about implementation. Of course, as a user of the data and reports generated by the accounting software, Bill would also be heavily involved in the decision process.

Today, Megan met with Roger Stales to get the ball rolling on the purchase decision. Roger indicated that the new accounting software would need to include accounting, billing, payroll, and budget planning capabilities. He suggested that Megan include staff members from each of these areas in the decision process to ensure the software chosen addresses their respective needs. He recommended four staff members for Megan to contact. She made a note to call them later that afternoon. Roger did have some suggestions regarding software suppliers to consider, and Megan jotted down that information. Megan asked about the timeline for the purchase, and Roger indicated the goal would be to implement the new software at the beginning of the next fiscal year, approximately ten months from today.

As Megan headed back to her office, she thought about the next steps. She needed to start gathering information quickly, as ten months is not much time to make such a complex decision. She needed to talk to potential users as well as influencers, the IT Director, the CEO, the CFO, and Roger to establish the decision criteria. Each person might have different requirements. She needed to familiarize herself with available products, gather as much third-party information and research as possible, and start contacting sales representatives, including the representatives recommended by Roger. She was excited to lead such an important purchase process but also recognized she needed to be fully prepared, as many people would have an opinion on the product ultimately chosen, and the risk of making a bad choice was high. Megan took a deep breath and sat down at her desk to outline a game plan.

1. In this situation, what is Megan's buying role?
2. Who seems to have recognized the need for a solution?
3. What role is CEO Brenda Everly likely playing in this decision process?

Application 2-2

Matt Winger is a new business development representative for TechSource Staffing. TechSource is a recruiting company that handles the candidate recruiting process for technology and engineering firms. TechSource develops relationships with talented engineers and information technology specialists; companies turn to TechSource when they are looking for a strong pool of potential employees to fill open positions in their firms. Companies become TechSource clients when they see the value

(Continued)

(Continued)

of partnering with a firm that can provide recruiting expertise, great talent, and add efficiency to the recruiting and hiring process.

By using TechSource services, companies outsource the recruiting function of the human resources department, freeing up those personnel to focus on employee training and development, among other things. TechSource offers three different employee options: contract, contract-for-hire, and direct placement. Contract employees are temporary employees hired to do a specific job or project; when the job or project ends, so ends the contract. Contract-to-hire employees are contract employees who can be hired by the client firm at the end of the contract if the client firm is impressed by the work of that employee and has an open position. Direct placement employees are hired full-time by the client firm. Providing three different hiring options allows TechSource to offer flexible, customized, and convenient solutions to hiring needs. TechSource is known for having industry-savvy recruiters who have developed strong relationships with early-career tech experts and engineers. As the #2 IT and Engineering staffing firm in North America, TechSource serves over 4,500 clients and places over 5,000 IT specialists and engineers each year.

As a new business development representative, Matt is responsible for identifying prospective clients and converting them to new clients for TechSource services. For the past six months, he has been talking to Wendy Harmon, the Director of Human Resources at Starfish Technology. Starfish creates technology and engineering solutions for manufacturers of technical products. Headquartered in Chicago, Starfish has been growing rapidly and is in the process of opening a new location in Dallas. Wendy needs to identify top technology and engineering talent quickly to meet the needs of this new Starfish location. Because Matt has been meeting with Wendy regularly to learn more about her business, they have developed a fairly good working relationship. As a consequence, Wendy called Matt to request that he submit a proposal to be considered for this opportunity.

Matt is meeting with Wendy tomorrow at Starfish headquarters to discuss the proposal. Also at the meeting will be CEO Sam Riley, CFO Andrea Marker, IT Director Pete Gomez, and head of Engineering Maria Champion. As he prepares for the meeting, Matt is outlining the features, benefits, and value he can offer Starfish and anticipating the different information needs of the different individuals who will be in the meeting. He is also trying to determine which role each person is playing in the buying decision process. He wants to make sure he can mitigate the risk associated with this purchase. Matt takes a gulp of coffee and scribbles furiously in his notebook—he has a lot of preparation ahead of him, and he is determined to be ready!

1. What stage of the buying decision process is illustrated in this example?
2. What is a benefit of TechSource's service offerings?
3. How would you describe the group of people meeting with Matt tomorrow?

Professionalism and Effective Communication

CHAPTER **3**

Learning Objectives

- Define professionalism in the workplace and within sales
- Explain and discuss the value of emotional intelligence (EQ)
- Summarize the value of communication skills in sales
- Analyze effective verbal and nonverbal communication skills
- Discuss adaptive selling and social styles
- Illustrate the connection between communication and technology

Employers require strong communication skills in their hires and especially from recent college graduates.[1] Take a look at any sales job posting and without exception, good communication skills are at or near the top of the list of requirements. Today, more than ever, customers demand that salespeople know and understand their concerns[2] and be able to provide and clearly communicate viable solutions. Meeting these high expectations can only be accomplished through professionalism and effective communication.

This chapter addresses the application of professionalism and communication skills to build trusting personal and business relationships in sales and how to improve each. We first explore what it means to be professional and how to become more professional. We next explore the role of emotional intelligence (EQ), its importance in any career, and ways to improve EQ. We then investigate the importance of communication skills in sales and identify ways to improve a salesperson's sales effectiveness through better communication skills.

What It Means to Be a Professional

Appropriately interacting with others, taking the initiative to become proficient in a chosen career, and correctly responding to challenges and adversity are all marks of *professional* behavior. Professionalism is also highly related to ethics and ethical conduct, which we will discuss in detail in Chapter 13. We include professionalism as a separate topic here because of its importance in setting a salesperson apart in a highly competitive business environment.[3]

Figure 3-1 identifies the conduct, purpose, and qualities of a professional. While different industries and organizations promote specific and unique norms for acceptable professional behavior, there are commonalities agreed upon by all. Professional salespeople make a personal commitment to develop and improve the skills required of the profession and exhibit integrity, competency, humility, accountability, self-regulation, and a professional image. Everyone can acquire these skills and make the choices required to truly be a professional.

Integrity

Integrity is a personal quality of fairness; in simplest terms, it exemplifies doing the "right thing" in the "right way" even when it means inconveniencing yourself.

integrity
a personal quality of fairness

Figure 3-1 Professionalism: Conduct, purpose, and qualities of a professional

Salespeople build trust when they exhibit integrity. Building trust, as discussed throughout this book, is essential to sales success. Salespeople make daily decisions that define who they are and what they believe in their own eyes and, importantly, in the eyes of their customers and co-workers.

For example, Shauna shows integrity when she makes sure that Megan's shipment is delivered on Friday if she has promised the shipment will arrive then. Shauna will call Megan to make sure that the shipment arrived. If Shauna discovers the components to be delivered are slightly damaged, even if the damage would not impair their performance, she will contact Megan to let her know the components were damaged. Shauna handles challenging situations immediately and appropriately regardless of how uncomfortable she feels. A salesperson exhibits integrity by doing what should be done, when it should be done, without compromising his or her values.

Integrity is the sum of a salesperson's daily choices and behavior exhibited throughout his or her career.

Competency

While integrity incorporates daily decisions regarding the right behavior, **competency** requires knowledge and preparation necessary for a salesperson to identify customer challenges, develop value-driven solutions, and deliver on promises made. Immediately after being promoted to the healthcare industry sales team, Rachel began researching the industry and her primary target customers and the chief information officer (CIO) role, who are decision-makers for telecom/technology purchases. This research helps her better understand both the industry and her customers. She sets aside five hours per week to continue research through online CIO discussion groups to keep up to date on industry trends, challenges faced by CIOs, and to network with technology leaders. She role-plays customer and prospect scenarios weekly with her manager and co-workers to improve her sales skills. Rachel makes the extra ongoing effort to become more competent and prepared to serve her customers.

> **competency**
> having the necessary knowledge and preparation

Becoming competent and staying competent is continuous. Oswald Chambers stated, "It is easy to imagine that we will get to a place where we are complete and ready, but preparation is not suddenly accomplished, it is a process steadily maintained."[4] A **profession**, strictly defined, requires specialized knowledge and skill set.[5] Professional salespeople continually update the knowledge required to understand their customers (industry, company, product, competitors, regulations, etc.) and skills that help customers move through their decision process. Reading this and other credible sales-related books, and then practicing and implementing the concepts ultimately contributes to the knowledge and skills that lead to professionalism. Professional salespeople develop competencies that allow them to help their customers identify their goals and overcome obstacles to those goals. These skills include listening, questioning, technological, analytical, and relationship development to name a few.[6] Preparation and homework do not end after graduation. Preparation and training must be a lifelong approach for professional salespeople.

> **profession**
> an occupation requiring specialized knowledge and skill set

Humility

Closely tied to competence is the trait of humility. While confidence is central to sales performance,[7] there is a difference between confidence and arrogance. Confidence is having an assurance of what you can accomplish; if you put in the effort, you are sure of having success. **Humility** is a state of modesty without an excess of pride. Because of the misconceptions of the sales profession and what is required to be successful, most do not associate successful salespeople with humility, which appears to be the opposite of confidence. Humble salespeople

> **humility**
> a state of modesty without an excess of pride

strive for continuous improvement. Confident salespeople do not have to be the center of attention and are *comfortable in their own skin*. Successful salespeople make the sales process about their customers, not themselves.

Accountability

Professional salespeople hold themselves accountable for their actions, words, and outcomes. **Accountability** means taking responsibility for success or failure. Professionals do not blame fate or others for their failures or attribute their successes to luck. Professionals understand that most of their successes and failures result from their own decisions and effort. Success is the consequence of daily actions and decisions over weeks, months, and years. Professional salespeople will lose sales when they do everything right and sometimes win sales when they make mistakes. Salespeople increase their chances of being successful by doing what should be done, when it should be done, whether they feel like it or not. Successful salespeople do not waste time blaming others. There are times when a salesperson's organization makes errors in order entry, delivering the product, or billing, among other things. Effective salespeople take the initiative to work with others in their organization to make sure value is delivered as promised rather than simply complaining. Holding yourself accountable focuses your efforts and energy on what can be done to improve and have success.

Self-Regulation

Self-regulation is the ability to maintain control of emotions and actions in adverse situations, and sales has its own unique pressures and challenges. Self-regulation requires salespeople to stay *professional* under pressure. They interact with their company's customers probably more than any other employee, and situations arise that may anger or frustrate the customer, and, quite often, the salesperson is the one that bears the brunt of those frustrations. These exasperations are sometimes warranted, and, at times, they are not. Regardless, the salesperson must maintain a professional demeanor and maintain a calm, businesslike approach to each situation and do what is required (not what they *feel* like doing, reacting rather than thoughtfully responding). This does not mean the customer is always right, but it means that the salesperson responds rather than reacts to the adverse situation. Professionals manage relationships in a mature manner and control their emotions as well as consider the emotions of the other party. Salespeople should exhibit a high level of emotional intelligence, which is addressed in the next section.

Professional Image

Having a **professional image** means simply acting and looking the part. Your image is conveyed in what you choose to wear, the cleanliness of your hair, and whether or not you have bad breath! Professionals are aware of their posture and body language, are well-groomed and clean, dress appropriately for the situation, and keep their vehicle presentable. Professional salespeople are well prepared for meetings with presentation materials that are error-free and in good condition. A professional image communicates confidence (not arrogance), which builds trust and credibility.

Emotional Intelligence

Michael has been with Allstate for eight months, his first job after graduation from college, and has begun specializing in selling supplemental health insurance targeting small to mid-sized companies. His first big sales meeting was with Krysten, the regional Human Resources manager for PolyOne, a global leader in polymer materials. Krysten has been an HR manager for 20 years. The meeting began with Krysten's asking Michael about his experience. Michael realized he was a little sensitive to his own age and inexperience, but Krysten's concern was legitimate. Krysten had probably been accustomed to working with older salespeople. Rather than getting offended, Michael provided evidence of expert support he had from Allstate and the value that the solution provided to PolyOne's employees and the company. Michael was mature enough to understand his emotions as well as Krysten's. He went on to make the largest sale of his young career. Michael exhibited a high level of emotional intelligence.

Emotional intelligence (EQ) is the ability to understand your and others' emotions and to use your awareness of those emotions to manage and control your behavior and relationships with others.[8] Research shows that EQ is twice as important as technical skills and IQ when it comes to high performance,[9] and the emotional challenges associated with the sales profession make EQ even more important.

> **emotional intelligence (EQ)**
> the ability to understand your and others' emotions and to use your awareness of those emotions to manage and control your behavior and relationships with others

How does EQ work? Why is it so important, yet so difficult to understand and manage? You are bombarded daily with stimuli—everything you see, hear, smell, taste, and touch creates electrical signals that travel through your cells and nerve endings and ultimately to your brain. These signals enter your brain through the spinal cord and eventually arrive at your **neocortex** or **frontal lobe** where logic and rational thinking occur.

> **neocortex/frontal lobe**
> the part of the brain where logic and rational thinking occur

However, before signals get to your rational thought center, they first travel through the limbic system where your emotions are produced. In other words, all stimuli you receive activate your emotions *before* you deal with them logically. So, when a prospect raises an objection ("Your price is too high!") the salesperson initially experiences the emotion (rejection; he doesn't like me; here we go again about price; I'm not going to make the sale; maybe our price is too high!) of the experience. In low EQ salespeople, the signal may never reach the neocortex. However, high EQ salespeople recognize this as a *trigger* event based on their knowledge of themselves, their history and personal experience, and they quickly engage the logic and rational thought center (that's okay, I know this prospect doesn't understand the value yet; I will be patient and discuss this with him; this happens often, and I look forward to sharing how my service can really help him and his organization). Everyone feels emotion. However, as you develop your EQ, you can respond rationally rather than react emotionally and lose control of the situation.

Importance of Emotional Intelligence

EQ explains a central element of behavior that is distinctly different from intellect. People with higher EQ levels outperform people with higher IQs more than 80% of the time. EQ accounts for 58% of performance in all types of jobs, and every point increase in EQ improves annual earnings by $1,300.[10] EQ is a significant factor in sales performance. Research shows that salespeople with high EQ significantly outperformed those with low EQ.[11]

> **personal competence**
> the sum of self-awareness, self-management, and self-motivation
>
> **social competence**
> the combination of social awareness and relationship management skills

Components of Emotional Intelligence

As illustrated in Figure 3-2 EQ includes personal competence and social competence skills. **Personal competence** incorporates self-awareness, self-management, and self-motivation skills. **Social competence** includes social awareness and relationship management skills.

Personal competence relates to how you understand and manage yourself. **Self-awareness** is the ability to recognize and understand your moods, emotions, and drives, as well as their effect on others. **Self-management** is the ability to control or direct disruptive impulses and moods, the capacity to suspend judgment and to think before acting. Personal competence also includes **self-motivation** or the propensity to pursue goals with energy and persistence. High EQ salespeople

> **self-awareness**
> the ability to recognize and understand your moods, emotions, and drives, as well as their effect on others
>
> **self-management**
> the ability to control or direct disruptive impulses and moods, the capacity to suspend judgment and to think before acting
>
> **self-motivation**
> the propensity to pursue goals with energy and persistence

Figure 3-2

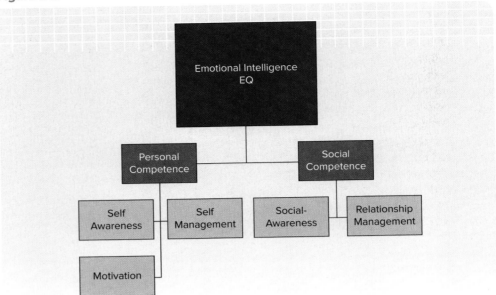

have a passion for work that goes beyond just making money or achieving status. This does not mean that they do not want to make money or have others recognize them favorably (status of title or position), but they have motivation that goes beyond these. Related to motivation but not strictly associated with EQ is **positive affectivity**, or positive emotions. Salespeople who strive to maintain a positive attitude and emotions tend to be more self-motivated and view difficult sales situations in a more positive light.[12]

Social competence includes **social awareness** or the ability to understand the emotional makeup of others and the skill to treat people according to their emotional reactions. **Relationship management**, another component of social competence, is the ability to proficiently manage relationships and build networks and includes the skill to find common ground and build rapport with others.

Improving Emotional Intelligence

The good news is that while IQ is fairly unchanging, EQ is a flexible skill that can be learned and improved. Your brain is a muscle, and when exercised its capabilities can improve. Increased use strengthens the connection between the rational and emotional centers of your brain. In other words, the more you rationally think about how you feel, the more developed the pathway, and the stronger your EQ becomes. Your brain continues to build new connections (a single brain cell can grow up to 15,000 connections with surrounding cells), and efficiencies as you reflect on your emotions and how you interact with others and then make conscious effort to act and manage yourself.

Importance of Communication Skills in Sales

Strong relationships are built upon effective communication. Most relationship breakups, arguments, divorces, and wars occur because of simple misunderstandings and poor communication. Historically, salespeople communicated to convey

positive affectivity
striving to maintain a positive attitude

social awareness
the ability to understand the emotional makeup of others and the skill to treat people according to their emotional reactions

relationship management
the ability to proficiently manage relationships and build networks

information about their products to their customers. Often sales representatives say that they are "teachers." However, the role of the salesperson has changed dramatically, and customers expect salespeople to understand their business and their concerns, and to be more consultative. Consultants solve business challenges based on the customer's situation, and salespeople must strive to do more than just convey information. They must first understand the customer's concerns. So the objective of communication is not simply to present information. The objective of communication is understanding. Thorough understanding can only be accomplished by using effective communication.

Developing Effective Verbal Communication Skills

How a salesperson delivers a message affects the customer's understanding of the message and perceptions of the salesperson. In this section, we will discuss how tone or inflection of a salesperson's voice, articulation, and choice of words, and use of abstract, filler words all influence the salesperson's ability to communicate clearly and effectively.

Vocal Qualities

Varying voice tone and inflection helps reduce monotony and assists the receiver in understanding the importance of what the salesperson is communicating. **Tone** refers to modulation of the voice to suggest attitudes or emotions such as anger, surprise, excitement, happiness, or fear, among others, whereas **inflection** is associated with the emphasis placed on a word, a part of a word, or group of words. Using variation in tone and inflection engages the customer emotionally and communicates the speaker's excitement, interest, and conviction and is more likely to create an emotional connection. For example, "this is a great deal that will save you 20% on your technology budget" can communicate boredom, whereas "this is a GREAT deal that will SAVE you 20% on your technology budget" can communicate enthusiasm and conviction. The same words are used, but by varying the tone and inflection of "great" and "save", the customer will probably be more emotionally moved to action.

tone
modulation of the voice to suggest attitudes or emotions

inflection
the emphasis placed on a word, a part of a word, or group of words

Being **articulate** means that a person expresses oneself readily, clearly, and effectively. More articulate salespeople are perceived as more credible and persuasive. Articulate speech is achieved by using appropriate concrete wording that has specific meaning. Generally, avoid **filler words**, those with no real function or meaning other than to fill space in the conversation. Some of these include like, you know, stuff, cool, uh, um, totally, actually, basically, well, you see, and they can include any other words used to fill a space in the conversation. Consider the difference between the following statements. Which is more effective?

articulate
expressing oneself readily, clearly, and effectively

filler words
words with no real function or meaning other than to fill space in the conversation

> This is a *very cool* iPhone, *you know*. It has a *lot of cool* stuff that customers like. I, *like*, love mine and all of my other customers **like, you know**, sell a *whole lot* of them.

> This iPhone is seen by your market as attractive and elegant. It has 15 new and distinct features that help your customers be more productive and connected. After carrying this line of iPhone, our other customers have increased their market share by 25% within 6 months.

Filler words, in moderation, are okay, but used in excess they can be annoying. Regardless of a salesperson's intelligence or capabilities, most customers will view them more positively if they are articulate, especially early in the relationship. Being

Table 3-1 Choose Your Words Carefully

Use	Rather than
Investment	Cost
Share	Show
Inexpensive	Cheap
Value	Low-cost
Challenge	Problem
Obstacle	Problem
Issues	Problem
Concerns	Objections
Definitely	Probably
We	I
More attractive	Better

negative connotation
negative feelings commonly associated with certain words or phrases

inarticulate may present obstacles to moving the relationship forward. Improving your articulation takes a conscious effort, and you are helped by improving your vocabulary and practicing when having any conversation.

Besides filler words, there are other words a salesperson should avoid. Some words have a **negative connotation**, meaning most people associate unfavorable feelings with those words. For example, customers often consider spending money on a *cost* to be negative, while spending money on an *investment* is more positive. People prefer to have a salesperson share information rather than to be shown or told about a product's features and benefits. Table 3-1 provides a partial list of more effective word choices.

Sending and Reading Nonverbal Messages

nonverbal
the unspoken transfer of messages or information through cues

Nonverbal communication is the unspoken transfer of messages or information through cues other than the spoken or written word. Some studies suggest that 80 percent of communication occurs nonverbally.[13] Nonverbal messages include body language (posture, gestures, distance), facial expressions, eye contact, and dress.

Body Language

body language
nonverbal messages from certain body movements and gestures

Also known as kinesics, **body language** sends nonverbal messages with certain body movements and gestures that express feelings about another person or situation and, often, one's self-image. A salesperson's relationship with customers is affected by the messages sent nonverbally. Because we are generally unaware of the signals we send nonverbally, we may be sending unintended messages. Generally, a more open posture communicates non-threatening cues and a more receptive attitude. Crossing arms or closed posture can suggest discomfort or defensiveness. Slumping or slouching can communicate disinterest while sitting up or standing straight will communicate engagement and interest.

mirroring
matching the stance and posture of the other person in the conversation

Mirroring is matching the stance and posture of the other person in the conversation. Mirroring often happens subconsciously and is a way to bond or build understanding. While you are in a public venue, watch people in conversations to see how they begin to mirror the other person through their body positioning, facial expressions, and gestures. A word of caution: too much mirroring may become obvious and can be annoying.

Facial Expressions

Facial expressions of emotion are universal to all cultures, can communicate numerous expressions of emotions, and are the principal way humans convey social information.[14] Involuntary facial expressions can occur in less than a second, and often provide cues to true thoughts and emotions. We previously discussed emotional intelligence (EQ), and with improvement in EQ, the ability to control some of these involuntary facial communications will improve. Remember, people experience emotions (lymbic system) before engaging logic (neocortex), which makes it difficult to guard against initial reactions and emotions of a situation or person before determining the appropriate response.

The most powerful nonverbal message is the use of a smile. Customers become more relaxed and consider you more trustworthy when you smile. They tend to be more open during conversations as well as perceive you as more friendly. Some research suggests that if you smile at the beginning of a meeting and the end, it shows that you are friendly, but not so friendly that you can be taken advantage of or manipulated. Smiling improves your mood, lowers blood pressure, provides stress relief, and improves relationships. Smiling and laughter also lead to a stronger immune function, pain relief, and, not surprisingly, a longer life.[15]

Eye Contact

Good eye contact can communicate confidence, trust, and respect. It also suggests that you are paying attention. Avoiding eye contact might also mean that you do not want the other person to know what you are thinking, thus encouraging distrust. Eye contact or lack of eye contact affects the way others think about you. Dilated pupils suggest that there is interest in the other person and, vice versa, restricted pupils suggest disinterest and also that you are less trustworthy. Therefore, you should consciously engage and focus on the other person and what they are saying. In other words, be interested. It is a choice.

Lack of eye contact can communicate non-interest, but too much eye contact (staring) can also be detrimental to a conversation and relationship. So what is the appropriate balance? Generally, one can break eye contact more often when speaking and maintain more eye contact when the other person is speaking. Consider maintaining consistent eye contact about 50% of the time when speaking and about 70% of the time when listening.

The Handshake

The handshake contributes to the first impression made when meeting someone. Shaking hands is traditional in the United States, but it dates back to the 5th century B.C. in Greece. It was a gesture of peace, indicating that neither person carried a weapon. Today, it is a global indication of friendship or courtesy. In business, it is considered rude not to shake hands when another's hand is extended. Some people may not shake hands for cultural or religious reasons (orthodox Muslims do not have social or physical contact with people of the opposite gender). However, this is rare and an exception. Salespeople engaged in sales internationally should research, respect, and follow the business etiquette of the country in which they are doing business. Salespeople should always extend their hand when meeting new people. What's so important about shaking hands? Touching another person (appropriately) breaks down one of the first barriers to communication. The touch releases hormones that create a sense of bonding and warmth, and it also has a calming effect. Some studies from medical researchers and journals suggest that primary care physicians who touch their patients during counseling (again, appropriately; on the shoulder, arm, back, etc.) promote healing.

Do's and Don'ts of Shaking Hands

Do
1. Always shake hands. Extend your hand even if the other person does not; if the other person does not shake your extended hand, simply drop your hand without getting upset. There may be a reason.
2. Look the other person in the eye.
3. Smile.
4. Shake firmly—no up and down movement is necessary, but more than one or two can be annoying.

Don't
1. Grasp too firmly—it is not a competition.
2. Grasp limply—known as a "dead fish" handshake.
3. Shake too long—be alert to when the other person releases, otherwise one firm grasp is appropriate.

Here are a couple of final answers to questions often asked. Yes, always attempt to shake hands with males or females regardless of your or their gender identity. If ill, one may excuse oneself from shaking hands by simply saying, "I'm sorry, I am sick, and I do not want to get you sick." It is okay to shake hands left-handed if the person is an amputee. Many amputees will still offer an arm to shake. Shake whatever is extended.

Appearance and Dress

The first nonverbals sent to a customer are general appearance and attire. Just as the salesperson is judged by articulateness, others' perception of the salesperson's credibility and trustworthiness is also substantially affected by clothing and appearance. What one wears matters. Fashions and "official" business attire are a moving target in today's culture, so it is a good idea to seek guidance from others in the organization regarding business attire. There are also useful resources available that provide guidance on professional business attire for sales professionals on the internet. Conduct a search for "Appropriate Business Attire for Sales Professionals." Because fashions do change regularly, below are some general tips on professional wardrobe and appearance.

- Ask for guidance from the manager and other sales reps in your organization.
- Generally, dress similarly to the way the customers dress.
- Always wear clean and pressed attire. If you can afford to dry clean, you should do so, or learn how to iron. Also, keep shoes in good repair and polished.
- Do not wear clothing that brings attention to your clothing or other aspects of your physique besides the face. Facial expressions are responsible for most of what is communicated nonverbally. Do not draw attention away from the face. Both males and females should avoid any clothing that is too tight, too short or reveals too much skin. This comes across the wrong way in a business environment, and one is less likely to be taken seriously.
- It is important to bathe (daily) and wear deodorant (daily). Go easy on the cologne or perfume. Don't smoke, especially before any business meetings. Brush your teeth at least three times a day and always carry breath mints. One is not often aware of one's own smell, so ask others about the strength of your cologne or perfume and general odor. An unpleasant odor can cost relationships and sales.

Listening to Sell

Despite the stereotypes of salespeople being avid talkers with the "gift of gab," as we discussed in Chapter 1, salespeople who listen more than they talk are more successful.[16] Many sales experts and researchers suggest the "80-20" communication rule. The highest performing salespeople listen 80% of the time and talk only 20% of the time. Listening is one of the more challenging obstacles salespeople face. Sherlock Holmes, the famous, fictitious private detective, famously said to Watson: "You see, but you do not observe." The same is true for listening; everyone hears, but not everyone listens. What is the difference? Hearing is accidental, involuntary, and effortless, whereas listening is intentional, voluntary, and determined.

The Role and Importance of Listening

Listening is important in developing good relationships. For salespeople, listening is critical for very practical and psychological reasons. Some practical reasons are that it allows the listener to gain information, involves the speaker in the conversation, motivates the speaker, helps the speaker resolve issues, and can lead to joint or mutual problem-solving. A less obvious reason is it gives the speaker a chance to just get something off their chest. Some comments do not require a response, and the speaker just needs to talk through an issue. Another practical reason is that listening allows the listener the chance to think and process information. A psychological reason important to a relationship and to salespeople is that when a person listens, it communicates that the person cares.

Active Listening

Why do we forget a person's name immediately after being introduced? The brain is a fascinating machine. People, generally, can hear and comprehend at a rate of around 800 words per minute. However, we can only speak at a rate of about 120 words a minute. This concept is called the **speaking/listening differential**, another cause of miscommunication. While someone is speaking to us, our brain is receiving millions of bits of data every minute in addition to what the person is saying.

Salespeople must consciously listen to what is said by a prospect or customer and then process their responses in order to problem-solve.[17] Listening can be broken down into passive listening and active listening. **Passive listening** is simply hearing. The receiver of the message is not engaged in the conversation and can easily misunderstand and incorrectly decode the message. This type of listening is not conducive to understanding (objective of communication) or developing good relationships. **Active listening** is the intentional effort on the part of the listener to understand, and to encourage feedback from the speaker. Salespeople engage in active listening by providing feedback and requesting feedback for additional information ("Could you tell me more about what you mean by durable?"), restating or rephrasing information ("So, if I understand what you're saying, durable means the filter will not need to be replaced for 24 months?"), and summarizing the conversation ("What you want, then, is a filter that will last for 24 months, is easy to store and easy to install? Is that right?"). These statements encourage the speaker to open up and provide additional information.

speaking/listening differential
the difference between the number of words people can speak per minute versus the number of words they can hear per minute

passive listening
simply hearing

active listening
the intentional effort on the part of the listener to understand

Adaptive Communication

Why are we able to connect with some people and not others? What is the difference between having productive communications and experiencing difficult failed interactions? One barrier to communication is that people are different in their social style or the way they prefer to communicate and the type of information they want when making decisions. People mentally process information differently. Wilson's Social Styles research, used by many sales training organizations, suggests that those with the ability to recognize differences in social style and communication preferences and adapt to them are able to make those interactions more productive. Salespeople who can connect, reduce tension, and put others at ease do so through their ability to both recognize and then adapt their communication style to that of their customers. This ability to adapt is the best predictor for setting appointments, gaining referrals, closing sales, and avoiding wasteful, disruptive relationship experiences.[18]

Social Style Matrix

People use various patterns of communication when interacting with others. Salespeople able to recognize these patterns and adjust to them have better relationships.[19] Two dimensions explain these social behaviors: *assertiveness* and *responsiveness*. The *Social Style Matrix* organizes individuals based on the dimensions of assertiveness and responsiveness. As depicted in Figure 3-3 each quadrant represents a basic social style and attitudes of each.

assertiveness
the degree to which people have opinions about different issues, and their need to express those opinions to others

Assertiveness

Assertiveness is the degree to which people have opinions about different issues, and their need to express those opinions to others. Less assertive people are more likely to try to avoid confrontations and keep their opinions to themselves. Those who are more assertive are more likely to dominate conversations, speak out, make strong statements, and less likely to try to avoid confrontations. Both low and high assertive people may have strong convictions, but lower assertive people are less likely to express those opinions. Table 3-2 provides some characteristics of assertiveness.

Figure 3-3 Social Style Matrix

	Low Assertiveness	High Assertiveness
Low Responsiveness	**Analytical** "What makes the solution work?" "How does the "clock work" • Serious • Organized • Thinker • Precise • Effective job more important than relationships	**Driver** "Show me the bottom line." "What time is it?" • Decisive • Efficient • Controlled • Task oriented • Results more important than feelings
High Responsiveness	**Amiable** "Do you care about me and my issues?" "What time to we get to play?" • Respectful • Personable • Trusting • Reserves opinion • People more important than results	**Expressive** "I need imaginative, best practices solutions." "Let's play now!" • Enthusiastic • Dramatic • Intuitive • Opinionated • What others think is important

Table 3-2 Characteristics of Assertiveness

Less Assertive	More Assertive
Avoids risk	Takes risks
Gets along	Takes charge
Expresses moderate opinions	Expresses strong opinions
Avoids direct eye contact	Makes direct eye contact
Makes decisions slowly	Makes decisions quickly
Cooperative	Competitive
Apologetic	Clear, direct statements
Speaks more slowly, softly	Speaks more quickly, loudly
Moves more deliberately	Moves more quickly
Soft handshake	Firm handshake
Low voice volume	Loud voice volume

Responsiveness **Responsiveness** is the degree to which people respond emotionally in social situations. Responsiveness is how a person emotionally responds to requests or demands of others on them. More responsive people are more emotional, while less responsive people control their emotions. Both low and high responsive people have emotions, but low responsive people control them.

responsiveness
the degree to which people respond emotionally in social situations

Drivers **Drivers** are high in assertiveness and low in responsiveness and are not concerned with how others will react, and they are straightforward and independent. They are more concerned about results, are practical, pragmatic, and bottom-line oriented. Drivers make decisions quickly and need only a few details, but they need to be convinced of the effectiveness of a solution. Drivers dislike inefficiency and indecisiveness. When in a stressful situation, drivers are more likely to take control of a situation. When selling to drivers, salespeople should be direct, less talkative, and more businesslike, and present bottom-line results of a solution. Drivers need to know how the solution will either improve revenues or lower costs.

drivers
individuals high in assertiveness and low in responsiveness. Not concerned with how others will react. Straightforward and independent

Analyticals **Analyticals** are low in both assertiveness and responsiveness and likely to ask a lot of questions about the details of a solution. Analyticals are cautious and deliberate when making decisions. Salespeople should provide tangible details of how the solution works, spend little time with small talk, and get to the point. Salespeople should be patient as analyticals process information.

analyticals
individuals low in both assertiveness and responsiveness. Likely to ask a lot of questions about the details of a solution

Amiables **Amiables** are low in assertiveness and high in responsiveness and appreciate getting to know people on a personal level. Amiables do not like uncertainty or change and want to avoid any conflict or risk. Salespeople should be more deliberate and be sure to take time getting acquainted. Amiables are more open to a salesperson's recommendations and guarantees where possible. Salespeople should be more direct when asking for an appointment or the sale.

amiables
individuals low in assertiveness and high in responsiveness and appreciate getting to know people on a personal level

Expressives **Expressives** are high on both assertiveness and responsiveness and like to make decisions based on their intuition or "gut feeling." Expressives are outgoing, enthusiastic, and they like being the center of attention. Salespeople should demonstrate how the solution could make the expressive look good and use creative graphics rather than details, tables, or many numbers.

expressives
individuals high on both assertiveness and responsiveness and like to make decisions based on their intuition or "gut feeling"

Table 3-3 Adapting to Social Styles

Analytical	Driver
Slow down	Keep quick pace
Provide detail – graphs & charts	Be brief
Be organized	Stay focused on agenda
Support solution with evidence – be factual	Be businesslike; professional
Provide balanced info – good and bad	Offer options
Amiable	**Expressive**
Slow down	Be enthusiastic
Take time building rapport	Use demonstration that gets them involved
Focus on user benefits – offer personal anecdotes	Provide references and testimonials
Provide assurances – provide testimonials	Be innovative
Listen, have empathy	Use stories

Understanding Social Style and Adapting to the Customer

The ability to adjust to various social styles is dependent upon understanding your own social style and tendencies or communication preferences. Recognizing your personal tendencies helps one adjust to a social style that is different. For example, an amiable will want to take time to get to know the prospect. However, if the prospect is a driver, he or she will want to get to the point and spend little time getting acquainted. The salesperson should adjust to the prospect. Get to the point, even when this is not what the amiable naturally wants. Whatever your personal style, be sensitive to how the other person wishes to communicate and adapt to that person's style. Suggestions for how to adapt to each social style are provided in Table 3-3.

Communication Using Technology

Technology can be fun and engaging, but it can also consume your day and valuable time when misused. This section provides insights about sales technology that salespeople use to leverage their time, strengthen customer relationships, and develop new sales opportunities. Since technology changes rapidly, salespeople need to invest time exploring different sales technologies regularly, yet be cautious of adopting technology for technology's sake. Bells and whistles are "cool," but carefully examine anything you consider adopting and only use tools that make you more efficient and effective, rather than just using a technology just because it is the "latest and greatest" innovation.

Salespeople communicate face-to-face and with the phone, text, email, tablets, web technology and social media. The use of alternative forms of communication technology can save time, allow salespeople to reach more prospects, more rapidly respond to customer concerns, and, generally, contribute to sales effectiveness and customer relationships. Customers are more connected than ever before through technology. However, misuse of technology can have negative effects on a salesperson's productivity.

Salespeople should know that technology cannot replace personal interaction when striving to develop close, cooperative relationships. Remember, up to 93% of communication is nonverbal, and most technology loses the ability to both send and receive nonverbal messages. Personal selling is effective largely through effective, real-time, two-way communication. Much of this can be lost when using technology, and some studies even show salespeople's use of communication technology can reduce performance.[20] A recent study from CareerBuilder revealed that the use of cell phone, texting, the internet, and social media are some of the worst killers of productivity.[21] Table 3-4 presents a comparison of the effectiveness of different communication methods across several criteria.

Knowing how and when to use the phone, email, texting, and social media effectively is important to building a successful career. Successful salespeople understand that technology is a tool, and they are wary of being distracted by any use not associated with building relationships and being efficient. Salespeople also need to understand and adhere to their customers' preferences regarding methods and timeliness of communication.

Phone and Voicemail

Since the patent of the telephone in 1876, Motorola's development of the first mobile phone in 1973, and the iPhone's emergence in 2007, salespeople have depended on it to set appointments and stay in touch with their customers. Before making a call, salespeople need to be organized and clearly understand their objectives. They should know exactly what they intend to say. Working from a script and practicing with others or in front of a mirror may be helpful. The goal is to be conversational, which requires practice and making the script your own.

Salespeople's nonverbals, even though not seen over the phone, do come across in their verbal communication. A smile affects a more pleasant and warm tone in the voice, and good posture affects a more professional and enthusiastic tone. One note on enthusiasm; customers want to work with a salesperson who is positive and has conviction about the company and product he or she represents. This does not mean an "over-the-top," "salesy zeal" as is often depicted in movies or television, but salespeople need to communicate their belief in their product or service. Some experts also suggest, and we recommend, wearing appropriate professional dress (business casual) for inside salespeople because it affects the level of professionalism that is communicated through tone, inflection, and articulation. Whether cold calling (leads are not expecting a call) or conducting

Table 3-4 Comparison of Sales Communication Methods

CRITERIA	Face-to-Face	Phone	Voicemail	Tele-Conference	Web/Computer Conference	Email	Texting
Verbal Feedback Capacity	Highest	High	Average	Average	Average	Average	Average
Non-Verbal Feedback Capacity	Highest	No	No	No	Average	No	No
Message Complexity	Highest	High	Low	Average	High	Low	Low
Amount of Information	Highest	High	Low	Average	High	Low	Low
Confidentiality	Highest	High	Average	Average	Average	Average	Average
Encoding Ease	Highest	High	Average	Average	High	Low	Low
Time-Decoding Ease	Highest	Average	Average	Average	Average	Average	Low
Cost	Highest	Average	Average	High	High	Low	Low
Warmth	Highest	High	Average	Average	Average	Low	Low

Adapted from Source: P.G. Clampitt, Communicating for Managerial Effectiveness (Newbury Park, CA: Sage Publications, 1991), p. 136

follow-up calls with prospects or current customers, being polite and considerate presents an opportunity to develop or successfully maintain a relationship.

General Phone Etiquette

- Speak clearly, articulately and professionally (reduce filler words)
- Be enthusiastic and positive (though not "salesy")
- Slow down the pace of speech a little
- Use active listening, encourage the speaker to talk
- Remember nonverbals: Use good posture, sit up straight or stand up
- Dress professionally: business casual, neat
- Do not take calls during the middle of any meeting: silence or turn off your phone

General Voicemail Etiquette

Salespeople often must leave voicemails. General phone etiquette applies, but additionally:

- Speak clearly and slowly, but not too slow
- Be aware of voice tone and inflection—when leaving several messages, it is easy to become monotone—and keep your enthusiasm for each call
- Be friendly and conversational, even when leaving a message
- Repeat your name, again, and repeat your call-back number *twice* and *slowly*

Texting

Texting is more common and accepted in sales and business settings today. Texting supplements other forms of communication in business and can create greater engagement. However, there are times to use and times not to use texting. When texting is used appropriately, research shows prospects who were sent text messages during the sales process convert at a 40% higher rate than those not sent any text messages. Very few prospects are sent text messages after contact is made, however. Less than 1% of contacted prospects are sent texts after that contact is made.[22]

Texting Etiquette and Tips

Remember, texting is an earned privilege.

- Timing: Send text messages only after contact.
- Gain permission: Always gain a prospect's or customer's permission before sending text messages.
- Text responsibly: Texts should be sent only when required. Three or more purposeful, meaningful texts appear to be appropriate.
- Content and timing: The content, timing, and the number of texts should be dictated by the lead's actions, preferences, and where they are in the sales process. Avoid using texts outside of business hours; remember your prospect's time zone.
- Worthy opportunities for texting: Texting should only be used when there is an important, timely message needed, and it can be said in few words.

  - A reminder of an appointment or when late for an appointment
  - Follow-up on a commitment made
  - Request for missing information
  - Acknowledgment of receiving a document
  - Checking availability for a call

- Formality: While one can get away with less formal grammar, punctuation, and abbreviations when texting, always use correct spelling, especially of the prospect's name. Do not be sloppy. Avoid using emojis.
- Length: Generally, if your message needs to be more than 300 characters, use email

Email

Email has become overused, and emails get opened much less than texts, but it remains a primary means of communicating with prospects and customers. Unlike texting, emails can be an effective form of reaching out to leads or prospects with whom the salesperson has not had previous contact. Suggestions and tips for using email in sales are below.

- Customer preference: Ask your customers or prospects how they wish to communicate. Phone, email, or texts?
- Grammar: Potential sales will be lost because of incorrect grammar, spelling, and punctuation in emails or other forms of communication. Most email platforms have spell check, but before hitting send, go back through and check for misspelling and punctuation. Know the difference between their and there, effect and affect, and to and too, as well as several other common spelling and word usage mistakes.
- Be brief: Three out of four emails are not read or opened. Studies suggest the ideal length of an email is between 50 and 125 words. Response rates for this length are above 50%. Emails of about 200 words have the highest click rates, so keep emails short and under 200 words.[23]
- Subject line: Subject lines should be enticing and short. The idea is to get the reader to open the email and read it. Be intriguing, but also be honest. Generally, use 30 or fewer characters, but ideally use 1- or 2-word subject lines; personalize the subject line when appropriate; avoid using "spammy" words such as Final, Complimentary, Help, Sales, Exciting, Solution, Unique, among others.

Professionalism in Social Media

Salespeople should follow the general rules of communication to use social media effectively. Content must be professional. Before posting any messages, images, or other content, review it to make sure they are error-free, communicate your message, and without unintended messaging. The ability to push content that captures a moment and tells a story in seconds is an advantage, but there can be miscommunication or misunderstanding if a salesperson is not vigilant in creating or identifying appropriate professional content to publish. Some final guidance regarding communicating through social media is provided below.

- Be professional: Develop a professional profile for each of your social media tools. Update the profile and use a professional headshot on each of your sites. Any messaging should be reviewed for accurate spelling, grammar, and punctuation—social is less formal, but mistakes affect your image and credibility. Never use vulgar, off-color, or suggestive language or images. Follow all the rules associated with each social media site.
- Review: Make sure to review content before reposting, sharing, or retweeting content. If forwarding, reposting, or sharing content you did not create, take time to read or examine the message, images, and all links that may be embedded before sending.

- Listen: Communicating relevant information is accomplished by determining the interests of your prospects and customers. Before sharing any content, make sure you know what your prospects value. Watch and listen before jumping into the conversation or beginning a conversation. Remember the 80-20 communication rule. Sharing a few very relevant messages and content is much more effective than sharing a lot of irrelevant content.

Technology and social media have value in many aspects of professional selling and especially prospecting. Clear and articulate communication through social media builds credibility and positively affects a salesperson's perceived professionalism and image and ultimately sales performance. Chapter 4 addresses ways to use these tools to prospect and develop relationships in more detail.

Applying this Chapter to Salesforce

A CRM like Salesforce helps the salesperson organize their communication with potential clients and customers in several ways. Since all contact, activities, meetings, and interactions are displayed in the *Activity Log* of Salesforce, the salesperson can follow natural next steps in the communication with customers without the risk of accidental duplication. The Activity Log makes it easier to pick up exactly where the last interaction ended, whether it was a sales call, meeting, presentation, or follow-up. Salesforce includes an *Activities* object that can be used to create a task, self-assigned to help the salesperson remember to complete it or assigned to someone else on in their organization. They can also schedule a *Calendar Event*, which can sync with Google or Outlook, among others.

Salesforce also enables the salesperson to send mass messages that appear to be personalized for potential customers using *Dynamic Content* fields. This means that the information being communicated changes based on what is known about the customer. For example, if a potential client is interested in blue shoes, while another client is interested in red shoes, the shoe image contained in the email to each client will change according to their preference. Email templates in Salesforce make it possible to send more emails to more customers without sounding "canned." To measure the impact of communication, Salesforce tracks open rates and read receipts on messages sent. This automated tracking helps inform which subject lines and messages are most effective. Salesforce will also show how many times links within messages have been opened. Before sending any message, Salesforce enables the salesperson to test email messages to see how they will appear on various devices.

Salesforce can be set to trigger communication to customers based on a certain action. For example, with *Lightning Dialer*, the salesperson can make a call by simply clicking on a customer's phone number. If the customer answers, the salesperson can take detailed notes of the call within the *Activity*. They can find answers to customer questions and view their previous history all within Salesforce. After the call, the salesperson can quickly trigger a personalized follow-up email from a template (like the blue shoes/red shoes example above). If the call goes to voicemail, Salesforce enables the salesperson to drop the call while sending a previously recorded voicemail. This saves time by allowing the salesperson to start a call to the next customer, while simultaneously leaving a message for the one who didn't answer.

Chapter Summary

- Professionalism requires salespeople to have integrity, be competent, have humility, be accountable, engage in self-regulation and carrying themselves in a professional manner
- Emotional Intelligence (EQ) is an attribute that can be improved upon and is associated with high performers
- Improving EQ requires gaining a higher awareness of the emotional makeup of others and the skill to treat people according to their emotional reactions. It also requires gaining an awareness of your own emotions and an ability to manage or control those emotions in any situation.
- Communicating effectively positively impacts relationships with customers.
- The goal of all communication is understanding.
- Communication is affected by verbal communication and especially through non-verbal communication made up of body language, facial expressions, eye contact, appearance and hand shaking.
- Listening is important to understanding the customer and also communicating that the salesperson cares about the customer.
- Active listening is more effective than passive listening.
- Being able to adapt communication style to the customer's style improves communication.
- Technology is an important tool for salespeople, but needs to be used appropriately.

Key Terms

accountability (p. 48)
active listening (p. 55)
amiables (p. 57)
analyticals (p. 57)
articulate (p. 51)
assertiveness (p. 56)
body language (p. 52)
competency (p. 47)
drivers (p. 57)
emotional intelligence (p. 49)
expressives (p. 57)
filler words (p. 51)
humility (p. 47)
inflection (p. 51)
integrity (p. 46)
mirroring (p. 52)
negative connotation (p. 52)

neocortex (p. 49)
nonverbal (p. 52)
passive listening (p. 55)
personal competence (p. 49)
positive affectivity (p. 50)
profession (p. 47)
professional image (p. 48)
relationship management (p. 50)
responsiveness (p. 57)
self-awareness (p. 49)
self-management (p. 49)
self-motivation (p. 49)
self-regulation (p. 48)
social awareness (p. 50)
social competence (p. 49)
speaking/listening differential (p. 55)
tone (p. 51)

Application 3-1

Michael has been with Allstate for eight months, his first job after graduating from college. Michael has begun specializing in selling supplemental health insurance targeting small to mid-sized companies. His first big sales meeting was with Krysten, the regional Human Resources manager of PolyOne, a global leader in polymer materials. Krysten has been an HR manager for 20 years.

Before the meeting, Michael researched Krysten on LinkedIn, where her photo showed her in a formal suit and showed her experience as an HR manager with two other organizations before joining PolyOne last year. Michael dressed in a suit and tie for the meeting.

As Michael introduced himself, he looked Krysten in the eye, smiled, and firmly shook hands with her. Krysten began the meeting by asking Michael about his experience. Michael realized he was a little sensitive to his own age and inexperience, but he also realized that Krysten's concern was legitimate. Krysten had probably been used to working with older salespeople. Rather than getting offended, Michael smiled and told Krysten about the tremendous expert support he had from Allstate and the value that Allstate solutions had provided to employees of other companies like PolyOne. He went on to make the largest sale of his young career.

1. By understanding his sensitivity to his age and experience, what is Michael demonstrating?
2. By understanding Krysten's concern about his age and inexperience, what is Michael demonstrating?
3. How did Michael attempt to build trust and confidence nonverbally?

Application 3-2

Jessica has been a pharmaceutical representative with GlaxoSmithKline for 10 years. Daniel, her regional manager, spent a day with Jessica in the field and had the opportunity to witness her working with several of her clients.

On a stop at Dr. Scott Inks' office, who is a regular client, Dr. Inks had Dr. Robin Forbes, another internal medicine physician, visiting his office to consult on one of his patients. When Dr. Inks introduced Jessica to Dr. Forbes, Jessica asked her questions about herself, her offices, and how she got started practicing medicine. Several times, Jessica said things like, "That's very interesting, why did you do that?" and "So, you really love taking care of your patients." Jessica mostly asked questions and talked very little. She quickly put the doctor at ease. Before Dr. Forbes left she gave her business card to Jessica and asked her to drop by her office. However, when Jessica began speaking to Dr. Inks after Dr. Forbes had left, she politely cut the meeting short and told Dr. Inks she would come back another day that week.

After leaving the office, Daniel complemented her on her ability to build rapport with the visiting physician and potentially gain a new client, but then asked why she had cut her visit short with Dr. Inks. Jessica said that Dr. Inks had a difficult patient (the reason for the consult) and that he gets a little frustrated when he has a tough patient on his mind and is distracted. She said that meeting at another time would be more productive.

1. Which communication skills did Jessica exhibited or used during her visit with Dr. Inks and Forbes?
2. Which components of Emotional Intelligence did Jessica exhibit during her visit?

CHAPTER 4

Lead Generation and Prospecting

Learning Objectives

- Discuss the importance of lead generation and prospecting
- Explain the two steps of successful prospecting
- Determine the ways in which sales organizations identify leads
- Define what constitutes a *qualified* lead
- Summarize who is responsible for lead generation and prospecting
- Explain how the sales pipeline contributes to the success of a sales organization
- Describe how a salesperson should prepare for the first appointment with a prospect

his chapter covers two closely associated terms: **prospecting** and lead generation. Some use these two terms interchangeably. For others, **prospecting** is broadly defined as any activity, successful or not, used to discover potential new customers. Whereas **lead generation** is a subset of all prospecting activities. Lead generation is the process of identifying potential customers—or in other words, to generate leads. This is a critical activity for all sales organizations, but especially for those newer firms that are trying to become established. Consider the example of Fastenal Company, based in Minnesota. Twenty-five years ago, salespeople from Fastenal spent a large percentage of their time making sales calls to firms that had never heard of them. In fact, they would often show up to these prospective accounts with no advance notice (what we learned in Chapter 1 is known as cold calling). Because these prospecting efforts were successful, Fastenal grew to become the largest distributor of fasteners in North America. This allowed the company to shift its focus away from lead generation and more toward servicing existing accounts. But still, Fastenal reps prospect on a regular basis. No sales organization can afford to forget about acquiring new customers.

We begin by defining the two steps involved with prospecting. The first step is **identifying leads,** which is the process of generating names of potential customers. The second step is **qualifying leads,** which involves evaluating these potential customers in terms of how likely they are to buy.

Identifying Leads

The first step of prospecting involves the acquisition of names and addresses of potential customers, which are most commonly called **leads**. This step is not necessarily focused on whether or not these are *good* leads (that's the second step). The idea is to generate a large number of names, and then, after that, the sales organizations should be concerned with prioritizing those names.

This initial list of names is sometimes called a contact list, but sales professionals differ in their definitions of various prospecting terms. In particular, there are differences associated with the meanings of the following three terms: **contacts, leads,** and **prospects.** Some sales professionals define these three terms in a hierarchical manner where contacts turn into leads, which they hope will turn into prospects and then customers. In other words, these people view contacts as those least likely to be customers, prospects as those most likely to be customers, and leads as being somewhere in the middle. This textbook, however, uses these three terms (contact, lead, and prospect) interchangeably, and views them all as being labels of potential customers that might or might not necessarily be good candidates for customers. We do use different terms to label two groups of potential customers that are more likely to become customers; specifically, we say that contacts/leads/prospects are qualified prospects or hot prospects as their likelihood of becoming customers increases. We clarify these prospecting terms and the prioritization process in more detail later in this chapter as we discuss the sales pipeline.

The remainder of this section describes the various ways that sales organizations can develop the names and contact information of potential customers. As shown in Figure 4-1, these lead sources include customer referrals, internal referrals, networking, cold calling, warm calling, email prospecting, and social media.

Referrals

Sales professionals generally agree that the best way to acquire new customers is through referrals. A **referral** is when a third party voluntarily provides the name of a potential customer. Ideally, the third party is a trustworthy person who is well

---

prospecting
any activity used to discover potential new customers

lead generation
the process of identifying potential customers

identifying leads
the process of generating names of potential customers

qualifying leads
evaluating potential customers in terms of how likely they are to buy

leads
names and addresses of potential customers

prospects/contacts/leads
potential customers that might or might not necessarily be good candidates for customers

referral
when a third party voluntarily provides the name of a potential customer

Figure 4-1 Lead Sources

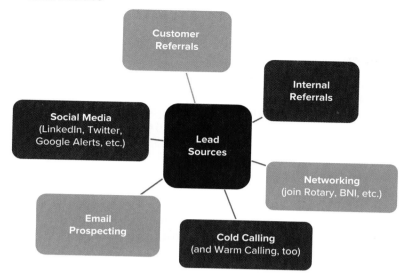

known by the sales organization. Most commonly, referrals come from existing customers; but they can also come from sources inside the sales organization.

Customer Referrals Salespeople responsible for generating their own leads indicate that their number one source of referrals is their existing customers. Salespeople typically ask for referrals from their best customers—those with whom they have a close, working relationship. Loyal customers are often happy to provide the names and contact information of their colleagues and peers who might also benefit from the products and services of the selling organization. A great time to ask these customers for a referral is *after* the salesperson has resolved a sticky situation.

Because this particular lead source is so valuable, many sales organizations create structured **customer referral programs**[1] in which customers are rewarded for referring potential new customers. For these programs to work, the customers that make referrals must be fully satisfied with the value they receive. If customers are only lukewarm toward the salesperson, they are not likely to refer the best names. Consequently, companies should review their customer base and organize them into segments. From this list, they should identify the best—most ideal—customers. Second, companies should be selective and solicit referrals only from these most valuable customers. One way to identify these most valuable customers is to include a question on their customer satisfaction surveys that asks: "How likely is it that you would recommend [company name] to a friend or colleague?" Interestingly, research shows that companies that do well with this question (that is, those that have lots of customers that make referrals) tend to have greater revenue growth.[2] This provides more support to the importance of customer referrals.

The customer referral program should continually and systematically track which customers are providing the best referrals. In addition, the program should keep these customers informed of any new business developments that are happening (e.g., new product releases). Finally, companies should *appropriately* thank or reward these customers for every referral. Different customers value different things, so companies should know what these things are. Some might prefer gift cards from their favorite retail store. Others might prefer discounts toward their next purchase.

customer referral program
a structured program for rewarding existing customers for referring potential new customers

internal referrals
referrals from employees, trade shows, and the internet

Internal Referrals **Internal referrals** come from two distinct sources, both of which are inside the organization. The first source is other people in the firm who have met or talked to people that they believe might be good prospects. This could include referrals from sales managers, members of the marketing department, participants of trade shows, and inside salespeople. For example, it is not unusual for salespeople to get referrals from the sales manager who is their direct supervisor or boss. Also, business-to-business firms often attend trade shows and collect business cards from those who walk by and express interest in the product. These business cards are passed on to salespeople by those employees who were attending the trade show. Another example of this is when the inside sales staff (or telemarketing team) identify qualified prospects from their phone calls, and then pass on these names to the outside salespeople.

The second source of internal referrals relates to internet technology, which is often used to gather information about potential customers' online behavior. This includes names of people who are searching for relevant products on the internet, or perhaps those who have responded to a salesperson's post on LinkedIn. The technology often gives specific contact information for these prospects. For example, Liberty Mutual Insurance provides price quotes on a variety of types of insurance to those visiting the company website. After receiving the quote, the website visitor can then request to be contacted by a Liberty Mutual agent, who is sure to follow up on this inquiry.

Networking

networking
developing professional and social contact with others

Salespeople often generate leads by developing professional and social contact with others. This activity is called **networking**. When exchanging information with friends and acquaintances, salespeople naturally learn about and meet new people who may be potential customers or who may be able to provide leads. There are many excellent places for salespeople to network. For example, salespeople can join professional and civic organizations, such as Chambers of Commerce, Kiwanis, Optimists, Rotary, Women in Business, and many others. Along these lines, networking connections can be made through volunteering with local service organizations, such as the American Red Cross, Humane Society, food pantries, youth sports, and others. Trade shows are also excellent places to network.

One networking organization formed for the express purpose of generating referrals is Business Network International (BNI), which has more than 200,000 members who meet weekly in thousands of local chapters around in the world. For example, Toledo, Ohio (population about 275,000) has more than ten local chapters. As a member of BNI, you are expected to find referrals for your fellow members as they try to find referrals for you. Interestingly, only one person from each profession is allowed to join each BNI chapter.

bird dogs
salespeople who network with individuals in high-visibility positions

Some salespeople strategically network with individuals who are in high-visibility positions and thus connected to a large number of people through their routine of daily work. These individuals are sometimes called sales **bird dogs**—especially if they are actively looking out for good prospects for their salesperson. The term comes from the hunting dog breed trained to help owners by pointing out birds. Salespeople use sales bird dogs as their eyes and ears on what is happening within an organization or out in the marketplace. Anyone in a position to observe and understand the business needs of others can be a bird dog. This includes lawyers, consultants, local politicians, hotel bellhops, receptionists, and many others.

Cold Calling

cold calling
making unsolicited calls to people or firms for the purpose of selling to them

As referenced earlier in this chapter, **cold calling** is defined as making unsolicited calls to people or firms for the purpose of selling to them. Cold calling can be done either in-person or by phone. In the typical cold call, the salesperson has never met and does not know the potential customer. In a sense, this technique skips prospecting as it can involve salespeople simply showing up in a neighborhood or business park and knocking on doors.

Cold calling was very common in years past. Salespeople would routinely make unannounced cold calls on businesses they thought *might* need the products they were selling. However, this technique is much less popular today, as many believe it is too time-consuming and not very cost-effective. Certainly, cold calling is associated with a high rejection rate. This is why many sales professionals believe cold calling is a technique of the past that is no longer relevant. The decline of cold calling is in part due to the advances in internet technology, which allows firms to identify and research potential customers before the initial contact is made—and thus, effectively eliminate prospects that are not likely to buy.

Some organizations, however, still cold call. In fact, advances in phone technology have enabled sales organizations to automatically and efficiently dial vast amounts of phone numbers in order to reach consumers and sell them something. These systems allow sellers to dial millions of consumers daily at little cost. Commonly, these automated telephone calls deliver *recorded* messages that explain how to buy a product or perhaps connect to a live person if interested. These robocalls are controversial as many people find them highly annoying and wish the U.S. Federal Communications Commission (FCC) would create more regulations to make them less common. Despite the opposition to this prospecting technique, the number of robocalls continues to increase significantly—and so do complaints about them.[3] Research shows that over one-third (37%) of these robocalls are from businesses that are trying to defraud consumers.[4] This is unfortunate as it gives legitimate salespeople a bad name. Table 4-1 lists those industries that are most likely to engage in phone scams using robocalls.

Even though many say that cold calling is fading out as a prospecting method, other sales experts maintain that cold calling can be effective by using the right techniques. Salespeople should identify themselves immediately and explain why they are calling. This should include a brief and specific value proposition. If possible, it is good to explain how they got the prospect's name (e.g., "I saw that we have a mutual connection on LinkedIn…"). Being friendly and conversational is important, and reading a script is never a good idea. Above all else, salespeople should position themselves as listeners more than talkers. Getting prospects to talk about themselves is key to the success of cold calling. More tips about how to contact prospects over the phone are presented later in this chapter.

Table 4-1 Estimated Volumes of Top Robocaller Scams by Industry

Category	Type	Volume
Interest rates	"0% interest rates"	122.9m
Credit cards	"Problem with your credit card"	82.5m
Student loans	"Forgive/lower student debt"	71.0m
Business loans	"Preapproved for business loan"	53.4m
I.R.S.	"Owe money to the I.R.S."	43.4m
Search listings	"Listing has a problem"	31.0m
Travel	"Free/discount trip"	27.0m
Preapproved loans	"Ready to wire—just need info"	26.2m
Home security	"Free service/installation"	26.1m
Utilities	"Save money—need your info"	19.2m

Source: Bernard, Tara Siegel. (2018). Yes, Those Calls You're Ignoring Are Increasing. *New York Times* (May 6, 2018): A1. Retrieved at https://www.nytimes.com/2018/05/06/your-money/robocalls-rise-illegal.html.

Warm Calling

warm calling
a variation of cold calling involving
some preliminary research on the
prospect

By definition, cold calling does not involve the *qualifying lead process* discussed in the next section. However, a variation that some call **warm calling** or smart calling involves doing preliminary research on the prospect before the call. This research allows the salesperson to make a genuine connection with the client, and perhaps build some rapport. The exact point at which cold calling becomes warm calling is not clear, but many sales experts claim that warm calling can significantly improve the success rate relative to traditional cold calling.[5] The goal of this preliminary research should be to develop familiarity with the business of prospects, and an understanding of their needs. Of course, the research also helps to identify prospects that are not likely to buy, so they may be eliminated from any contact list. Advances in internet technology have made this research possible; and as described in the next sections, the process can include both email and social media.

Email Prospecting

email prospecting
sending unsolicited emails out to
a contact list in order invite them
to find out more information about
your product

Email prospecting involves sending unsolicited emails out to a contact list in order to invite them to learn more about the product or service. Those who respond to these emails are good prospects to follow up with. Because these emails are unsolicited, this is a variation of cold and/or warm calling, depending on how much research has been done in developing the email list (or actually, the terms *cold emailing* and *warm emailing* are commonly used).

Contact lists (for both cold calling and emailing) can be purchased from a variety of lead generation companies. Names of several of these companies can be found by entering terms such as "sales leads" and "email marketing" in Google. Most of these companies have millions of emails that they sell for pennies per name. Further, customers can buy lists that match their target markets by filtering on a number of characteristics of consumers or business customers. For example, entering the search term "email list of doctors in California" generates a similar list of lead generation companies—although this one includes a number of companies that apparently specialize in providing contact information for the health care industry.

Consequently, it is easy and relatively inexpensive to purchase a targeted list of emails; however, the quality of these emails is sometimes questionable. The internet is full of bad reviews of these companies, and it is often not as easy as it sounds to engage in email prospecting. Emails on these lists are notoriously inaccurate, undeliverable, or get blocked as junk mail. Further, emails are easy to ignore, delete, and forgotten. One option is to purchase a list of "opt-in" emails, in which the owners of the email addresses have agreed to have their information sold. However, opt-in emails can be expensive, and do not necessarily include the best customers.

At the same time, there are a number of advantages of email prospecting. Many sales organizations find it an effective means to connect with customers. Unlike phone calls, emails give prospects plenty of time to research the product and seriously consider the offer. Further, technology allows salespeople to see how the audience is responding. This includes who is opening the email, who is clicking on the various links within the email, and what they might be interested in. This information can be used to identify and follow up with those most likely to buy the product.

Finally, some argue that the key to successful email prospecting is to *develop* a good list of contacts—as opposed to *purchasing* the list. The best way to develop a list is to engage with potential customers on social media.

Social media

social selling
using social media to interact with
potential customers by answering
their questions and introducing
them to useful content

Social media allows salespeople to interact with potential customers by answering their questions and introducing them to useful content. This is called **social selling**. Once they have received something of value through this interaction, prospects are often happy to fill out contact forms containing email addresses or phone numbers.

This resulting contact list, which is developed and refined, rather than purchased, is generally of much higher quality. These people have demonstrated an interest in the sales organization, and they have essentially opted-in to being contacted by either phone or email. Further, internet technology provides information about their interaction history within the website and social media pages of the sales organization. This provides insight into the needs and interests of their business. This is useful information for salespeople as it helps them better prepare for their sales calls by customizing the presentation to more effectively meet the unique needs of the prospect.

Facebook, LinkedIn, Instagram, and Twitter are the most common platforms for social selling. The use of these platforms as part of a digital sales strategy will be covered in greater detail in a later chapter.

LinkedIn Most sales experts point to LinkedIn as being the best social media platform for lead generation and prospecting. In fact, LinkedIn has an optional, fee-based prospecting tool called Sales Navigator, which generates leads in an impressive manner. Sales Navigator not only keeps salespeople up to date on what their current prospects are doing, but it analyzes current contacts and suggests potential organizations that fit a similar profile. This includes potential customers that the salesperson may have never heard of. LinkedIn also points salespeople to good prospects by showing them who has viewed, liked, commented on, and shared their posts. This is why some salespeople commonly post content that they believe will be helpful to their clients. This content, which is often in the form of a short article, provides an opportunity for salespeople to build their reputation as an expert in their field.

Prospects tend to be open to being contacted through LinkedIn—or at least, they are open to being contacted by people that come across as legitimate and trustworthy on the social media platform. LinkedIn gives potential customers insight into the trustworthiness of salespeople in a number of ways. First, the LinkedIn profile provides background on the salesperson's work and education history. LinkedIn also shows their business interests, recommendations, mutual contacts, posts, and a variety of other information that helps prospects determine whether this is someone they might want to do business with.

Twitter Salespeople are less likely to use Twitter than LinkedIn. This is likely because LinkedIn users make up a strictly professional network of people, whereas Twitter users are generally there for personal reasons not related to their business careers. So, the challenge of using Twitter is finding the right target audience among the hundreds of millions of users—as most of them have no interest in connecting with the salesperson. However, this is a challenge that it may be worthwhile to overcome, as many sales experts argue that Twitter is a powerful tool for prospecting. In fact, studies show that business-to-business companies that use Twitter get twice as many sales leads.

The way to use Twitter to connect with customers starts with an understanding that Twitter users do not respond to a hard-sell strategy. Rather, it is a soft-sell approach that strives to engage with prospects, but not close the deal. It is important to be responsive and helpful—but at the same time, salespeople must tweet frequently and consistently in order to find their audience and be visible. Salespeople should identify and search for keywords and hashtags that potential customers tend to use. Also, salespeople should follow their competitors, and identify who these firms are following and who is following them. This can lead to connections with excellent prospects.

Salespeople should be careful who they follow. Followers should be restricted to those that are a good fit with the salesperson's product. Pay special attention to those followers that are especially influential in the industry. It is a good idea for salespeople to cultivate close connections to these high profile influencers by retweeting their posts—and be sure to thank them if they happen to share one's tweets. A single tweet from one high-profile influencer can enhance the reputation of salespeople such that they become quite well known in their industry.

Like LinkedIn, Twitter allows users to create and share their own content. However, Twitter is more about sharing and retweeting relevant content that others have posted. If done right, adding thought-provoking comments to this content can generate interest among the right group of potential customers. Although salespeople are advised to not post many personal stories (which should be saved for a separate, personal Twitter account), it is important to behave like a human—not an online robot. That is, salespeople should make a point to personally communicate real messages to their followers, and stay away from automated services, like automated "welcome" tweets for new followers.

Google Alerts   Google Alerts is available for free to Google users. This service interacts with social media platforms, such as Twitter, to provide salespeople with useful information for finding good prospects. Google Alerts can be used to automate a number of repetitive sales, marketing, and business tasks—including lead generation and prospecting. In general, this service allows users to set up an alert for anything that interests them. Whenever Google detects new web content about that topic, the user is informed about it through an email.

Google Alerts can generate useful prospecting information about potential customers in a number of ways. For example, salespeople for 3M Healthcare could set an alert for the names of major hospitals in their geographic region. The salesperson would then get an email whenever a news story, press release, or post is generated with the name of one of these hospitals.

Google Alerts can be set to alert the salesperson whenever specific questions are asked on forums or blogs. For example, a salesperson for North Sails might get notified whenever anyone on a specific forum for sailing enthusiasts asks the community for a recommendation for replacing their old sails.

Qualifying Leads

After identifying leads, the next step is to qualify leads. This is the process that determines whether or not the lead has a reasonable chance of becoming an actual customer. This process is important because salespeople become discouraged if they spend too much time with prospects that have no need for their products. This is not only frustrating, it is also quite expensive for salespeople to call on customers who do not need, do not want, or cannot afford the products they sell.

Specifically, leads (or prospects or contacts) become *qualified* when these four **ANAR conditions** are met:

ANAR conditions
authority, Need, Afford, and Receptive

1. They have the **Authority** to buy the product
2. They **Need** the product that is being sold
3. They can **Afford** to buy the product
4. They are **Receptive** to being called on by the salesperson

The first condition for qualifying is that the prospect must have the authority to buy the product. It is not always easy to find the person in the firm that is authorized to make the buying decision. Salespeople can waste a lot of time talking to people (i.e., unqualified leads) who do not have this authority. Consequently, successful salespeople are sure to ask about this early in the first sales call. They might ask, "Are there any other colleagues that participate in the decision-making process for this product? And if so, can we invite them into this meeting?" Salespeople must be diplomatic in asking these questions, and be careful not to offend the client by suggesting that they would rather be talking to someone more important.

The second condition for qualifying is that the prospect should have a genuine need for the product. In years past, salespeople engaged in high-pressure tactics in order to trick prospects into buying—even if they did not need the product. This is no longer the case for a variety of reasons. First, salespeople strive to be more ethical. Second, selling today is more about creating long-term relationships, and high-pressure sales tactics work only in the short term. Third, buyers are more sophisticated today and are not willing to buy products that they do not need. Of course, sometimes prospects might need a product but not know they need it; perhaps they are not yet aware of the product, so they have no understanding of its value. This is why professional salespeople today ask probing questions to uncover problems, and then demonstrate how their product can serve as a solution.

Shutterstock/UfaBizPhoto

Being able to afford to buy the product is the third condition that must be met to ensure that the lead is qualified. In business-to-business sales, this gets at the issue of what the prospect's budget is. Frequently, prospects will raise the objection that they do not have the budget for a particular product. If true, this would make that prospect unqualified. However, salespeople may be able to get past this concern if they can show how expensive the current problems and concerns are for the prospect's firm. This is why salespeople should be equipped to demonstrate the return on investment (ROI) associated with buying their product.

Finally, the lead can consider buying the product only if the lead is receptive to being called on. As leads become more senior in rank, it becomes increasingly more difficult to schedule an appointment with them. This is a common problem. Really expensive products are generally only purchased if the CEO of the company signs off—but, of course, CEOs are too busy to meet with most salespeople. Successful salespeople do not immediately give up when confronted with this news. One way around this is for salespeople to arrange for the CEO of their own firm to occasionally accompany them on sales calls. Executives from the customer firm are more likely to make an appointment with salespeople when other executives will be there.

Another way to meet with a prospect who is initially not receptive to being called on is to make a favorable impression with that person's gatekeeper, which is typically a secretary or administrative assistant. Gatekeepers often control the schedules of their boss, and it is their job to keep unwanted calls away. Salespeople should not try to assert their own authority to push past gatekeepers. Rather, salespeople should be polite and respectful, and focus on building rapport with the gatekeeper. Asking gatekeepers for advice about the company is typically a good idea. Not only does this show respect, but gatekeepers generally know a lot of "inside information" about what is going in their firm. As explained earlier, some gatekeepers make excellent sales bird dogs!

When done properly and thoroughly, the qualifying leads process results in gaining access to better leads—because they are much more likely to buy. This translates to greater sales performance by the sales team and greater revenue for the firm. However, this process is not always done well. A common complaint by salespeople is that the leads they receive are poor or weak. But if the leads are weak, whose fault is this? The next section discusses this issue.

Responsibility for Generating Leads: Sales vs. Marketing

Who is responsible for prospecting? Much of the preceding discussion presumes that it is the salesperson's responsibility to generate and qualify leads. In many firms, however, the qualifying leads process is the responsibility of both marketing and sales. The process ideally begins in the marketing group, which generates marketing qualified leads, and then moves to sales, which generates sales qualified leads.

The behavior of potential customers on the internet is a key factor in assessing the quality of leads. The marketing department is typically responsible for monitoring this behavior. Consequently, **marketing qualified leads (MQLs)** are defined as potential customers who have intentionally shown interest in a product through their online actions or behaviors. These actions might include filling out an online form on the company website, adding items to their shopping cart, clicking on an internet advertisement to find the company website, and downloading trial software or a free ebook. Marketing departments typically analyze these behaviors and then give a score to each lead to indicate their sales-readiness (or likelihood of buying). Leads that score high enough are then passed on to salespeople. This approach to prospecting is consistent with the inbound marketing techniques described later in the chapter.

After acquiring the MQLs, salespeople then proceed to analyze them with respect to the four ANAR conditions described previously. That is, they evaluate whether or not the MQLs (1) are authorized to buy, (2) have a need for the product, (3) have a budget that enables them to afford the product, and (4) are receptive to being called on. Consequently, **sales qualified leads (SQLs)** are leads that have been vetted by salespeople and judged to have a high potential to actually purchase the product. This second step of the process is sometimes done by inside support salespeople who make this assessment through phone calls. In this case, once the inside salesperson determines that the MQL is now an SQL, the lead is passed on to an outside salesperson who schedules an in-person sales call with the SQL.

The marketing department is often frustrated by the fact that salespeople do not follow up with the leads that they give to them. One study reports that up to 70% of sales leads are ignored by salespeople.[6] A typical counterargument by salespeople is that the leads provided by the marketing department are not worth pursuing ("The leads are weak," they say). To solve this problem, these two functional groups need to collaborate in order to improve the system used to score or evaluate the leads. A key tool in prioritizing leads is the sales pipeline.

Sales Pipeline

The **sales pipeline** is a visual representation of where all the prospects are in the purchasing process (see Figure 4-2). The sales pipeline includes a complete listing of the names and contact information for all prospects, categorized by how likely they are to purchase the product. As the figure suggests, the sales process turns leads (or prospects or contacts) into qualified prospects, hot prospects, and eventually customers. Sales pipeline diagrams—with considerably more detail—are generated automatically by several customer relationship management (CRM) systems, such as Salesforce. Tracking prospects in this way keeps the salespeople focused on developing new clients, which is important for a firm's survival. After all, even the best companies lose customers from time to time. Further, sales managers understand that turning a lead into a new customer takes time, and thus trying to fill up the pipeline at the last minute is nearly impossible. Successful sales organizations keep the sales pipeline full because they understand that a well-managed and continuous process of prospecting is critical to sales success.

Of course, in order to personally meet with the prospect, the salesperson has to call and make an appointment. As pointed out earlier, research shows that salespeople only pursue about 30% of the leads provided to them by the marketing department.[7] The remaining 70% of potential customers that are being ignored is

marketing qualified leads (MQLs)
potential customers who have intentionally shown interest in a product through their online actions or behaviors

sales qualified leads (SQLs)
leads that have been vetted by salespeople and judged to have a high potential to actually purchase the product

sales pipeline
a visual representation of where all the prospects are in the purchasing process

Figure 4-2 Sales Pipeline

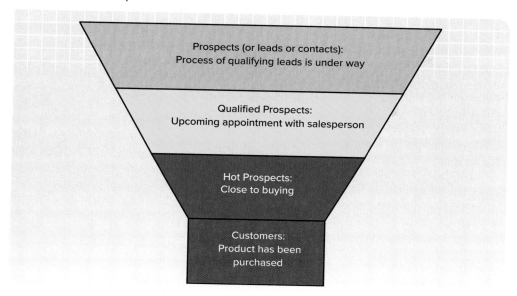

referred to as the sales lead black hole. This is often a point of contention between the sales force and the marketing department.

Prospects, Leads, and Contacts

People and firms in the first category of the sales pipeline are called prospects (or leads or contacts). These are potential customers that are going through the firm's qualifying leads process; so, not much is known about them at this stage. A large number of names should be in this category. The philosophy behind prospecting is to first cast a wide net and get essentially as many reasonable names as possible. You never know who might be a good customer until you attempt to qualify them. This is at the start of prospecting.

Qualified Prospects

The second category is **qualified prospects**, who are the potential customers that meet the four (ANAR) conditions of the qualifying leads process. That is, salespeople have made a preliminary determination that these potential customers (1) have the authority to buy, (2) have a genuine need for the product, (3) can afford to buy, and (4) are receptive to being called on. Consequently, qualified prospects have typically agreed to meet with an outside salesperson for an upcoming appointment. What happens during that appointment will determine whether or not they advance to the next category.

qualified prospects
potential customers that meet the four (ANAR) conditions of the qualifying leads process

Hot Prospects

A **hot prospect** is a potential customer that is not quite ready to buy—but they are close. There is no consensus among sales experts as to precisely when a qualified prospect turns into a hot prospect. This is a judgment call to some degree. However, we define a hot prospect as someone who has met with the salesperson at least once and has agreed to meet with them again. Of course, some qualified prospects might agree to buy during the first sales call, and thus move directly to the customer category (and skip over hot prospect). However, it is much more likely that the salesperson will have to follow up with the customer—perhaps several times—before closing the sale.

hot prospect
a potential customer that is not quite ready to buy—but is close

Customers

If all goes well, the prospect eventually buys the product and becomes a customer. Of course, a lot goes into this. In fact, the details and techniques of how to turn a prospect into a customer require the next several chapters of this textbook to explain.

Managing the Sales Pipeline   A sales pipeline is not just an interesting picture of what is going on with lead generation and prospecting. Rather, it is a tool that can be used to drive revenue for the firm. However, there is evidence to suggest that sales organizations could do a much better job at using their sales pipeline in this way. One study found an 18% difference in revenue growth between companies that actively managed their pipeline and those that did not.

There are several best practices associated with effectively managing a sales pipeline, especially when data for the pipeline is available through the firm's CRM program. First, each salesperson should be sure to have a full pipeline. This means there should be a good number of names in each of the four categories. In order to know this information, salespeople must keep their pipeline up to date by regularly keeping track of all sales calls. As explained later in this chapter, recording information about sales calls typically involves the firm's CRM system. Salespeople should keep track of this information on a continual (daily) basis. This does take time, and some salespeople resent this. However, this is generally time well spent that results in higher sales performance.

An overall review of the sales pipeline should occur at least once per week. One metric to keep an eye on in this review is the length of the **sales cycle**. The sales cycle is defined as the average amount of time that it takes a new prospect to become a customer. In other words, the sales cycle starts when a prospect first enters the sales cycle, and it is over when that prospect makes the first purchase. Salespeople who carefully manage their sales pipeline tend to shorten their average sales cycle. Shortening the sales cycle results in increased sales performance for the rep, and more revenue for the firm.

Other important metrics include **conversion ratios**, which are calculations in percent of how many prospects become qualified prospects, how many qualified prospects become hot prospects, and how many hot prospects become customers. Figure 4-3 shows an example of how these numbers can be managed to drive revenue. Note that the conversion ratios in example 2 result in four customers, which is twice as many customers as those in example 1. This is occurring even though the conversion ratio of prospects to qualified prospects is four times bigger in example 1 (20% vs. 5%). Why would this happen? One possibility is that too many prospects are being designated as qualified prospects in the first example, which makes it difficult to accurately assess which ones are hot prospects. This points to the benefits of quickly eliminating bad prospects.

By closely managing their sales pipeline, salespeople tend to focus on their best, most high-value leads. This makes sense because not all deals are equal. By sorting prospects by the size of the potential deal, salespeople can quickly see which leads are the most valuable for their business. These leads should become the top priority. Similarly, the pipeline illuminates which leads are dead and should no longer be pursued. Giving up on prospects can be hard for some salespeople, especially if they have invested considerable time in trying to form a relationship with them. However, sometimes salespeople need to stop working unproductive prospects to make time to focus on better leads. Sales pipeline management makes these circumstances clear.

Another best practice relates to the importance of consistently following up with the prospect in order to make the next appointment. That is, the pipeline software can show data on the best time to follow up under various

sales cycle
the average amount of time that it takes a new prospect to become a customer

conversion ratios
calculations in percent of how many prospects become qualified prospects, how many qualified prospects become hot prospects, and how many hot prospects become customers

Figure 4-3 Conversion Ratios

Pipeline Category	Example 1		Example 2	
	Number in Category	Conversion Ratios	Number in Category	Conversion Ratios
Prospects	1,000		1,000	
		20%		5%
Qualified Prospects	200		50	
		10%		40%
Hot Prospects	20		20	
		10%		20%
Customers	2		4	

circumstances. Research indicates that it typically takes more than eight calls to close a sale, but salespeople often give up after two calls. Sales pipelines keep track of who has been called on and when. Reminders can be set to notify salespeople when it is time to follow up. Some sales pipeline software allows salespeople to automatically send follow-up emails to new customers. For example, an email might be programmed to be sent two weeks after the purchase, to assess satisfaction levels.

Effective management of the sales pipeline not only keeps salespeople up to date on the details of all customers and potential customers, but it also leads to a better understanding of the entire sales process. Further, this process identifies the indicators of success and clearly communicates this to all members of the sales team. As stated above, entering and reviewing information takes time. However, research shows that companies that spent at least three hours per month managing each salesperson's pipeline saw 11% greater revenue growth compared to those that spent less than this. To some extent, salespeople can do this themselves. They have access to all relevant information through the CRM system. However, it is ideal when sales managers meet individually with their salespeople to go over each rep's pipeline, the primary focus being on developing strategies to help salespeople move their deals forward.[8]

Preparing for the First Contact

A key objective of the lead generation and prospecting process is to make the first appointment with clients. The remaining chapters of this textbook get into more details about what to do during and after that first meeting, but the topics of this chapter are centered on making that first meeting happen. Of course, this process is also about finding prospects that have a genuine need for the product. However, prospects that might truly need and benefit from a product will never buy unless they first *meet* with the person who can inform them about it.

Not surprisingly, making an appointment with qualified prospects is usually not easy. These people are important decision-makers who almost always have many demands on their time. There are techniques, however, to increase the chances of setting up that first meeting. This section elaborates on how to effectively reach out to these people and achieve this goal. We discuss both phone and email.

Phone Calls

Compared to the many high-tech options that have emerged in recent years, most customers still prefer speaking to a live person. So, if executed properly, phone calls can be an effective way for salespeople to make in-person appointments with new clients. One factor to consider is when to call. Research done by an online phone service found that the best day to call prospects is Wednesday and that the best time to call prospects is between 4 p.m. and 5 p.m. (with the second-best time to call prospects being between 11 a.m. and 12 noon).[9] This study also showed that it pays to be persistent if a connection is not made on the first call and that salespeople tend to give up too soon. Further, the findings indicate that salespeople should attempt at least six calls to try to have a conversation with prospects.

Build Rapport   If this persistence pays off and salespeople make contact with the prospect, then the first step in this conversation should be to build rapport. **Rapport** is defined as the sense of connection between two people who like and trust each other. Prospects are much more likely to hear out salespeople if there is some human connection between the two of them. This is why warm calling is so much more effective than cold calling, and why phone calls can be more effective than emails. This connection could be based on a number of things, such as mutual acquaintances or common schools attended. Important to building rapport with people is to find common ground and to create shared experiences. Also important is the salesperson's empathy, which is about understanding other people's emotions and being able to see things from their perspective. In other words, meaningful two-way communication has to happen for effective rapport. This communication involves asking questions and truly listening and paying attention to what the prospect says in return. Table 4-2 includes other suggestions for how to build rapport over the phone.

rapport
the sense of connection between two people who like and trust each other

Focus on Helping (Not Selling)   In this initial phone call, salespeople also should make clear that they are there to help, not just sell. Prospects will only make an appointment with salespeople who are in a position to provide value to them. At this early stage, it is not possible to explain exactly how they will do this (salespeople must first meet with them and do a thorough needs assessment). Salespeople, however, should be able to give a high-level overview of how their product can benefit the prospect. The benefit might be in the area of generating more revenue with a specific product or gaining efficiency and lowering costs associated with a particular business function. When explaining these benefits,

Table 4-2 Tips for Building Rapport over the Phone

1.	Be friendly and smile as you are speaking
2.	Sit with good posture
3.	Mirror the tone, tempo, and volume of other person's speech pattern
4.	Be conversational (never read a script)
5.	Address people in the way they introduce themselves
6.	Don't rush—take your time
7.	Stand up and walk around while talking
8.	Maintain a positive attitude
9.	Adopt a similar mood and temperament
10.	Ask open-ended questions
11.	Be a good listener

salespeople should do it with an attitude of helpfulness and professionalism. This makes a more positive first impression, which leads to the scheduling of an appointment.

Make the Appointment   Early in the phone call, salespeople should be sure to state that a key reason for the call is to schedule an appointment. Being clear on that objective is important. They might say, "The purpose of this call is to get 20 to 30 minutes to discuss how we can help you with this issue and reduce your costs of this service by 20%." Some salespeople are tempted to ask for only 5 or 10 minutes; thinking prospects would be more willing to meet for a short time. Suggesting such a short meeting time, however, indicates that the product is unimportant and serves to undercut the value of what the salesperson is selling.

When the prospect appears to be interested in the benefits of the product, it is time to ask for an appointment. In doing this, the salesperson should suggest a couple of specific meeting times. "Can we meet at this same time on Friday? Or would Monday at 2 p.m. work better with your schedule?" Giving prospects options keeps them engaged in the conversation and makes them choose, which is more likely to make that first meeting happen.

Email

Making the first contact via email is quite a bit different from doing this by phone. However, there are at least some similarities. Again, salespeople should try to connect with the prospect in a way that builds some rapport. That is, the email should feel personable, warm, and human. It should not come across as an automated robot. Using a more conversational writing style tends to work better. Like with the phone call, the goal should be to help prospects—not just sell to them.

Research shows that the subject line of the email is important. About half of all emails get deleted based only on the subject line. Emails are more likely to be opened if the subject line is casual and short. Because they are different from headlines, only the first word of the phrase should be capitalized so it reads more like a sentence. Using humorous subject lines is generally not advisable as they work only for some people—as a sense of humor varies greatly among people. Table 4-3 shows a list of one person's suggestions for humorous subject lines. Some experts argue that emails are more likely to be noticed (and thus opened) with bold, risky subject lines like these. Other ways to be bold are to express a contrary opinion ("The customer is not always right") or to create a sense of urgency ("You don't want to miss this"). Again, this is a risky approach that will only work in certain industries and situations.

Salespeople should pay careful attention to the first line of the email. This line is especially important, considering it often is displayed in most inboxes below the subject line (before the recipient has opened the email). Sales lingo should be avoided in this first line. A good way to open is to use the prospect's name, along with a brief comment showing that time was taken to invest in the situation (e.g., "Hi Seth, I loved reading your recent blog post about...).

Personalizing the email is very important, and there are a variety of ways to do this. If the prospect's name is not known, it can often be found (e.g., using LinkedIn). Also, salespeople should add such details as commenting on a recent company development in the news or extending holiday wishes. If possible, salespeople should demonstrate an understanding of the particular business of the prospect. They should also briefly provide an overview of how their product will benefit the prospect. Some salespeople embed short videos in their emails to explain how the product can help the prospect. If done well, such videos can set salespeople apart from their competition.

Table 4-3 Humorous Email Subject Lines

Would you be more likely to open these emails?	
"Need a day at the beach?"	"What's your Uber rating?"
"3 bizarre steps to being better at your job"	"Mom's gonna love this"
"Pairs nicely with spreadsheets"	"C'mon, it's Friday and you're killing time anyway..."
"HBO GO Password?"	
"Dad jokes. I've got 'em."	"Is Twilight the best movie ever made?"
"You have this in common with Steve Jobs"	"Coffee's for closers"
"Swipe right on us"	"The most important meal of the day"
"Is it too late now to say sorry?"	"I like you better than my nephew right now."
"How to organize your VHS collection"	"Confession: I watched Harry Potter 1-4 this weekend"

Source: Prater, Meg. (2018). 23 Funny Email Subject Lines Begging to Be Opened. *Hubspot blog.* Retrieved at https://blog.hubspot.com/sales/funny-email-subject-lines.

Finally, there should be a clear call to action followed by a warm signoff. This call to action should be in the form of a question: "Do you have 20 minutes tomorrow to talk about how this product can help you?" The signoff can be a bit tricky. Experts debate on the pros and cons of using various signoffs. "Yours truly" sounds old-fashioned and overly formal to some. "Best" seems impersonal to many. Good options for signoffs include "Thank you," "Best regards," "With gratitude," "Respectfully," "Looking forward to hearing from you." Of course, there are many clearly bad options: "Love" is not professional, "Ciao" seems pretentious (unless you are Italian), and "As ever" does not make any sense. Some sales experts assert that salespeople should use a unique, creative signoff that makes them stand out (e.g., "Hakuna Matata"). Although some salespeople can likely use these to good effect, we see these as an unnecessary risk that might come across as sarcastic or unprofessional.[10]

Inbound vs. Outbound Marketing

outbound marketing
the traditional approach to marketing, including radio, television, telemarketing, direct mail, and print and outdoor advertising

A recent trend in the discussion of lead generation and prospecting is to make a distinction between inbound and outbound marketing. **Outbound marketing** is defined as the traditional approach to marketing, and it includes radio, television, and print and outdoor advertising, as well as telemarketing (e.g., cold calls) and direct mail. The word *outbound* is used because traditional advertising *pushes out* messages to people who may or may not have a genuine need for the product. Although traditional advertising does identify and focus on a target market, there is still at least some waste as many people receiving the message have no interest in buying the product. Further, even if these messages do reach the right people, they are often ignored because these potential customers either are engaged in other activities or are using modern communications technology that facilitates this (e.g., skipping over commercials, streaming entertainment without ads).

inbound marketing
efforts that utilize internet technology to find potential customers who are actively searching for a product

Not surprisingly, these criticisms of outbound marketing are voiced most strongly by those who practice **inbound marketing**, which are those efforts that utilize internet technology to find potential customers who are actively searching for a product. The assets of inbound marketing include blog posts, search engines, internet ads, social media, and mobile apps. Some say that inbound marketing uses pull tactics, whereas outbound marketing uses push tactics. Table 4-4 shows a comparison of inbound and outbound marketing from the website of an inbound marketing company. Consequently, this figure might be a bit biased!

Table 4-4 Inbound and Outbound Marketing

Inbound Marketing	Outbound Marketing
Permissive	Interruptive
Pull tactics	Push tactics
Two-way communication	One-way communication
Marketers provide value	Marketers provide little to no value
Customers come to you	Customers are sought after
Channels: Search engines, referrals, social medias	Channels: Print ads, TV ads, radio, telemarketing...

Source: This comparison is taken from the website of SEOPressor, which is an inbound marketing firm that specializes in search engine optimization. Retrieved at https://seopressor.com/blog/inbound-vs-outbound-marketing-more-effective.

An interesting exercise is to evaluate the various lead sources from the beginning of the chapter (see Figure 4-1 on lead sources)—on whether they are more representative of outbound or inbound marketing tactics. There is a mix of both. For example, classic cold calling is consistent with outbound marketing, which is probably why proponents of inbound marketing claim that cold calling is no longer relevant. Googling "Is cold calling dead?" results in many websites with strong arguments on both sides. That is, many argue for why cold calling is still a viable prospecting method if done correctly. Not surprisingly, the inbound marketing websites present arguments for why cold calling is inefficient and a waste of time.

The tactics that turn cold calling into warm calling are generally consistent with inbound marketing methods. Much of the discussion of how to use social media to generate leads comes from the inbound marketing group. Leads from internal referrals are generated by inbound marketing methods if they come from internet searches, but they are generated by traditional methods if they come from the suggestions of salespeople or other employees. According to most sales experts, customer referrals are still the best source of leads—and this has been true since long before internet technology made inbound marketing methods possible.

Recall that the first step of lead generation and prospecting is to generate a large number of names. We maintain that the most effective way to do this is to use a combination of both inbound and outbound marketing techniques.

Role of CRM

The main purpose of a company's CRM system is to organize information about both prospects and customers. Consequently, CRM has played an increasingly important role in prospecting—especially with regard to the qualifying process of moving prospects to customers. As explained previously, most CRM systems automatically generate a sales pipeline for each salesperson. The systems also provide several metrics to assess the strength of the pipeline. For example, many CRM programs calculate quantitative numbers or scores for each prospect. These scores direct salespeople to who the best prospects are.

A good CRM can remind the salesperson *when* to follow up and can provide them with guidance on *how* to follow up. It can even be programmed to follow up for them. The result is quicker, more accurate decision making that speeds up the sales cycle. This enhances sales performance for the salesperson and drives revenue for the firm.

One word of caution is that the validity of CRM information is only as good as the quality of the data that has been inputted. This means that if salespeople want to take from their CRM, they also must give. In other words, salespeople should conscientiously and accurately enter information about each sales call. In addition, salespeople should make the effort to learn all they can about their CRM. The system might seem complicated at first, but they are designed for users not necessarily proficient in technology. Understanding the full capabilities of CRM is key to successful lead generation and prospecting.

Applying this Chapter to Salesforce

Much of the prospecting and lead generation process can be managed with Salesforce. To focus time and energy on the best prospects, Salesforce can help by prioritizing them in *Tiers*. Salesforce can also provide information about a prospect's use of the seller's website. Important information about their location, site searches, and click path can all be reviewed with Salesforce's *Web* and *Mobile Analytics* dashboard. This information provides the salesperson with insight about what the prospect wants before they speak, turning cold calls into warm calls.

Tracking open and click rates on sent email is another good way to generate better leads. A prospect who opens an email is signaling more interest than one who doesn't. Even better is someone who opens the email multiple times and clicks on links to additional information. If the email includes a video clip, Salesforce will report how much the prospect watched before closing it.

Triggers can be set so that if a prospect opens an email, a task is automatically created for the salesperson or someone else on their team to call the prospect. Salesforce can also be set to automatically follow up with anyone who has interacted with your messaging. For example, if the prospect clicks a link in the email to watch a video, a follow-up email will automatically be sent with more information or a call to action.

Another helpful feature within Salesforce is *News*, which provides instant access to relevant news activity related to any customers, partners, competitors, or prospects the salesperson is following. The *News* feature includes articles from the past 30 days. This information can be presented on the salespersons home page or can be displayed within the *Account*, *Contact*, or *Lead* tab, providing useful background information when reaching out to speak to a new lead.

Chapter Summary

- Prospecting is the method or system used by the sales force to find new customers—or in other words, to generate leads. This is a critical activity for all sales organizations, but especially for newer firms that are trying to become established.
- The first step is identifying leads, which involves the acquisition of a large number of names and addresses of potential customers.
- Sales professionals generally agree that the best way to identify leads is through referrals from existing customers.
- Other good ways to identify leads is through internal referrals (sources from inside the sales organization, such as salespeople, sales managers, employees of the marketing department, and workers at trade shows).
- Salespeople often generate leads through networking, which involves developing professional and social contact with others in civic organizations such as Rotary, Kiwanis, and Business Network International (BNI).
- Cold calling, which was once a very common way to generate leads, has become much less popular in recent years.
- Newer techniques of generating leads include warm calling, email prospecting, and social selling.

- Once the leads are generated, the second step of prospecting begins. This step is called qualifying leads. It involves evaluating each potential customers in terms of how likely they are to buy.
- Leads become qualified when prospects meet the four ANAR conditions. That is, prospects have the <u>A</u>uthority to buy; have the <u>N</u>eed the product that is being sold; can <u>A</u>fford to buy the product; and are <u>R</u>eceptive to being called on by the salesperson.
- The sales pipeline is a prospecting tool that is a visual representation of where all the prospects are in the purchasing process.
- A key objective of the lead generation and prospecting process is for salespeople to make the first appointment with clients—and then build rapport with them.
- There is a trend away from outbound marketing and toward inbound marketing.
  - Outbound marketing is defined as the traditional approach to marketing, and includes radio, television, outdoor and print ads.
  - Inbound marketing uses internet technology to analyze web traffic in order to identify potential customers who are actively searching for a product.

Key Terms

ANAR conditions (p. 72)
bird dogs (p. 68)
cold calling (p. 68)
conversion ratios (p. 76)
customer referral programs (p. 67)
email prospecting (p. 70)
hot prospect (p. 75)
identifying leads (p. 66)
inbound marketing (p. 80)
internal referrals (p. 68)
leads (p. 66)
lead generation (p. 66)
marketing qualified leads (MQLS) (p. 74)

networking (p. 68)
outbound marketing (p. 80)
prospect (p. 66)
prospecting (p. 66)
qualifying leads (p. 66)
qualified prospects (p. 75)
rapport (p. 78)
referral (p. 66)
sales cycle (p. 76)
sales pipeline (p. 74)
sales qualified leads (SQLS) (p. 74)
social selling (p. 70)
warm calling (p. 70)

Application 4-1

John Dubach is an account manager for Account Staff, Inc., which is a staffing firm in Louisville, Kentucky. John spends two hours a day contacting companies to see if they are in need of hiring an accountant or bookkeeper. He reaches out to these companies over the phone, randomly dialing numbers that he obtains from the membership list of the local Chamber of Commerce.

When these companies say "Yes," John is able to provide a list of names and resumes of candidates for the job. Typically, he makes an appointment to personally deliver this list to the prospect. During this meeting, he uncovers specific needs, talks over the pros and cons of various candidates, and makes recommendations. If these companies find someone on the list that they interview and ultimately hire, then he has successfully made a sale—and he earns a nice commission.

John, however, feels that this process is very inefficient and mostly a waste of time. For every 1,000 phone numbers that he dials, he talks to only about 60 people—and on average only two of these 60 people end up hiring one of his candidates. John believes there must be a better way!

(Continued)

(Continued)

1. What is John's process of generating leads called?
2. Rather than the current process, let's say John contacted qualified leads that were generated by inbound marketing methods. What would this new process of generating leads be called?
3. Recently, this process of generating leads resulted in a sale because John happened to contact someone who went to the same university he did. Because John and the prospect had this common experience, what kind of connection did they have?

Application 4-2

Betty works as a sales representative for Cactus State Insurance, which is a business-to-business insurance company that specializes in liability coverage for public swimming pools. Her territory includes both Arizona and New Mexico.

Betty is currently in a meeting at Cactus's national sales convention in Orlando, Florida. She is attending a session on the sales pipeline, and is given a report about the number of prospects and customers in her pipeline. The report indicates that she is currently dealing with 3,000 prospects, 900 qualified prospects, 90 hot prospects, and 9 customers.

A friend and colleague of Betty is Fred. Fred's territory is North Carolina, which is about the same size as Betty's territory. Fred's pipeline report indicates that he has 3,000 prospects, 300 qualified prospects, 150 hot prospects, and 24 customers. Betty is frustrated that Fred has more than twice the customers she does. She wonders if the analysis of the two sales pipelines might give her a clue as to what her problem is.

1. What is Betty's conversion ratio from prospects to qualified prospects?
2. What is Fred's conversion ratio from hot prospects to customers?
3. Based on a comparison of the numbers in these two sales pipelines, what would be a logical reason why Betty has fewer customers than Fred?

CHAPTER

5

Planning Sales Calls and Presentations

Learning Objectives

- Explain the value of planning for successful sales calls
- Evaluate what pre-call information salespeople should collect about their customers
- Determine where salespeople can find valuable pre-call information
- Illustrate how salespeople should set goals for their sales calls
- Describe what is involved in planning sales calls for complex buying decisions

Successful salespeople recognize that planning before the sales call is critical to their performance. In the absence of planning, salespeople often miss opportunities to connect with the buyer, present information that does not align with the buyer's interests, or push for an outcome that is unrealistic for the expectations of the sales call context. These unfocused sales calls provide little value to the customer and often lead to distrust. However, by creating a plan, salespeople are more likely to generate interest from their buyers and improve their likelihood of succeeding.

Return on Planning

Just as the buyer's time is valuable, so is the salesperson's. Planning helps salespeople spend time efficiently on calls that meet their own performance objectives. Additionally, planning sales calls also makes them more predictable in terms of how long they should last. This predictability allows salespeople more time to invest in other call plans, make additional calls, complete administrative tasks, and avoid falling behind in their daily schedule. Top salespeople know that proper planning gives them more control of their time and greater likelihood of meeting their performance objectives. In this chapter, we illustrate two major areas of sales call planning: gathering pre-call information and presentation planning. We first elaborate on three key areas of pre-call information, which should be used to guide the development of the sales call presentation (Figure 5-1).

Gathering Pre-call Information

Gathering pre-call information can often make the difference in gaining customer commitment. The more information salespeople have about their customer, the higher their chance of developing a relationship and uncovering needs. However, there are diminishing returns for the time spent gathering information for the call so it is wise to prepare efficiently. In light of this, we emphasize three key areas to gather pre-call information and prepare for a sales call: customer knowledge, product knowledge, and market knowledge. In many cases, these areas require research about the customer while at the same cultivating the right mindset.

Figure 5-1 Important Information for Pre-Call Planning

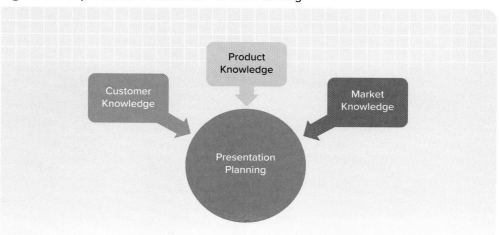

Customer Knowledge

Today's salespeople are encouraged to align all their actions in the context of building customer relationships. The increasing need for relationships comes at a time of dynamic change in the sales ecosystem. Salespeople across industries are experiencing mounting competition (e.g., international firms and new channels such as Amazon) and greater **role complexity**, defined as a large number and diversity of customer and organizational tasks. By the same token, customers are also experiencing greater complexity in the buying process (see more in Chapter 3), which means that customers need help to understand how to buy what they need. As a result, the difference between closing a sale and walking away empty-handed is often defined by how the customer perceives you, the seller. Customers value salespeople who demonstrate their preparedness in the sales call, which can be accomplished in multiple ways. Key among these are the ability to build a relationship and show thoughtful insights regarding the customer's business.

role complexity
a large number and diversity of customer and organizational tasks

Preparing for a Relationship   Sellers must prepare to build a relationship with each customer. Any relationship starts with finding familiarity with the other person. The initial meetings between a salesperson and customer are very important in establishing familiarity. During these first meetings, customers form an impression of the salesperson that either facilitates or distracts from the salesperson's intended message. Top salespeople capitalize on these impressions as opportunities to build common ground with their customers. We highlight three areas salespeople should examine before the call to increase familiarity with their customers and begin cultivating a relationship.

Develop a Genuine Interest in the Customers   Before customers meet with a salesperson, they are just like anyone else you might meet on the street. They have a desire to be perceived as important and understood. However, salespeople often overlook this need by prioritizing a focus on convincing their customers to understand their offering. This focus typically causes salespeople to hear their customers selectively, and ignore subtle aspects of the customers' situation, and thus miss the meaning of the customers' story entirely. Clearly, most salespeople are well-intentioned, so why does this happen? Author Stephen R. Covey finds that this problem happens because people do not listen with the intent to understand; they listen with the intent to reply.[1] Salespeople fall into this trap often. During customer conversations, salespeople continually prepare in their minds what they want to say, questions they want to ask while filtering the customer's answers through their own experiences and product strengths. Consequently, salespeople form an inaccurate impression of the customer's needs before they have a deep understanding.

Salespeople must prepare for sales calls with a mindset to first understand their customer's situation. Research often describes this mindset as a **customer orientation**. Customer orientation reflects a deep concern for others, low-pressure selling, and problem-solution selling approaches.[2] Indeed, findings show that salespeople with customer orientation increase customers' perception of trust, satisfaction, and relationship development. This evidence suggests that focusing on customers' needs first, rather than their solutions, helps salespeople become better at understanding how they can help their customers. To evaluate your own customer orientation before each sales call, ask yourself: Do I genuinely want what's best for this customer?

customer orientation
a high concern for others, low-pressure selling, and problem-solution selling approaches

Mutual Connections or Interests   Another important avenue for connecting with customers is to find friends, colleagues, or interests you share. As humans, we are all drawn to connection. As a result, business relationships are often formed by establishing some form of common ground between parties. Salespeople can prepare for a customer meeting by searching for shared connections that are already known. Technology has made this process even easier with tools such as LinkedIn, Facebook, and other similar sites. For example, salespeople can search for a customer's profile and quickly find connections in common.

These common contacts can provide deep knowledge about the customer's background, network, and goals that can shape the nature of the sales call and help add value even during the introductions. If any relationship has been established in the past, the salesperson's company's customer relationship management (CRM) database (e.g., Salesforce.com, Hubspot.com) is also likely to have valuable information about these factors.

Many profiles include other areas that may uncover mutual interests, such as the college they attended, or groups to which the customer belongs. These potential customers may actively post content on social media as well. The salesperson may wish to make a note of these postings in preparing for the sales call. The customer may mention recent activities, hobbies, or notable experiences that would offer great conversation starters to build rapport. The information may also provide an opportunity to point out related interests or friends in common or to avoid topics that would make the customer uncomfortable. Plus, customers take note of diligence in learning about them and providing common ground to start the conversation.

Other sources of information about mutual interests are offline. While gatekeepers, like receptionists or administrative assistants can often be skeptical of salespeople's wanting a meeting, they can be valuable sources of information to learn deeper information about the customer. Additionally, since noncompeting salespeople may have already visited with the customer, they can also provide valuable insights about your customer's personality, communication style, and interests. Be mindful that this information is unlikely to be given to just anyone. Cultivating these sources of customer intelligence requires diligent networking and relationship building behavior over time.

Cultivate a Mindset of Integrity   Every salesperson projects an image that is defined by the qualities perceived by the customer. Too often in the selling field, this image has been one of mistrust and manipulation spawning the many stereotypes and general suspicion of salespeople across industries. While these are more exception than rule, untrustworthy salespeople create a stigma for the rest of the sales population. Top salespeople recognize that to overcome these biases, they must show integrity with their customers to build relationships. Experts describe a person to have integrity "when there is no gap between intent and behavior."[3] Salespeople who can be trusted to do what they say they will do inspire trust in their relationships. Customers feel the person is dependable and committed to positive results and validates their confidence. An integrity mindset also drives humility. Humble salespeople do not get caught up in arrogance, manipulation, or win-lose power plays. They are quick to see their errors and learn from customer interactions that go poorly.

Integrity is the "root" of every person. Many salespeople have great capabilities, but if they lack integrity, customers will quickly see through these salespeople's hollow relationship-building efforts.

Integrity is composed of honesty, congruence, humility, and courage. To cultivate an integrity mindset, ask the following questions:

- Am I honest in all my interactions with my customers?
- Am I open to learning new truths that cause me to rethink my relationship approach?

- Am I able to consistently make and keep commitments with my customers?
- Is there anything about this customer or account that might bias my integrity?

Learn the Customer's Business   Today's salespeople are well-advised to become as knowledgeable as possible about their customer's business and financial standing. One primary way to become fluent in the customer's business is by reviewing financial statements and earnings reports. Trends identified in these documents can offer great opportunities for understanding challenges the customer may be experiencing, or openings for the salesperson to help them continue to grow. These types of insights can speak volumes to knowing about the customer before meeting them.

If a customer works at a publicly-traded company, the first stop for this type of information is the "Investor's Relations" section of a company's corporate website or on the U.S. Securities and Exchange Commission (SEC)'s EDGAR (Electronic Data Gathering, Analysis, and Retrieval) website for publicly traded companies.[4] A great place to start is the company's income statement, which details the operational performance over a specified period. From a high level, the income statement provides an overview of how the company captured revenue, the expenses incurred to do so, and the resulting profit or loss. Table 5-1 provides an example of an income statement from Cisco Systems. The top and bottom of the income statements reveal the initial story. What's going on with revenues? You can see that they increased compared to the same quarter last year for both products and services. At the same time, net income (or profitability) grew in comparison to last year. Both are good signs, but there are important details in between that can provide opportunities for the salesperson to help the customer's business.

For example, taking a closer look at revenues by percentage growth can tell a story. By looking at percentage growth, we can see that overall revenues grew by 7.7% compared to last quarter. However, when breaking down by category, product revenue grew more than 9% while services grew only 3.2%. This shows that sales of services are not growing as fast as products, indicating that there may be some challenges for the sales force in going to market with these offerings. Let's also look at what **gross profit** really means in the context of a year-to-year comparison. Gross profit is the difference between the total revenue generated and cost of sales (also called cost of goods sold). Another perspective to consider for this metric is **gross margin,** which is gross profit as a percentage of revenue (i.e., (revenue − costs)/revenue). For Cisco, we can see that their gross profit increased from $7,427M up to $8,146M between years indicating a successful growth period. However, Cisco's gross margins for the same periods are 82.0% and 82.4%, respectively, indicating that they essentially gained the same rate of revenue returns on the amount spent to produce those goods and services. These examples represent a portion of many areas to research a potential customer's income statement. Salespeople should also feel comfortable reviewing the company's balance sheet and cash flow statements as well. Most importantly, this review should help salespeople identify areas where they can make a strategic difference in the customer's business.

Another way to learn more about the customer's situation is to research recent news about the company. This approach is especially important for private companies that are not required to disclose financial statements. Company webpages routinely provide updates about changes to its people, products, and organization, usually found under tabs titled "Newsroom" or "Press Room." E&J Gallo, for example, announced that it will acquire over 30 wine and spirits brands from Constellation Brands, a competing firm.[5] This is clearly a sign of change for many parts of the organization at Gallo and can potentially create pain points for

gross profit
the difference between the total revenue generated and cost of sales (also called cost of goods sold)

gross margin
gross profit as a percentage of revenue

Table 5-1 Income Statement

CISCO SYSTEMS, INC.
CONSOLIDATED STATEMENTS OF OPERATIONS
(in millions, expect per-share amounts)
(Unaudited)

	Three Months Ended	
	October 27, 2018	October 28, 2017
REVENUE:		
Product	$ 9,890	$ 9,054
Service	3,182	3,082
Total revenue	13,072	12,136
COST OF SALES:		
Product	3,799	3,615
Service	1,127	1,094
Total cost of sales	4,926	4,709
GROSS MARGIN	8,146	7,427
OPERATING EXPENSES:		
Research and development	1,608	1,567
Sales and marketing	2,410	2,334
General and administrative	211	557
Amortization of purchased intangible assets	34	61
Restructuring and other charges	78	152
Total operating expenses	4,341	4,671
OPERATING INCOME	3,805	2,756
Interest income	344	379
Interest expense	(221)	(235)
Other income (loss), net	(19)	62
Interest and other income (loss), net	104	206
INCOME BEFORE PROVISION FOR INCOME TAXES	3,909	2,962
Provision for income taxes	360	568
NET INCOME	$ 3,549	$ 2,394
Net income per share:		
Basic	$ 0.78	$ 0.48
Diluted	$ 0.77	$ 0.48
Shares used in per-share calculation:		
Basic	4,565	4,959
Diluted	4,614	4,994

many of its leaders. For a marketing leader, how will Gallo ensure these new brands are aligned with their current go-to-market strategy? For a production manager, if these new brands will continue to be produced in their current facilities, how will those processes be integrated with their current distribution system? For a sales leader, how will Gallo salespeople represent these new brands while maintaining the performance of the existing brands in their portfolio? As you can see, there are many potential opportunities for your own products, processes, or people to help with these challenges.

Traditional secondary sources may also be helpful in this area. Data providers such as Hoover's, Moody's, and Standard & Poor's provide several informative documents that can include key contacts, historical information, the situational outlook for the firm and industry, locations, and other information. Other online sources such as ZoomInfo, InsideView, and Datanyze extract information from the web to provide salespeople with enriched customer contact information. The value of this information may vary based on the timeliness and costs to acquire.

Product Knowledge

The next major factor for sales call planning is knowing the product's advantages. Domestic and global markets are filled with a wide array of goods and services. In some industries, the number of new offerings introduced each year is staggering. The marketing technology industry, for example, grew from around 150 offerings to over 5,000 between 2011 and 2017.[6] For customers, this creates more choices, but the resulting increase in choices and the amount of information required to learn about the choices makes purchasing more difficult.[7] One of the most important roles for today's salespeople is to simplify the customer's decision-making process by crafting a solution that adds value. In this section, we examine the types of information needed to help salespeople communicate the value from their offering by understanding its benefits and advantages.

Understanding Benefits

The importance of benefits to the selling is so significant that it is worth revisiting. A benefit is how an attribute of the salesperson's offering helps customers eliminate a problem or improve an existing situation. The benefits should help customers answer the question, "How will buying this product or service help me?" A feature is a description of the attribute of the salesperson's product or service. Features often characterize the design, quality, speed, technical, or other operational aspects of the offering.

One may notice that features are product-focused— describing aspects of the product— while benefits are customer-focused— describing how the product uniquely helps the customer. For example, the CRM software company Hubspot might describe one of their key features, such as "Automated logging and updating of customer deals and sales activities." This description tells what the offering does but not necessarily how it helps the customer. A savvy salesperson might describe a benefit stemming from this feature as "this helps salespeople spend more time contacting customers and less time performing data entry."

General and Specific Benefits

In his seminal book, SPIN Selling, author Neil Rackham points out that a salesperson's offering provides a benefit only when it meets a buyer's specific need.[8] A general benefit describes how a feature can be helpful to a customer in a broad sense, but it does not clearly link to the specific needs of the customer. Many times this occurs when customers have varying interests and goals. Some sales practitioners have highlighted that customer accounts typically have different **buying influences**— someone who has a positive or negative impact on your selling activity— and thus different specific needs. While there are multiple types of buying influences, two of

buying influences
someone who has a positive or negative impact on your selling activity

the most common types are: **economic buyer**— the person(s) who has final approval to make the purchase, and **user buyer**— the person(s) who make judgments about the impact of salesperson's solution on their own performance.[9]

When examining these two types of buyer influences, each likely has different specific needs to be addressed by the salesperson's solution. A generic benefit would be unlikely to satisfy either influence. To plan for these different types of customers, salespeople should prepare specific benefits to address each buying influencer's specific needs. Here is an example of a generic benefit from a sales training solution that is translated into specific benefits catering to each buying influence:

- Generic benefit: "Our sales training helps your salespeople improve customer retention."
- Specific benefit for Economic buyer: "Our sales training will help you (sales leader) improve your recurring revenue by decreasing the number of lost customer accounts."
- Specific benefit for User buyer: "Our sales training will help you (salesperson) build greater customer loyalty and blow past your quota every quarter."

Create Bridge Statements

A deep analysis of the salesperson's solution helps identify the primary features and customer benefits. Once all the important features and benefits are identified, arrange them in a logical order based on priority and buyer influence type. We know that customers purchase benefits, not features, so it is important to prepare a statement that connects how the features will provide the benefits to help the customer. This statement, often called a **bridge statement**, is a transitional phrase to connect the feature descriptions with the benefits of the offering. In planning the sales call, prepare a series of bridge statements to connect all the features and benefits to the buying influences to be called. By using this approach, an HR payroll service that is rolling out a mobile application developed feature-benefit worksheets (Table 5-2). Notice how each feature is translated into a specific benefit that would be relevant to each buying influence involved in the purchase decision.

Aligning Benefits Against the Competition

Achieving sustained success in today's competitive markets requires that salespeople actively communicate the value of their offering. This can become difficult when competing products and substitutes are introduced to the market and take away the product's advantages. As a result, top salespeople constantly monitor their customer's perceptions of their products, not in isolation, but relative to competitors. This preparation helps salespeople to consistently deliver value in how they communicate their offering's value. In this section, we review how positioning and differentiation are two factors that drive value communication.

Positioning

Positioning refers to the firm's activities intended to create a certain concept of the offering in the customer's mind. While positioning is often performed through the firm's marketing activities, every salesperson needs to invest time to understand how their offering is positioned in the marketplace. Good positioning means that the product's name, reputation, and value are well recognized. Salespeople can often rely on these positive customer perceptions to gain credibility and improve the odds of a purchase. However, good positioning does not last forever. Weak or bad positioning can damage the product's reputation and make the salesperson's efforts to sell much more difficult. In an age where information about products is

Table 5-2 Feature-benefit worksheet example

Feature	Economic Buyer Benefit	User Buyer Benefit
Our mobile application allows users to process payroll anytime, anywhere via a mobile device...	...gives all of your employees a common user interface to access payroll regardless of role or location, removing the need for additional terminals to access this information.	...lets you quickly address any payroll transactions and get back to serving customers.
Our mobile application provides real-time reporting...	...helping you minimize the risk of over-drafting for payroll expenses.	...giving you notifications when funds are available to you.

readily available, salespeople who cannot positively position their products with their customers will quickly lose value.

When assessing a product's positioning, it is important to consider that customers evaluate factors beyond the product. Today's savvy customers are seeking multiple benefits from their solutions and typically look to factors stemming from the company and salesperson, as well as the product when evaluating their choices. Figure 5-2 provides a framework of these three dimensions that can make up the solution's positioning in the market.

Differentiation   One of the foundational principles of marketing and sales is **differentiation**. Differentiation refers to the ability to distinguish your solution from that of competitors. Competitors in most industries are all trying to distance themselves from one another on some or all of the factors in Figure 5-3. As a result, differentiation is a core activity for salespeople to create a competitive advantage when meeting with customers. Consistent feedback from customers, in addition to their company's marketing knowledge, helps salespeople prepare to communicate how their solution is different from the competition. This type of information is often called **competitive intelligence**, defined as salesperson knowledge about competitors and the market environment. It is key for salespeople to communicate the differentiated value of their offering.[10] Without this distinction, customers are likely to compare solutions as commodities and choose the provider with the lowest price.

To illustrate how salespeople can differentiate their solution in a real-world setting, let us examine a complex buying decision. Adrienne McDonald, a sales representative for a commercial insurance provider, sells insurance and risk management solutions for small and middle-market businesses. Over a period of nine months, she frequently called on a prospect who had a long-established business relationship with a local provider. However, she knew the prospect had the potential to become a valued customer based on the differentiated value she felt she could provide. At first, the business's decision-maker refused to schedule a meeting with her. Frustrated, but not discouraged, Adrienne collected information about the business's history and the current provider, and she also conducted her company's proprietary risk assessment process on the business's building. These efforts led her to uncover a significant risk to the business that was not currently covered by the policy in place. With a plan ready, Adrienne approached her decision-maker again, armed with insightful expertise that generated interest in an initial meeting. She conveyed how her company's assessment process (company factor) combined with her own expertise (salesperson factor) led her to uncover a problem with their current provider. These aspects of her presentation provided differentiated value to the decision-maker and opened the door for Adrienne to

differentiation
the ability to distinguish your solution from that of competitors

competitive intelligence
salesperson knowledge about competitors and the market environment

Figure 5-2 Framework for solution positioning

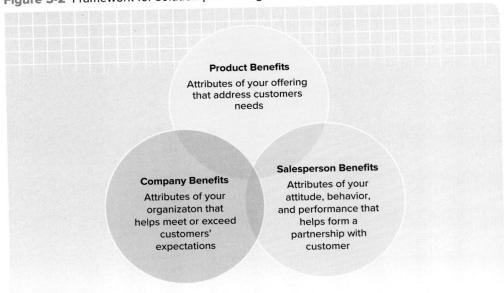

expand upon the unique aspects of her solutions (product factor). Within the month, Adrienne had become the business owner's most trusted advisor, winning the business and also getting referrals for associated businesses in the area.

This example provides clear evidence that salespeople who plan on how to differentiate their solution are more likely to be successful. Preparation helps salespeople clearly communicate their solution differentiation with each customer and convey their value. The differentiation planning worksheet (Table 5-3) can help the salesperson discover ways to position the solution choice over the competition's product, company, and the salesperson's attributes relative to the competition. Table 5-3 provides an example set of attributes for evaluating the value of the salesperson's offering in the marketplace. How would the customer rate these attributes?

Market Knowledge

To effectively prepare for a sales call, it is also important to gain a broader understanding of the market. Every market will consist of different customers who could buy an offering; however, their reasons for doing so vary widely. This can make planning difficult if salespeople are preparing to address too many different kinds of needs. Market knowledge helps salespeople align their preparation to focus on a set of core customer needs. For example, if salespeople are selling solutions to relationship customers, salespeople should plan to address items such as longer selling cycles, frequent customer requests, and custom requirements within their sales calls.

Ideal Customer Profile Salespeople should spend time researching their markets to understand their **ideal customer profile**. An ideal customer profile is a description of a company that creates mutual value when using the salesperson's solution. This definition highlights that ideal customers are ones that experienced success using the salesperson's solution and have also been customers from which the salesperson's company received value as well. Experts find that surprisingly few companies clearly define these criteria and suggest salespeople should adopt a process to identify these core customers to align their selling efforts.[11]

Salespeople should define these customers by conducting a careful review of current and prospective accounts based on the type of industry, size, location,

ideal customer profile
a description of a company that creates mutual value when using the salesperson's solution

Table 5-3 Differentiation planning worksheet

	My Firm	Competitor A	Competitor B	Competitor C
Product Value				
Quality				
Brand				
Performance				
Service				
Company Value				
Locations				
Market reputation				
Ordering system				
Return policy				
Salesperson Value				
Expertise				
Responsiveness				
Integrity				
Adaptive selling				

annual revenue, and other distinguishing characteristics that make them a good fit. For example, which industries seem to receive the most benefit from the salesperson's solution? For what size companies does the solution provide the most benefits? At the same time, these sets of customers should also be categorized by which ones are most aligned with salesperson and company goals. Which types of customers are most profitable? While customers remain the longest? Which customers are more costly to serve?

By identifying ideal client profiles, salespeople can efficiently keep track of key types of customers, their most likely challenges, and their resulting needs. This preparation provides multiple benefits for salespeople. Ideal customer profiles increase salesperson capacity by reducing the variety of customer types and increased focus on fewer indicators. Ideal customer profiles also improve close rates because salespeople are more knowledgeable about the challenges and needs of their key customers. It also reduces the amount of preparation for each call and reduces the number of likely objections raised.

Gaining Business Acumen Another key aspect of market knowledge is business acumen. Restating the definition, business acumen is the practical awareness of the various characteristics, processes, and roles that comprise a successful business in a given market. Many salespeople fail at building meaningful customer relationships because they do not grasp the fundamentals of how businesses in their markets operate. Conversely, salespeople who develop business acumen have a better understanding of the risks and opportunities in a market that helps them guide customer actions toward positive outcomes. Unfortunately, business acumen typically takes time and experience to develop, but salespeople can focus on a few specific areas to accelerate their development.

Experts find that in even the most complex companies, the same core business drivers are found: cash, profit, assets, growth, and people.[12] These first three core drivers are typically found in financial statements such as the income statement, balance sheet, and cash flow statement as mentioned in the previous section. Thus, reviewing the 10-Q (quarterly reports) and 10-K (annual reports) of companies in an industry, which include managerial discussions of these metrics, can quickly get salespeople up to speed. Growth is a common goal for any company although the shape and form of it can vary from revenues, profits, repeat business, number of customers, or earnings per share. Lastly, people represent the value of employees and leaders within a company, which is typically a core driver of the other four metrics.

While all of these core drivers are common, the metrics and strategy that they fall into vary depending on the industry. As a result, salespeople must immerse themselves in the thought patterns of leaders in the industry to understand the specific attributes that are applicable. This involves continuous learning for salespeople through many types of resources such as conferences, books/trade magazines, podcasts, or courses.

Preparing for the Presentation

Once salespeople have gathered pre-call information and prepared themselves for the call, they can use this information to guide the strategy for the presentation (i.e., how the sales call should be executed). In this section, we outline the steps salespeople take to effectively plan out the presentation, given their pre-call information and context of the upcoming sales call.

Define the Objective(s)

After reviewing pre-call information, the most important activity to complete before planning the call is to set an objective. Customer decision-making processes involve several steps and can be complex. As a result, setting an objective to "make a sale" on every call is unlikely to be achievable. Similarly, setting an objective to "present our products" lacks any action from the customer. Salespeople need to undertake a thoughtful process to isolate the best goal for a given sales call.

Despite the importance of this activity, salespeople often overlook this important task. Considering salespeople's focus on results, frequent meetings with customers, and a dynamic environment, it is not surprising many salespeople want to "just make a call" rather than spend time planning. But in the absence of a plan, salespeople end up wasting more time on poorly executed sales calls.

The best starting point for setting the call objective is to review what one has learned about the customer, the product advantages, and the business environment. However, call objectives should not be created in a vacuum. Keep in mind that some customers may not want a salesperson relationship.[13] In fact, spending time with these customers makes one appear less trustworthy and inefficient. Objectives should be flexible enough to adapt to customers who may or may not become strategic partners. At the same time, objectives should also take into account the company's goals, management's emphasis, the sales team's goals, and individual aspirations. For example, new product introductions are often dependent on the sales force promoting the product to customers. It may be easier to set objectives to align with selling existing products, but this would run counter to the company's goals of a successful market entry for the new offering. Regardless of the type of goal, the only way to achieve it is by securing incremental customer commitments along the way. When the call objective includes a customer commitment, each and every sales call moves the salesperson closer to the goals.

customer commitments
the customer's promise to do something concrete to move the sales process forward

Shutterstock/Kostiantyn Voitenko

Goal for Customer Commitments

Customer commitments represent the customer's promise to do something concrete to move the sales process forward. During each call, the objective should include a customer commitment that marks the near-term accomplishment. It may seem obvious that salespeople should have a customer commitment in mind on each call. However, even experienced sales professionals' objectives are typically too general, unrealistic, and salesperson-focused rather than customer-focused.[14] Instead, objectives should meet several criteria in order to ensure customers make commitments following the sales call.

Is the Call Objective Specific?

An objective must be specific to be effective. It should clearly guide what needs to be accomplished, when it will be accomplished, and who will be involved. Specific objectives help salespeople from "winging it" during the call, which may ultimately confuse the customer. In setting an objective, ask, Does it define the who, what, where, and when of the action? Attention to all these specifics can prevent many unforeseen problems. For example, you may set an objective for the customer to provide a referral to their vice president (the who), but if you do not set a time frame for this action, the customer may put off the commitment and ultimately forget. These types of oversights result in significant delays throughout the buying process.

Does the Call Objective Focus on a Customer Action?

If the salesperson is not receiving effort in exchange for the salesperson's own efforts, the customer does not see the value, and it is a waste of the salesperson's time. They need to ensure that an objective includes an action for the customer to complete for mutual benefit. The customer's action must also be more than just something the customer wants to do. It must also be something they are able to do. Often, salespeople commit their customers to agree to bring in additional decision-makers without the authority to influence their involvement. Sensitivity to the individual customer's role and authority will provide additional guidance on defining an objective.

Is the Call Objective Measurable?

Once the customer completes the action within the salesperson's objective, how do they know it was completed? Customers are busy and have many additional responsibilities; they may unintentionally forget or overlook completing their commitment. Therefore, part of the objective should include a contingency to ask for evidence of the customer's action after the call. By all means, do not stalk the customers for feedback. But if one plans on providing value, expending effort, and gaining a commitment, then customers should not hesitate to fulfill their obligation. If there is hesitation, consider whether your interests are truly aligned.

Does the Call Objective Move the Sale Forward?

Regardless of the actions the customer commits to perform, and despite the level of commitment to performing those actions, ultimately, the relationship exists under the foundational premise that the salesperson will complete an exchange. Often, customers may be more than willing to provide information and set up meetings, but these may not be pertinent to supporting the case for providing value and closing a sale. A classic example of this type of misguided action is committing the wrong customer to attend a demonstration. While well-intended, the customer may not be the individual with the expertise, authority, or relevance to provide any meaningful progress as a result of the demonstration. As a result, the salesperson wastes valuable time preparing and delivering a presentation to the wrong audience. Consider before setting the objective: If the customer commits this action, will we be closer to making a sale?

Is the Call Objective Realistic?

Objectives must be realistic for the call to be successful. Inexperienced salespeople often have over-optimistic expectations about the customer's response to the sales call presentation. For example, if BMW currently uses the same advertising firm for all of its commercials, a competing advertising firm's salesperson who expects BMW to change firms after the first few calls is demonstrating an unrealistic objective. Objectives are most often unrealistic because they overestimate what can be expected given the time allocated to the sales call.

One way to test whether an objective is realistic is to summarize the other four criteria above. A realistic call objective is specific, focuses on what the customer can and will do, can be measured when complete, and moves the sales forward. If the next meeting with the customer's vice president is set at some vague point in the future, if it's not clear whether the customer has the authority to connect with the vice president, or if there is no way to confirm that the vice president is relevant to the offering, then by definition the sales call objective is not realistic.

When in doubt about how realistic the objective is for the next sales call, ask. On the call, ask questions to help clarify the customer's view of the process moving forward in order to get on the same page about what the customer is committed to accomplishing, what can be accomplished, and when. This type of intelligence can be gathered using the questioning process found in Chapter 6 and help you get aligned with the buyer's decision-making process.

Your Plan for Capturing Interest

Just as important as an objective(s) for the next sales call is the plan for capturing the customer's interest. Many salespeople's best-laid plans are wasted because the customer never developed any interest in the meeting agenda. Before walking into a sales call, consider, "What is the customer's reason for meeting with me?" Whenever someone schedules some time, that person is making a conscious decision to give up a precious resource in exchange for what the salesperson has to offer.

Capturing the customer's interest sounds obvious enough and is not a new concept. But it is habitually overlooked in sales calls, as well as many other familiar activities such as giving a speech, creating an advertisement, making a new friend, or scheduling a team meeting. How many of these types of scenarios have we been involved in where our interest was high? How often did we feel our time was wasted? Time is valuable in all these scenarios, and the audience concentrates their attention, for a short period of time, to determine whether they will benefit from this experience.

Openings   Customers often spend the first few minutes of a sales call determining whether they will benefit from a salesperson. This includes nonverbal factors such as when the salesperson walks in, makes eye contact, shakes hands, and selects a seat. Notably, the first few words out of the salesperson's mouth can set the customer's expectations for the rest of the sales call. This is where the **halo effect**— the tendency for an impression created in one area to positively influence opinions in other areas— can be helpful for salespeople. If the salesperson is perceived to be capable during the first part of the sales call, the customer is more likely to perceive the salesperson as effective during the rest of the call.

A successful way to demonstrate confidence and capabilities during the early part of the sales call is to plan an effective opening. An **opening** is a brief series of statements or questions designed to get the prospect's attention and interest quickly and smoothly transition into the next part of the presentation. Every selling situation is unique and requires that salespeople be adaptable to using many different types of openings to gain a customer's interest. In Chapter 6, we will examine different types of openings to gain a customer's interest at the start of a meeting. In any scenario, salespeople must plan on how to effectively engage the customer's interest in what they can provide later.

halo effect
the tendency for an impression created in one area to positively influence opinions in other areas

opening
a brief series of statements or questions designed to get the prospect's attention and interest quickly and smoothly transition into the next part of the presentation

Opening for a Meeting in the Future Salespeople may often be introduced to a customer at an inconvenient time that prohibits a longer conversation, perhaps through an introduction, networking event, the cliché elevator meeting, or even an email. In these situations, salespeople need to have prepared an opening that can gain the customer's interest in a sales call in the future. The focus of this prepared opening should be on the **valid business reason** for the customer to meet in the future. A valid business reason is a motive for why a potential customer should want to meet. Too many openings focus on product pitches, social agendas, or ambiguous lunch meetings that do not provide the customer a compelling reason to invest time with the salesperson.

valid business reason
the motive for why a potential customer should want to meet

The point of every valid business reason is to encourage customers to meet because it benefits their situation. Put oneself in the customer's shoes and ask, "If I attend this meeting, what's in it for me?" The challenge in setting up a meeting is to communicate a focused reason that would interest a buyer in that account. This is especially critical for executive-level meetings, when having a valid business reason helps one think through the logic for why customers would share 20 minutes of their time. For example, Steve Martin is a senior account manager for ABC, which provides data and power management solutions for Fortune 1000 clients. Steve is responsible for one of ABC's major accounts, XYZ networks, a telecommunications leader throughout the Southeast. ABC offers a wide array of products and services— from server hardware to energy management systems— in which XYZ could be interested. Steve knows that having a focused reason that the customer sees as important makes all the difference in getting a meeting. Fortunately, Steve has been following the news on XYZ and discovered that they recently made an acquisition of a smaller telecommunications firm with its own data storage facilities. This fact suggested an obvious valid business reason. Given the new data facilities likely being added to XYZ, Steve developed a strategy to meet with their CIO to show them how their energy management systems could efficiently reduce power consumption and improve data security across different facilities at one single location. For the CIO, resolving the uncertainties of the additional data facilities was top of mind.

Initial Questions to Assess Need

When preparing for any sales call, whether for a first-time meeting or an established relationship, it is vital to establish the customer's current needs. Research suggests that correctly assessing customers' needs is one of the most critical aspects that distinguishes top salespeople. Indeed, an analysis by Huthwaite, Inc. of more than 35,000 sales calls around the globe over 12 years revealed that the distinguishing characteristic of high-performing salespeople was their ability to discover customer needs. This confirms that of all the parts of the selling process often thought to be most critical (e.g., closing, objection handling, demonstration), the single factor repeatedly shown to influence salesperson performance is discovering customers' needs. Any salesperson desiring to develop a win-win solution that benefits the customer and the company must have a plan to assess their customers' needs.

Identifying needs begins before the sales call, while conducting pre-call research and preparing objectives and openings. These activities will all contribute to being able to narrow down the customer's most likely needs. While the salesperson's intuition and prepared questions may change after beginning the conversation with the customer, this preparation is invaluable in reaching a deeper understanding of the customer's situation and buying motives.

Preplanned Questions to Assess Needs   Anyone can write down a set of questions and conduct an investigation to find out information. Similarly, identifying customers' needs is not complicated. But successfully delivering needs-assessment questions without the customer's feeling uncomfortable requires that salespeople perform several tasks very well. It is very tempting for salespeople to keep control of the conversation and stick to a scripted set of questions. Top salespeople know that this annoys customers. Instead, asking the right questions at the right time, listening deeply to the responses, and recognizing customers' hesitations are key skills to effectively assess needs. It is important to remember that customers perceive a salesperson as someone wanting to bring change, which is true. Needs-assessment questions can bring up uncomfortable topics for customers who may feel threatened by the idea of addressing known problems. For example, a sales manager being asked about ways to improve salesperson efficiency may foresee future layoffs if a solution is brought in to reduce costs. Therefore, salespeople need to be prepared with a set of questions to create a conversation with customers to uncover needs. Chapter 6 explores the use of different types of questions to help uncover needs.

Reviewing Questions Before the Call   For all types of questions, it is important to follow a few guidelines. First, review them before the sales call. A question may appear fine on paper but not align with your delivery style or customer context. Questions that appear scripted, or misaligned with the conversation, will only do more harm than good. Second, prepare in advance for the likely answers. Remember that the hope is for the questions to uncover information about customer needs. The pre-call information should help with how to respond to the customers' answers. However, keep in mind the possibility that the customers are not aware of or are unwilling to divulge their needs. In these cases, customers are unlikely to make a buying decision soon.

When preparing questions for the sales call, also keep in mind that the answers may make the customer uncomfortable. This is important to consider because customers cannot develop urgency for change if there is not a feeling of dissatisfaction with their current offering. However, the customer may resent the implication that the choices they have made or the roles they are in are performing worse than expected. When facing evidence that things could be better, the customer may be afraid to share information or be forthcoming. Also, make note that depending on the complexity of the business and solution, the time needed to assess needs varies greatly.

Different Preparation and Agendas for First Calls, Multiple Calls, and Group Presentations

Another key factor for determining sales call objectives is the salesperson's expectations for the buying decision process. A number of characteristics, such as deal size and solution complexity typically define the buying decision process. In general, larger deal sizes and more complex solutions require a longer period of time to make a purchase decision because they involve a greater commitment for the customer as well as a larger number of buying influences. These are important considerations when preparing for the sales call. Research finds that these factors and others are likely to define whether the salesperson is entering into a one-time purchase with limited relational involvement versus a relationship.[15] Relationships entail multiple activities between buyer and seller with the intent of engaging in long-term, committed exchange. We focus here on how salespeople should plan for building relationships.

Planning for the First Call Planning for the first call of a longer buying decision process should focus on setting objectives aligned with building a long-term relationship. This is often called the **exploration phase** of a buyer-seller relationship and is characterized by each side's considering the benefits, obligations, and likelihood of doing business together. For a salesperson entering into this phase via the first call, the nature and scope of the goals will focus on developing trust and setting relationship expectations. Customers in this phase will be looking for red flags that indicate the risks of entering into a business relationship with the seller. As a result, sample goals for the first call tend to be:

exploration phase
the buyer and seller considering the benefits, obligations, and likelihood of doing business together

- Gain customer commitment to contact previous customers
- Attain customer provided goals and needs
- Motivate customer to agree to a demonstration
- Set up a future meeting to meet additional team members on site

Planning for a Series of Calls Planning for a series of calls requires salespeople to develop a series of objectives as well as an overall strategy for achieving those objectives. This approach is especially important in long-term relational exchanges and is often referred to as the **build-up phase** of the relationship. The build-up phase is marked by increasing investment and commitment between the salesperson and customer as they increase their satisfaction and trust with each other's performance and future rewards. Salespeople planning multiple calls are wise to keep this in mind and should plan objectives that gain increasing commitments from their customers. Agreement to more significant commitments are signals that the customer is moving forward in their buying process and shows interest in making a purchase. Planning for objectives in this phase might resemble the following:

build-up phase
increasing investment and commitment between the salesperson and customer as they increase their satisfaction and trust with each other's performance and future rewards

- Have customer gain approval from executives to join a meeting
- Secure customer commitment to a 60-day trial
- Gain agreement from customer to share information about their current solution
- Have customer purchase a small or partial order of the solution

Preparing for Group Presentations In some cases, salespeople must prepare for meetings that include multiple people from the buying organization. Planning for group presentations requires that salespeople address and satisfy the individual and collective concerns within the group. This can be challenging given that the diversity of the attendees might be executives, front-line employees, buying committee members, and others. As mentioned earlier, the salesperson should attempt to define the various buying influences based on their role, amount of influence, and reason for attending. Careful observation during the sales call can uncover who is most likely to use the solution (user influence) versus who has more authority over the purchase decision (economic influence). Regardless of which influence one identifies, it is important to make all attendees feel engaged. Plan to ask direct questions for each attendee to ensure their involvement should they remain silent. Remember, any member of the presentation who feels left out could prevent the sale. Additionally, note that there may be buying influencers who are not on the sales call. These silent members are often higher-level employees who may have prior commitments or are waiting to get involved depending on the group's approval. Planning for group presentations should include a question to determine whether any other decision-makers exist and establish a way to communicate with them in the future.

Preparing the Team

Team selling has become a prominent approach in today's environment to sell and support complex and customized offerings. This approach is ideally suited to environments where communication between multiple customers and technical experts is required. It can be cumbersome for salespeople to remain an expert on the customer as well as all aspects of the product offering in industries with very complex solutions or frequent new product introductions. By having a group of diversified expertise, sales teams can uncover problems and craft solutions that no individual salesperson could do alone. For example, a salesperson might receive a technical question from the customer that the salesperson is unable to answer. Similarly, a salesperson may propose a solution that imposes requirements on the solution that the company cannot provide. A sales team approach would include multiple members from the selling organization (e.g., technical solution expert, service and installation consultant) who have the deep expertise to address these concerns on the sales call. These additional resources not only provide greater credibility for the seller but also speed up the selling cycle, define more precise needs, and improve the product selection.

Team selling does have its drawbacks. Preparing for a team selling presentation requires more detailed planning than individual sales calls. Each member of the team must have a clear understanding of roles and responsibilities during the call. Members should all have detailed pre-call information about the customer and the capability to add value to the sales process. Further, the sales call objectives must be understood and agreed upon before the call. Without this preparation, the sales call can quickly become unorganized, unprofessional, and throw customers off their decision-making process.

Applying this Chapter to Salesforce

Important sales calls and presentations often require collaboration with others from the salesperson's firm. To optimize this internal collaboration and communication, Salesforce offers a native internal network called *Chatter*. Chatter feeds work the same way as other social media in that they can be used to post images, articles, files, links, videos, polls, questions, tips, feedback, and more. Each posting can be tagged for a specific team or colleagues to see and respond.

For example, let's say you find an article that provides important insight to a client's business. You could email the article to your coworkers. But it may be months before some of them interact with the client, and they may not remember the article or they misplace it by then. Any email exchange among coworkers may be difficult to locate later, especially for new members joining the team in the future. With Chatter, you can share information with anyone, and they can easily respond and collaborate. And by linking the Chatter feed to the client's account in Salesforce, the collaboration remains visible for anyone who needs information about the client's account in the future.

Another powerful application of Chatter is in sharing information and documents to benefit other salespeople. Let's say you created a particularly successful PowerPoint presentation, and you would like to share it with others. By posting in Chatter, your colleagues can access, duplicate, and modify it for their next presentation.

If you have information that is only relevant to specific people in your organization, Salesforce allows for the creation of *Groups* within Chatter. Groups allows you to make a Chatter post that is only visible to members of the Group. Groups also makes it easy to share a post with a large number of people without needing to tag each individual.

In preparation for sales calls and presentations, it is often necessary to delegate responsibility. Using *Tasks* in Salesforce, portions of a presentation can be assigned to each member of the sales team. Each task can be directly linked to *Leads*, *Campaigns*, or just about any other object within the Salesforce. As your teammates complete the task, they can mark them as completed and add their contribution in the shared Group. This allows everyone to keep track of the progress made toward being prepared for the presentation.

Chapter Summary

- Planning for sales calls provides greater value for salespeople and customers.
- Salespeople should gather pre-call information from three key areas: individual customer, product/service offerings, and the market environment.
- Information about the individual customer helps salespeople customize their messaging, delivery style, and information relevance.
- Product and service information helps salespeople understand the aspects of their offering that are unique and prepare the strongest value proposition.
- Marketplace information guides salespeople to be more knowledgeable about the interests, goals, and business outcomes that are important to customers.
- Setting a pre-call objective is often overlooked, but it is essential to ensuring each sales call moves the decision process forward and gains customer commitment.
- Effective salespeople develop plans to capture customers' interest and uncover needs through effective questioning,
- Sales calls fall under many different contexts that require salespeople to plan differently for first calls, group calls, chain of calls, and team-based calls.

Key Terms

bridge statement (p. 92)
build-up phase (p. 101)
buying influence (p. 91)
competitive intelligence (p. 93)
customer commitments (p. 96)
customer orientation (p. 87)
differentiation (p. 93)
economic buyer (p. 92)
exploration phase (p. 101)

gross margin (p. 89)
gross profit (p. 89)
halo effect (p. 98)
ideal customer profile (p. 94)
opening (p. 98)
positioning (p. 92)
role complexity (p. 87)
user buyer (p. 91)
valid business reason (p. 99)

Application 5-1

Standard's Annual Income Statement (reduced)			
Year ended December 31	2020	2019	2018
Sales Revenue	$8,000,000	$6,500,000	$5,500,000
Cost of Goods Sold	$3,400,000	$2,500,000	$2,000,000
Gross Profit	$4,600,000	$4,000,000	$3,500,000
Operating Expenses			
Selling, General, and Administrative	$1,500,000	$1,200,000	$800,000
Net Income	$3,100,000	$2,800,000	$2,700,000

(Continued)

(Continued)

You work for a consulting firm that provides manufacturing process improvement and training to help businesses reduce waste in product production and also help improve their sales force efficiency. The Standard is a components supplier firm in South Carolina that supplies parts to businesses in the automotive and aviation industries. Over the years, you developed a strong relationship with the Standard's owner, Joe, and he recently asked you to review his business to find areas to improve. Upon reviewing the income statement, you see that Joe's business looks healthy, with steadily increasing revenues and profits. However, you know that's not the whole story and dig a little deeper to understand how well the business is operating.

1. How would you respond to Joe regarding the efficiency of his production?
2. How would you respond to Joe regarding the efficiency of his sales and marketing expenditures?
3. What factors should be considered in your next sales call with Joe EXCEPT:

Application 5-2

EcoBiz provides hygiene, sanitation, and maintenance products and services for a wide array of customers, including the hospitality, restaurant, and commercial real estate industries. Thanks to a market-leading R&D department, EcoBiz customers enjoy reliable and cost-saving products and services that are well known for reducing health hazards. EcoBiz services its customer base using a sizable sales force with company vans and equipment to service customer sites.

EcoBiz is known for its ability to cater to its customers' needs, including on-call maintenance, custom accommodations, and hygiene audit consultants. Juan Bustamante is a salesperson for EcoBiz and is currently planning his first visit to Susan Wright, a front-line operations manager on one of Caribbean's ships. Caribbean serves international customers worldwide on their many cruise ships, stopping at large urban cities as well as small local ports. Unfortunately, they have recently experienced several food-borne illnesses from passengers on board. With this and other factors in mind, Juan believes that EcoBiz can provide outstanding benefits to Caribbean Cruises.

1. What would be the best objective for this sales call?
2. What would be the most helpful product information to gather before this meeting?
3. After careful planning, Juan meets with Susan and includes the following statement in his opening: Susan, one reason I'm here today is to learn how we might work together to reduce the number of health risks on your ship by 50%. Which type of opening is Juan using?

6   The Sales Call

Learning Objectives

- Understand the components of a sales call
- Learn to successfully conduct an approach and build rapport with a buyer
- Comprehend and apply basic processes that ensure a successful discovery conversation with the prospect or customer
- Understand how to convert information found in the discovery phase into a presentation through value propositions and recommendations
- Identify and understand the use of various types and categories of questions commonly used in the sales call
- Recognize the complementary nature of the discovery process

sales call is an interaction that a salesperson has with a prospect or current customer. The sales call may take on many forms, especially in the digital age. For example, a sales call may take place face-to-face, on the phone, or even using video conference software. However, most sales calls share two common components: the sales call is usually pre-arranged and the purpose is to generate a sale or to progress to the next stage of the sales process. As noted in Chapter 5, research and preparation are the cornerstones of a successful sales call.

In this chapter, we explore how the sales call is the crescendo of all the preparation and research that has been done prior to the actual meeting. The importance of the sales call cannot be overstated. It is more than simply a meeting. It is a complex interaction where the salesperson must use both the science and art of selling to progress the prospect or customer to the next stage of the buying process.

Purpose of the Sales Call

sales call
an interaction that a salesperson has with a prospect or current customer

The purpose of the sales call is to either close the sale or progress into the next stage of the sales process. Depending on the type of product(s) or service(s) a salesperson offers, there may be many sales calls before the deal is closed. Business-to-business products and services are notorious for having long, complex sales cycles. For example, if a salesperson is selling slot machines to casinos, years may pass before closing a deal with a new prospect based on the wear and tear of the slot machines and possible contracts that the casino has signed with other providers of slot machines. In other words, the sales process and the types and numbers of sales calls a salesperson makes is dependent upon the type of product or service being sold and the nature of the prospect's or customer's industry. With this in mind, although the goal is often to close a sale, many salespeople make sales call visits to build relationships or check on the status of the buyer's situation, ultimately progressing the relationship and increasing the potential of closing the sale when the timing is right for the prospect or customer.

Components of the Sales Call

approach
the first stage of a sales call, when the salesperson introduces themselves, builds rapport, gains the buyer's attention, and sets an agenda

Most successful sales calls begin with an **approach**, during which the salesperson introduces themselves, builds rapport, gains the buyer's attention, and sets an agenda. When they meet for the first time, the salesperson and the buyer are essentially strangers. The purpose of the approach is to develop a common connection and move the relationship from a place of uncertainty to one of comfort, credibility, and value. Using an approach, the salesperson can influence the development of the relationship.

discovery, needs identification
when the salesperson uses strategic questioning to uncover the prospect's or customer's needs and wants

The **discovery** or **needs identification** phase of the sales call is when the salesperson uses strategic questioning to uncover the prospect's or customer's needs and wants. Discovery is the strategic use of questions to uncover the prospect's or customer's needs and wants. Note the importance of the word *strategic*. In other words, no question should be asked just to kill time during the sales call. Additionally, no question should be asked that has an answer that can easily be found on the company's website, social media, or anywhere else online or in past interactions. Instead, the questions asked during the discovery phase should focus on answers that can only be found in the prospect's or customer's head. For example, the answer to the question, "How many locations do you have?" is something that is very likely to be found online or on the company's website. Although the needs discovery phase may be shorter or longer, depending on the sales call, this phase should be dominated by the prospect or customer,

Figure 6-1 Components of the Sales Call

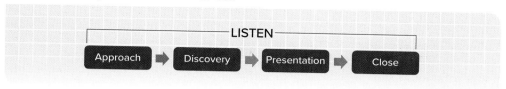

and the salesperson should talk significantly less. A good rule of thumb is that the prospect or customer should be talking at least 60% of the time.[2] A successful discovery phase makes the following phase of the sales call, the presentation phase, much easier and more efficient.

These same needs and wants will act as the foundation for the salesperson's response during the **presentation** phase, where the salesperson proposes the potential value the prospect or customer will receive by using the product or service in a value proposition. **Value propositions** are statements that emphasize the unique value and benefits a product or service provides for someone (often the prospect or customer). **Recommendations** are the best course of action that the salesperson proposes to achieve the proposed solution. Similar to how a doctor prescribes medicine for an illness, salespeople often "prescribe" a solution through value propositions and recommendations. Although a salesperson may be able to identify hundreds of potential value propositions and recommendations for the customer, it is the salesperson's responsibility to select the value propositions and recommendations that are customized to the information that was uncovered in the discovery phase. This doesn't mean that the salesperson can't mention value propositions that the customer may be unaware of, such as new product offerings or innovations, but most value propositions and recommendations should be tailored to the customer's needs and wants.

And finally, every sales call will conclude with the salesperson attempting to **close**, or asking for a commitment from the buyer.

This chapter will focus on the approach and discovery phases of the sales call, as well as some aspects of the presentation. Chapter 7 will go into greater detail on presentations. And chapter 8 is devoted to overcoming objections during a sales call and closing. Figure 6-1 presents an overview of components of a sales call.

presentation
the salesperson proposes the potential value the prospect or customer will receive by using the product or service in a value proposition

value propositions
statements that emphasize the unique value and benefits a product or service provides for someone

recommendations
the best course of actions that the salesperson proposes to achieve the proposed solution

close
asking for a commitment from the buyer

Approach

The goal of the approach is for the seller to create a connection with the buyer, build trust and credibility, break down barriers to communication, and get the buyer's attention so they are motivated to listen. Creating comfort and credibility is essential. The buyer is more likely to answer the salesperson's questions during discovery if they are comfortable and trust the salesperson. After a successful approach, the buyer is much more likely to conscientiously answer the salesperson's questions. And with more meaningful answers from the buyer, the salesperson is more likely to present more valuable solutions. After the introduction, **rapport building** is the first phase of the approach, and is focused on making personal connections with the prospect or customer to ultimately set a friendly tone for the sales call[1]

rapport building
making personal connections with the prospect or customer to ultimately set a friendly tone for the sales call

Rapport Building

At the beginning of the sales call, the salesperson must be prepared to ease the pressure of the interaction by building rapport with the prospect or customer. Salespeople should not be trying to sell during this stage of the sales call. This stage of the sales call is all about building trust. As noted, rapport is a mutual understanding and connection between two individuals and is founded on trust and empathy. Often, the longer the salesperson has known the prospect or customer, the easier building rapport will be, but initial meetings can be uncomfortable and awkward because of a lack of familiarity with each other.

Consequently, the salesperson should prepare a few rapport topics based on customer intelligence found in the preparation phase. For example, a salesperson may find out, through social media, that the prospect is an alumnus of the same school and is a foodie. The salesperson can use these as rapport topics by mentioning their alma mater and asking for good restaurant recommendations in the area. Potential rapport topics are endless, so the salesperson should have three to five topics ready to chat about in case the first two fail. Regarding the amount of time spent rapport building, the salesperson should cue in on the prospect's or customer's verbal and nonverbal responses when deciding to move on from rapport topics. Some personality types tend to prefer less rapport, while others prefer more. A general rule of thumb is to focus on rapport building for three to five minutes, but salespeople must be careful to take cues from the prospect or customer as to when rapport building is ending. At this point, the salesperson can start asking more specific sale-related questions to transition into the discovery phase.

Transitioning to the Discovery Phase

As we mentioned in Chapter 5, openings are useful for gaining a customer's interest at the start of the sales call. Time is valuable to your customers, and they will quickly decide whether the commitment to meet is worth their time. In this chapter, we use openings to set the stage for what the customer should expect to focus on during the meeting and establish a clear idea about the topics for discussion. This approach also serves as a transition from rapport to needs identification and helps gain permission to move forward into this portion of the sales process. When well-executed, the opening sets up the rest of the sales call in order to move the buying process more efficiently and effectively.

Table 6-1 provides several different types of openings for salespeople to plan for their first part of their sales call. Note that each type of opening focuses on an aspect of improving the customer's business or learning more about how their

Table 6-1

Opening Type	Description	Example
Agenda	• Review the meeting goals • Establish your preparedness and professionalism	Today, I'd like to spend about 20 minutes to learn about how you currently recruit new talent and then determine whether we can work together to improve that process.
Referral	• Offer a third party to provide credibility for your meeting • Support your relevance from mutual connection	A colleague of yours at State Farm, Susan Richards, shared with me that you were dealing with significant turnover and were looking for new ideas to improve engagement.
Trial	• Provide a free trial or sample of product • Creates ownership by using the product	Now that you have had some time to try it out, I'm here to help ensure you see the value our other customers receive when implementing the solution.
Insight	• Generate curiosity about a topic of interest • Provide a new way of thinking about an issue	As a marketing leader in the retail industry, can you help me understand your strategy for dealing with the drastic rise in rent and employee wages across your region?
Benefit	• Lead off with your primary means of helping the customer • Direct way to detect customer's interest	Mr. Smith, I'm here today to learn how we might work together to reduce your paper usage by 20% or more.

business could potentially be improved. A consistent focus on the customer's interests will ensure the opening is on target. As with all of the openings, the key to success is advanced preparation. Customers are annoyed when they enter a meeting without direction. We provide a brief description of each type.

Agenda   The agenda opening is one of the most effective methods to create interest and transition smoothly from rapport building to the focus of the meeting. One of the primary benefits of this opening is that it is applicable in almost all sales calls and leaves little risk that the customer reacts negatively. Briefly, the agenda opening starts by thanking the customer for the time to meet and then reviews the objectives you plan to address during the call. This opening shows you value the customer's time and also demonstrates your professionalism in having an explicit plan for the call. Note, however, that it is important to establish the customer's commitment to the agenda to ensure there are no changes to the topic or time allotted for the call. Customers also welcome this opening in multi-call situations.

Referral   Research demonstrates that people are far more impressed with your points if they are presented by a third party rather than by you. As a result, the referral opening is a very useful technique to leverage a previous customer or mutual connection (with a positive relationship) who believes the customer can benefit from your offering. Like the agenda opening, the referral opening has universal appeal with very little risk of annoying the customer.

Trial   The trial opening focuses on providing customers with some form of temporary ownership of the product, like a sample, limited selection, or time-bound usage, in order to build a foundation of interest for the sales call. For example, a software company might provide a free version of their product, but only for a limited number of users. A very common example is from textbook publishers who give faculty members free or discounted materials to convey the educational value for their students. The trial opening can be a very effective means to elicit customer's interest, but it runs the risk that the customer may be dissatisfied with their initial usage. Top salespeople using this opening nurture their customers using the trial to ensure they extract value from usage.

Insight   The insight approach focuses on asking a customer a question that generates a new way of thinking about a topic. This technique has multiple benefits. First, a well-posed question creates an opportunity for the customer to elaborate and become engaged in conversation about the topic. Second, the question should not only spark the customer's curiosity, but also create an opening for the salesperson to potentially address a problem that they are prepared to solve.

For example, Minnie Thompson, a sales training consultant, conducts training classes for sales leaders who want to improve their retention. She starts by asking a question about some recent information that is relevant to a potential customer: "As a matter of curiosity, how does your sales organization respond to the high levels of voluntary turnover in your industry?" Minnie knows that this topic is something a sales leader has definitely thought about but may not have a great answer. As a result, this question not only lets the customer illustrate their current retention situation but also allows the Minnie to understand the likelihood that there is a problem that her training can solve.

Benefit   Another way to gain the prospect's attention is by immediately pointing out the benefits of the offering during the opening. As mentioned previously, the benefits could stem from aspects of the product, but also the salesperson's company and the salesperson themselves. The pre-call research should help provide guidance about the most important issues likely facing the customer. This should point out the key benefits that are likely to stimulate the customer into deeper conversation. For example, a company benefit for the financial services context could be: "Our firm provides an array of mutual fund options that have no transaction fees even while working off the advice of our investment counselors."

Discovery or Needs Identification

discovery
the strategic use of questions to uncover the prospect or customer's needs and wants

Discovery is the strategic use of questions to uncover the prospect or customer's needs and wants.[3] Some refer to discovery as needs identification or needs assessment. The discovery phase is a complex but extremely helpful element of the sales call that should be adapted based on the prospect or customer. Salespeople should recognize that making assumptions about what the prospect or customer needs or wants is a barrier to this stage. Consequently, the salesperson must go in with an open mind and eagerness to learn about the prospect's or customer's perspective.

Preparation is key to a successful discovery phase. Salespeople should bring a list of thoughtful and customized questions based on the prospect's or customer's personality, goals, industry, products, and so on. However, it is also critical that a salesperson is willing to and ready to deviate from their scripted questions and be adaptable. Although a salesperson should arrive at the sales call with prepared, strategic questions, the prospect or customer may lead the salesperson on a different discovery path than was planned. Lastly, listening can be a really difficult challenge for salespeople during the discovery phase. Without efficient and effective listening, it is impossible for the salesperson to create value propositions based on a prospect's or customer's needs and wants. Effective listeners are good at not only hearing what the prospect or customer says, but also hearing what they don't say. This means that salespeople can also "read between the lines" of what is said and find connection points between the customer's comments.

Purpose of Needs Discovery and Questioning

Although all salespeople are familiar with questions, many have never had to use them prior to their careers to strategically uncover an individual's wants and needs. Needs discovery is both a science and an art.[4] The purpose of the discovery phase is to not only uncover a prospect's or customer's known needs and wants but also help the prospect or customer see challenges or issues they didn't see before and to establish how the consequences of those issues might affect their role. In other words, salespeople who excel at asking strategic questions not only uncover what is in the prospect's or customer's mind, but they are also able to guide the prospect or customer to come to nuanced conclusions on their own. For example, if a salesperson asks the customer, "How does the machine failure affect your day?" this guides the prospect or customer to consider the implications of that type of event. This is merely one example, but there are many categories and types of questions that can be used to uncover needs and wants, while also strategically guiding the prospect or customer to think about events, issues, and challenges in a way that they may not have considered before. The next three sections discuss how we might categorize questions (by structure, by type, or by purpose). These categories are not mutually exclusive. Depending on the specific question, the question may fall into multiple categories.

open-ended questions
questions that do not provide an answer choice, but instead, have an infinite number of possible responses

Structure of Questions: Open-Ended vs. Closed-Ended Questions   The first category of questions is deceivingly simple, but still has a strategic purpose. All questions are structured as open-ended or closed-ended.[5] **Open-ended questions** do not provide an answer choice for the customer. Instead, these types of questions have an infinite number of possible responses. Open-ended questions can either be broad-scoped or narrow-scoped. For example, "Tell me about your typical day" is a broad-scoped open-ended question, whereas "What are the specific challenges you face with your current computer provider?" is narrow-focused. Broad-scoped open-ended questions tend to be used to get the prospect or customer talking or to diagnose a situation, whereas narrow-scoped open-ended questions are more precise in nature and help uncover specific needs and wants of the prospect or customer. Although strategic in purpose, all types of questions have a trade-off. For example, although broad-scoped open-ended questions encourage the customer to talk, they can be very time consuming and unpredictable, depending on how the prospect or customer responds. Consequently, the salesperson should be intentional when choosing the types of strategic questions for the sales call. A salesperson with only a 15-minute appointment may choose to limit the use of broad-scoped open-ended questions. Unlike open-ended questions, **closed-ended questions** offer the customer a response choice or choices, such as yes or no. Often these questions are used near the end of the discovery phase to either provide customer buy-in or get specific information and encourage a positive response. These questions should be used less often because they tend to discourage dialogue and can derail the presentation if the customer responds with an unexpected "no."

closed-ended questions
questions that offer a response choice or choices, such as yes or no

Types of Questions: Circumstances, Challenges, Consequences, and Values In addition to structure, salespeople must consider the types of questions they ask. Discovery questions generally fall into four types: circumstances, challenges, consequences, and values.[6] Circumstance questions are used to gain insight regarding facts, data, and other basic information. These types of questions are the most basic form of discovery. Salespeople must be careful not to ask circumstance questions that could have easily been found on the company's website or that were asked in previous interactions. Doing so would signal poor preparation. Challenge questions are used to uncover challenges, problems, and issues. These questions may be used to uncover both known challenges and unknown challenges that the prospect or customer hasn't recognized yet. Next, consequence questions are used to explore the implications of these challenges. In other words, consequence questions uncover how the prospect's or customer's challenges affect day-to-day activities and goals. Often, prospects and customers haven't thought in depth about the implications of problems, due to focusing on daily issues, which makes consequence questions very powerful when used successfully. Last, value questions help uncover the benefits that the prospect or customer will receive if their challenges are solved. These questions encourage the prospect or customer to act urgently to solve the problem in order to reap the benefits of the solution, which often means more time, money, or mental well-being.

Questions with Specific Purposes Another way to think about questions is to categorize them as having specific intentions or purposes. This section focuses on three types of commonly used purposeful questions: rapport-building questions, tactical questions, and reactive questions. Rapport-building questions are used with the intention of building a connection or relational bond between the prospect or customer and the salesperson. These questions can be great at helping ease the potential pressure or tension that arises during the beginning of sales calls. Examples of rapport-building questions are "How did you get in your current role?" or "Are you originally from here?" As the individual responds to these questions, the salesperson should be looking for mutual connections. When used authentically, these types of questions can set the tone for a friendly sales call. The second type of purposeful question is a tactical question. A tactical question is used to shift the direction of the conversation. These types of questions can be used to get the

Table 6-2 Strategic Discovery Questions

Tell me about your day-to-day role. What goals do you have in this role?
What goals is your firm most focused on right now?
What seems to be a daily challenge you face? A problem you need to solve?
What is the source of this challenge or problem?
How are you evaluated? What metrics matter the most in your role?
Why do you think the problem hasn't been addressed in the past?
If you could fix one thing today, what would that be?
What do you think a potential solution for the problem looks like?
If this problem isn't fixed, what are the implications for you and your organization?
Do you have a "back up" plan for not choosing a product?
What's your timeline for implementation?
Do you already have a budget allocated?
Are you looking at other solution providers at the moment?
Do you have resources for the problem? A budget? Personnel?
Are you the sole decision maker or do you have a team involved in the decision-making process?
What do you look for in a vendor?
Do you have certain criteria that must be met in regard to a vendor?
What does the purchasing process look like in your organization?
If you decide to partner with us, how can I help make the buying and implementation process easier for you?
If you implement this solution, how do you hope things are different in one year?

Source: Kaski, Timo, Ari Alamäki, and Ellen Bolman Pullins. (2019). Fostering Collaborative Mind-Sets Among Customers: A Transformative Learning Approach. *Journal of Personal Selling & Sales Management,* 39 (1): 42–59. doi:10.1080/08853 134.2018.1489727.

Karaman, Jason. (2017). 25 Engaging and Strategic Discovery Questions. Retrieved at https://expertcaller.com/25-engaging-and-strategic-discovery-questions.

conversation back on track. "Can we talk more about the buying process you mentioned earlier?" is an example of a tactical question. Tactical questions are used to navigate the conversation. Lastly, reactive questions are used as a direct result of information the prospect or customer has shared and are a direct reaction to the information previously provided by the prospect or customer. The purpose of tactical questions is to gain more insight regarding a particular topic. For example, "You mentioned that the manufacturing floor can get crazy when you miss a shipment, can you give me an example of what you meant?" encourages the prospect or customer to elaborate on previous information that was given. All questions should be strategic and have a purpose; however, rapport building, tactical, and reactive questions have specific purposes of building a connection or bond with the customer, shifting the focus of the conversation, or probing the customer for more information. These are three very important and skillful ways to ensure an efficient and thorough discovery phase. See Table 6-2 for more examples of all three categories of questions.

Presentation: Value Propositions and Recommendations

After discovering the prospect's or customer's needs and wants, the salesperson should then provide a customized solution. As noted earlier, during the prescription phase, the salesperson uses value propositions and recommendations to "prescribe"

Table 6-3 Examples of Value Propositions

"The textile industry is highly competitive, however, companies who have managed to improve their supply chain strategy with our product have seen an overall 3% increase in revenues and 19% increase in efficiencies. I believe, based off your need for a whole new logistical system, that we would be able to double these numbers for you with our newest technologies."

"We help small companies reduce the cost of their employee labor without impacting the level of quality. With rising competition today, this is a critical issue for most manufacturers. One of our recent clients, a small, privately owned manufacturing company similar to yours, was struggling with how to reduce labor costs. We saved them over $3,000 a week, and ultimately about $150,000 per year. We did so by streamlining processes, and adding software that ultimately increased the quality of the end product. Based on the numbers you provided me, and your focus on labor costs, I believe we can save you similar amounts and cut your labor costs significantly, while maintaining the current level of quality.

"We have been able to partner with other engineering firms to provide web content that is both meaningful and easy to digest. A company similar to yours recently had a 700% increase in their web traffic, ultimately leading to, on average, six more proposals each week. Being a family owned business ourselves, we want to help business like yours thrive through authentic, consistent touchpoint with your customers."

a remedy for their situation. The value propositions and recommendations should directly reflect the information that was uncovered in the discovery phase. Salespeople need to be cautious not to "information dump" in this stage, simply naming off all the great values the product has to offer. Instead, value propositions should be customized and specialized. A value proposition is simply a statement salespeople use to communicate the unique values a product or service offers.[7] Common value propositions focus on important prospect and customer values such as increasing revenues, reducing labor, increasing efficiency, increasing quality, or saving time. Recommendations are suggestions, or a course of action the salesperson provides to attain the intended outcome or solution.

It should now be evident why a salesperson who is unsuccessful in the discovery phase will find it difficult to craft customized value propositions and recommendations. Often, an unsuccessful discovery phase leads to a generic sales pitch, leaving many of the prospect's or customer's needs and wants unmet. In sum, during the presentation phase, salespeople have an opportunity to share with the prospect or customer how their product or service brings value and does so uniquely. See Table 6-3 for examples of value propositions.

How Does a Salesperson Know What Their Product's or Service's Value Propositions Are?

To understand what value propositions are unique to a product or service, salespeople must do their research. By studying target markets and existing customers, salespeople will be able to understand what the prospect or customer views as potential pros and cons of the product or service. Eliciting consistent feedback from current customers ensures that the salesperson is aware of the customer's perceptions of the unique value offered by their product or service. Salespeople should also be researching potential customers, or target markets, helping them to understanding common pain points and barriers to buying. Additionally, keeping track of competitors and their unique value propositions is also critical to understanding which of the value propositions are best.

Basic Components of a Value Proposition

There are four basic components of a value proposition: outcome, process, implications, and tools. The salesperson should begin crafting the value proposition with a focus on the intended prospect or customer outcome. The outcome is simply the specific need, want, or desire the prospect or customer expressed during the discovery phase. The salesperson then explains the process, or how their product or service can achieve this outcome, for the customer. Next, the salesperson should explain the implications, either the benefits that will come with switching to the new product or the cost of not switching. Tools, the last component of the value proposition, can be used throughout the conversation. **Tools** provide evidence supporting the claims made by the salesperson. The following sections go into greater detail regarding each of the four components of a value proposition.

tools
evidence supporting the claims
made by the salesperson

Outcome   Value propositions should be based on the outcomes that the prospect or customer wishes to achieve. These outcomes should be uncovered during the discovery phase. Typical prospect or customer outcomes include increased revenues, reduced labor, increased efficiency, increased quality, or time saved. However, these are very broad in nature. During the discovery phase, the salesperson should pinpoint the details surrounding the intended outcome. For example, the prospect or customer may share that the goal is to save time, but "saving time" could have various meanings and motivations. Consequently, the salesperson must drill down into the details of what the prospect or customer means so that a specific, customized value proposition can be created. Additionally, a salesperson must decide the ways in which the intended outcome can be achieved. This is where the process component of the value proposition comes into play. The following section outlines the next important component of the value proposition, the "how" of achieving the outcome, also known as the process.

Process   The process component of the value proposition tells the prospect or customer "how" the intended outcome can be achieved. This is usually done by talking about the features and the benefits of the product or service using the bridge statements covered in Chapter 5. While salespeople often prepare many bridge statements, they must be very strategic in selecting which features and benefits to emphasize because there may be many possibilities to choose from that can lead to the intended outcome. However, listing off all the features and benefits is overwhelming and time consuming for the prospect or customer. It is the salesperson's responsibility to present the most valuable features and benefits, based on the prospect's or customer's intended outcome. See Table 6-4 for a common list of general product features and the general benefits that are often associated with those features.

Table 6-4 Common Features and Benefits

Features	Example of associated benefits
Price	Saves the prospect or customer money
Warranty	Peace of mind for the prospect or customer, decreases risk
Quality	Prospect or customer doesn't have to replace the item for an extended period of time and doesn't have to worry about it breaking
Packaging	Packing may protect fragile items, assuring they arrive in pristine condition; packaging may be easy to assemble or use, saving labor time and ultimately money
Convenience	Product or service is available when prospect or customer needs it, decreasing inventory, ultimately saving money
Customer Service	Customer service provides the prospect or customer access to help and peace of mind; Ensures problems can be fixed quickly

Implications   When an outcome is achieved, there are often multiple consequences (usually beneficial) that the prospect or customer may experience. For example, if a product quality problem is solved, the prospect or customer may find themselves with more time and money, along with decreased stress. Often, customers may not consider these implications without the salesperson leading them to do so. The salesperson should highlight implications in the proposed value propositions. For example, a salesperson may say, "Based on what you told me, if I fix this issue, you will have an extra two hours a week to focus on other tasks such as payroll and mentoring." Helping the customer understand the added positive implications connected to the solution will add value to the proposition. Following implications, the salesperson must provide evidence for the claims through tools.

Tools   Tools are used to provide support or evidence for the claims made by the salesperson regarding the benefits and features of the products or services. The salesperson must "prove" the claims they made regarding the features and benefits. For example, if the salesperson claims that the company's product is well made and durable, that claim is stronger with a statistic, backed by research, that suggests the average life span of the product is twice that of competitors. Other examples of tools a salesperson can use to provide evidence for the claims are demonstrations, samples, testimonials, product specifications, and references. Not all claims will necessarily require evidence, nor will evidence be available for each feature or benefit, but the salesperson should take great care to build the prospect's or customer's trust through the use of tools. Trust places prospects and customers in a better position to make a confident purchase. See Table 6-5 for a list of common tools and descriptions.

Crafting a Complete Value Proposition   When presenting value propositions, a salesperson must be able to adapt to the prospect's or customer's conversation style, meaning that although the salesperson may start with the outcome, the customer may then ask about the implications or even ask for supporting evidence (i.e., tools). A salesperson must recognize that sometimes the

Table 6-5 Common Value Proposition Tools

Demonstrations—product demonstrations can be used to increase understanding of the product or service and provide evidence of the possible benefits of using the product features.

Samples—samples can be used to allow customers to decrease perceived risk by trying out the product before they buy it and allows the customer to personally explore the features and benefits of the product.

Videos—videos can be used to provide evidence of processes, benefits, and features and be used to show how a complex product or service works when trials or demonstrations are too costly.

Product specs—product specifications are tools that allow the prospect or customer to ensure that the purchase will be logical and appropriate for their needs and wants.

References—references are a list of current, active customers that can be called upon by the prospect to ask questions about the product, customer service, etc. References can be used to decrease the prospect's or customer's perceived risk or concerns.

Scientific studies and statistics—research and statistics provide empirical, numerical evidence for the salesperson's claims. This allows the salesperson to go beyond opinion and to decrease the prospect's or customer's perceived risk.

Testimonials—testimonials are often videos or quotes from current, active customers that endorse the product or service. These are similar to referrals, but prerecorded and documented, as opposed to real-time.

Charts/graphs—charts and graphs provide visual, numerical evidence for the salesperson's claims. This allows the salesperson to go beyond opinion and to decrease the prospect's or customer's perceived risk.

value proposition pitch may get derailed, moving in a non-linear fashion. The main goal of the value proposition is to share the outcomes, process, implications, and tools with the prospect or customer, ultimately influencing the customer's decision-making process, while adapting to the natural flow of the conversation.

Components and Crafting of Recommendations

Recommendations are the final step of the presentation phase. Recommendations are the proposed mix of products and services the salesperson makes based on the value propositions. Similar to the value propositions, a salesperson may be able to provide multiple recommendations, based on the prospect's or customer's needs and wants; however, it is the salesperson's job to offer the prospect or customer the best recommendation for the person's specific situation. Recommendations should be directly tied to the foundational needs and wants uncovered in the discovery phase of the sales call (see Table 6-6). Although recommendations may be structured

Table 6-6 The Complementary Nature of the Sales Call Components

Discovery Questions	Customer Response	Value Proposition	Recommendation
"What is the largest challenge you face using your current payroll system?"	"It is hard to use and isn't intuitive."	"Our product has 24-hour customer service and best of all a new, easy-to-use interface."	"I recommend the basic interface initially and when you get comfortable with it you could upgrade to the pro interface."
"If I could solve one day-to-day problem for you, what would that be?"	"I have to manually input numbers into our payroll system. It is frustrating and inefficient. I would want you to fix that."	"We just rolled out new technology that allows you to upload an excel spreadsheet into the system with a single click. No manual entry is required."	"Let's set you up for an introduction training session with our experts to ensure that you learn multiple ways to avoid manually inputting the numbers."
"What factors go into your decision to choose your payroll processing provider?"	"I want to be able to trust the software. My employees need their paychecks!"	"I completely understand that. We have a double auditing process within the software that alerts the user of any suspicious looking output. Additionally, in the rare case of an emergency, we have a 24-hour expert in your area that could be here within 30 minutes if something unexpected happened."	"I will ensure the expert shows you what the error warning look like. I will include the area expert in our next meeting so you can get familiar with her."
"What is your company's main priority this year?"	"To save money. We aren't investing in a lot of new technologies this year."	"Our payroll system should pay for itself within the first two months of every year, as you won't have to spend hours of your time manually inputting numbers, or paying someone else to do so. The software also ensures that you are receiving the largest possible tax credits based on your total payroll."	"I think our system will not only save you time and money, but will allow you to contribute to the company's main savings goal. Our experts will also walk you through the best practices to ensure you and your company are using the software optimally."

Figure 6-2 Shifting Concerns Throughout the Sales Cycle

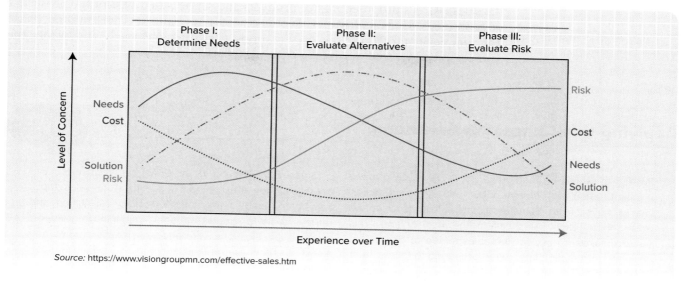

Source: https://www.visiongroupmn.com/effective-sales.htm

differently, a recommendation often includes a tangible solution and actionable next steps. For example, the salesperson may recommend that the customer use their product training services and suggest a time frame for this training to happen. After the recommendations are proposed, the salesperson can close with questions, proceed to negotiations, or attempt to close, depending on how the sales call has gone and their confidence in closing. Remember that the salesperson's product(s) may not always be a good solution for the customer's problem. A salesperson who is certain this is the case should recommend a solution from another company. Although this seems counterintuitive, by doing so the salesperson builds trust with the individual, making them more likely to do business with the salesperson in the future. Conversely, if the salesperson proposes a solution while knowing that it will not work for the customer, the customer will likely not want to work with the salesperson again, feeling that they have been cheated.

Considerations of Time and Dynamics of the Sales Call

The buying process is dynamic. Prospects and customers will be more concerned with specific needs and wants based on the sales cycle stage. Early in the buying process, customers are often fixated on the product's price. Whereas, after the prospect or customer has a set of alternatives that are both within budget and meet basic needs, the best solution for the problem may be of more concern. Near the end of the sales process, risk will be more of a concern because the prospect or customer is about to decide on a solution and sign a contract. The salesperson must remember that the stage of the sales cycle or buying process will influence the emphasis on certain features and benefits. For example, if the prospect is about to sign a contract, the salesperson, being aware that the buyer is concerned about risk, could emphasize the 30-day money-back guarantee or the warranty to minimize the feeling of risk in the customer's mind. See Figure 6-2 for a summary of shifting concerns during the sales process.

Putting It All Together

The approach, discovery, and presentation are all critical components of the sales call. During the discovery phase, the salesperson uncovers the prospect or customer's needs and wants. These same needs and wants are used as the foundation for the next phase of the sales call, the presentation. The presentation is the salesperson's proposed mix of products and services that best fit the prospect's or customer's needs and wants. The discovery phase and the presentation phase are complementary, with the presentations mirroring the needs and wants the salesperson uncovered during the discovery phase.

Applying this Chapter to Salesforce

Instead of relying on memory, a good CRM should make it easy to enter and retrieve notes from every interaction with a buyer. With Salesforce, the salesperson enters notes about each sales call in the *Activity Log*. This feature makes it easy for the salesperson to review the collected information later when preparing to follow up or in preparation for the next call.

Another useful feature to drive sales productivity within Salesforce is *Path*. Path is a customizable section within *Leads* or *Opportunities* that provides the salesperson with information to make each sales call more effective.

A company can use Path to focus each salesperson on exactly what needs to happen during each call to move prospects and leads through the pipeline. For each stage, Salesforce can provide *Guidance for Success* boxes, which may include checklists, recommended questions to ask, and topics to keep in mind while talking to a potential customer. Path can also be used to outline what information needs to be gathered to qualify a prospect and move toward a recommendation.

Since Salesforce and all CRMs work as an active database, they are an ideal place to store sales tools. Salesforce enables the salesperson to easily find and retrieve tools to support the sales call, including videos, product specifications, references, scientific studies and statistics, charts, graphs, and testimonials. The salesperson can pull up these sales tools on their smartphone or laptop and immediately share them during a sales call or forward them by email directly from Salesforce.

Over time, through a feature called *Analytics*, Salesforce can use the information entered by each salesperson to reveal powerful trends about which tools, tactics, and methods are most successful. Analytics can answer questions like: Do salespeople close more business when opening with an agenda or a referral? How frequently is a sale made when providing a free trial, and what was the average time to closure? Has a scientific study or a customer testimonial been the more effective tool? The information provided by Salesforce Analytics can improve the likelihood of the sales call ending successfully.

Chapter Summary

- The purpose of the sales call is to close or to progress into the next stage of the sales process, but a sales call can be used to build a relationship, ultimately increasing the potential of closing the sale when the timing is right for the prospect.
- Discovery is the phase of the sales call that uncovers the needs and wants of the customer.
- Presentations should be based on the needs and wants uncovered in the discovery phase.
- Questions should be used strategically, which means uncovering information that cannot be found online or in past interactions with the prospect or customer.
- Value propositions are unique features and benefits that serve as solutions to the prospect's or customer's needs and wants.
- Outcomes, processes, implications, and tools are components of the value proposition.

- Recommendations are the final step of the value proposition and often provide actionable next steps.
- A successful sales call takes a lot of preparation and research; however, asking strategic questions, listening well, and customizing solutions are an art that then often make or break the sales call.

Key Terms

closed-ended questions (p. 111)
discovery (p. 110)
open-ended questions (p. 110)
presentation (p. 107)
discovery phase (p. 106)
approach (p. 107)

rapport building (p. 106)
recommendations (p. 107)
sales call (p. 106)
tools (p. 114)
value propositions (p. 107)

Application 6-1

Patterson Parking is a medium-sized, boutique provider of parking services such as parking garage management and valet services. They offer two ways for their customers to make revenue. First, Patterson Parking can incur 100% of the operational expenses (e.g., pay for labor, uniforms, signage), but give 20% of the revenue to the customer. Or the customer can incur all the expenses and give Patterson Parking a flat rate for running their parking operation. Although often not the cheapest provider of parking, Patterson Parking is known for its top-quality service and ability to handle all parking issues and headaches, easing the customer's stress load. Patterson Parking is also known for their progressive use of technology in parking solutions, such as a "call ahead" mobile app that ensures shoppers' cars are waiting for them when they arrive at the valet stand.

Evan is a Patterson Parking sales representative. He is going to meet with Taylor, the president of a large portfolio of luxury shopping malls, and Shawna, the vice president of Mall Operations. On their website, Evan sees that they have 65 retail locations in 47 cities. Following is a summary of the questions Evan used to uncover needs and wants and the customer responses:

Evan: What is the one thing you are most concerned within your day-to-day role?

Customer Response: Similar to the rest of the country, mall foot traffic is down, but anchor stores (i.e., department stores) and high-end restaurant traffic have increased over the last three years. There is a need to either increase foot traffic or find other revenue streams.

Evan: How does parking fit into your current revenue stream?

Customer Response: 70% of the malls in their portfolio already have a valet operation, but only 20% of them are generating revenue. They currently pay a flat rate to their parking provider and pay for all the operational expenses such as uniforms and signage.

Evan: Where do you see the biggest room for improvement in regard to your current parking provider?

Customer Response: Taylor and Shawna haven't had any major issues with their current valet provider, but they feel like their current company isn't living up to what they promised regarding revenues and quality of service.

Evan: What effect would it have on your day-to-day role and time commitments if you didn't have to deal with the parking operation?

(Continued)

(Continued)

Customer Response: Taylor and Shawna are so busy that they don't want anything to do with the parking operation, but they don't think that is an option with their current provider. The thought of not having to deal with the parking operation sounds like a dream to them.

Evan: Does your current provider use any technology to streamline your valet parking processes? If so, how well does it seem to be working?

Customer Response: None that they know of.

Evan: Do you have any future plans that involve parking operations at your malls?

Customer Response: Within the next five years, all the malls will have a "VIP" self-parking lot that is close to the main entrance of the mall. Taylor wants to charge a fee for customers to park in this lot.

Evan now has a significant amount of information to pull from and craft a presentation for Taylor and Shawna. Following is a summary of Evan's presentation. Take special note of how Evan uses the outcomes in Taylor's and Shawna's responses to craft value propositions (through benefits and features) and recommendations. Also, take note of the tools Evan uses to provide evidence for his claims.

Evan: Based on what you have told me, I think we can collaborate to not only save you a lot of time, by taking 100% of the parking responsibilities off your hands, but also by providing you with a new revenue stream. Patterson Parking offers a revenue share service, where we incur all the costs and operations of the parking programs at your shopping malls, and simply write you a check each month for the 20% of the total revenue. Based on the car counts you provided me earlier, that would be a 40% revenue bump from what you make with your current provider. Additionally, over 90% of your malls would be bringing in significant revenue under this new revenue share setup. Additionally, we could add another 5% revenue this year by implementing the VIP lots at your top 10 malls. We actually do this for some of our other malls, and would be happy to take the lead on this project. Here is a list of referrals you can call where we currently provide operations, including VIP lots. As you will note on the referrals list, we provide parking services for the luxury mall in the next city over and at many local restaurants and businesses. Also, through technology, we can increase efficiency and decrease labor by offering your shopping guest a "call ahead" mobile app that ensures their cars are retrieved in a timely manner, with little to no wait time. This technology has allowed us to staff one fewer person on most shifts. Let me show you how this app works (as Evan walks them through the app on his phone). I recommend that we plan to transition into your parking operations by fall, which will ensure everything is in place for the busy holiday shopping season. Would you like me to send the proposal to both of you tomorrow?

After seeing an example of how the discovery phase and value proposition phase are connected, try to answer the following questions:

1. What questions should Evan have asked?
2. "What effect would it have on your day-to-day role and time if you didn't have to deal with the parking operation?" What type of question is this?
3. What are some examples of tools that can be used to provide evidence for claims made by the salesperson?

Application 6-2

Sam, a sales representative for Mobile One, is meeting with Rashida and Tim, co-founders of a technology start-up. Mobile One offers mobile product solutions (phones, tablets, etc.) for businesses. Rashida and Tim are expanding from 15 people to 120 within the next year, and they need to provide every employee with both a phone and a tablet. Often, complex purchases like this can't be completed in one meeting, meaning that salespeople often meet multiple times with the prospects or customers. Salespeople must be aware that the buyer may be more concerned about specific issues based on the stage of development of the sale. For example, prospects and customers typically care more about the cost of the product or service at the very beginning and very end of the sales process. Conversely, in the middle of the decision process, also known as the evaluating alternatives phase, the prospect or customer may be less focused on pricing and more focused on solutions. The following are Sam's notes from the three meetings he had with Rashida and Tim:

Meeting 1, April 2nd: Determining Needs
Rashida and Tim seemed to be focused on the cost of the products, the brand of the products, and processing efficiency. At this meeting, they wanted to make sure that the purchase will fit within their budget and meet their specific needs and wants. I focused on providing value propositions and tools that speak to price and product benefits associated with the high processing speed our phones and tablets offer.

Meeting 2, April 28th: Evaluating Alternatives
At this meeting, I found out that Rashida and Tim have a set of three possible providers and they are currently focused on which provider would offer the best solution for their upcoming expansion. Price didn't come up, as they know that each provider can offer a solution within their budget. Instead, they were focused on what products and services would be optimal for their specific situation. Also, they are starting to be concerned about the risk of deciding (or choosing the wrong provider), so they want to know more about customer support and possible tools that mitigate these possible risks. I told them about our 24-hour customer service center and 3-year warranty.

Meeting 3, March 17th: Evaluating Risk and Purchase
Rashida and Tim chose us! Because they are about to actually sign a contract with us, they are most concerned with risk and total cost. We spent a lot of time talking about the warranty again, and the 30-day money-back guarantee. This seemed to calm their concerns. After negotiations, I provided them with a 20% discount for the first year since they are a new customer. This will save them over $2,000 per month, as compared to their next best alternative. I need to go back next week with a service technician to install and train all the employees.

Sam's notes highlight that needs, concerns, and values are dynamic and dependent upon the stage of the sales cycle. Salespeople must be aware of the prospect's or customer's stage of the decision-making process and adapt the sales call based on this information.

1. In the initial stages of the buying process, what are prospects and customers often most concerned with?
2. When evaluating alternatives, what are prospects and customers often most concerned with?
3. Are prospect's and customer's concerns usually dynamic, static, or solely based on price? Explain your answer.

7

Making the Presentation

Learning Objectives

- Summarize the indicators of an effective presentation
- Identify the key salesperson factors that create value for customers during the presentation
- Compare and contrast the most effective methods for salespeople to offer recommendations to their customers
- Summarize what kinds of tools are available for the presentation
- Explain how salespeople can create compelling presentation content
- Outline the next steps to take after the presentation to close a deal

his chapter focuses on the role of the presentation component of the sales call as the primary means to add value when communicating benefits to potential buyers. Once goals have been set and the customer's needs have been identified, then persuasion can and should be a very targeted and effective approach that recommends a solution. When salespeople clearly define how their customers will benefit from their offering, a persuasive presentation will deliver value.

Goals of Effective Presentations

Successful presentations do not happen by chance. Salespeople must not only prepare for the expected topics to be covered, but also find creative ways to involve the customer and adapt to unforeseen questions. It is important to note that many new salespeople are tempted to present their offerings without a meaningful understanding of customers' needs. While salespeople perceive to have made progress toward a sale, this approach often frustrates customers and reduces the presentation to little more than a generic pitch. Ultimately, salespeople should demonstrate the value of their offering based on an understanding of their customer's needs. Salespeople should deliver on several key factors for a successful presentation that increases the likelihood of solving customers' problems.

Speak to the Customer's Situation

Customers know that the presentation should be the most polished part of the sales call. Any competent salesperson is expected to clearly communicate how their offering solves the customer's problems. These kinds of "canned" presentations can be recorded and shared on the company's website. However, we discussed in Chapter 5 how benefits should not be limited to just the product, because there are many benefits that stem from salespeople as well. With this knowledge, top salespeople view the presentation as another opportunity to demonstrate the value of partnering with them. For example, a salesperson will customize all of the benefits to speak to each customer's unique interests whether they be personal ambitions (e.g., promotion), financial (e.g., cost reductions), or other improvements (e.g., improved morale).

Improve the Buyer's Understanding

A typical buying decision will be filled with multiple conversations, discoveries, setbacks, and adaptations. All of these can be distracting for customers and make it difficult for them to conceptualize the proposed solution. This can be especially difficult for customers to rely on the spoken word to understand very complex solutions. Effective presentations find useful ways to improve the buyer's understanding of the salesperson's proposed solution. Customers who are unsure about whether they understand the product are unlikely to move forward with a purchase decision.

Focus the Buyer's Attention

Unfortunately, we have all been in meetings wishing we were somewhere else. What do we do in this scenario? Do we pull out our phone? Do we think about what else we need to do that day? Probably so, which means that our presenter has lost our attention and we have missed part of the message. Rest assured, this is not the fault of the audience. The presenter did not focus on ways to keep our attention. In contrast, effective presentations typically find creative ways to keep the audience involved through interesting visuals, stories, and active discussion, among other ideas.

The same premise rings true for salesperson presentations. Salespeople must find ways to involve their customers in the presentation and keep their interest beyond just hearing about the features and benefits. It is important here to understand the audience. What interests the people seeing the presentation? A technical audience will be unlikely to appreciate customer satisfaction improvements. Similarly, a marketing audience will lose focus during a deep technical dive into the scientifically researched efficiencies of a solution. The customer's personality and social style can also play a role here. Analytical styles are more appreciative of a detailed and slower pace presentation with opportunities to ask questions, while drivers will probably be annoyed at the lack of high-level outcomes and slow pace. Thus, salespeople should keep the audience in mind when designing their presentation to hold the audience's attention.

Leave an Impression

Customers are busy. Customers also meet with many different people each day and each week—all with different agendas. So, how likely is it that they recall what they saw in an average presentation? This is what today's salespeople face when preparing their presentation. They must find ways to leave an impression on customers. Heightening this point, salespeople often need approval from multiple people, and so most buying decisions today rely on customers' relaying the presentation message to others in the organization. So it is critical that salespeople vividly communicate their offering's benefits in ways that help their message stick. For example, salespeople can include templates for customers to take notes, review material, and answer questions during a presentation. Customer involvement, which includes note-taking and review is a highly effective way to improve recall, even as much as three weeks later.[1]

Creating Value During the Presentation

After salespeople gather the right information, uncover customer challenges, and isolate specific needs, the stage is set for a persuasive presentation. Many people initially recoil at the idea of persuading someone, because they feel it is manipulative. However, **persuasion** is simply a communication process by which you motivate someone to voluntarily take a beneficial action.[2] Note here that persuasion involves voluntary and beneficial action, which means that true persuasion occurs when someone not only chooses your recommendation but also feels good about it afterward. In line with this, the goal of a **persuasive presentation** is to influence the customer's beliefs, attitudes, and behaviors to encourage buyer action toward an improved outcome. Persuasive sales presentations typically include a transition stage where dialogue shifts from a rational emphasis (or logical appeal) to an emotional appeal. This is in contrast to an **informative presentation**, which emphasizes factual information often drawn from marketing produced literature, technical specifications, or other company-prepared reports. While informative presentations can be an effective tool to introduce new offerings or explain technical details, it is important to note that today's sellers do not add much value in the sales process with an informative presentation since this information can be distributed through a number of other channels, such as emails, websites, social media, or videos.

persuasion
a communication process by which you motivate someone to voluntarily take a beneficial action

persuasive presentation
a presentation to influence the customer's beliefs, attitudes, and behaviors to encourage buyer action toward an improved outcome

informative presentation
a presentation emphasizing factual information often drawn from marketing produced literature, technical specifications, or other company-prepared reports

Align the Customer's Problems with Solution Benefits

Shutterstock/Dusan Petkovic

Customers will not change from their status quo unless they perceive a problem, as well as a solution to fix it. However, many salespeople may identify customer's needs but miss the mark in addressing them in the presentation by offering too many or unrelated solution benefits. These mistakes typically result in backtracking the buyer's decision process, leaving the salesperson in limbo and in danger of losing the sale. Consultative salespeople must have the mindset that they exist to solve customers' problems, which starts by helping customers select a customized solution for their situation.

The challenge of guiding customers to select the right solution is growing. In today's information age, product information is widely available and often makes purchasing decisions difficult for buyers when they are not experts on the solution or buying process. Salespeople must become trusted advisors who comprehend customer's unique issues and make valuable recommendations. This process requires time, effort, and expertise but creates significant value for the customer. Here are some helpful tips for staying focused on addressing customer needs:

- Review notes from the needs identification process. What key issues stand out the customer? Prioritize these issues and isolate which of the solution's benefits resolve them. High-performance salespeople present benefits that are tailored to the customer's needs.
- Compare and contrast the salesperson's tailored benefits with the competitors' offerings. Where is a differentiated advantage? Are they on equal footing or even at a disadvantage? The customer will perceive the most effective solution as the one that provides the most favorable points of difference from the next best alternative.
- Research indicates that appeals given at the beginning and end of a conversation are more effective than those made in the middle. Therefore, the salesperson should prepare to lead off with the strongest benefits to clearly distinguish the salesperson's offering and also end with a flourish as preparing to close.

Configuring the Solution

Most salespeople sell a variety of products and services. As we discussed in Chapter 5, salespeople should become well versed in their product advantages and plan to communicate how their different offerings provide customized benefits. For example, a territory manager at Ecolab has offerings varying from products such as cleaning products and dishwashers to services such as repair maintenance and hygiene audits. There is a clear advantage for Ecolab salespeople to have such a variety of offerings available to help their customers. Yet, it is rare that a customer needs all of these different solutions. Rather than overwhelm and annoy customers with a canned product pitch that covers an entire portfolio of products and services, Ecolab salespeople add value by leveraging their knowledge of the customers' problems and needs to guide them to the proper solutions. This means that salespeople must adapt to the customer's uncovered needs to recommend which offerings are best for the given customer. This process of helping customers select the right solution is typically called **solution configuration**.

Many complex sales involve multiple decision-makers, along with varying challenges and needs to resolve. As a result, solution configuration can become

solution configuration
the process of helping customers select the right solution

complicated for salespeople and take significant time and effort. For example, video recording and management software like *Ensemble* helps universities capture lectures to enrich student assignments. In this context, Ensemble's solutions typically involve many options for university customers such as hardware (video cameras, servers), installation (wall-mounted, cloud-based), training (professors, students), and support choices (in-house, website). Salespeople will need to carefully guide the decision-makers toward the right combination of offerings in order to satisfy their needs. Any salesperson who offers solutions with this type of complexity is likely to face challenges in configuring the solution. There are two key factors that can aid salespeople in this tedious process.

In complex selling situations, salespeople can often create value in the solution configuration process by co-creating the solution. Here, **co-creation** refers to the salesperson and customer combining their expertise and knowledge to define the solution with the optimal value.[3] Co-creation prevents salespeople from defaulting to predetermined solution configurations that may not provide the most value to customers. It also helps customers better understand their own needs and potentially conceive of innovative solutions as well. However, customer involvement is critical for co-creation in the solution configuration process. Customers are more motivated to participate in co-creation when they share a strong relationship, mutual goals, and meaningful dialogue with salespeople.[4] These factors emphasize the importance of relationship-building for salespeople to co-create the solution with their customers.[5] Ultimately, this process helps the customer make smarter buying decisions while meeting the specifications of the salesperson's offerings—it creates value for both the salesperson and customer.

co-creation
when the salesperson and customer combine their expertise and knowledge to define the solution with the optimal value

Another factor to help salespeople be more successful in solution configuration is the use of technology. Today, many companies offer software applications to help salespeople configure-to-order, quote, and sell unique combinations of their solutions. For example, Saleforce CPQ (Configure, Price, Quote) is software that creates a digital user interface for the salesperson to automate the configuration process—regardless of the complexity of their products, processes, or services.[6] This application also includes current inventory and pricing information so that salespeople can communicate timely and accurate solution offerings. Electronic catalogs also provide help to salespeople during the solution configuration process. Software programs such as eCATALOGsolutions (https://partsolutions.com/ecatalogsolutions/) enable salespeople to access their database of offerings via a web-based portal. This application helps salespeople quickly find and configure solutions faster, often while with the customer. Companies have also benefitted from providing customers access to their electronic catalogs to help them plan for future usage in their designs, processes, and business.

Make Recommendations

At this point in the sales process, consultative salespeople have established rapport, explored the customer's needs, and configured a solution to improve the customer's situation. It is clear that the time and effort required to support these activities are significant when compared to a transactional (simple one-time purchase) customer. However, this investment earns salespeople the right to make a recommendation about the best way to move forward.

In many ways, the recommendation is the essence of the salesperson's role in the consultative selling process. Every recommendation stems from the salesperson's accumulated expertise (market knowledge, company knowledge, product knowledge) combined with unique customer insights. Essentially, the salesperson becomes the critical link between the company's offering and the customer's needs. There are essentially three ways to move forward with the recommendation.

Table 7-1 Examples of Buying Signals

Type of Buying Signal	Statement Form	Question Form
Possessive	"Andre will be the lead when this gets implemented."	"Would you recommend having 4 or 5 people oversee this new process?"
Service and Delivery	"It will probably take at least a week before we could have the install team on site."	"With 50 people in the org, how soon would we be fully operational?"
Expressions of Desire	"This tool would definitely decrease our downtime."	"It would work for us, but how about a team at a different location?"
Risk Minimization	"Ah, so this is where I fix this potential problem."	"What happens when we have questions?"
Next Steps	"Tell me where we go from here."	"Would you be ready to present this to the leadership team?

Source: Retrieved at https://blog.hubspot.com/sales/phrases-signal-prospect-is-ready-to-buy.

buying signals
indications the customer is ready to purchase

Recommend Solution and Close   At any point in the sales call, the customer may exhibit **buying signals**—indications the customer is ready to purchase—that indicate strong buy-in to the offering (see Table 7-1 for examples). When these signals are present, salespeople may provide a brief recommendation of the proposed solution and attempt to close. These types of situations are unlikely in complex selling environments, such as enterprise sales or strategic partnerships, where larger deal sizes and multiple decision-makers will impede the process. Note that salespeople still must have a clear understanding of the customer's needs and how the solution will address them. While customers may offer little resistance to moving forward, this does not necessarily mean they fully understand the solution. It is ultimately the responsibility of the salesperson to ensure that the solution implemented will satisfy the customer.

Recommend Solution and Present Problem Resolution   This recommendation offers the proposed solution followed by a presentation of product benefits that includes evidence of how the proposal helps the customer. Salespeople should also be prepared for in-depth questions and potential objections under this alternative. This type of recommendation is most applicable in complex sales, when buying influences with hidden agendas exist, or when the salesperson perceives that the solution is not well understood. We discuss the problem resolution presentation in the next section.

Recommend Another Source   After a careful needs assessment, it may become evident to the salesperson that no potential solution will address the customer's needs. Salespeople should refer the customer to potential alternatives that may help resolve their issues, potentially a competitor. While this is not an optimal conclusion to the sales process, it is an opportunity to demonstrate the value of the salesperson's expertise and integrity. Imagine the alternative. The salesperson makes a solution recommendation which does not help the customer. These situations damage the salesperson and the company's reputation. Research supports the real consequences of this poor choice, showing that salesperson reputation is strongly related to customer loyalty.[7]

Transition to Presenting Problem Resolution

The presentation marks a shift in the communication dynamic between customer and salesperson. While the focus at the start of the sales call centers around uncovering information from the customer, the focus in the presentation shifts to the salesperson's communicating how to resolve the problems that were found. This means there is a notable increase in the proportion of time salespeople spend

Figure 7-1 Salesperson/Customer Speaking Time During the Sales Process

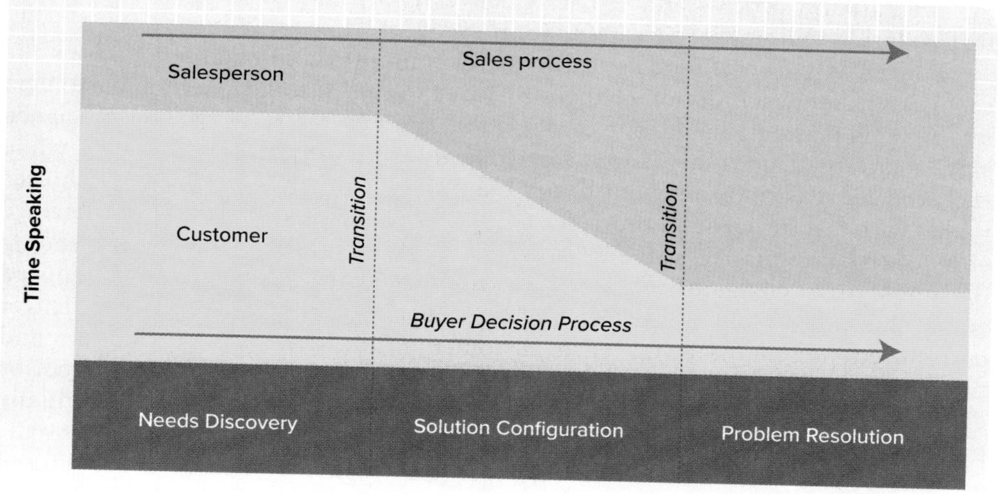

talking, compared to the customer, in this phase of the sales call (see Figure 7-1). As a result, salespeople need to find an effective way to transition from needs discovery and product configuration to the presentation.

If the solution configuration and problem resolution occur as part of a single sales call, simple statements that emphasize the customer's expressed needs alignment with the presentation work well.

- "Since you emphasized the issues with accessing your payroll out of the office, I would like to show you how our mobile app gives you the freedom to see payroll anywhere, anytime."
- "I agree that the extended time you are losing with your current performance management process is problematic and would benefit from our streamlined coaching tools."

If the presentation takes place as the beginning of a separate sales call, salespeople should spend time to recommit the customer to their needs. This can be done by recapping a summary of the customer's needs followed by a closed confirmation question to confirm their agreement. Salespeople who conduct multi-call, complex sales routinely summarize and confirm previous conversations because it increases customer buy-in and uncovers hidden objectives. For example:

"In our last meeting, you shared with me that you spend many late hours at the office filling out your payroll and that paycheck errors have been increasing recently. We planned to focus today's meeting on how our mobile payroll application addresses both of those challenges. Should we cover anything else?"

Note that this ending confirmation question allows the customer an opportunity to bring up additional challenges or new information that has changed their situation since the last meeting. If the customer agrees to move forward, they have assured the salesperson they are still bought-in to resolving the issues discussed.

Present Problem Resolution

After delivering several successful presentations, it is tempting for many salespeople to become reliant on the same structure and message. This mechanization of the presentation process seems efficient, but experts know that customers will quickly detect the lack of customization. Top salespeople avoid this depersonalization of the presentation process and strive to deliver a customized message about how their solution will improve their situation.

Boeing sells several models of commercial aircraft with countless options for each airline, and each option changes its value to the customer. Certain customers like Qantas Airlines, based out of Australia, are very focused on fuel efficiency since many of their routes cover very long distances. On the other hand, while fuel efficiency is important, a customer like Southwest Airlines, which flies shorter flights with fast turnaround times, focuses more on the durability and maintenance costs of the aircraft. The value propositions can also change over time depending on supplier part changes (e.g., new composite materials for lighter planes, reduced engine maintenance). As a result, Boeing sales teams come prepared to deliver customized presentations for each customer airline that provide relevant and timely information about the latest capabilities of the aircraft. A structured, or canned presentation would ignore the needs of each customer and potentially misrepresent the actual capabilities of the aircraft if the information is out of date.

Salespeople add value to the sales process when they deliver a customized presentation of how they resolve customers' needs. They accomplish this by selecting the right presentation tools, leveraging a unique value proposition, and quantifying the solution.

Visual Presentation Tools

Salespeople today have more visual presentation tools than ever before. However, the value of the tool greatly depends on the effective use of the right tool, for the right customer, in the right context. This section offers an overview of various tools along with a summary of the various ways available to display content.

Salesperson Enablement Tools   The fast pace of new product introductions and increasing competition requires that sellers have more support to deliver value in the presentation. Continually updating content that is accurate with the latest information would be overwhelming for salespeople in complex selling environments. In response to this environment, many organizations have developed a sales enablement process to help salespeople provide the right information to the right customer at the right time. **Sales enablement** is the process of providing the sales force with information, content, and tools to help salespeople be more effective. Many organizations have dedicated employees who work in sales enablement to achieve several objectives:

- Connect sellers to the relevant content for each unique customer
- Increase adaptability in presenting content to customers
- Tracking, reporting, and learning from the results of content given to sellers

Sales enablement can provide a portfolio of visual aids to help sellers communicate value. Often, this portfolio is kept within a **sales asset management system**. A sales asset management system helps to store, categorize, and find digital media when needed. This type of system contains a collection of all content designed to generate sales many of which we elaborate on in this chapter (e.g., brochures, fact sheets). It is important to emphasize that salespeople should not intend to use everything in the portfolio of visual tools available for every sales call. Rather, salespeople should gain a deep understanding, often through training delivered by sales enablement, of the unique benefits of each visual tool.

In many presentations, charts, figures, and graphs offer a clear way to communicate large amounts of information. For example, charts may offer project timelines, forecasted revenue growth, or types of solution configurations. These visual aids help sellers develop a shared understanding with their customers. Charts and graphs may often come in the form of a presentation slide

sales enablement
the process of providing the sales force with information, content, and tools to help salespeople be more effective

sales asset management system
a system to store, categorize, and find digital media when needed

deck like PowerPoint. While this type of visual content is relatively standard in many presentations, it can encourage one-way communication. Salespeople are encouraged to not merely progress from one slide to the next but leverage the graphic content to stimulate conversation with the customer.

Enablement may also provide sellers with access to catalogs and brochures. Complex selling environments may include a vast array of products and services with prices that frequently vary. Salespeople who can access up-to-date catalogs with potential buyers help reduce any friction in the sales process. Similarly, brochures often summarize key points and support for buyers' typical concerns, or questions that come up often. Brochures can also have creative designs and innovative packaging to inspire and maintain customers' interest even after the salesperson has left.

With new forms of media being introduced every year (3D viewing, holograms, etc.) sales enablement also helps provide additional supplementary content through varied media options. However, salespeople are encouraged to be selective about utilizing the right media option for the right context. For example, video has become a popular tool for salespeople. Salespeople use video to demonstrate how service delivery works for another customer (e.g., showing the catering outlays and food from a similar event) as well as branding material that illustrates the values of the company (e.g., showing an upcoming TV commercial). Videos should be short, concise, and to the point to ensure they do not lose customers' interest. Longer videos give the impression that the salesperson is more interested in promoting their offering rather than solving customers' problems.

Salespeople also are equipped with laptops, tablets, phones, and other portable devices capable of displaying visual content for presentations. Imagine being a PepsiCo representative discussing a product display with a grocery store manager. It can be difficult to convey the dimensions and appeal of an in-store display without actually setting up the promotional material. Fortunately, an iPad app helps the representative visually depict how the Pepsi display will look within the store's confines, providing a realistic idea of the space needed, along with the aesthetic appeal, or a potential in-store promotion.

Portable devices are especially suited to collaborate with sales enablement processes where digital content can easily be updated and displayed. Imagine you are a Merck pharmaceutical salesperson who meets daily with medical professionals. Salespeople in this role are tasked with providing trusted advice and insight about product developments and treatment options, many of which are highly technical and change quickly. In this context, portable devices such as iPads help Merck representatives access a large database of information, such as product specifications and medical research, helping supplement their knowledge needed for a consultative presentation.

Product Performance Demonstrations When possible, the strongest tool to convey the value of an offering is to show how it works. As customers cultivate an interest in a product offering they also develop a natural desire to test a product's claims.

Consider potential customers for a new Honda Odyssey. Advertisements and salespeople can convey the benefits of the roomier seating in their interior. However, some customers may not buy into the benefits until they take a test ride.

This form of tangible evidence can be even more persuasive as the risk of product performance becomes heightened. Consider the case of Arthrex, a leading medical device manufacturer. Arthrex representatives work with surgeons to improve their patients' treatment. These surgeons are often likened to carpenters of the human body: they repair damaged tissue and build new skeletons. As a result, surgeons want more than claims about new device alternatives; they want to see them in action. Arthrex representatives play a key role here in sharing knowledge about new devices and their applications, and they also act as a resource in the

Shutterstock/Anton Gvozdikov

operating room to answer important questions. Arthrex reps may also accompany surgeons to their own facilities to demonstrate new devices. Arthrex routinely invites surgeons from around the world to their facilities to demonstrate the applications and procedures associated with their offerings. These surgeons can attend an educational seminar on their products, receive guidance on new procedures, and even try out the new device on cadaveric specimens. This type of hands-on and tangible product demonstration approach clearly conveys the value of their offering and increases commitment to using Arthrex devices.

Here are some key tips for preparing and executing effective product performance demonstrations:

- Practice. Practice. Practice. Your demonstration should be very organized and professional. Think about how you will transition to different topical points. Plan for ways that things could go wrong (e.g., loss of power, lack of technology, critical parts are not on site)
- Choose an appropriate location for the demonstration. Make sure there are no distractions or conditions that may weaken your product's performance. For example, demonstrating a sound system in a cramped office may not convey the benefits of the sound quality.
- Keep the demonstration simple and concise. Long, cumbersome demonstrations can quickly sap your customer's interest and distract from the core benefits the product delivers. Limit your use of technical jargon to audiences who desire this type of performance specification.

Lastly, remember that despite your best-laid plans, product demonstrations can still go wrong. Do not be embarrassed or frustrated. A humble perspective here is important because the customer will pay attention to your reaction. Simply apologize for the problem and propose an alternative way or time to demonstrate the product. Remember, customers who desire a long-term relationship will want to know how you will react when things do not go according to plan. Difficult situations are likely to come up in buyer-seller relationships, and your ability to handle stress will be a strong indicator of your future behavior in those scenarios.

handouts
documents that offer guidelines and summaries for the content in the presentation

Complementary Visual Tools   For some presentations, it is helpful to provide complementary visual material to support your own communication. **Handouts** are helpful documents that offer guidelines and summaries for the content in the presentation. These tools are especially helpful in longer presentations for customers to reference key points. Handouts can also improve buyer retention by having a reinforcing medium (visual learning) along with your communication (audio learning) as well as a quick way for customers to reorient themselves after the meeting.

Top salespeople ensure they are strategic about how they use handouts. First, handouts can be interactive tools. An example is to walk a customer through a graph or infographic by linking key points with arrows or notating subtle linkages that support their sales message. Second, handouts can include many types of visuals to engage customers. Recent reports, charts, websites, case studies, or a copy of the content all provide valuable tools to increase customer interest and involvement. Here are some additional recommendations for your handouts:

- It is critical that handouts do not become the "star of the show" during the presentation. Handouts should always be a complement to strengthen the message, not a device to convey the benefits for the salesperson.

- Provide time for customers to process the information on the handout. When referencing handout content, provide a pause to let customers orient themselves separately and review the content.
- Ensure that the handouts support the sales call objective. It may be tempting to include the latest technical performance specifications in the handout but this is not helpful for an economic buying influence.

Another type of complementary visual tool is a written proposal. In many industries, written proposals are a critical part of the selling process. Some proposals act as brochures developed by the marketing department, while others summarize a complex solution. In industries that require competitive bidding, a written proposal is usually a requirement for the buying process. When buying processes involve formal proposals from multiple providers, this is usually called a **request for proposal (RFP)**.

An RFP contains the customer's specifications for the solution as well as timelines, deliverables, and logistics (e.g., installation, delivery). When salespeople get involved in an RFP process, they should be aware that customers already have a firm idea of the needed solution. Thus, it is to the salesperson's advantage to be engaged with the customer early in their decision process to ensure the buying criteria in the RFP aligns with their potential solutions. Top salespeople also ensure the criteria put competing offerings at a disadvantage.

request for Proposal (RFP)
the customer's specifications for the solution as well as timelines, deliverables, and logistics (e.g., installation, delivery)

In addition to communicating the seller's intentions and rationale for helping the customer, proposals communicate a customized message to the buying influences outside of the salesperson's actual presentation. Proposals also can be shared between customer buying influencers helping to build a consensus opinion regarding the proposed solution. However, there is also some risk to the persuasive ability of the proposal since the salesperson is not present to answer questions. Customers may misinterpret or develop bias regarding particular parts of the proposal and form a negative evaluation of the solution. Rather than building support for the solution, sellers may face a hidden source of opposition after sharing a proposal.

Virtual Presentations Many presentation tools today provide the ability to present to audience members remotely at different locations. **Virtual communication platforms** such as Webex, Skype, Zoom, GoToMeeting are communication tools that allow simultaneous video and audio communication among multiple parties. These platforms allow the seller to make their computer display visible to the audience members, regardless of their location. The presenter can use the screen-sharing technology to demonstrate software, or share documents, video, graphics, data, and PowerPoint slides. Sellers use virtual platforms to schedule and conduct meetings that require far less investment in time and cost than that required for a face-to-face environment. However, many sellers would argue that virtual communication is often unable to deliver the intimacy, authenticity, and deepened trust that stems from in-person meetings. This challenge may be overcome as these tools continue to evolve. Virtual communication platforms are beginning to include holographic projections as well as haptic feedback (e.g., gloves to simulate handshakes). These new offerings may one day be able to simulate virtual meetings that feel as though the attendees are in the room.

virtual communication platforms
communication tools that allow simultaneous video and audio communication among multiple parties

In addition to meetings, sellers are also utilizing virtual platforms to conduct **webinars**. A webinar is a preplanned presentation given to a virtual audience usually followed by a question-and-answer session. Webinars differ from a typical sales call meeting in that they can include a wide array of audience members with varying interests and needs. Because of this context and lack of unique knowledge about the audience members, webinars are often used as prospecting tools to provide an overview presentation that communicates general benefits. Interested

webinars
a preplanned presentation given to a virtual audience usually followed by a question-and-answer session

customers are often invited to ask questions and then provided with a call-to-action to set up a personal meeting to discuss their specific situation.

Verbal Tools

Salespeople should ask themselves before any presentation: How can I deliver my message clearly and convincingly to make a vivid impression on my customer? Salespeople must have a strong command of their verbal communication toolset to accomplish this goal. We cover a set of verbal tools to help salespeople positively influence their customers during presentation.

Persuasive Vocabulary Research looking into the use of persuasion finds that people's use of certain words can be more effective in persuading others.[8] For example, phrases that include the word "you" are important for influencing a discussion partner. Salespeople can leverage this knowledge with phrases such as "You expressed your dissatisfaction with your current costs..." or "If you are anything like me, then I'm sure you receive too many emails." Other words like "advantage" or "new" also were shown to convey strong persuasion influence and should be incorporated into the presentation communication when applicable.

Metaphors, Stories, and Testimonials Top salespeople are adept at conveying abstract concepts to their customers. The benefits of many complex solutions can be difficult to understand through technical jargon and ROI. Instead, salespeople sometimes need to employ the use of metaphors, stories, and testimonials to convey a vision of their offering.

metaphors
phrases that suggest a relationship between objects, concepts, or ideas

Metaphors are phrases that suggest a relationship between objects, concepts, or ideas. Metaphors are highly persuasive sales tools that allow salespeople to build vivid conceptual pictures for customers that command their interest and attention. For example, a salesperson trying to convey the luxurious feeling customers experience when using one of their rental cars might say, "We are the Ritz-Carlton of rental car agencies." Here, the metaphor's value rests on the customer's understanding of Ritz-Carlton as a brand that represents luxury. The success of any metaphor depends on establishing common ground between the associations being made. If the customer was unfamiliar with Ritz-Carlton Hotels, or has never stayed there, the power of the metaphor is probably lost.

Every salesperson also needs to be able to tell a story. Neuroscience research shows that stories offer a way to tap into three different pathways (habits, beliefs, and emotions) to the subconscious mind. Stories deepen and enrich relationships with customers by creating positive associations between the salesperson and the story elements. Insurance agents often benefit greatly from the use of stories.

Shutterstock/Chirvas Anatol

"A husband and father like you initially balked at a life insurance plan out of a belief that he was healthy and unlikely to suffer illness. However, after a brief scare following a car accident that threatened his ability to work, the man experienced great relief with a new policy and now knows that his family would be financially independent if he were ever to be unable to work."

This type of story focuses the customer's attention on common associations between habits, beliefs, or emotions that are experienced in the story elements. Some other tips for sharing stories:

- Ensure that the story is relevant to the customer. You need a reason to relate the story to the customer.
- Use a transition to link your story back into your presentation.
- Pay attention to your audience during your story. Vary your pace, delivery, and tone to keep their interest.
- Select stories that align with your personality and style. Stories are ineffective if the delivery falls flat.

Third-party references can also be a powerful tool for salespeople. Customers always know in the back of their mind that salespeople are there to sell something. Even in the best cases where salespeople are truly helping the customer, some customers will still exhibit a bias toward being skeptical of everything the salesperson says. Third-party testimonials offer salespeople a trusted source of evidence that customers have little reason to doubt. Third parties can be extremely valuable to convey confidence because they are often current clients who have experienced a positive outcome with the salesperson. Indeed, research finds that salespeople who associate information from previous clients help their customers understand their buying situation better and improve their buying outcomes.[9]

Humor   Humor is a valuable verbal tool for salespeople to keep customer's attention, increase likability, and put everyone at ease. Research indicates that well-executed humor also improves salesperson creativity, customer trust, and even sales performance.[10] On the other hand, Burt Teplizky, author of *Sell It with Humor*, suggests that poorly executed or off-the-cuff jokes can quickly distance a person from the customer. He suggests always planning and practicing the use of humor.

Humor works best when it stems from personal experience and does not come at the expense of someone else. Remember, customers are constantly forming an image of the salesperson, and an inauthentic or tasteless joke can leave a lasting negative impression. Some other tips to keep in mind:

- Deliver humor with confidence. Do not apologize or start a joke by under-selling its ability to generate a humorous response ("This probably isn't that funny, but let me tell you this story anyway.")
- If you are unsure about the audience's reception to humor, it may be best to leave it out. In group settings, it can be particularly difficult to appeal to all parties' sense of humor.
- Express your own enjoyment from sharing humor. Smile and provide animated gestures to support the delivery.
- If possible, practice your jokes on acquaintances. This is a safe space to try out untested jokes with individuals that are not too close to you to overlook problems.

Leverage the Unique Value Proposition

A well-planned and well-executed presentation is a hallmark of top salespeople. In the best cases, it provides resolution and hope for the customer to resolve their important business challenges. This is especially true if the presentation can match the customer's interests.

Illustrate Company Results and Customer Success   Regardless of the product or service, customers do not make purchases for the offering itself, but for the expectation of how it makes them successful. Think about the last major purchase you made—not an impulse buy, but a major buying decision that required

Table 7-2 Examples of customer results vs. success

	Customer Results	Customer Success
Description	The impact of the offering on the customer's business processes	The fulfillment of an individual's personal intentions to change a situation for success.
Typical Attributes	Tangible, Measurable, Quantifiable	Intangible, Immeasurable, Unquantifiable
Examples	Reduce costs, Improve efficiency, Grow profits	Gain recognition, Increase growth potential, Achieve more influence

some thought. When you made this purchase, you had specific expectations in mind for what it would help you accomplish. For example, let us assume you recently invested in a professional wardrobe for interviews or a new job. This purchase rests not on your need to own more clothes, but on the expectation that the clothes will resolve your problem of looking unprofessional and your desire to secure future success. These expectations represent the **customer's vision** of what they believe the product or service will accomplish for them.

It is important to focus on the individual customer's vision of success because it is subjective and different for each customer. The basic point here is to broaden the salesperson's presentation to address each customer's reasons for buying. This is especially critical in B2B and complex selling environments. For example, the salesperson's offering may offer clear improvements to the customer's business results, but not offer a compelling vision for helping the individual customer be more successful. Table 7-2 illustrates how customer success is distinct from customer results. Furthermore, if selling to a company with multiple decision-makers the salesperson has to address multiple customer visions. Both cases emphasize that salespeople should identify and presentation how their offering aligns with their customer's vision of success.

customer's vision
what the customer believes the product or service will accomplish for them.

Clarify with Proof Devices

The salesperson's presentation should be focused on the most distinctive advantages and biggest sources of value. But in a crowded market with lots of competitors, this can be difficult to communicate with only feature-benefit statements. Customers want something more tangible in order to trust they are getting the value promised by the salesperson. **Proof devices** help enhance salespeople's credibility in the presentation by provided evidence of their value. Proof devices are any form of evidence such as a statement, testimonial, research study, or customer feedback that conveys the value of an offering.

Panopto is a leading video recording and management software company. A salesperson for Panopto selling the broad service applications and support provided might use the following proof device in the form of a customer testimonial: "For the team here at Nike, Panopto has two major benefits. First, the Panopto video platform really helps us meet all our video needs. And second, Panopto's customer service has been just amazing."[11] Later, the salesperson shows a customer the application recording video and live streaming during a virtual meeting. The customer testimonial and usage visualization proof devices help build the customer's confidence in the offering and its value.

proof devices
any form of evidence such as a statement, testimonial, research study, or customer feedback that conveys the value of an offering

Involve the Customer

While the focus in the presentation is on building effective product configurations and demonstrating value, it is important to not lose sight of the relationship with the customer. Customers can feel unimportant or even ignored during presentations with little interaction. When the presentation focuses on telling and showing, Salespeople can enhance relationships with their customers by communicating value in compelling and creative ways.

Table 7-3 Example of a presentation worksheet

Feature	Advantage	Benefit	Proof Device	Actions
What part of the offering to present?	*How does this stack up against competitors?*	*What does this deliver to resolve customer needs?*	*How will I provide evidence of the benefit?*	*How can I involve the customer?*
Patented "Sleep on Air" Mattress	Only mattress in the industry with cooling gel technology	This mattress improves the quality of your sleep and delivers faster recovery from long workouts	Display mattress in showroom or customer testimonials	Have customer lie down on mattress or take home for 30-day trial
Downtown location for hotel and conference center	Only hotel and conference facility located within walking distance of downtown attractions, restaurants, and nightlife	Improve your attendee satisfaction by providing easy access to an array of downtown amenities such as parks to relax or highly rated restaurants	Map of hotel location in relation to downtown amenities	Have customer visualize attending the conference and/or visit hotel facilities

One way to accomplish this is by developing a presentation worksheet (see Table 7-3). A presentation worksheet provides salespeople with an overview of how to present a unique benefit that also incorporates customer involvement. The first three columns focus on the key characteristics of your offering that resolve customers' unique needs prepared from the salesperson's pre-call preparation, needs identification, and solution recommendation: Features, Advantages, and Benefits. The fourth column includes the specific proof device(s) to be used to illustrate the offering's value. Finally, and importantly, the fifth column pinpoints specific actions for the salesperson or customer to create presentation involvement. Notice that the worksheet outlines multiple ways to communicate with the customer. Sharing the benefit communicates through "telling," using a proof device communicates through "showing," and creating actions for the salesperson and customer communicates through "involving." Not only does involvement improve customer's reception to the presentation, but also creates a sense of ownership over the product. This temporary ownership can potentially create what researcher's call **loss aversion**,[12] or people's tendency to prefer avoiding losses to acquiring equivalent gains. For example, a customer who tries out a comfortable mattress may feel more compelled to purchase (to avoid losing the feeling of comfort) compared to a similar customer who did not have a trial.

loss aversion
the tendency to prefer avoiding losses to acquiring equivalent gains

Another way to involve the customer is to obtain reactions throughout the presentation. After stating benefits or having the customer perform an action, ask the customer a confirmation question to obtain their reaction. Simple questions such as, "Does this resolve the inefficiencies we have been talking about?" or "Now that you've tried it, is this an application that would help increase win rates in your sales organization?" These questions are sometimes referred to as **trial closes**, which are questions to assess the customer's incremental commitment to the offering. One should always include questions to obtain reactions from the customer to ensure you both have the same understanding about the value of the offering and its application to the customer's situation.

trial closes
questions to assess the customer's incremental commitment to the offering

Quantify the Solution

We use the term *value* throughout this textbook to describe the benefits that salespeople deliver to customers. However, the term can become vague and lose its meaning quickly with customers if it is not clear what benefits they receive relative to the price. This is especially problematic for solutions that require significant investment or impose risk on the customer.

Figure 7-2 Quantifying the solution or documenting value

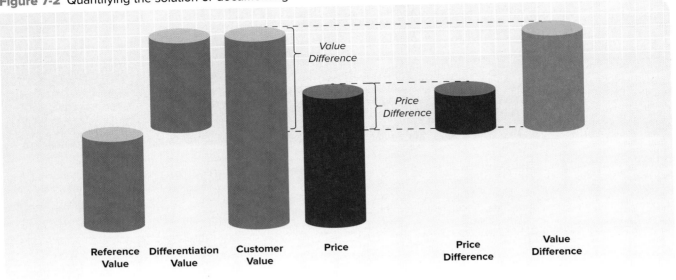

Reference Value   Differentiation Value   Customer Value   Price   Price Difference   Value Difference

Source: Hinterhuber, A., & Snelgrove, T. C. (Eds.). (2016). Value First Then Price: Quantifying Value in Business to Business Markets from the Perspective of Both Buyers and Sellers. Taylor & Francis.

Salespeople can increase the likelihood their customers perceive value in their offering by presenting how the benefits received by the customer outweigh the price. This presentation process is often called *quantifying the solution* or *documenting value*, and we provide a visualization of this in Figure 7-2. In this section, we cover multiple ways salespeople can quantify a solution as a proof device during their presentation.

For all of the methods we cover, we emphasize that presenting metrics that do not align with the customer's interests or situation will weaken rather than strengthen perceived value. The metrics used to document value must align with the customer's situation, needs, and interests. This means that salespeople must convey enough credibility and trust so that the customer is willing to share details about their finances, costs, revenues, or other metrics that are relevant to documenting value.

cost-benefit analysis
the comparison of costs to benefits

Cost-Benefit Analysis   The most straightforward way to quantify a solution is to directly compare the costs and potential savings (or improvements) the customer can expect from making a purchase. This comparison of costs to benefits is called a **cost-benefit analysis.** Important here, the costs and benefits delivered from a proposed solution must be drawn from an analysis of the customer's business or situation. Figure 7-3 offers an example of how a salesperson conducted a simple cost-benefit analysis for a series of training implementations for a sales organization.

The method in figure 7-3 works well for new product purchases, but sometimes salespeople are faced with a customer using a competing solution, or an existing solution with the potential to upgrade. In these situations, a related method for quantifying value called the **comparative cost-benefit analysis** can be performed. Here, salespeople contrast the customer's current value (e.g., costs, revenues) with the value of the proposed solution. For example, a Hershey's retail representative may justify a larger purchase of the higher-priced Reese's candies on the basis of drawing in additional foot traffic and add-on purchases during a holiday season. The Hershey's rep here can provide evidence of purchase behavior from similar

comparative cost-benefit analysis
contrasting the customer's current value with the value of the proposed solution

Figure 7-3 Cost-benefit analysis

Costs			
	Units	Rate	Total
Trainer Compensation (hourly)	100	$200	$20,000
Training Facility	20	$500	$10,000
Annual Retainer Fee	1	$30,000	$30,000
	Sum of Costs		$60,000
Benefits			
			Total
25% reduction in lost customers			$200,000
5% reduction in salesperson turnover			$50,000
	Sum of Benefits		$250,000
Benefit-to-Cost Ratio	4.17		

stores to provide evidence that the added cost will actually improve the revenue production in the grocery aisle and potentially prevent discounting.

Return on Investment Most B2B buyers want to know what type of return, or improvement in their business, they can expect when investing in the purchase of product or service. **Return on investment (ROI)**, captures the net benefit expected from a given investment. This metric is most often measured as the net profits expected from a given purchase, expressed as a percentage of the purchase. For example:

return on investment (ROI) the net benefit expected from a given investment

$$ROI = \frac{Net\ Profits}{Purchase\ Price}$$

A salesperson may offer a new software application that costs $10,000 but saves the company $14,000 in paper expenses each year. The $14,000 drop in paper expenses translates into the buyer's net profits. Thus, the salesperson could quantify the ROI of this solution as:

$$ROI = \frac{\$14,000}{\$10,000} = 1.4$$

Drawing from this example, it is important to note that many customers may be more familiar with the term "ROI of 1.4X" where this means the customer can expect the purchase investment to multiply the return by 1.4. Many companies set a minimum ROI for new solution purchases and may leave the purchase process if the ROI is too low. Salespeople should discover whether their customer has minimum ROI expectations to ensure their proposal does not get rejected outright.

In addition to uncovering customers' minimum ROI criteria, salespeople should also be aware of different ROI interpretations. For example, salespeople selling solutions to recruiting organizations may need to focus on a different type of ROI such as the number of hires per dollars spent on the purchase. Marketing companies may be focused on increasing the number of customer touches (interactions with an ad) per dollar spent on the offering. A common understanding of the customer's ROI helps salespeople ensure they clearly communicate value to the customer.

Time to Break-even For large purchases such as capital expenditures on construction equipment or building material, it may be important to quantify value in the form of time. **Time to break-even** helps salespeople in this regard, capturing

time to break-even the length of time for an investment to be returned

the length of time for an investment (i.e., cash outflow) to be returned (i.e., cash inflows, savings). This form of time-focused value is often appropriate for high-level decision-makers and financial officers who are concerned with strategic decision making and financial management. To estimate the time to break-even, divide the investment cost (cash outflow) by the sum of all the projected cash returns.

$$\text{Time to Break-even} = \frac{\textit{Investment or Purchase Price}}{\textit{Savings (or Profits) per Period}}$$

Note that the time to break-even depends on the focused period for the investment, which could take the form of days, months, or even years. For example, suppose a new machining tool costs $659,000 but will save the manufacturing plant $95,000 each year by reducing the number of parts made that do not meet specifications. The time to breakeven here is:

$$\text{Time to Break-even} = \frac{\$659,000}{\$95,000 \text{ per year}} = 6.93 \text{ years}$$

Salespeople can indicate to the customer in this scenario that the investment will pay for itself in just under seven years, leaving any savings after that period as added value. Clearly, customers take on significant risk with these large purchase decisions and pursue options with a shorter time to break-even where possible.

Opportunity Cost   **Opportunity cost** is the return a customer would have earned from using the same investment for a different purpose. College students deal with opportunity cost each day in determining how to use their time. For example, many students work part-time, participate in on-campus activities, build a community of friends, and all while attending and studying for classes. The decision to spend one hour at work, while producing a return in the form of compensation, comes at the cost of preventing the student from studying or participating in their other interests. Clearly, these can be difficult decisions, and many students struggle with balancing opportunity costs as they work to attain their degrees.

opportunity cost
the return a customer would have earned from using the same investment for a different purpose

Salespeople must be cognizant of their customer's opportunity costs as potential reasons that derail their proposal. For example, a customer could outlay $50M for business improvements in the coming year such as updating the sales force's fleet of vehicles, building infrastructure for their data networks, or upgrading the computing hardware for employees. Top salespeople uncover these other potential purchase options that, while not necessarily direct substitutes for their offering, may detract from the likelihood of customers committing to a certain purchase option. As a result, salespeople should offer realistic comparisons (e.g., cost-benefit, ROI, time to breakeven) of the customer's potential options to help educate the customer about the best solution.

Quantifying Value for the Customer's Customers   Many salespeople sell to customers, such as retailers and distributors, who then sell that offering to end-users. These resellers are focused on how many, how often, and for what price their own customers will buy their offering in their purchasing channels (e.g., store, ecommerce). In these cases, salespeople should quantify value by documenting how their offering increases profit margin or inventory turnover among other metrics.

Schneider Electric is a Fortune 500 company that sells data and energy management products and services. When a Schneider Electric salesperson meets with a distributor partner to sell data backup protection products, the salesperson provides data showing how profitable the backup units are for similar distributors, as well as evidence that the distributors' customers (e.g., construction contractors, IT infrastructure managers) show demand for the product. The distributor gains valuable insight from this quantifiable value and is more likely to make space for this product over competitors in the same category.

Setting the Next Steps

Toward the end of the presentation, it is the salesperson's responsibility to gain the customer's commitment to move forward in the sales process. The ending of the presentation should establish a vision of how their situation could be improved and motivate the customer to buy. However, many presentations may cover a large amount of material and involve significant discussion. Thus, it may be difficult for the customer to recall the core value of the offering. A summary of benefits helps overcome this challenge by helping customers assemble a clear picture of how the offering delivers on its core benefits. Summarizing the offering's benefits at the end of the presentation is also a great way to transition forward.

Here's an example from the hospitality industry. Kurt Rogers, the sales development representative for a luxury conference hotel in Atlanta, recently presented their facilities to Coach Herb Swinney, a football coach for a collegiate-level program. Following the presentation, Kurt summaries the major benefits of his hotel as, "Mr. Swinney, I'd like to recap how our offering addresses your biggest needs for your leadership conference. First, our larger hotel rooms and California king beds offer the best option to comfortably host your players who often find their lodgings inadequately sized. We can also provide you with a conference room and five smaller workshop rooms that are perfectly sized for your planned activities and will be kept inaccessible from other guests to reduce distractions. Lastly, our hospitality team will personally oversee the awards dinner that offers our chef's exclusive menu while costing less than $30 per person. Would these benefits provide the value to achieve your goals for this conference?" Notice that after summarizing the core benefits of the offering, Kurt ended with a confirmation question to gain the customer's commitment to these benefits as adding value. A confirmation question is critical here to definitively establish the customer's agreement with your vision of the solution.

Applying this Chapter to Salesforce

The success of a presentation can hinge on who is making it. While the salesperson may be very knowledgeable, it is often necessary for them to get help with the presentation from sales engineers or other colleagues with specialized knowledge or skills. Finding the right participants and organizing their participation can be very time-consuming. Fortunately, Salesforce enables companies to automate the process. The salesperson can simply submit a request in Salesforce for presentation support. Based on the criteria of the request, it is instantly routed to the person or group of people with the skills and availability to help.

When presenting to more than one person, it is very helpful to know the role of each person, the issues that matter to each of them, and the degree to which each will influence the buying decision. Being armed with this information enables the salesperson to adapt the presentation and speak to each attendee specifically about the issues most important to them. While it's possible for the salesperson to remember all of these details, it isn't realistic if they are simultaneously working on sales opportunities with several customers.

Reports available from Salesforce provide a summary of key information and findings entered by the salesperson during the discovery phase and any other customer research or interaction leading up to the presentation. These reports can serve as quick reference guides and reminders about each audience member, allowing the salesperson to personalize elements of the presentation. The value of these reports is especially high for co-presenters, who may have no prior experience with or knowledge of the customer.

If a "canned" presentation is appropriate, the salesperson can use Salesforce templates with links to video files or other previously created material. The salesperson can send these canned presentation templates in real-time, or they can arrange for Salesforce to send them automatically in the future, based on date or event triggers.

Chapter Summary

- The first step in the presentation process is a meaningful understanding of the customers' needs.
- Effective presentations are marked by several indicators, such as being memorable, improving understanding, and catering to the individual customer's needs.
- Salespeople should consider how they will recommend a solution and demonstrate problem resolution during a presentation.
- Software tools and co-creation are two options to help guide salespeople to develop solutions. These factors shape the recommendation salespeople offer to customers and set up a transition to present how the solution will resolve problems.
- Top salespeople focus their presentation on not just outcomes, but also on benefits. These presentations are most effective using proof devices that involve the customer and quantify the solution's impact.
- The salesperson is responsible for gaining the customer's commitment to move forward in the sales process. The ending of the presentation should motivate the customer to buy.

Key Terms

buying signals (p. 128)
comparative cost-benefit analysis (p. 138)
cost-benefit analysis (p. 138)
co-creation (p. 127)
customer's vision (p. 136)
handouts (p. 132)
informative presentation (p. 125)
loss aversion (p. 137)
metaphors (p. 134)
opportunity cost (p. 140)
persuasion (p. 125)
persuasive presentation (p. 125)

proof devices (p. 136)
request for proposal (RFP) (p. 133)
return on investment (ROI) (p. 139)
sales asset management system (p. 130)
sales enablement (p. 130)
solution configuration (p. 126)
time to break-even (p. 139)
trial closes (p. 137)
virtual communication platforms (p. 133)
webinars (p. 133)

Application 7-1

Harrison Becker is sitting in the lobby of Taylors Painting, waiting to meet with the owner, David Taylors. Harrison is a sales representative for Picasso Paints, a regional paint manufacturer known for their innovative paint products. He's in David's office today because Taylors Painting was just awarded a contract to paint the interior and exterior of a new mixed-use development. The development includes three commercial buildings along with two restaurants and an art installment park located as a center point between the buildings. The business potential for this meeting is large, and Harrison wants to make sure he communicates the value of Picasso Paints products as the best choice for this project. In his six months with Picasso, Harrison has never pitched a deal of this size and is a little nervous. Harrison also knows that Taylors has been a long-time customer of a competing paint company in the area, Rival Paints. Fortunately, Harrison feels that he

(Continued)

has a good understanding of David's needs based on previous sales calls. After a few minutes, Harrison is called into David's office for a presentation.

> Harrison: *Thanks again for meeting with me today. As we discussed last time, based on your needs for the new development I would recommend our QD Delux exterior and interior finish lines for your upcoming project. These two paint portfolios offer the most durable finish with just a single coat helping to reduce your labor costs from the initial application as well as maintenance.*

> David: *I appreciate your recommendation. But you know, I just had a call with Rival Paints yesterday and their paint line I've been using for a while offers the same benefit at a lower price. Why should I switch?*

1. Harrison was expecting this comment from David because he's known about Rival's performance promises in the past. He knows that Rival's paints do not really live up to their promises and ends up costing more overall. How should Harrison proceed?
2. As the presentation continues, David states that, "So, this seems like these paints could really shave off some time for us to finish the project faster. How many people would you recommend I hire on to complete the project in two months?" What kind of signal is David giving Harrison?
3. Harrison is doing well in his presentation but then realizes that he forgot to review his presentation worksheet before entering the meeting. He's trying to remember the different components but feels as if he's leaving one out. What information should be on his presentation worksheet?

Application 7-2

In your first year as a salesperson for Salesforce, you have learned a lot. Because Salesforce is a leading provider of customer relationship management software, you spend a lot of time talking with your customers about how to improve their business. You know that among the many applications, Salesforce's offerings help salespeople increase their productivity by helping keep track of the customers they call. In addition to notifications that help salespeople know when to contact an account, the software can track account information regarding what has been purchased in the past, who was involved in the decision process, and details about people involved in the account. Plus, sales managers love implementing Salesforce because it can generate reports automatically to help track activity and performance.

As you start another day, you notice you have a few planned calls today that will involve presentation. You recognize the importance of planning and practicing your presentation before your calls. Some of the decisions you have to make are prepared below.

1. The first call on your list is with Michael, a sales leader in the paper industry. On a previous call with Michael, he shared that a big concern of his was the up-front cost to switch and implement Salesforce's software in his organization. He felt like it would take *too long* for the investment to bring any return. Which type of value quantification tool would be best used here?
2. Your second call today is with Martha, a department head in the development office at a university. Martha has expressed an interest in Salesforce to help keep track of

(Continued)

(Continued)

their donors' information and development officer's progress and performance. You recently conducted a needs assessment with Martha and you feel like you have good handle on her most important issues. What is the next step you should take?

3. Your last call of the day is on the chief operating officer of Chicago Business Press, who tells you she's impressed with the benefits you've demonstrated. However, they are currently weighing whether to update their CRM system or their warehouse automation system instead. What kind of criteria is Chicago Business Press applying to the buying decision?

CHAPTER

8 Objections and Closing

Learning Objectives

- Understand the role of objections in the selling process
- Prepare for the type of objections buyers will raise and when they are likely to raise them
- Learn the most appropriate methods to respond to various objections
- Assess whether an objection has been overcome
- Know when it is appropriate to attempt to close
- Learn the various methods for closing
- Understand what to do after a successful or unsuccessful attempt to close

I n the history of business, many truly great products and services have been brought to market. Yet, even the best still required salespeople to help buyers understand them. Effective interactions between the salesperson and the buyer are not one-way pitches by the salesperson. Instead, it should be a dialogue, a two-way conversation that brings the seller closer to understanding the buyer's needs, and brings the buyer closer to understanding how the value of the product or service benefits them. In this chapter, we cover the fundamentals of handling objections and closing and explain why they are integral to the selling process.

The Value of Objections and Addressing Concerns

objection
any concern or question raised by the buyer

When a buyer expresses a concern or question about whatever is being sold, we call this expression an objection or concern. In simpler terms, an **objection** is any concern or question raised by the buyer.[1] Although an objection sounds like a buyer's negative reaction, they are actually quite positive and constructive for the salesperson. Objections are positive because they demonstrate a buyer who is engaged and interested enough to be thinking of reasons why the salesperson's product or service may not work for them. The traditional term for a salesperson's attempt to answer or resolve a buyer's objection or concern is **overcoming objections**, while others call it **addressing concerns**.

overcoming objections, addressing concerns
a salesperson's attempt to answer or resolve a buyer's objection or concern

Objections are also constructive in that they provide the salesperson with concrete clues about what is important to the buyer. By overcoming the buyer's objections, the salesperson is addressing the criteria important to the buyer's decision and their misunderstandings about the product or service being sold. Without objections from the buyer, the salesperson would be virtually blind to the criteria important to the buyer or what they accurately understand about the product or service.

When and Why Buyers Raise Objections

Buyers can raise objections for any reason and at any time. It's one of the most interesting challenges of professional selling—that every call can be different. That said, in the following section, we will cover some of the common themes of when and why buyers raise objections.

Appointment Setting or Initiating a Sales Call

It may come as no surprise that everyone is busy. Virtually everyone has more to do than time to do it. This is especially true for buyers. Those with the authority to make a purchasing decision usually also have many other demands on their time, and, as a result, their time is very valuable. So, they protect their time carefully, accepting meetings only with those they believe will have a positive impact on them and their organizations.

Appointment-setting is the stage of the selling process where the salesperson has the least amount of information about the buyer and the least amount of time to succeed. Learning to think and respond quickly to overcome appointment-setting objections is critical. After all, without appointments, the salesperson will not have opportunities to make sales.

Most of the objections salespeople experience with appointment-setting are the result of, not only the buyer's scarce time, but also the lack of perceived value of the product or service being sold. Common objections to attempts to set appointments are: "We're satisfied with our current vendor," "We tried a product or service like yours before and it didn't work out," or simply, "We're not interested."

Sales Calls and Presentations

A buyer may raise objections at any time during the sales call, but most often, they will do so in response to something said by the salesperson. That means the buyer may raise objections as early as the beginning of the call, when the salesperson is explaining the purpose of the call, trying to position their firm's history with other customers, or making a general value proposition statement. More often though, the buyer will raise objections during the salesperson's presentation.

Again, an objection might sound like a negative interaction. But it is actually a positive sign that the buyer is engaged and trying to understand how the product or service may or may not benefit them. Each objection provides the salesperson with clues about what specific issues need to be addressed to make the sale. By comparison, the potential buyer who doesn't ask any questions or raise any objections might seem like an easy sales call. But their lack of response and objection is more likely a sign of lack of interest.

Attempt to Close

Ideally, the salesperson has conducted a thorough sales call (or series of sales calls) and asked enough questions to identify and overcome all objections by the time they attempt to close the sale or obtain a commitment. If they have, their attempt to close will be met with agreement or commitment. Generally speaking, the more experience the salesperson has, the better they are at anticipating all possible objections and asking questions to reveal and overcome them before they attempt to close. However, it's not unusual for the salesperson's attempt to close to be met with another, previously unmentioned objection.

Common Objections

Although buyers use objections to essentially express their needs or understanding of how the salesperson's product or service matches their needs, objections can come in a few common forms (See table 8-1 for examples). Understanding these common types of objections helps the salesperson be better prepared to respond to them effectively.

Need Objections

There are, in fact, companies that do not have a real need for the product or service being sold. The office manager for a law firm that just signed a five-year lease on their office space has no need that can be addressed by the person selling office space in a newly constructed building. An expensive piece of machinery capable of high-volume output and 24-hour operation is probably not needed by a small, specialized manufacturer with only a few customers. What matters more to the successful salesperson is the ability to identify and overcome a *perceived* need objection.

A prospective buyer with no perceived need might express this **need objection** by saying, "We already have a supplier for that," "Your product doesn't apply to us," "We tried something like that before and it didn't work," or the universal "We're not interested." All of these objections demonstrate that the buyer does not immediately see a benefit from the salesperson's product or service that meets a need of their business.

The need objection occurs most often when the buyer doesn't understand how the features of the product or service might be applied to benefit the buyer—

need objection
the objection expressed by a buyer with no perceived need

Shutterstock/fizkes

product objection, service objection
an objection raised by a prospective buyer who perceives their need is not met by the features or characteristics of the product or service

effectively addressing needs they didn't realize existed. The challenge for the salesperson is to ask questions and provide information that helps the buyer recognize a need met by the product or service.

Product or Service Objections

A **product objection** or **service objection** is one raised by a prospective buyer who perceives their need is not met by the features or characteristics of the product or service. Put another way; the buyer will raise an objection if the product or service lacks something they need. For example, the buyer needs a printer that can print 50 pages per minute while the printer offered by the salesperson only prints 30 pages per minute. A buyer might also need 24-hour availability, while the seller is only open Monday through Friday 9-5. In either of these situations, the buyer would likely express an objection.

In some cases, the product or service being sold does not meet the buyer's needs. In these cases, the salesperson may need to present an alternate version or configuration or add optional features to match the buyer's need. In these cases, the objection is very helpful in providing the salesperson insight about the buyer's specific needs, improving their likelihood of presenting a product that meets them. There will be times, however, when the options available for the salesperson to present don't meet a buyer's specific need. When this happens, skilled salespeople ask more questions to determine the importance of the unmet need relative to other needs met.

Here are some examples of product or service objections:

"I don't think that your service can deliver as quickly as we need."

"I am happy with the 24-hour service of our current supplier."

"I am not sure if the quality of your product will meet our needs."

"I have been told that your product breaks down rather quickly."

Source or Company Objections

source objection, company objection
an objection expressed when the buyer is reluctant to proceed based on their perceived reputation of the salesperson's company, industry, location, or even the salesperson themselves

A **source objection** or **company objection** occurs when the buyer is reluctant to proceed based on their perceived reputation of the salesperson's company, industry, location, or even the salesperson themselves. Company objections generally come in one of two forms; either the buyer has never heard of the salesperson's company, or the buyer has heard of the salesperson's company and doesn't like what they've heard.

Salespeople representing small or new companies competing against large, better-established firms will more often have to overcome a company objection like, "I've never heard of you." The underlying concerns that are often being expressed with this type of company objection have to do with the risk to the buyer for choosing an unknown company; financial stability, reliability, or support capability compared with larger companies. Company objections don't apply only to small firms though. Salespeople representing large companies might also face a company objection for being too big. A buyer might assume that they won't receive the same kind of attention and service from a large supplier as they will by being a more important customer to a smaller supplier. It's also possible that the buyer has had a negative experience with the salesperson's company, or has heard about negative experiences. Lastly, a buyer might also have a source objection against the salesperson's industry, location, or even the salesperson specifically.

Price Objections

To make the best use of their time, the salesperson needs to qualify each prospect's ability to pay, early in the sales process. Few things are as discouraging as spending

Table 8-1 Examples of Objections

Need Objection	*"We don't need that."*
Product or Service Objection	*"That feature won't work for us."*
Source or Company Objection	*"My neighbor used your company and wasn't happy"*
Price Objection	*"Your product is just too expensive."*
Time Objection	*"I'll need to think about it."*

considerable time with a prospect only to learn later that they have no budget to make the purchase. But assuming the potential buyer has been qualified sufficiently, a price objection will still be the most common.[2]

Any way the buyer expresses an opinion that the price is too high for the product or service is a **price objection**. The buyer will most often make a price objection for one of three reasons. First, the price is higher than the value they believe they are receiving from the purchase. Second, the buyer might believe that a comparable competitive product or service is available for a lower price. And third, many buyers assume that all prices are negotiable. Even if they perceive the value to be greater than the cost, many buyers feel asking for a lower price is part of doing their job well.

Some examples of price objections are:

> *"Your price is about 20% more than what we currently pay."*

> *"We just don't have the budget for the rates you charge."*

price objection
an objection that the price is too high for the product or service

Time Objections

When a potential buyer responds that they don't have time to meet or they need time to think about their decision, these are both **time objections**. So, salespeople most frequently experience time objections when they are prospecting and when they are attempting to close.

The time objection will exist for virtually every cold call. So, it is important to have a concise value or benefit statement that quickly conveys why a meeting would be worth the buyer's time. Time objections are also common in response to the attempt to close or gain commitment. Time objections at this stage might sound like, "I need time to think about everything we've discussed." "I need to go over my findings with my manager." "I need to speak with other suppliers before we make a decision." The salesperson needs to be careful not to be too pushy or overly aggressive in overcoming a time objection. Otherwise, they risk damaging their rapport and relationship with the customer.[3]

time objections
when a buyer responds that they don't have time to meet or they need time to think about their decision

Responding to Objections

Regardless of the type of objection raised by the buyer, it is important for the salesperson to remain calm and listen carefully before responding.[4] Accurately hearing and understanding the objection is critical to formulating an effective response. The salesperson should never interrupt or finish the buyer's sentence.

Successful salespeople should also develop the ability to quickly evaluate objections before responding. In addition to evaluating the kind of objection the buyer is expressing and deciding on the best response, the salesperson may also need to determine whether the buyer is expressing a genuine objection or an excuse. **Excuses** are false objections expressed by the buyer instead of their true objection. For example, a buyer might be embarrassed to say, "I can't afford your product." So, instead, they might raise an unrelated objection that is preventing them from buying.

excuses
false objections expressed by the buyer instead of their true objection

However the salesperson responds to an objection; honesty is an absolute necessity. Aside from being unethical, deception or manipulation will eventually undermine the relationship with the buyer.

Listen, Acknowledge, Assess, Respond, and Confirm

LAARC Method
listen, acknowledge, assess, respond, and confirm

With experience, responding to objections becomes almost second nature. Hearing and responding to an objection is just another form of communication that, when conducted effectively, results in a clearer understanding between buyer and seller. On the way to mastering handling objections, many find it helpful to use the **LAARC Method**. LAARC stands for listen, acknowledge, assess, respond, and confirm.

Listen   As with every other aspect of successful selling, listening is the most important skill to apply when dealing with an objection. When a buyer objects, they are revealing more detail about what they want or don't want. Resist the urge to interrupt or finish their thought. And make eye contact as they are speaking.

Acknowledge   The first response to an objection is to acknowledge it, showing the buyer that their objection is important. The polite and respectful acknowledgment is also an opportunity to set the tone for a polite, professional exchange. Many salespeople acknowledge an objection by repeating it back to the buyer to confirm they heard it correctly. For example, the salesperson might say, "So, to make sure I understand you correctly, you're concerned about the maintenance cost of our product. Is that right?"

Assess   The purpose of the assess step is to make absolutely certain the salesperson understands the objection. One outcome of the assess step is to gather more specifics about the buyer's objection. Using the previous example of the buyer's concern about long-term maintenance, the salesperson might assess by asking, "What maintenance are you expecting?" "What are you currently spending on maintenance?" or "How long would you normally maintain a product like this before replacing it?" Conducted effectively, the assess step ensures that the salesperson's language and criteria for the objection are the same as the buyer's. Another objective of the assess step is for the salesperson to use questions to better understand if there are other objections beneath the one expressed by the buyer. Continuing the example, asking more questions about the buyer's experience with maintenance costs might actually reveal that their concern is less about the cost of maintenance as it is about poor service or reliability they've experienced.

Respond   The salesperson should only respond after being absolutely certain they clearly understand what the buyer is objecting to and why. There are several types of responses. But none of them are more effective than the others without a thorough and accurate understanding of the objection. Later in this chapter, we'll discuss a variety of techniques for responding.

Confirm   Immediately after making the response, the salesperson should ask the buyer whether their objection has been addressed. One outcome is that the buyer says no or acts unconvinced. In either case, the salesperson should further assess the objection. While it's possible that the salesperson cannot completely overcome the objection, it is also possible that further assessment will reveal additional information. The other outcome of asking the buyer if their objection has been addressed is that they confirm or agree. For some sales calls, this type of positive response means the conversation will move to another (maybe many) objections the buyer needs to have answered. But the buyer's response to the salesperson's confirmation might also include **buying signals**, the verbal or nonverbal cues that indicate a readiness to buy or commit.

buying signals
the verbal or nonverbal cues that indicate a readiness to buy or commit

Be Prepared

Objections are a natural part of the buyer/seller dialogue. Accepting that objections are normal and expecting them is the first step in being prepared. Most companies are also keenly aware of the most common objections their salespeople will face and prepare them through training and practice. Knowledge of the product or service being sold is also very important to successfully overcoming objections. Although training will provide some of this knowledge, it is also important for the salesperson to know where to find answers they haven't committed to memory.

Response Methods

Because there is an almost unlimited number of ways a buyer might express an objection, there is equally an almost unlimited variety of ways in which the salesperson might respond. And there is no perfect response to match each objection. That said, in the same way most objections are similar to the types previously described, there are also some common types of effective responses. This section will cover those most common response types.

Forestalling **Forestalling** means to address a likely objection before the buyer voices it. Most companies have a clear understanding of how their products or services are different from their competitors. They may be smaller, more expensive, or have fewer features than their competitors. Knowing the most common objections, forestalling minimizes the number of objections the salesperson will need to respond to. Some buyers will feel a need to defend objections they raise. By forestalling, or preempting the buyer raising the objection, the buyer may be more willing to change their thinking. Forestalling should only be used for objections that buyers are very likely to raise.[5]

forestalling
addressing a likely objection before the buyer voices it

Questioning and Assessing Although we've already discussed the value of good questions within the context of the LAARC Method, a good question can also be the most effective response to some objections. Responding with the right question will help assess the objection. But sometimes, the right question can completely defuse and overcome the objection. Table 8-2 provides examples.

The buyer's answer can quickly clarify for the salesperson whether there is a simple misunderstanding to be corrected, alteration of the product or service required, or alternative product to present to improve the odds of making the sale.

Direct denial In some cases, the buyer's objection is based solely on their misunderstanding of facts. Responding to this kind of objection by directly correcting the buyer's mistake or misunderstanding is called a **direct denial**. By definition, a direct denial may be as blunt as, "That's not true." or "I'm afraid you're wrong about that." But since many people don't respond well to being told they are wrong, the salesperson needs to use direct denials sparingly. Often, the better the relationship between the salesperson and the buyer the more frequently a direct denial can be used.

direct denial
responding to an incorrect objection by directly correcting the buyer's mistake or misunderstanding

Indirect denial With an **indirect denial** the salesperson first responds to the buyer's incorrect understanding by agreeing that the objection is important or

indirect denial
responding to a buyer's incorrect understanding by agreeing that the objection is important or expressing understanding before correcting them

Table 8-2 Examples of Questioning and Assessing

Objection	Salesperson's response
That's too expensive.	*How much were you expecting to spend?*
I don't like the color.	*What color would you prefer?*
Your delivery wouldn't be fast enough for us.	*How fast do you need it to be?*

expressing understanding before correcting them. The salesperson may soften the denial by first saying, "Oh, that's a common misunderstanding, but the fact is…" or "I talk to a lot of people who think that way, but the reality is…" or "You're not the first person I have talked to who had gotten bad information. Let me show you how this really works." Or "I can see why you might think that, but a lot has changed in just the last year. Let me explain.…"

Compensation   It's very rare for the features of a product or service to perfectly match a buyer's needs and budget. Most companies make conscious decisions about which features are most important to the customers they are trying to serve, and the price those customers are willing to pay. As a result, it is common for a buyer to raise an objection to real shortcomings of a product or service, relative to their needs.

An effective way to respond when a buyer raises a valid objection to a shortcoming is with the **compensation method**, showing how other features compensate for or outweigh the shortcoming.

The first step in the compensation method is for the salesperson to recognize and agree with the buyer's valid objection. The second step is to explain the compensating feature. For example, let's say a buyer objects to the price of a printer, noting accurately that a competitor's printer is less expensive. Responding to the objection with the compensation method, the salesperson might say, "You're right. Our printer is more expensive to buy. But our toner cartridges are half the price of our competitors, so you will save more on our toner in just the first year than you would save buying the less expensive printer."

Using the compensation method, the salesperson might also respond with multiple smaller features and benefits to compensate for the objection. Using again the objection that the price of a printer is more expensive than the competitor's, the salesperson might respond by saying, "You're right. But remember that our toner is less expensive, our printers are faster, and our warranty is better."

Another situation where the compensation method can be applied is with the buyer who is postponing their decision. In a case where the buyer wants to "think about it," the salesperson can use the compensation method to encourage a decision now by explaining the cost of waiting. For example, the price might be higher later because a special promotion may be ending, the product may not still be available later, or the savings or productivity gained by the purchase is great enough that every month delayed is lost savings or gains.

Referral Method/Third-Party Reinforcement/Feel-Felt-Found   When a buyer's objection is based not so much on facts, but on their personal attitude or opinion, an effective response can be the **referral method**, also known as **third-party reinforcement** or **feel-felt-found**, where the salesperson provides examples of other people with similar objections, who changed their mind after using the product or service. The salesperson might also support their response with data or assessments from independent sources like Consumer Reports, J.D. Power, Gartner, or other third-party research.

An effective way to organize this response is with a feel-felt-found statement like, "I understand how you *feel*. Steve Moore at Ace Ventures *felt* the same way the first time we met. But after just two weeks into the free trial we offer, Steve *found* the results so positive that he placed an order for twice the amount he was originally considering."

Revisit, Translation, or Boomerang Method   With some objections, the salesperson can **revisit**, **translate**, or **boomerang** a response that uses the buyer's objection, but with a different rationale that provides a reason for the prospect to buy. Table 8-3 shows examples of this. At the very least, this method allows the salesperson to offset the objection by providing an equal benefit.

compensation method
showing how other features compensate for or outweigh the shortcoming

referral method, third-party reinforcement, feel-felt-found
the salesperson provides examples of other people with similar objections, who changed their mind after using the product or service

revisit, translate, or boomerang method
a response that uses the buyer's objection, but with a different rationale that provides a reason for the prospect to buy

The appropriate use of this method requires the salesperson to have a good sense of their customer and the situation. Used at the wrong time or with the wrong person, this method can appear arrogant or pushy. Table 8-3 provides examples of this method.

Table 8-3 Examples of the Revisit/Translation Method

Buyer	Salesperson
Your product looks cheap.	Exactly! Our engineers know that how the product looks has no bearing on how it performs. So, we invested less making it look better in order to reduce the price to you.
Your product has a lot of features we won't use.	It does. But those are features you could be using in order to grow and improve your business.

Acknowledge Method   There will be times when a buyer expresses an opinion or concern that is beyond the salesperson's control. When this happens, the buyer is not so much raising an objection, but venting their frustration. When the salesperson senses this is the case, the best approach is the **acknowledge method**, where the salesperson lets the buyer talk, acknowledges that they've been heard, pauses, and then steers the conversation toward something they can control. Table 8-4 provides examples.

In both these examples, the pause allows the buyer the opportunity to ask a more specific question or raise a more specific objection for the salesperson to answer. If the buyer doesn't take the opportunity, it's a good indication that they just needed their opinion to be acknowledged.

acknowledge method
the salesperson lets the buyer talk, acknowledges that they've been heard, pauses, and then steers the conversation toward something they can control

Table 8-4 Examples of the Acknowledge Method

Buyer	Salesperson
I can't believe how much all the companies in your industry charge these days! It doesn't seem like that long ago that we were paying half what we do now!	I understand your frustration. The cost of everything that goes into making our product has risen...PAUSE... Your time is important, so let's get back to your specifications so I can price this bid.
Your markup is 30 percent!?	I know. It seems like a lot. But that's what we need in order to pay our staff, rent, and all the other costs of providing this service...PAUSE... So, what's your ideal schedule for getting this work done?

Postpone or Coming-to-That   It's not unusual for a buyer to raise an objection early in the sales call or presentation that the salesperson would prefer to respond to later, not out of avoidance, but because the response might make more sense in the context of a topic they haven't discussed yet. Using the **postpone method** or **coming-to-that** method, the salesperson asks permission to respond later. Table 8-5 provides an example.

postpone method or coming-to-that
the salesperson asks permission to respond later

Table 8-5 Example of Postpone Method

Buyer	Salesperson
What do you charge for personalization?	If you don't mind, I'd like to answer that question after I've learned enough about your needs to give you an accurate figure. Our personalization charge will also make more sense when you see it with the other costs I'll go over later.

The salesperson should ask permission to postpone in a way that doesn't sound like they are postponing the question because it isn't important. If they acknowledge the importance of the question and provide a sound reason why it will be better answered later, most buyers will agree to wait. The postpone method should almost always be used for a buyer who asks about price before any discussion of features and benefits. Talking about price without first confirming the buyer's understanding of the value they are receiving is almost always counterproductive.

There are two occasions when it does not make sense to postpone. The first is when the buyer insists on an answer now, and by not providing one, the salesperson appears evasive or uncooperative. The other is if the salesperson senses that the buyer will be distracted by the unanswered question, and won't pay full attention to the conversation or presentation until their concern is addressed.

Which Response Method Is Most Effective?

First and foremost, effective salespeople adapt to every buyer and situation. The response that worked well with one buyer, time, or place may not work with another. Similarly, a response that worked well early in the process may prove less effective later with the same buyer. If one method fails with a buyer, it is usually best to switch to another method.[6] That said, recent research has found that more benevolent methods, like indirect denial, LAARC, and third-party reference are more effective than techniques that assert more expertise, like direct denial and revisit.[7] Table 8-6 provides a summary of all the response methods.

Table 8-6 Summary of Response Methods

Response Method	What It Does	Example
Forestalling	Answer an objection before the buyer expresses it.	*If you're like many people, you might assume we are the highest priced option. If so, you'll be pleased to know we have a wide range of pricing options to match every budget.*
Questioning and Assessing	Use probes to accurately understand the buyer's objection.	*When you say our output isn't fast enough, how fast do you need it to be? Why?*
Direct Denial	Bluntly correct a buyer who makes an incorrect statement.	*That's simply not true. Our support is among the best in the industry.*
Indirect Denial	Use more diplomatic terms to correct a buyer.	*I understand why you might think that. There's a lot of misleading information out there. But the fact is...*
Compensation	Outweigh an objection with a benefit.	*While it's true we don't offer that feature, our price is substantially lower. And you said price was your most important criteria.*
Referral/Third-Party/ Feel-Felt-Found	Uses independent opinion or experience to overcome objections	*I understand how you feel. Dave Matthews at YYZ felt the same way the first time we talked. And now he's one of my biggest customers.*
Revisit/Translation/ Boomerang	Convert a reason not to buy into a reason to buy.	*I understand you think my firm is too small to provide the support you need, but because we're small, you will instantly get VIP treatment as one of our largest customers.*
Acknowledge	Express sympathy for an issue beyond the salesperson's control, then move on.	*I don't disagree. I wish there was something we could do about that. But it's beyond our control. So, you were saying...*
Postpone/Coming-to-that	Telling the buyer that their objection will be answered later.	*I'm glad warranty terms are important to you. You will really like my answer. But it will make more sense if I answer your question later, when I talk about support and maintenance. Do you mind if I answer your question then?*

Assessing Whether the Objection Has Been Overcome

The last step in responding to an objection is to confirm whether the buyer has accepted the response. Doing so involves asking any variation of questions like these: "Have I answered your question?" "Did that make sense?" "Does that work for you?"

It is always possible that the buyer will respond with additional questions or that they will provide verbal or nonverbal signals that they are not completely satisfied by the response, meaning their objection remains. When this happens, the salesperson needs to ask more questions to understand the objection better and provide additional responses. It is also possible that some objections cannot be completely overcome. When this happens, the prudent salesperson will apply a version of the compensation method to help the buyer see how their one objection is compensated for or outweighed by all the other features and benefits discussed.

But when the salesperson receives an affirmative response from the buyer that their concerns have been addressed, the salesperson can move on with their sales call or proceed to securing a commitment or closing the sale.

Securing Commitment and Closing

Closing means asking for and securing a commitment from a customer or prospect. Unfortunately, in the history of sales advice, many have portrayed closing to be something the salesperson does *to* the buyer. Countless pages have been written about techniques that are supposed to help salespeople close more sales. But the salesperson who focuses too much on closing techniques alone will likely be disappointed with their performance—not to mention their unfavorable standing with customers. In fact, salespeople who focus on closing instead of thoroughly identifying needs and presenting solutions experience less success.[8] An overemphasis on closing can also insult buyers or at least make them uncomfortable, instill distrust, and lay a poor foundation for any long-term relationship.

closing
asking for and securing a commitment from a customer or prospect

Instead, the savvy professional salesperson understands that securing commitments and closing are part of the buying process. Each time the salesperson asks for a commitment or attempts to close, they are essentially testing or validating their understanding of the conversation with the buyer. A positive response to a request for commitment indicates the salesperson is on track to making the sale. A negative reaction to an attempt to close may only be an indication that the salesperson needs to invest more time and effort into understanding the buyer's needs.

Most importantly, salespeople close and ask for commitments because people generally feel an obligation to do what they said they would do. Without asking for a commitment, there is no responsibility on the buyer to play a part in moving the relationship forward. However, the potential buyer who agrees to try a sample product before the next meeting is more likely to do so, simply because they said they would. And when it matters most, the buyer who has committed or made a promise to purchase from one salesperson is far less likely to consider options from other salespeople.

When to Close

While closing the customer on the final commitment to buy is still critical to a salesperson's success, professional selling involves a sophisticated and nuanced understanding of how to apply closing skills throughout the selling process.

Shutterstock/fizkes

The very first attempt to close in most sales processes is securing a commitment to meet for the first time. Simply setting that first appointment requires asking for a commitment. Assuming the first meeting goes well, the salesperson may need to close the prospect on scheduling a second meeting to collect more detail or conduct a demonstration. It may be helpful for the prospect to talk with existing customers or references. In this case, the salesperson should secure the commitment from the prospect to make the calls. If co-workers or supervisors will influence the buyer's decision, it may be wise for the salesperson to ask the buyer to commit to invite those influencers to the next meeting. And of course, once it is clear that the salesperson's product meets the buyer's needs, they should ask for the ultimate commitment...the commitment to buy. In short, there are reasons to seek commitment and close throughout the selling process.

The best time to close is when the buyer is ready to be closed. Novice salespeople often think they need to complete the sales call and presentation first and save the close until the very end. However, at any point during the sales call or selling process, the buyer may send buying signals that they are ready to commit.

trial closes
questions to check the buyer's attitude or readiness

Throughout the sales call, the effective salesperson will also use **trial closes**, or ask questions to check the buyer's attitude or readiness. Trial closes also help the salesperson clearly understand the buyer's priorities so they can present their offering in a manner that matches what's most important to the buyer. Let's say the salesperson and buyer have just discussed a specific feature. The salesperson might attempt a trial close such as "How valuable is this feature to you?" or "Do you think your co-workers would find this feature useful?" There are occasions when a trial close can even be used in an attempt to secure an early commitment to buy; before the salesperson is certain they have all the facts. In some cases, these early trial closes succeed, saving time for both the salesperson and buyer. But even when they don't succeed, the buyer's response usually provides a very clear direction about what information they really need in order to become a customer.

Closing Methods

Regardless of the closing method, the salesperson needs to remember that no closing method should be used to manipulate a buyer. The objective of professional selling is to match the right product or service with the buyer's needs. And successful salespeople use a variety of closing methods to serve that objective. In addition, successful salespeople are mindful of how each buyer wants to buy. The methods that follow will apply in a wide variety of situations, but they also need to be tailored to the pace, style, and personality of the buyer in order to be effective.

Direct Request

direct request
asking for a commitment in the most straightforward and plain terms, leaving no room for interpretation

As the name implies, a **direct request** means asking for a commitment in the most straightforward and plain terms, leaving no room for interpretation of what the salesperson is asking the buyer to do. The direct request works when the salesperson is confident they have the information necessary to justify the request. If not, the direct request may sound blunt or even inappropriate to the buyer.

Here are a few examples of direct requests:

How many units would you like to order today?

Can we schedule a time for me to come back and conduct a demonstration?

Would you introduce me to the other person involved with the decision?

Benefit Summary

Over the course of a sales call or multiple sales calls, the salesperson will likely talk with the buyer about multiple needs and how the salesperson's product or service offered features and benefits meet each need. As they presented each benefit, the salesperson should have confirmed with the buyer that the benefit did indeed meet the need. Summarizing those agreed-to benefits before asking for a commitment is called the **benefit summary method.**

Although the discussion about particular features and benefits may be fresh in the sales representative's mind, consider that the buyer may not remember everything as clearly. This is especially true at the end of long meetings or selling situations involving multiple meetings. The benefit summary method reminds the buyer of all the positive points discussed previously, which will increase their likelihood of agreeing to the request for commitment that follows.

> **benefit summary method**
> summarizing those agreed-to benefits before asking for a commitment

Balance Sheet Method

Also known as the **T-account method,** the **balance sheet method** provides the customer a visual list of the pros and cons of buying now or waiting, buying the salesperson's product versus a competitor's, and buying versus not buying. Regardless of the comparison, the method starts with the salesperson's drawing a large "T" or two distinct columns on a piece of paper, laptop, or tablet. As the salesperson summarizes the benefits and reasons to buy, they write them in the left column. Then they do the same with the right column. It's best if the buyer is participating and contributing their own ideas for reasons to add to each column. In fact, the process may uncover new information they didn't previously mention.

As pictured in Figure 8-1, if the list of reasons to buy on the left is visibly larger than the list on the right, the balance sheet method can help get the buyer past their reluctance to make a decision. It may go without saying that the salesperson should not introduce the method unless they are confident that the number of reasons to purchase their product or service outweighs the number of reasons not to.

> **T-account method, balance sheet method**
> a visual list of the pros and cons of buying now or waiting, buying the salesperson's product versus a competitor's, and buying versus not buying

Figure 8-1 Example of Balance Sheet or T-account

Reasons to Buy	Reasons not to Buy
More output (feature) allows you to get more done (benefit) Lower operation cost 24-hour support (feature) means you'll have help no matter when you need it (benefit)	Need to learn to operate

Probing Method

Probe is another word for a question that helps uncover a buyer's situation, motivation, or reluctance. The **probing method** is the use of probes (questions) by the salesperson to understand why the buyer is reluctant to commit. The most appropriate use of the probing method is after an unsuccessful attempt to close.

The objective of the probing method is to understand why the customer won't commit. If the salesperson understands why the buyer is reluctant, the salesperson may be able to alter the offer or provide additional information that resolves the reluctance. So, one of the most important words to keep in mind for the probing method is *Why.*

> **probing method**
> the use of probes (questions) by the salesperson to understand why the buyer is reluctant to commit

Example of Probing Method

Salesperson: So, this seems like the best mattress for you. Would you like to buy it?

Buyer: No, I'm just looking. I'm not ready to buy yet.

Salesperson: Oh? Why's that?

Buyer: I didn't realize mattresses were so expensive.

Salesperson: We do accept all credit cards and offer our own financing. Does that help?

Buyer: No, not really.

Salesperson: Oh? Why's that?

Buyer: The interest rate on my credit card is really high, and I'm sure your finance charge is pretty high also.

Salesperson: Aside from financing the purchase, is there anything else that would prevent you from buying this mattress today?

Buyer: Well, I'm not sure how I would get it home.

Salesperson: Okay. So, if I can finance your purchase with a low-interest rate and arrange delivery, will you buy the mattress?

Buyer: Sure.

Alternative Choice

alternative choice method, legitimate choice method
the salesperson asks the buyer to choose from a set of options

With the **alternative choice method,** sometimes called the **legitimate choice method,** the salesperson asks the buyer to choose from a set of options. An example of an alternative choice close might sound like this: "Will our Series 70, Series 80, or Series 90 analyzer work best for you?"

Trial Offer

trial offer
the salesperson allows the buyer to try the product or service for a limited time, often at no charge

If the product or service is easy to implement and use and the benefits are immediately experienced, a trial offer can be effective. With a **trial offer** the salesperson allows the buyer to try the product or service for a limited time, often at no charge. The rationale for the trial offer is that once the buyer experiences the benefit of the product, they will commit to purchasing it. The trial offer does not work well for products that are complicated, difficult to learn to use, or that deliver longer-term benefits.

Other Methods

minor-point closes
seeking to convince the buyer to decide on a trivial element of whatever is being sold

continuous yes closes
the salesperson persistently asks they buyer questions they would logically answer with a Yes

assumptive closes
the salesperson assumes without asking that a buying decision has been made

standing-room-only closes
attempts to create some urgency in timing by describing the end of an opportunity or limited availability

There is an almost infinite number of closing techniques and variations. The right one to use depends on the product or service being sold, the salesperson's personality or selling style, their relationship with the buyer, and the buyer's situation and personality, just to name a few.

Minor-point closes seek to convince the buyer to decide on a trivial element of whatever is being sold. For example, the salesperson may ask a buyer to decide on their favorite color before asking them to commit to buying a car.

Continuous yes closes involve the salesperson persistently asking the buyer questions they would logically answer with a yes. The thinking is that the buyer becomes so accustomed to saying yes that they are more likely to say yes when the salesperson attempts to close.

Assumptive closes occur when the salesperson assumes without asking that a buying decision has been made. They may begin to complete the order details or place a contract in front of the buyer to sign. Alternatively, they might make a statement like, "I'll go ahead and tell my warehouse that you want your order delivered Friday."

Standing-room-only closes are attempts to create some urgency in timing by describing the end of an opportunity or limited availability. For example, a salesperson might say, "We only have three of these items left. If you don't act today, I doubt I'll have one for you tomorrow." Salespeople should never describe a limited opportunity or availability that is untrue.

Benefit-in-reserve closes involve the salesperson's discounting the offer or improving the terms when the buyer rejects the first attempt to close. Immediately offering a pricing discount or extending the warranty or payment terms would apply to benefit-in-reserve closes.

Emotional closes attempt to create fear or sympathy by describing a consequence of not buying for either the buyer or salesperson.

> **benefit-in-reserve closes**
> the salesperson's discounting the offer or improving the terms when the buyer rejects the first attempt to close

> **emotional closes**
> attempt to create fear or sympathy by describing a consequence of not buying for either the buyer or salesperson

If the Attempt to Close Is Accepted

Having a buyer accept the attempt to close can be very exciting. The sense of accomplishment, even victory, can be so great, that it can be easy to forget that there is still more to do in order to complete the sale. In this section, we will describe some of the activities and responsibilities that follow a successful close.

Now that the customer has agreed to buy, it is time to set expectations for when the product will be delivered, when service will start, and any steps the customer will need to complete to finalize the purchase and successfully start using the product or service.

A critical step toward having a satisfied customer is confirming the details of the product or service they are buying to make sure that it matches the salesperson's understanding. Confirming the details of a large sale of a complex product or service may even require additional meetings.

The buyer's signature represents a formal commitment, if not legal, commitment to make the purchase. Seen in those terms, it can appear to be a weighty task. However, collecting the buyer's signature on an order or contract should be approached as a natural and routine matter.

It is common for people to have doubts about their decisions, regardless of how rational or thoroughly informed they are. In their worst case, these doubts can become **buyer's remorse**, the buyer's sense of regret about a purchase, also known as **post-purchase dissonance**.

> **buyer's remorse, post-purchase dissonance**
> a buyer's sense of regret about a purchase

Successful salespeople compliment buyer's decisions and provide affirmation that they made the right choice, telling them how happy they will be with what they've chosen.

Everyone likes to be appreciated. Buyers are no different. Successful salespeople find ways to express their gratitude for each sale. Gratitude can be expressed to a buyer verbally, by email, or by text. In fact, expressing gratitude in these manners should be done often. Those forms of gratitude are easy and cost the salesperson nothing. But in an age where handwritten communication is increasingly rare, a handwritten card can be one of the most memorable forms of expressing gratitude.[9] Whatever method the salesperson uses to express thanks, doing so consistently is a cornerstone of goodwill and a positive relationship.

Review Any Open Tasks or Next Steps

Once the buyer has agreed to the salesperson's attempt to close, it is important for the salesperson to summarize any tasks that need to be completed to proceed. In doing so, the salesperson also needs to identify which tasks are their responsibility and which are the responsibility of the buyer. This is especially important if the commitment gained was for another meeting. In this case, it's critical to identify what both parties will do to prepare for the next meeting.

Shutterstock/fizkes

Plan for the Future

How the salesperson treats the customer during the first sale is the most significant determinant of future sales.[10] In many industries, salespeople succeed with repeat sales to existing customers more than on constantly finding new customers. The salesperson's professionalism, ability to solve a problem or provide a benefit for the buyer with their product or service, and ability to exceed expectations will all affect the buyer's likelihood of being a future customer. So, successful salespeople think of a successful close not as the end of the selling process, but as the beginning of a relationship.

If the Attempt to Close Is Rejected

When attempting to close, the salesperson might also encounter more objections. These objections are no different from those we described earlier, except that they occurred during the attempt to close. Often, it takes the attempt to close for a buyer to reveal an objection they haven't previously mentioned or that the salesperson didn't recognize for its importance to the buyer. In this case, the salesperson can use any of the objection responses. But it is usually best to start with probes to make sure they accurately understand the true nature of the objection.

When a buyer rejects a close, and their objection cannot be overcome, it can be useful for the salesperson to think of the buyer's reaction as "not now" instead of "no." Just because an opportunity does not exist now does not mean it never will. The ability and willingness of the salesperson to politely persist and remain available can often make a difference later when circumstances change for the buyer or their company.

But the fact of the matter is that salespeople do not always succeed in closing. In fact, in many fields, the fact of the matter is that even good salespeople will fail to close more often than they succeed, because of several factors beyond their control. Some salespeople and companies are so thorough in tracking their sales efforts that they know how many failed closes an average salesperson will experience for every successful close. Knowing this, the salesperson can think of every unsuccessful close as one step closer to a successful close.

The most important thing to do when an attempt to close is rejected is not to take it personally. A certain amount of rejection is just part of the job for anyone making a career in sales.

Applying this Chapter to Salesforce

While listening, acknowledging, accessing, responding, and confirming, one of the most valuable things a salesperson can do is keep a record of it all. Variations of similar objections will often be repeated multiple times throughout the course of multiple calls with the same buyer. A consistent response is critical to earning trust. Being able to quickly find and review notes from previous calls helps the salesperson identify objection trends and maintain consistency in their response.

Information is power when attempting to overcome objections. Salesforce and other CRM systems enable organizations to put massive amounts of information at their salespersons' fingertips. Filters make it easy for salespeople to find specific information to help overcome objections of need, product or service, source, or price. For example, a recent news article posted to the Salesforce home tab about economic pressure in a customer's industry might help the salesperson overcome a need objection. The salesperson might also filter their customer contacts to quickly locate a referral to overcome the objection of a prospective buyer.

When the buyer's attention turns to price, Salesforce can also serve as an easily assessable source for the salesperson to locate and quote pricing or pre-approved discounts. For cases when the buyer is seeking a deeper discount, Salesforce can also be configured so the salesperson can submit a request for additional discounts. Smaller discounts may be programmed to receive automatic approval, while discounts for larger amounts will automatically route for approval to the appropriate managers. In either case, the request, approval, or denial are recorded for future reference. The automation of this process saves time, avoids internal miscommunication, and improves accuracy between prices quoted and prices actually charged.

For many sellers, once the salesperson closes the business, processes need to start internally to complete the order, schedule the service, send an invoice, etc. Salesforce can automate the next step or sequence of steps that need to happen to turn a commitment to buy into the delivery of product or service.

Triggers can be set to automatically put each next step in motion. And data captured during the sale and each step and after it can flow to the next person who interacts with the customer. This information flow improves the quality and accuracy of the delivery or implementation of the product or service sold and spares the buyer having to repeat things with each new person they encounter from the salesperson's firm. In short, Salesforce can be used to manage and automate many of the factors that contribute to customer satisfaction and retention after the sale is closed.

Chapter Summary

- A buyer raising a concern or objection is a normal part of the selling process. The salesperson's answer to the buyer's concern is often called overcoming an objection.
- Objections may be raised at any time, but they are most common when the salesperson is first attempting to set an appointment or initiate a sales call, during the presentation as they try to understand the value of the product or service to them, and when the salesperson attempts to secure a commitment or close.
- A prospective buyer making an objection such as, *We don't need that* or *We already have a vendor for that* doesn't perceive a need and is expressing need objection.
- A product objection or service objection is one raised by a prospective buyer who perceives their need is not met by the features or characteristics of the product or service.
- A source objection or company objection occurs when the buyer is reluctant to proceed based on their perceived reputation of the salesperson's company, industry, location, or even the salesperson.
- Any way the buyer expresses an opinion that the price is too high for the product or service, that is a price objection.
- When a potential buyer responds that they don't have time to meet or they need time to think about their decision, these are both time objections.
- One of the most important principles in handling objections is the LAARC Method. LAARC stands for listen, acknowledge, assess, respond, and confirm.
- In responding to objections or answering concerns, the salesperson must listen carefully and adapt to find the most appropriate response method, often using a variety of methods during the course of the sales call.
- It is necessary for the salesperson to assess and confirm that the buyer's concerns have been answered or objection overcome before attempting to close or secure a commitment.
- Closing is a term used to describe securing a commitment from the buyer to take the next step in the buying process or make a purchase.
- There are a variety of closing methods and a salesperson must learn to read each buyer and situation to determine which method has the best chance of succeeding.

Key Terms

acknowledge method (p. 153)
alternative choice method, (p. 158)
addressing concerns (p. 146)
assumptive closes (p. 158)
balance sheet method (p. 157)
benefit-in-reserve closes (p. 159)
benefit summary method (p. 157)
buyer's remorse, post-purchase dissonance (p. 159)
buying signals (p. 150)
closing cues (p. 155)
coming-to-that method (p. 153)
company objection (p. 148)
compensation method (p. 152)
continuous yes closes (p. 158)
direct denial (p. 151)
direct request (p. 156)
emotional closes (p. 159)
excuses (p. 149)
feel-felt-found (p. 152)
forestalling (p. 151)
indirect denial (p. 151)
LAARC method (p. 150)

legitimate choice method (p. 158)
minor-point closes (p. 158)
need objection (p. 147)
objection (p. 146)
overcoming objections (p. 146)
postpone method (p. 153)
price objection (p. 149)
probing method (p. 157)
product objection (p. 148)
referral method (p. 152)
revisit/translation/boomerang method (p. 152)
service objection (p. 148)
source objection (p. 148)
standing-room-only closes (p. 158)
third-party reinforcement (p. 152)
time objection (p. 149)
trial closes (p. 156)
trial offer (p. 158)
T-account method (p. 157)

Application 8-1

Alec is an account executive for Apex Document Storage, a Houston-based firm that specializes in the secure storage of important documents for large companies and law firms. He learns that the city of Austin, Texas is conducting a request for proposals for exactly the services Apex provides.

Alec makes a cold call to the RFP coordinator, Jean Simmons. Upon hearing Alec's introduction and purpose for the call, Jean replies, "I'm really too busy to talk to you right now."

Alec politely convinces Jean that a few minutes on the phone with him will be worth her while. But upon hearing that Apex is based in Houston, Jean says, "I'm sorry Alec, but we're only considering Austin-based vendors for this project."

After listening carefully to Jean's objection about Apex' location, Alec says, "I understand why using an Austin-based vendor would be important. But our costs are so low in Houston that we will likely be far less expensive than any Austin-based vendor. Does that outweigh your concern about our location?"

Jean replies, "No. We are assuming we will get better service from a vendor with a local presence."

1. What kind of objection is Alec dealing with when Jean says, "I'm really too busy to talk to you right now?"
2. what kind of objection is Jean expressing when she says, "...we are only considering vendors located in Austin"?
3. In Alec's reaction to Jean's objection about Apex' location, what important step of the LAARC method does he skip?

Application 8-2

The following is an excerpt from a conversation between Ayalla, an office furniture salesperson and Mike, a project manager responsible for outfitting a new office for a fast-growing tech firm.

Ayalla: So, Mike, I've been thinking about our last conversation and your criteria to use material on the chairs that will be both durable and environmentally-friendly. And I think our new bamboo fabric meets both of those objectives very well. Now I know you're thinking, bamboo fabric would be scratchy and uncomfortable. But here, feel this sample, I think you'll agree that it feels like any other fabric.

Mike: That was my first thought. But it does feel like a lot of other fabrics I've considered.

Ayalla: Great! How many chairs would you like to order?

Mike: I'm not ready to place an order, Ayalla.

Ayalla: Oh? Why's that?

Mike: Well, I don't have any experience with bamboo fabric. I have my doubts about how durable it is.

Ayalla: That's understandable. Sheila Atkins at The Boring Company had the same concern when we furnished their offices three years ago. And she now orders only bamboo fabric.

Mike: I guess that's good to know. I'll need to think about it.

Ayalla: How about this for our next step? If I give you the contact information today for my other clients who have used bamboo fabric, would you have time to call or email them by the end of this week?

Mike: Yes

Ayalla: Great! I'll send you that information as soon as possible. Are you available Monday at 11 am to meet and go over the responses?

Mike: That sounds good.

1. In Ayalla's opening statement about bamboo fabric, what response method is she applying?

2. When Ayalla says, "Great! How many chairs would you like to order?", what closing method is she attempting?

3. What kind of response method is Ayalla using when she introduces the experience of Sheila Atkins?

CHAPTER

9

Sales Negotiation

Learning Objectives

- Introduce concepts underlying sales negotiation
- Learn the differences across distributive and integrative bargaining contexts
- Learn about different bargaining styles and how personality traits influence which style an individual is prone to use
- Develop self-awareness of your own style
- Discuss six building blocks for understanding sales negotiation
- Understand the four basic stages of a sales negotiation
- Discuss how the situational matrix can be used to improve the salesperson's effectiveness
- Refine skills for dealing with multiple issues by understanding parties may have similar, integrative, or divergent levels of values on each issue being negotiated

s G. Richard Shell, Wharton professor and author of a classic business text on negotiation titled *Bargaining for Advantage* asserts, "All of us negotiate many times a day."[1] Each and every time we seek to reach an agreement with others when our interests or priorities conflict—and we seek the resolution to such conflicts, we negotiate to reach a path forward that is deemed acceptable to everyone involved. Introducing the science, art, and practice of sales negotiation is the intent of this chapter.

Negotiation Fundamentals

Negotiation is a core competency required of any effective sales organization. Not surprisingly, instilling an understanding of negotiation, and refining your skills therein is of vital importance to effective sales organizations. Moreover, given that professional sales jobs represent one of the largest professions in the world with, for example, over 10% of the labor force in the United States, there is a great demand for training programs on sales negotiation.[2]

Negotiation Defined

negotiation
a process by which a joint decision is made by two or more parties

In a broad sense, **negotiation** can be defined as a process by which a joint decision is made by two or more parties.[3] For professional salespeople, the two parties of interests are, of course, the buying and selling organizations. Both buying and selling organizations pursue interests that often depend on some measure of collaboration from another organization.

While salespeople serve as agents who seek to implement the goals of the selling organization, buying organizations employ buying agents (or purchasers) to represent their interests. Outside of exclusivity arrangement (which are typically negotiated agreements as well), it is very rare that two such organizations have interests that are perfectly compatible.

sales negotiation
the process by which a joint decision is made between a seller and one or more of its buyers

At the most rudimentary level, a buyer seeks to buy the seller's wares at the lowest possible price, whereas the seller often seeks the highest possible price. This example points to an inevitable conflict that emerges with economic exchanges between organizations—and it highlights why negotiation is often considered as a process whose purpose is simply stated as conflict resolution. While some organizations negotiate with upstream, downstream, or other organizations in the conduct of their business, the focus here is on the role of the professional salesperson and their interactions with buyers. As such, **sales negotiation** refers to the process by which a joint decision is made between a seller and one or more of its buyers.

Basic Approaches to a Sales Negotiation

Not all negotiations between buyers and sellers are of the same type—and it's worth considering two general methods for conducting a sales negotiation, each of which requires a different approach by the salesperson to the negotiation task. The two basic approaches for sales negotiation are distributive and integrative, as they reflect the nature through which the resources involved in the negotiation are allocated across the parties involved.

Characteristics of Different Types of Negotiation Approaches

Business-to-business (B2B) sales negotiation occurs in various, and often complex, sales contexts—and may involve large- or small-scale exchanges. To begin thinking about the issues underlying a sales negotiation, consider first a B2C sales context, such as a consumer purchasing a car. Of course, price represents one issue that the two parties must negotiate, but other issues arise in this simple sales situation. For example, buyer and seller priorities may differ on the car's color, stereo system, or loan financing terms. Each issue represents a potential source of conflict in priorities and importance and represents key components of a negotiated agreement or deal. While identifying issues of potential conflict is an important element of the pre-call sales plan, not all sales processes are as simple as this example. In particular, they may vary on important characteristics such as the number of issues comprising a negotiated deal or the sales process best suited to reach such an agreement.

Other factors, such as the economic scale and desired post-negotiation relationship, may represent key characteristics that influence the best negotiation approach, or sales process the salesperson might employ. For example, consider the negotiation between Procter & Gamble (P&G) with Kellogg associated with P&G's selloff of the Pringles potato chip brand for $2.7 billion in 2012.[4] The value exchanged in the car purchase discussed earlier is likely less than $50,000—the ultimate price reached in the deal for the car purchase. Contrast the economic scale confronting the P&G negotiation team for the Pringles acquisition to that of the simple B2C car purchase. Not surprisingly, the sales process, including the number of people involved and their levels of functional expertise, when selling a major consumer brand is not identical to that which occurs during the sales process associated with selling cars to consumers. Yet, thinking about these two very different contexts based on the salesperson's need to identify the relevant negotiation issues associated with the exchange is a helpful sales planning exercise.

Another consideration, the desired relationship following the sales negotiation, warrants consideration. For many car purchases, the buyer and seller may be focused more on that single transaction than upon any long-term relationships. B2C sales negotiation objectives can focus more on building long-term relationships—and is common in B2B markets. While P&G may be less concerned about their long-term relationship with Kellogg, let's consider the more typical role for the P&G sales organization in managing relationships with key accounts. In particular, consider that the P&G sales team responsible for selling to its largest customer account, Walmart, generates over $10 billion in annual business.[5] Of note, then, even when compared on an economic scale to a large-scale brand acquisition or selloff, the economics for maintaining long-term business relationships may far exceed those of such acquisitions. In this example, annual revenues from the Walmart account are over three times larger than the single transaction associated with selling a large consumer brand. These facts highlight the importance of a professional salesperson as the account manager for such B2B relationships with key customers.

Importantly, of note in comparing the P&G selloff of the Pringles brand to that of its Walmart strategic account team, the nature of the post-negotiation relationship desired by P&G across the two different buyers is quite divergent. Specifically, while Kellogg may never buy another brand from P&G, maintaining a productive long-term relationship with Walmart is of vital strategic importance to P&G. That is, P&G has a strong desire to maintain a positive relationship with Walmart (a long-term, more relationship-forging focus), but it may have been less concerned about the post-transaction exchange with Kellogg (a short-term, more transaction-based focus). This contrast in B2B situations for the same sales organization (P&G) foreshadows a discussion of the two general types of negotiation contexts that arise in sales practice.

Using a Distributive Negotiation Approach to Resolve a Single Issue Conflict

The number of issues (or interests) under consideration represents a key defining characteristic of a negotiation. A **distributive sales negotiation approach** is characterized by a focus on a single-issue, such as reaching an agreement on

distributive sales negotiation approach
a focus on a single-issue, such as reaching agreement on the selling price of the product

Shutterstock/fizkes

zero-sum game, win-lose negotiations
the reality of gains on one side equating to losses on the other

hard-bargaining
the salesperson yields only in ways considered to improve the seller's interest

integrative sales negotiation approach
a focus on resolving more than one issue of which the buyer and seller may have different priorities

the selling price of the product. While the seller seeks to optimize the price attained for the product being sold, the buyer seeks to minimize the price. In this way, any resulting agreement represents a trade-off in which the seller's gain equates the buyer's loss, or vice versa. Both sides seek to maximize their share of the resources obtained through the agreement—and, while such a negotiation may characterize their first interaction with one another, it is often approached as if it will be their last.

A common analogy to such a context is one focused on the notion of slicing a pie into two parts—and the idea that the objective in such a context is to maximize the resulting share of the pie through the negotiated agreement. Accordingly, this type of bargaining is often called a *fixed-pie* negotiation. Given the reality of gains on one side equating to losses on the other, this type of negotiation is also referred to as a **zero-sum game** or **win-lose negotiations**. A zero-sum game is also called a strictly competitive game. The conventional negotiation mode employed in a distributive context relies more upon competitive bargaining style and as the context becomes more complex, strategies associated with optimizing *pie-sharing* outcomes evolve.[6]

Considering the short-term focus of distributive sales negotiation combined with little, if any, concern for continuing a relationship beyond the achievement of a negotiated agreement, the conventional approach in a distributive sales negotiation is to bargain very competitively. The salesperson seeks to maximize the seller's profits (or benefits) attainable from the negotiated agreement. This involves using a **hard-bargaining** stance in which the salesperson yields only in ways considered to improve the seller's interests.

Using an Integrative Negotiation Approach for Resolving Multiple-Issue Conflicts

It's worth noting that some negotiations are unavoidably distributive—and even when they involve multiple issues, some of the individual issues may be distributive. In professional selling, while distributive negotiation contexts are common to transactional selling, they are less common in contemporary sales where collaboration is often the common goal for the buyer and seller. Thus, since the sales profession was once far more transactional, distributive bargaining was once the norm. However, in the era of relational selling, sellers, and thus their salespeople, are often very concerned about maintaining relationships with customers—and the long-term potential afforded through effective customer relationship management.

When such collaborative interests are of focal concern, a key characteristic of an effective sales negotiation involves the salesperson's efforts to introduce considerations that get beyond the exchange price. For example, instead of a focus only developing agreement on a selling price, the negotiation may include resolving logistical concerns, such as how quickly the seller can deliver the product from its plant to the buyer's warehouse. The resulting process is referred to as an **integrative sales negotiation approach**, which is characterized by a focus on resolving more than one issue of which the buyer and seller may have different priorities.

Not surprisingly, many sales organizations train salespeople on how to broaden a negotiation with a buyer from a focus on a single issue, like price, to the consideration other aspects of the exchange, like quality differences in alternative solutions. By expanding the negotiation to consider more than one issue, the salesperson can alter the negotiation in ways that present outcomes that may be mutually beneficial to both the selling and the buying organizations. Given the potential for mutually beneficial gains, this type of negotiation is also referred to as or a win-win negotiation. The conventional negotiation approach in a distributive context is to be more collaborative in dealing with the negotiation partner. The general outlook in an integrative negotiation is that by working together, negotiating partners can find synergies that will help them achieve outcomes beyond that which would be possible if they worked alone. Accordingly, this type of bargaining is often called *expanding the pie*, in reference to expanding the resource outcomes possible through the negotiation process. As the context becomes more complex, strategies associated with optimizing *pie-expansion* outcomes evolve.[7]

Even when dealing with multiple issues, some of those issues (like price) may follow a process common to distributive negotiation—wherein the settlement of such issues imposes a zero-sum distribution of resources.

Cooperative Bargaining Styles in Integrative Negotiations

An integrative sales negotiation takes a long-term view. It involves sincere concern for continuing a relationship beyond the reaching a negotiated agreement. The salesperson seeks to maximize the both seller's and the buyer's profits (or benefits) attainable from the negotiated agreement. This involves using a **soft-bargaining** stance in which the salesperson yields in ways to improve mutually beneficial outcomes.

soft-bargaining
stance in which the salesperson yields in ways to improve mutually beneficial outcomes

Building Blocks for Effective Sales Negotiation

As summarized in Figure 9-1, effective sales negotiation benefits from an understanding of six building block domains: bargaining styles, personality factors, goals and expectations, interests and priorities, inter-organizational and personal goals, leverage, and relationship norms.[8]

Figure 9-1 The Building Block for Effective Sales Negotiation

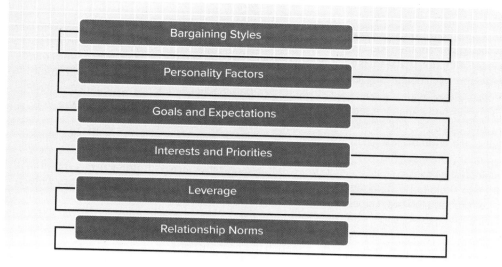

- Bargaining Styles
- Personality Factors
- Goals and Expectations
- Interests and Priorities
- Leverage
- Relationship Norms

The first two of these domains (bargaining styles and personality factors) are aided by the negotiator's development of self-awareness and the ability to understand and apply the concepts to their negotiating partners. The first can use self-assessments to help the negotiator develop a better understanding of their bargaining styles and how they can adapt it to negotiations with other bargaining styles. The second centers on how personality factors may influence the negotiator's tendencies in negotiations, such as preferences to use different bargaining styles.

Self-awareness of your tendencies may be best assessed prior to engaging in sales negotiation training—and some instructors may have done this before assigning this chapter. Role plays and practicing negotiating is a great way to learn how to assess the bargaining styles and personality traits of others while adapting your style to improve the outcomes from your sales negotiations. Before turning to the other foundations, we'll focus on these first two domains.

Bargaining Styles

Individuals have tendencies that help guide the way in which they approach a negotiation with someone else. Hopefully, *What's Your Bargaining Style?* caused you to think about different tendencies and to start developing an awareness of your own.

What's Your Bargaining Style?

Imagine that you have been searching for a new sales job for the past few months. You've had a few leads for opportunities that seem interesting, but you finally got a call from a large consumer packaged goods company, which is not only headquartered in a desirable city, but also has jobs available in several geographies where you would love to work. In fact, because it offers so much to fit your career interests, the company has become your most desired employer—and they too have noticed you. After meeting them at a local career fair, where you felt you had a great conversation and were able to pass along your resume, you got a call inviting you to come in for an interview.

Of course, you accepted their invitation, and today is your big day to visit for your initial interviews. Oddly, after arriving at the designated location, you were directed not to talk with anyone, but to enter a room with a dozen chairs forming six pairs of seats facing one another. You are instructed to pick any available seat. Although you want the job and ensured that you arrived about 10 minutes early for your interview meeting, you notice a few other strangers already sitting in the chairs. Everyone had chosen a seat facing the entrance that you came through—and no two people have chosen chairs facing one another. You follow the norm and don't sit across from anyone else.

However, after another ten minutes, all twelve seats are filled with strangers to you, who also seem to be strangers to one another—and someone just grabbed the seat across from you. Everyone looks somewhat bewildered, and a little anxious, but shortly thereafter, a company representative walks in, and with a huge, warming smile, stands behind a podium at the front of the room, thanks everyone for showing up on time, welcomes all to their headquarters, and states, unequivocally, while there are twelve of you, I can assure you that we have more than twelve openings. We're so delighted you chose to come—and consider sitting with us this morning. You could cut the excitement in the room with a knife. It seems everyone could be your new best friend at work, but then a strange thing happens as the representative discusses a "fun" exercise.

The company representative explains, "Now that all twelve of our seats are filled and everyone has someone sitting opposite you, we'd like to start the day with a fun exercise. The person sitting across from you is your new partner for this exercise. You could think about your partner as your new buyer. However, after this exercise, you may never see your new partner again. Please don't ask any questions of me, but work with your partner on this potentially rewarding task. Is everyone ready? Okay, then, starting now, the company will give an Amazon gift card worth $500 to the first two people who remain sitting after you have persuaded your partner to run to the front of the room and gently tag me on the arm."

Before reading further, close your eyes and think about how you'd try to negotiate a solution with your new partner, that person sitting across from you who you may never see again after this exercise. You may want to write your thoughts on what you would do on a piece of paper for reference later. The approach you choose will likely approximate one of the five generic bargaining styles discussed in the next section.

Thomas-Kilmann Instrument (TKI)   Research on leadership in the 1960s established two key dimensions upon which an individual leadership style could be described. Those two dimensions were a "concern for production" and "concern for people."[9] These dimensions generally captured how managers viewed the trade-offs between caring for their employees and getting the job done. Years later, those two dimensions were adopted to describe the two driving factors associated with how different people approach negotiation tasks. In the negotiation framework, as part of his doctoral dissertation, Ken Thomas began to describe the dimensions underlying a negotiator's approach, one's "concern for production" became the "assertiveness" dimension, and one's "concern for people" became the "cooperativeness" dimension.[10] In conjunction, one of his colleagues, Ralph Kilmann, refined his interest in developing self-report measures to capture attitudinal dispositions. Their work led to the development of an instrument that captured five bargaining styles based on the interaction of those two dimensions—and a widely used assessment tool referred to as the Thomas-Kilmann Conflict Mode Instrument (TKI). The TKI projects five generic bargaining styles, which are referred to as avoiding, compromising, accommodating, competing, and collaborating.[11]

Competing, Collaborating, Compromising, Accommodating, and Avoiding   While salespeople may sometimes represent their interests over the sales organizations' interests (a central tenant of agency theory when applied to the sales context), for this chapter, we'll assume the salesperson's interests in the negotiation align with the seller's interests. That is, the agent (salesperson) dutifully represents the principle's (sales organization's interests).

From the professional sales standpoint, a salesperson's **assertiveness** refers to the extent to which the salesperson seeks to satisfy the sales organization's interests. A salesperson's **cooperativeness** refers to the extent to which the salesperson seeks to satisfy the buyer's interests.

As shown in Figure 9-2, the five generic bargaining styles can be constructed upon the salesperson's assertiveness in competing to secure the seller's interests juxtaposed against the competing force of cooperativeness toward accommodating the buyer's interests.

assertiveness
the extent to which the salesperson seeks to satisfy the sales organization's interests

cooperativeness
the extent to which the salesperson seeks to satisfy the buyer's interests

Figure 9-2 The Five Generic Bargaining Styles

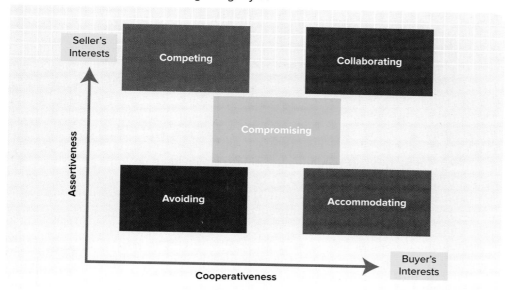

avoiding
a negotiator who decides to be neither cooperative nor assertive

compromising
a bargaining style with a balanced focus on cooperative and assertiveness without being too extreme (high or low) on either dimension

accommodating
a bargaining style involving a full concession to cooperate with the buyer's interests

competing
a bargaining style in which a salesperson is very assertive toward securing the seller's interests

collaborating
a bargaining style entailing a strong commitment to both the seller's and the buyer's interest

At this point, before elaborating on the five generic styles, it's worth reflecting on your thoughts about how you would handle *What's Your Bargaining Style?* Reflection on how you would approach the situation will help you build some self-awareness of your own tendencies.

One possible response to the representative's call to action in *What's Your Bargaining Style?* would be to remain seated and do nothing. You might suspect the company is trying to trick you into giving up your seat and may not want to ask the person facing you to give up his, as you sense that he's concerned about looking foolish going to the front of the room. This bargaining style is called **avoiding**, and it is characterized by a negotiator who decides to be neither cooperative nor assertive. An avoiding strategy is a good strategy when you are happy with maintaining the status quo, but, otherwise, it may not be the best approach.

Another response is to offer to split the value of the gift card with the person sitting across from you. To you, this solution appears simple, quick, and fair. This style is called **compromising**, and it represents a balanced focus on cooperative and assertiveness without being too extreme (high or low) on either dimension. However, you start to wonder, which of the two of you will run to the front of the room? There is no equitable way for either of you to run to the front as someone must concede, and thus you need an additional strategy to resolve the dilemma.

A third response, then, is to follow your offer to compromise with a sprint to the front of the room to tag the representative. This style is called **accommodating**, and it represents a full concession to cooperate with the buyer's interests. However, given that others may have implemented this strategy immediately, without wasting time with the compromising offer, the two chances at earning a gift card may have already been claimed by the lucky partners who just happened to have been sitting in the room across from those accommodators. Those two now have $500 Amazon gift cards, even though the accommodators have nothing. But, at this point, those lucky winners face a problem too. Will they keep all the money to themselves, or not?

A fourth response to the task is to think about how you can keep the full value of the gift card. This bargaining style is called **competing**, which occurs when a salesperson is very assertive toward securing the seller's interests. Competing styles may challenge a salesperson's ethical values as one way to achieve the outcome is to make a promise to split the money evenly, and then later renege. Another unethical approach might be to lie and tell your partner that you are physically disabled—and you can't run, begging your partner to do so, while having no intention of honoring any agreements required to get your partner in the running mode. Competitive strategies, on the other hand, can be fully ethical, as discussed later in this chapter, but, for now, the task fits well as an introduction to how ethics have a key role in professional selling, and are thus discussed in more detail in a later chapter.

The final approach is called **collaborating**, and it entails a strong commitment to both the seller's and the buyer's interest. In this task, the collaborator needs to be clever—and consider that both parties have the potential of getting the two gift cards. The solution requires one to run quickly to tag the instructor while the other sits followed by an exchange of roles between the partners. If executed quickly after the game begins, the collaborating partners have a chance of both getting the full $500 gift card for themselves through working together. As business problems are often more complex, such collaborating strategies often require salespeople to work diligently and, often, analytically when preparing for their sales calls. Yet, while collaborating strategies are often the most time-intensive, they can be the most rewarding to both buyers and sellers.

While working through this exercise may have provided a quick self-assessment of your tendencies to use these different bargaining styles, for a more detailed understanding of individual tendencies, your instructor might direct you to an administration of either the TKI assessment discussed earlier, or Shell's adaptation of the TKI for a negotiation context that is provided as an appendix in his book, *Bargaining for Advantage.*[12][13]

Personality Factors

The second domain of importance to negotiation involves personality factors, and how they might influence your approach to sales negotiation. Personality can help explain individual differences in thinking, feeling, and behaving. While there is a rich literature on personality, the Big Five Inventory (BFI) provides a framework that centers on five traits comprising the structure of an individual's personality: extraversion, agreeableness, conscientiousness, neuroticism, and open-mindedness.[14]

Shutterstock/ALPA PROD

Extraversion is characterized by a focus on the external world. Extraverts (individuals who score high on extraversion) exhibit high energy and enjoy interacting with people. They like to talk and assert themselves during social interactions. On the other hand, introverts (those who score low on extraversion) are less likely to talk during social interactions and tend to be quieter, more deliberate, and less involved in the social world. They have a more inward focus and may be less influenced by the external world. Extraverts tend to talk too much during sales negotiations and may need to practice actively listening. On the other hand, introverts are often good listeners, but they may need to talk more during sales negotiations. Generally, an individual's personality combines elements of extraversion and introversion—and some recent research suggests there may be an ambivert advantage afforded to salespeople who can balance their introversion with extraversion.[15]

extraversion
a focus on the external world

Agreeableness reflects the extent to which an individual is concerned with social harmony. Agreeable individuals like to get along with others. Agreeable people are often very trusting and trustworthy—and they are willing to compromise on their interests. They often exhibit an optimistic outlook. On the other hand, disagreeable individuals place self-interests above social harmony—and they are generally unconcerned with their negotiating partner's interests.

agreeableness
the extent to which an individual is concerned with social harmony

Conscientiousness refers to an individual's tendency to strive for achievement against goals and expectations. Conscientious people are often high in self-discipline and very capable of regulating their impulses. They prefer planned activities over spontaneous activities. Age may provide a general indicator of one's conscientiousness as individuals tend to become more conscientious as they grow older. In sales negotiations, your tendencies represent how much you may need to work to incorporate sales planning into your work habits, and your buyer's tendencies may influence their preferences with how they prefer to operate in their decision-making responsibilities.

conscientiousness
an individual's tendency to strive for achievement against goals and expectations

Neuroticism, or **negative emotionality**, refers to the tendency to experience negative emotions, such as anger, anxiety, or depression[16]. Those exhibiting high neuroticism are often emotionally reactive and vulnerable to stress, and they may seem somewhat flippant in their expressions of emotion. In ordinary situations, high neuroticism manifests as threatening. Dealing with minor frustrations may seem more challenging. On the other hand, individuals low in neuroticism are less emotionally reactive, tend to be calm, and stable, although they do not necessarily experience excessively high positive emotions. As such, it may help to assess whether your emotions are excessively positive, or negative, while seeking to understand those of your negotiating partner.

neuroticism, negative emotionality
the tendency to experience negative emotions, such as anger, anxiety, or depression

Openness, or **open-mindedness**, refers to individuals who are open to new experiences and emotions. They are often intellectually curious and willing to try new things. This trait helps with creative thinking, which can tremendously aid in problem-solving abilities—which is an important element in developing and proposing integrative solutions to buyers. It's also wise to understand how open-minded your buyers may be toward the alternative solutions you may propose—and, at times, vital to first increase their open-mindedness toward solutions that may seem new to them by framing the solution effectively before introducing it during the sales negotiation.

openness / open-mindedness
individuals who are open to new experiences and emotions

Goals and Expectations

The third domain of importance to negotiation involves an understanding of setting goals and expectations for a sales negotiation while seeking to understand those held by the buyer. In fact, **good faith** in the negotiation process refers the idea that parties have some capacity and will to compromise in ways that accommodate the other party's interests. Bad faith is the opposite and occurs when a party enters a negotiation with no intent to compromise on their interests in any way.

Among the first lessons of many sales organizations' onboarding processes, conveying the mantra of "seek first to understand" proves useful when meeting with buyers. Beyond seeking to understand their bargaining styles and personalities, you as the salesperson need to understand what goals and expectations they have for the person-to-person and business-to-business relationship.

In many relational contexts, the objective of the relationship will be for the salesperson to forge better business relationships with the buyer—and his or her organization. In B2B contexts, both the salesperson and the purchasing agent perform their duties on behalf of their organizations. While the individual actors may have goals related to their personal relationships, and salespeople are known for developing strong personal bonds with purchasing agents, the buying and selling organizations often have long-standing business relationships as well.

The focus of such B2B negotiations centers on how well the solutions proposed by the salesperson and implemented by the buyer ultimate compare to the goals and expectations the two organizations had when they negotiated an agreement. Thus, an important step in preparing for an interaction with the buyers, and in developing a sales proposal, is to fully understand what your organization seeks to accomplish. At the same time, in preparation and interaction with the buyers, a key element of the relationship hinges on how well you understand the buying organization's goals and expectations.

If the intent is to negotiate collaboratively, understanding both the selling and the buying organization's interests is paramount. Some of that understanding may be based on the history of the business relationship and interactions which may be included in the selling firm's contact management system. The inter-organizational relationship may both precede your involvement as the agent for the sales organization and continue beyond your relationships with purchasing agents whenever responsibilities or assignments change.

When setting your goals and expectations, think carefully about what you want to achieve through the negotiated agreement. Set optimistic, but justified, goals, noting that much research shows that optimistic goals are effective only if they are feasible. Be as specific in identifying the different aspects, or issues, of the agreement that you hope to achieve. It may help you to commit to your goals by writing them down but be aware to avoid an "escalation of commitment," which often leads to spending too much time and money to get what you want.

As Shell notes, to be an effective negotiator, you must commit yourself to achieve specific, justifiable goals[17]. You need to transform your targets into genuine expectations for your negotiation. The key is to have high but attainable expectations—and the more specific you can be about your interests and priorities, the better you can remain focused and collaborate, when appropriate, on those outcomes during the negotiation.

Interests and Priorities

Once you have your higher-level goals and expectations refined, you need to add layers of specificity by identifying the specific negotiable issues associated with those goals—and develop a prioritization scheme to help guide

your sales negotiations. That is, you want to enter the negotiation with a set of issues about which you have determined the relative importance across those issues.

One of the first steps in negotiating involves understanding your own, or the sales organization's interests and priorities, while also identifying those of your negotiating partner, or the buying organization. In B2B selling contexts, interests may exist at either the agent (salesperson or purchasing agent) or the organizational level (selling or buying organizations).

The authors of the most-cited and best-selling book on negotiation, *Getting to Yes*, note the importance of focusing not on the person, but on the problem—and not on their positions, but on their interests. Sales negotiations can become intense, and the resulting intensity can inject more emotions into the negotiation than is ideal for achieving rational outcomes. By focusing on the problem instead of the person, a sales negotiator can properly channel the emotional aspects toward a more constructive path, and toward more rational outcomes.

Interests often yield the key issues of concern to a negotiated agreement. For example, pricing is a common concern in which the seller seeks the highest possible price, while the buyer seeks the lowest price. Similarly, delivery time required may create an issue in which the buyer seeks the fastest possible delivery while the seller prefers more time to complete the delivery of exchanged goods. Try to separate the "what" from the "why" of the different sides.

Positions can be considered the "what." They are summary statements that approximate what a negotiator seeks, and they may not provide much insight into underlying motivations, incentives, or priorities.

Interests, on the other hand, represent the "why." They represent the negotiator's underlying reasons, motivations, or priorities. Understanding the interests from both the selling and buying organization—and focusing your efforts therein—can be vital to the ultimate development of mutually beneficial sales proposals.

Leverage

Leverage, in a negotiation context, represents the "situational advantage" that different parties have toward securing their side's interests. Leverage represents the power not just to reach an agreement, but to obtain an agreement on your terms. Three types of leverage are worth noting: positive leverage, negative leverage, and normative leverage.

Positive leverage refers to having something of value that the other side wants. This is the most common type of leverage. For example, the seller manufactures high-quality products (e.g., Coca-Cola products) that the buyer wants to purchase and resale), while the buyer has the operational capacity to sell the manufacturer's products to its customers (e.g., Walmart retail stores.)

Negative leverage exists when one side has the power to take something away from the other side that they already possess. Negative leverage is often used in a threat-based application—and can be very effective in motivating. **Prospect theory** argues that we often see losses as much more significant than we view gains of equal value.[18] **Framing** refers to the way a proposal is presented, relative to other issues or factors. Prospect theory has implications for the way a sales proposal is best framed can impact a buyer's response to your proposal.

Relationship Norms

As humans, we share a psychological drive to maintain consistency and fairness in our words and deeds. Therefore, we tend to negotiate based on authoritative norms and standards. For example, the single most common tactic for closing a negotiation is to split the difference. Keep in mind, your role as a salesperson is to first, and foremost, be an advocate for the selling firm's interests—and you should work to achieve the

positions
summary statements that approximate what a negotiator seeks

interests
the negotiator's underlying reasons, motivations, or priorities

leverage
the "situational advantage" that different parties have toward securing their side's interests

positive leverage
having something of value that the other side wants

negative leverage
when one side has the power to take something away from the other side that they already possess

prospect theory
seeing losses as much more significant than we view gains of equal value

framing
the way a proposal is presented, relative to other issues or factors

goals and expectations inherent to those interests. Fortunately, many sales firms have goals that include collaborating with their buyers—and thus expect you will develop proposals that are mutually beneficial to the buying and selling firms.

Fairness   As individuals, we often perceive and strive for outcomes that are considered fair to ourselves and others affected by our actions. In buyer-seller exchanges, equity theory explains how fairness is often assessed. **Equity theory** argues that to maintain equity, people seek to balance the outcomes they receive from a negotiation using a ratio of their inputs to outcomes versus their partner's ratio of inputs to outcomes.[19] That is, equity exists when outcomes from a negotiated agreement are proportional to the inputs from the parties involved. Thus, to achieve fairness, sales negotiators strive to achieve equity in their negotiated agreements.

Reciprocity   The **norm of reciprocity** refers to the tendency to give back to those who have given to us. That is, we typically feel that we owe something to another person or organization, who has given something to us in the past. This norm of reciprocity can be used to create an expectation that a person will respond favorably to another by returning benefits for benefits. Importantly, since issues and priorities differ, some benefits we seek may not be that important to our buyers, and vice versa. As such, there may be issues upon which we are willing to concede to the buyer's interests that may result in the buyer's giving back on other issues.

While the norm of reciprocity provides the logic and drives the underlying process of this approach, differences in priorities between the buyer and the seller can present opportunities for both parties to concede on issues of lesser importance to them, while receiving concessions on issues that are of more importance. An important negotiation tactic called **logrolling** involves conceding on an issue that is valued lower to you while bundling it with an issue that is of higher value to you.

Trust   Building trust with buyers may take time—and it often results from proposing solutions that are credible and benevolent toward the buyer's interests.[20] Trust has a basis in cognition and emotion. **Cognition-based trust** is a rational evaluation or calculation as to whether we have enough knowledge to trust. Effective salespeople can build cognitive-based trust and strengthen business relationships by sharing knowledge that is beneficial to the buyer.[21] In buyer-seller relationships, cognitive-based trust may work on more of an inter-organizational level, with respect to considering inputs (e.g., relationship investments) and outcomes associated with achieving organizational interests. **Affective-based trust** stems from the emotional bonds between individuals—and thus may work on a more interpersonal level in buyer-seller relationships[22]. Showing compassion, demonstrating kindness, and behaving in a likeable way when interacting with buyers are examples of how salespeople build affective-based trust.

The Sales Negotiation Process

The **negotiation process** represents the steps that are followed from conception to completion of a negotiated agreement. The suggested sequence of steps includes the following: planning, exchanging information, opening bids and making concessions, and closing to gain commitment. Figure 9-3 previews the four major stages of the negotiation process.

Sales Planning

An effective sales negotiation requires good planning and preparation before beginning the sales interaction with a buyer. Salespeople can plan for distributive negotiations by centering their knowledge on the sales organization's product

---

equity theory
to maintain equity, people seek to balance the outcomes they receive from a negotiation using a ratio of their inputs to outcomes versus their partner's ratio of inputs to outcomes

norm of reciprocity
the tendency to give back to those who have given to us.

logrolling
conceding on an issue that is valued lower to you, while bundling it with an issue that is of higher value to you

cognition-based trust
a rational evaluation or calculation as to whether we have enough knowledge to trust

affective-based trust
trust stemming from the emotional bonds between individuals

negotiation process
The steps that are followed from conception to completion of a negotiated agreement

Figure 9-3 The Sales Negotiation Process

Figure 9-4 Sales Negotiation Situational Matrix

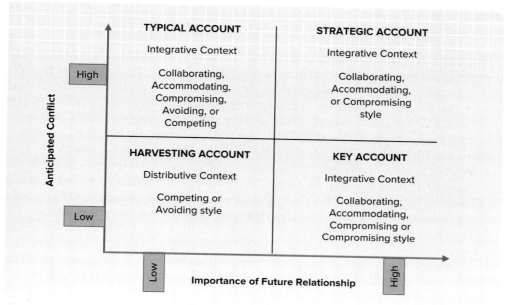

and interests and may spend less time considering the buyer's interests; as such, a negotiation may not involve developing solutions through a collaborative process centered on mutually beneficial gains. However, proposing integrative solutions requires the salesperson to understand their buyer's interests, and planning for an integrative sales negotiation requires the salesperson's understanding of their customer's customers. Such planning, referred to here as **customer-centric** sales planning refers to the extent to which the salesperson anticipates, collects, and evaluates information relevant to understanding their buyer's interests[23]. By understanding both the seller's and the buyer's interests, the salesperson is much more capable of understanding how different sales proposals affect the prospective outcomes for buyers and sellers. Such an understanding becomes vital to developing equitable solutions that ensure proportional returns to buyers and sellers based on their inputs, or required investments, toward accepting a negotiated agreement.

Situational Matrix Of course, not all sales negotiations involve identical situations. And, while there are countless variations, an understanding of two major factors defining the negotiation may help salespeople plan for different negotiation strategies. Those two factors are the perceived conflict over the negotiated issues and the perceived importance of future relationships with that buyer.

Figure 9-4, the sales negotiation situational matrix, provides general guidance for salespeople confronting divergent situations driven by these two considerations—and should help with planning for which types of bargaining styles might work best across different types of accounts.

customer-centric
the extent to which the salesperson anticipates, collects, and evaluates information relevant to understanding their buyer's interests

While there is no universal solution to what type of style works best, considering the alternative before a sales negotiation can help managers to assign salespeople to accounts in addition to helping salespeople plan for interactions with their assigned accounts.

BATNA   When planning for any negotiation, one of the key considerations is the negotiator's assessment of the **best alternative to a negotiated agreement (BATNA)**. The BATNA is the lowest acceptable value to an individual for a negotiated agreement. The best alternative to a negotiated agreement may be maintaining the status quo, selling a solution or product to another buyer, or recognizing that the timing for a negotiated agreement may be better on a future date. The salesperson should never sell below the BATNA as it represents the line below which walking away from a negotiated agreement is the best option for the sales organization.

Zone of Potential Agreement (ZOPA)   As discussed earlier, when parties enter a negotiation, they should be entering in good faith—that is, both the seller and the buyer should be willing to compromise in some way on whatever position exists absent any negotiation. Said another way, both parties enter with an intent to change the status quo. For most established buyer-seller relationships, good faith is implied—and it's common for buyers and sellers to work toward mutually beneficial outcomes. However, complete knowledge of the other party's interests is rarely known.

In a negotiation, both sides have reservation points. A **reservation point** is the minimum needed for a deal to be deemed acceptable, and it is related to, but may not be exactly equivalent to, the BATNA. A **zone of potential agreement (ZOPA)** would include the outcomes or terms both party's reservation points have in common.

The easiest way to understand how the ZOPA and the reservation point operate, consider Figure 9-5, which provides a graphic of a new car purchase and would represent a single issue (price) negotiation between a buyer and a seller. Assume a buyer seeks to purchase a new car and has a target price of $39,500 (which is based on insight discovered through a website providing the dealer's invoice price paid for the car). The buyer is still willing to pay more for the car than their target price as the best deal found at another dealership is $40,500, a price

BATNA
the lowest acceptable value to an individual for a negotiated agreement

reservation point
the minimum needed for a deal to be deemed acceptable

zone of potential agreement (ZOPA)
the outcomes or terms both party's reservation points have in common

Figure 9-5 Zone of Potential Agreement for New Car Purchase

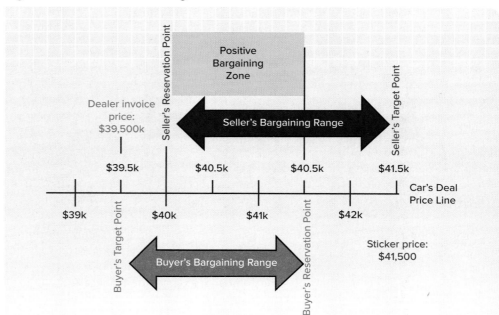

that, in the case, will represent both the buyer's reservation price and her BATNA. On the other side of the bargaining table, the dealer's target price for the car is $41,500, which is the car's sticker price. However, this dealer is willing to settle for a profit of $500, which represents a seller's reservation price of $40,000. As shown in the figure, this creates a positive zone of agreement (between the reservation points), and thus, a deal should be reached.

The bargaining surplus is calculated as the difference between the BATNA and the settlement, or deal price, reached through the negotiated agreement. Using the positive zone of agreement in Figure 9-5, if a settlement deal was research at $41,200, the buyer's surplus is the difference between the buyer's BATNA ($40,500) and the deal price, which equates to a $700 bargaining surplus for the buyer. At that same sales price, the seller's bargaining surplus would be the difference between the seller's BATNA ($40,000) and the deal price, which equates to $1,200. Yet, both sides should be somewhat satisfied with the deal as they achieved a surplus over their respective BATNA prices.

In contrast, Figure 9-6 depicts a negative zone of agreement, which is a condition under which the buyer and the seller should not reach an agreement. Any deal reached would fail to satisfy either one of both the buyer's or seller's BATNA price and represent a negative surplus.

Sharing and Exchanging Information

Once all planning is complete, the interaction with the buyer often begins with the second stage, the process of sharing and exchanging information. Sharing and exchanging information during a negotiation may help build trust between the negotiators and often follows a pattern evoking the norm of reciprocity. That is, one side shares some information of value to the other side, which provokes a norm to return the favor by sharing information of value in return. This *quid pro quo* (translation: something for something) exchange should help both sides of the negotiation to better calibrate the interests and priorities of the other side.

For the salesperson, there are three main functions to achieve during this stage of the negotiation: establishing rapport, assessing the goals with associated issues

Figure 9-6 Negative Zone of Agreement for New Car Purchase

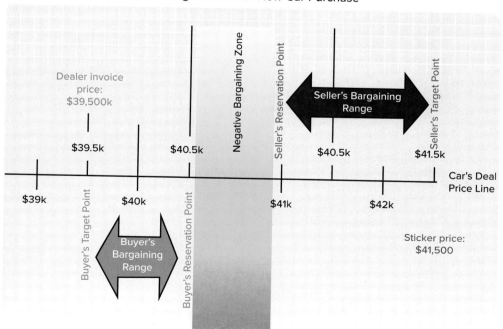

and prioritization of the buyer, and signaling your goals, with associated issues and prioritization of the buyer.

First, establishing rapport may be conditioned on your past relationship and interactions with the buyer. Many salespeople maintain established rapport with their buyers, and they simply do not need to re-establish rapport at each meeting, although starting the conversation with friendly ice-breaking conversation may help create an atmosphere that is receptive to a productive negotiation.

The second component of this stage entails developing an understanding of what the buyer seeks to accomplish during the negotiation, including any major goals and expectations the buyer may have for the negotiation. Adding details to those goals by understanding the issues and their prioritization can only help with considerations on opening bids and proposals, although much of that detail may occur in the next stage, when you are co-creating solutions that integrate your desired outcomes with the buyer's desired outcomes.

Finally, the third component of this stage of the sales negotiation involves signaling your goals, key issues, and prioritization of those issues with the buyer. The top-level understanding of what is important to you, combined with your understanding of what is important to the buyer, can only help with co-creating solutions in the next step.

Opening Bids and Making Concessions

The third major stage in the negotiations process involves opening bids and making concessions. This stage represents the heart of the sales negotiation process. It is during this stage that the salesperson and the buyer began sharing specific details on what agreements they are willing to make.

Opening bids should be reasonable—and you should open if you have developed a firm understanding of an idea that you feel can meet your major objectives in a distributive bargaining context and meet the buyer's objectives in an integrative context. However, novice, or overly competitive negotiators, often open with irrational bids. It's important to be prepared for such an opening.

anchoring effect
causing one to rely too heavily on the first piece of information received

In negotiations, opening bids can cause an **anchoring effect,** which causes one to rely too heavily on the first piece of information received. The anchoring effect can have a strong impact on the outcome of a negotiation. Research shows that the closer you are to an optimistic but attainable outcome with your opening bid, the better the ultimate settlement. However, some will use unrealistic or irrational opening bids in an attempt to anchor the negotiation in their favor. The tactic used by experienced negotiators when confronted with an unrealistic or irrational opening bid is to **re-anchor,** or adjust the opening bid with a counteroffer that balances the extent of irrationality in the opening bid.

re-anchor
adjusting the opening bid with a counteroffer that balances the extent of irrationality in the opening bid

During this stage, you should also insist on using objective criteria, particularly with respect to assessing the proportional equity of proposed solutions. For example, if the buyer states they are only willing to pay $4 per case on your product ($2,400 per truckload), you should pivot by asking how your buyer arrived at that number.

For negotiations that involve multiple issues (e.g., those that present opportunities for integrative negotiations), this is the phase for developing, typically through co-creation, proposals that couple issues. The coupling of issues follows the logrolling process discussed earlier in this chapter, in which an issue of high importance to you but low importance to the buyer is coupled with an issue of low importance to you, but high importance to the buyer.

Closing to Gain Commitment

The final stage of the negotiation involves securing agreement on the negotiated issues and outcomes. As covered previously, closing refers to asking the buyer to commit to the next steps suggested through your negotiation. In complex B2B sales, this may not represent a commitment to buy, but instead a continuation of the negotiation in a future interaction that seeks to resolve concerns developed during the sales negotiation process. In all cases, the salesperson should confirm the commitments of the negotiated agreement, and, in some cases, such agreements may result in formal, written contacts. The formality, or informality, of the contractual agreements, often follows the norms of the relationship or the industry standards. These are typically represented by your firm's requirements for fulfilling the agreements to which you were authorized to make commitments.

Applying this Chapter to Salesforce

A CRM like Salesforce will help in all four stages of sales negotiation. The reports and dashboards available with Salesforce provide immediate access to a wealth of data to inform both the seller and buyer during negotiations. For example, the salesperson can generate a report of the details for sales to customers similar to the buyer in size, industry, and needs. At a minimum, the salesperson can use these reports to determine the likelihood of a successful outcome of a specific negotiation by comparing the buyer's expectation to other sales. These reports also serve to remind the salesperson what discounts or alterations were previously approved. Knowing the details of previously approved sale terms enables the salesperson to negotiate with confidence about which compromises are normal. And lastly, Salesforce reports can inform the buyer's expectation for a rational opening bid. By sharing with them the terms and pricing of similar sales, the salesperson can set a rational starting point for negotiation.

If the salesperson has been careful to capture all of the information discovered leading up to the negotiation, Salesforce will help them accurately recall the previously discussed needs, benefits, and overall value of the solution relative to price, resulting in more productive negotiations.

Even when the customer seems ready to buy, there are often additional steps remaining before the salesperson will gain a commitment to buy. This is especially true with complex products or solutions. Salespeople can use Salesforce *Path* to plan the movement of the buyer through these final steps. Whether the next step is a continuation of the negotiation, resolving further concerns discovered in the process, or a commitment to send the customer a contract, Path outlines exactly where they are in the process of the sale. Because Path clearly defines each step, the salesperson is better able to communicate and confirm commitments made to the customer at each stage.

Even when the buyer has agreed to purchase, there are often additional terms to be negotiated; Will they pay upfront or in installments? Will they need to finance the purchase? If so, for how long? Do they want an extended warranty or service-level agreement? For ongoing services, will they pay invoices within 30, 60, or 90-days? All of these variables, and others, can affect the cost for the seller, and the resulting price to the buyer. Salesforce CPQ (Configure, Price, Quote) is a very valuable tool for negotiating these details. CPQ gives salespeople the ability to change the details of a quote to match each customers' needs and immediately see how the changes impact the quote.

Chapter Summary

- There are two general approaches to a sales negotiation: distributive and integrative.
- Most contemporary B2B sales calls involve an integrative negotiation approach as the long-term relationship of the sales organization with its buyer is of paramount importance.
- There are six foundational building blocks for developing effective sales negotiation skills and practices: bargaining styles, personality factors, goals and expectations, interests and priorities, leverage, and relationship norms.
- A typical sales negotiation process follows four basic stages; sales planning, sharing and exchanging information, opening bids and making concessions, and closing to gain commitment.

- Tips for *slicing the pie* in competitive negotiations
  - Know your BATNA as it tells you when to "walk away" and seeks ways to improve it prior to commencing the negotiation
  - Determine your optimistic but attainable goals and expectations
  - Develop a list of negotiable issues and prioritize them, including planning concessions.
  - Determine your reservation point, but do not reveal it.
  - Research and estimate your buyer's reservation point.
  - Insist on using objective criteria
  - Make the first offer, if you feel you are prepared—and keep it approximate to your target expectations.
  - Immediately re-anchor if the buyer starts with an unreasonable opening bid.
  - Think and act competitively at the negotiation table
  - Sit on the opposite side of the table when possible
  - Do not reveal too much about your interests
  - Use the buyer's interests and incorporate as leverage into your proposals
  - Stay positive and ethical
- Tips for *expanding the pie* in cooperative negotiations
  - Know your BATNA as it tells you when to "walk away" and learn as much as possible about your buyer's BATNA
  - Determine your goal and expectations, prioritize your key issues, and seek to understand your buyer's
  - Insist on using objective criteria
  - Make the first offer, if you feel you are prepared—and keep it approximate to your target expectations.
  - Immediately re-anchor if the buyer starts with an unreasonable opening bid.
  - Think and act collaboratively at the negotiation table
  - Sit on the same side of the table when possible
  - Signal your interests effectively
  - Understand their interests and incorporate them into your proposals
  - Use logrolling to couple issues noting which issues require different inputs and yield different outcomes for both parties
  - Stay positive and ethical

Key Terms

accommodating style (p. 172)
affective-based trust (p. 176)
agreeableness (p. 173)
anchoring effect (p. 180)
assertiveness (p. 171)
avoiding style (p. 172)
best alternative to a negotiated
   agreement (BATNA) (p. 178)
cognition-based trust (p. 176)
collaborating style (p. 172)
competing style (p. 172)
compromising style (p. 172)
conscientiousness (p. 173)
cooperativeness (p. 171)
customer-centric (p. 177)
distributive negotiation (p. 167)
equity theory (p. 176)
extraversion (p. 173)
framing (p. 175)

good faith (p. 174)
hard-bargaining (p. 168)
integrative negotiation (p. 168)
interests (p. 175)
leverage (p. 175)
negative emotionality (p. 173)
negative leverage (p. 175)
negotiation (p. 166)
neuroticism (p. 173)
negotiation process (p. 176)
norm of reciprocity (p. 176)
open-mindedness (p. 173)
positive leverage (p. 175)
reciprocity (p. 176)
re-anchor and adjust (p. 180)
situational matrix (p. 177)
soft-bargaining (p. 169)
zone of potential agreement
   (ZOPA) (p. 178)

Application 9-1

Imagine you landed a highly desirable sales internship for the summer between your junior and senior year of college. The sales position is with a company that sells new cars to businesses who use them as part of their corporate fleet. After completing your onboarding training, you and your manager schedule a meeting with a buyer who represents a small business in the local area.

The buyer's company bought three cars from your firm in the past, but that was more than ten years ago—and neither your company nor the buyer wanted to continue the relationship after that transaction. Apparently, both the representative from your company and the buyer used hard bargaining to reach a deal that neither side appreciated, but that both sides accepted as a negotiated contract.

The time to meet with the buyer is now—and after shaking hands and exchanging greetings, you both agree to get down to business. You know the buyer wants to buy three more cars and that the buyer purchased an invoice report indicating that you paid $35,700 for each car. You don't know what color, sound system, or financing terms the buyer prefers, but do know the manufacturer is planning a $500 discount next month on the car the buyer wants.

Consider the following alternative as to how the buyer opens the negotiation, once your conversation gets down to business.

1. The buyer says, "I'll offer you $35,000 for each car. You can take it or leave it, and our company really doesn't care either way. We're ready to walk now, in fact, if you want a penny more for the car."
    Which bargaining style do you think this buyer is using?
2. The buyer says, "I'll offer offer you $30,000 for each car. Can you make that happen?"
    How should you respond?
3. The buyer says, "I know your company needs to make a profit—and you do an out-standing job of preparing and delivering the cars. Our executives especially appreci-ate the demonstration your reps provide on how to operate their new cars. My esti-mates show that your cost for each car is $37,500. We'll offer you a profit of $300 per car, or $37, 800 each. Can you work with that?"
    Which bargaining style do you think this buyer is using?

Application 9-2

Imagine you're interviewing for a sales position for a major consumer packaged goods firm. They have several major retail grocery chains who buy more than a billion dollars worth of product each year from them. In some cases, the sales company's strategic priorities align well with those of the grocery chain (buyer). For those accounts, the company wants to forge long term relationships.

You are preparing for a set of interviews with company executives who hire new sales reps to help manage relationships by negotiating contracts with these large, strategic accounts.

In preparing for the interviews, you reflect on your experiences during college. You were the leader of a successful pre-business organization—and have several examples of how you negotiated deals with other college organizations. Some of the examples demonstrate that you know how to use an integrative approach with a collaborative

(Continued)

(Continued)

bargaining style and other examples help show you can adapt and use a distributive approach with a more competitive stance.

Your meeting with the hiring executive begins.

1. The hiring executive says, "I see you led a business organization at your college. I'd imagine you had to work with other organizations on campus to get things done, and in some cases, you wanted to have lasting relationships with those organizations after you resolved any differences you may have had. As you know, building relationships with our retail customers is an important objective for our sales negotiations. Can you give us an example of how, in your leadership role, you negotiated a resolution with some other organization on campus?"
   What example would you give in response?

2. The hiring executive says, "imagine that you have an offer from us for $60,000 starting salary and other benefits such as starting date, location, vacation, health benefits, a company car, and so on. Our competitor offers you all the same details except they offer you $10,000 more per year in starting salary. You know from a friend's experience that the most our company will offer is $5,000 more, and you realize that we have another candidate equally as impressive as you who is willing to accept our offer with that salary and supporting package."
   What negotiation strategy would you use?

3. The hiring executive says, "imagine that you have an offer from us for $60,000 starting salary and other benefits such as starting date, location, vacation, health benefits, a company car, and so on. Our competitor offers you all the same details except they offer you $10,000 more per year in starting salary. You know from a friend's experience that the most our company will offer is $12,000 more, and you realize that we have another candidate equally as impressive as you who is willing to accept our offer with that salary and supporting package."
   What negotiation strategy would you use?

Shutterstock/DiMadra

CHAPTER 10

Territory, Time, and Resource Management

Learning Objectives

- Identify several different types of sales territories
- Understand the importance of goal setting in territory management
- Explain why a territory management strategy will require trade-offs
- Explain the importance of time management for salespeople, prioritizing, scheduling, and making route/travel plans
- Identify different company resources that can help a salesperson be more efficient and effective
- Recognize the importance of "self-management" in sales, including the nature and importance of working hard and working smart in territory management

alespeople must wear many hats simultaneously. That is, the salesperson's role is wide-ranging and complex. Among other things, effective salespeople:

- Develop healthy personal relationships with several people inside of a buying organization
- Are good communicators (good question-askers, good listeners, persuasive)
- Understand their buyers (reading body language, understanding communication styles and personalities)
- Prospect (identify and qualify potential new customers)
- Create written proposals
- Pre-call plan (do their homework)
- Deliver effective sales presentations
- Overcome objections and close
- Provide excellent service after the sale

In addition to the activities above, the salesperson's role also includes an executive function. The salesperson often becomes the CEO of his or her sales territory. As territory CEO, the salesperson is responsible for setting territory goals and developing and executing a strategy to achieve those goals. Accordingly, this chapter "steps back" and discusses the salesperson's role as an executive or territory manager. The salesperson's ability to make decisions about goals and resource allocation is an often-overlooked factor that separates the successful from the unsuccessful.

In this chapter, we first discuss the nature of territories and describe different types of sales territories. Next, we discuss the importance of goals in sales territory management. From there, we move to a discussion about resources and strategy. The discussion of resources is separated into personal resources and company resources. The chapter closes with a discussion about self-management. The section about self-management is separated into discussions about the importance of both working hard and working smart.

Territories and Territory Management

Very rarely are salespeople responsible for a single customer relationship. More often, salespeople are responsible for a group of customers and prospects. The group of customers and prospects for whom the salesperson is responsible is called the salesperson's **territory**. Just as no two customers are the same, no two territories are the same. To some degree, each territory will require a unique sales approach. We will use the term **territory management** to refer to the decisions a salesperson makes regarding resource allocation and day-to-day activities that affect territory-level outcomes like revenue. Because time may be the salesperson's most critical resource—and because the salesperson's activities require time—it is also common to hear the term *time and territory management* in a discussion about salespeople or sales managers.

Types of Territories

The group of customers and prospects for which the salesperson is responsible are often similar in some way. If not, sales territories can be designed to allow the salesperson to gain and leverage some expertise or specialized knowledge. With these factors in mind, different types of sales territories include the following.

territory
the group of customers and prospects for whom the salesperson is responsible

territory management
the decisions a salesperson makes regarding resource allocation and day-to-day activities that affect territory-level outcomes like revenue

Geographic   To envision a geographic sales territory, imagine a pharmaceutical salesperson responsible for covering ten U.S. zip codes, or five adjacent cities, or the northwest region in a particular state, etc. In geographic territories, salespeople are responsible for selling all of a company's products to all potential customers. For example, a pharmaceutical salesperson might sell all four company products (hypertension medication, acne medication, osteoporosis medication, diabetes medication) to various types of doctors (cardiologists, family practice physicians, dermatologists). Geographic territories are common across different types of sales jobs. From the organization's standpoint, this type of territory is simple and reduces uncertainty or confusion about each salesperson's responsibilities.

Product-Based   In product-based territories, salespeople are responsible for selling just one or two company products to all potential customers. Product-based territories are useful because they allow the salesperson to specialize and develop expertise (which is important in developing credibility and trust). To envision a product-based territory, imagine a pharmaceutical salesperson who specializes in one or two medications (only the company's acne medication). This pharmaceutical salesperson might sell only the acne medication but sell it to various types of doctors (pediatricians, family practice physicians, dermatologists).

From the organization's standpoint, one downside of product-based territories is an increased need for communication between salespeople and between sales managers. For example, imagine a situation in which a single doctor is being called on by three salespeople from the same pharmaceutical company, each selling a different medication. In this situation, it becomes very important that the three salespeople share relevant information. Imagine, for example, if one salesperson learns that the doctor's office is planning to expand, close, move, or make other changes that affect the prescriptions they order.

Customer-Based   In customer-based territories (or territories based on customer segment), salespeople are responsible for selling to only *a single type* of customer. Like product-based territories, customer-based territories are useful because they allow the salesperson to develop specialized knowledge or expertise. As we will note later in this chapter, salesperson expertise is critical to success. To envision a customer-based territory, imagine an advertising salesperson for Gannett who focuses only on the advertising needs of car dealerships, or sporting goods retailers, or hospitals, etc. This salesperson might sell all company products (newspaper advertising, online banner advertising) but sell only to car dealerships. In this situation, you can imagine that, over time, the salesperson will more fluently "speak the language" of their customers and see their customers' needs with a perspective improved by their industry-specific experience.

Key/Major/Strategic Account   Some organizations have sales territories that include a small number of *key*, *major*, or *strategic* accounts. These accounts are important because they generate a disproportionately high amount of revenue. More plainly, these accounts spend a lot of money. To envision a "key account" territory, imagine an advertising salesperson for Gannett who is responsible for only four customers: Verizon, Walmart, Macy's, and Lowe's. This advertising salesperson would sell all company products but sell only to these four customers.

Salespeople managing territories with key accounts must have high levels of knowledge about the customer's goals, operations, strategies, problems, and

Shutterstock/damann

products. As such, key account management usually requires high levels of cooperation internally and coordination externally. With high levels of customer knowledge and deeper customer relationships, salespeople responsible for key accounts should be able to better identify and satisfy the evolving needs of these important customers.

Inside vs. Outside Sales Almost any territory can be covered by either an inside salesperson or an outside salesperson. Although these concepts were introduced earlier, they are worth revisiting in the context of territory management. **Inside sales** is defined as selling and relationship building that is not conducted in-person or face-to-face. Inside salespeople generally manage relationships remotely by phone, email, and with video conferencing platforms. From the organization's standpoint, one common benefit of an inside sales approach is cost-effectiveness (especially for smaller or low revenue customers). **Outside sales** is selling that is conducted in-person. Outside salespeople must make plans to travel to see the customers and prospects in their territory. In many organizations, all sales territories are covered by either inside salespeople exclusively or outside salespeople exclusively. That said, some companies cover territories with a mix of inside salespeople and outside salespeople.

inside sales
selling and relationship building that is not conducted in-person or face-to-face

outside sales
selling that is conducted in-person

territory goals
territory "results to be achieved."

Territory Goals

Before making decisions about "how," effective territory managers must first decide "what" important outcomes are to be accomplished. That is, territory goals are first; territory strategy is second. We can think about goals as desired end-states. From an executive point of view, salespeople can think about **territory goals** as territory "results to be achieved."[1] Such goals motivate and guide behavior.

Without clear territory goals, salespeople:

- may naturally and slowly shift from minor activity to minor activity, engaged in easy-but-less-productive tasks.
- will have difficulty deciding where to go next or where to begin.
- will have difficulty determining the most appropriate territory strategy.

Goals Set By Salespeople for Themselves

Different types of goals that salespeople, as territory managers, may set for themselves include the following (also see Figure 10-1):

- *Revenue* goals at the customer level (e.g., $50,000 for Company A), product-level (e.g., $500,000 of Product E), or territory-level (e.g., $8,000,000 next fiscal year)

Figure 10-1 Types of Territory Goals at Different Levels

Goal Level	Goal Type			
	Revenue Goal	Activity Goal	Growth Goal	Unit Sales Goal
Customer Level	$50,000 with Company A	Visit Company B in person each week	Grow revenue with Company C by 50%	5 units with Company D
Product Level	$500,000 of Product E	Make 15 sales presentations each week that focus on Product F	Increase revenue for Product G by 50%	400 units of Product H
Territory Level	$8,000,000 next fiscal year	Make an average of one cold call per day	Sign up two new customers per week	Increase unit sales across the territory by 30%

- *Activity* goals at the customer-level (e.g., visit Company B in person each week), product level (e.g., make 15 sales presentations each week that focus on Product F), or territory-level (e.g., make an average of one "cold call" per day)
- *Growth* goals at the customer-level (e.g., grow revenue with Company C by 50%), product level (e.g., increase revenue for Product G by 50%), or territory-level (e.g., sign up two new customers per week)
- *Unit sales* goals at the customer level (e.g., 5 units with Company D), product level (400 units of Product H), or territory-level (e.g., increase unit sales across the territory by 30%)
- *Customer satisfaction* goals (e.g., achieve a 95% customer satisfaction score based on a company survey)
- *Customer retention* goals (e.g., retain 95% of last year's customers)

Making Territory Goals S.M.A.R.T.

Not only should salespeople as territory managers have goals, but the territory goals should be **S.M.A.R.T.**,[2,3] which is an acronym suggesting that goals have five characteristics. Goals should be Specific, Measurable, Attainable (or achievable), Relevant, and Time-bound (or time-limited).

S.M.A.R.T
Specific, Measurable, Attainable (or achievable), Relevant, and Time-bound (or time-limited)

Specific Territory Goals Goals such as "Have a successful year in the territory," "Grow territory revenue," and "Have the best territory in the region" are not specific. These vague goals can mean different things to different people. For example, what does "success" mean exactly? Grow revenue by how much exactly? The best territory in the region according to what criteria exactly? Without specificity, the exact goal to be pursued is unclear.

Measurable Territory Goals Imagine a salesperson who has the following goal: "Make sure that the customers in my territory are always satisfied." This goal could be measurable if, for example, the salesperson planned to email surveys every three months to all customers in the territory. However, in this example, if there are no email addresses and no online surveys, then it could be difficult to know whether the "satisfaction" goal was attained or not.

Attainable Territory Goals Goals should motivate or drive effort. Unfortunately, goals that are too high or unattainable do not motivate. Effort levels will depend on the "Can I do it?" question.[4] If we think we can do it, then we will be more motivated to achieve the goal. To illustrate, imagine a difficult annual sales territory goal: "Quadruple last year's territory revenue." In most circumstances, it will quickly become evident to a salesperson that this goal is unrealistic; and the unattainable goal will fail to drive the salesperson into action.

Relevant Territory Goals Most likely, salespeople will not be setting irrelevant goals. To illustrate a territory goal that is probably irrelevant, imagine a salesperson setting the following goal: "Have a better year than John," where John is a salesperson in a different division of the same firm. Most likely, a salesperson's performance will not be evaluated by sales management or by customers based on the performance of another colleague, especially one in a different division of the firm. As such, this goal would likely be insignificant or irrelevant.

Time-Bound Territory Goals It is important to have a date or time before which goals must be accomplished. For salespeople as territory managers, making goals time-bound adds a necessary level of urgency. For example, imagine two goals: "Sign up three new customers" and "Sign up three new customers by the end of the week." The goal with the "due date" is more likely to stimulate action.

The bottom line: Salespeople should be managing their territory according to (S.M.A.R.T.) territory goals. Goal setting is critical to success in many areas of life, and sales territory management is no different. Many successful sales professionals, such as Eddie Haislop at AutoiPacket Agree: "In sales, goal setting is key. At the end of the day, the way that I manage my territory is based on the goals that I am trying to accomplish. To me, a goal represents a map, where the destination is success. Without this type of direction, it's very easy to get lost."

Territory Strategy as a Resource Allocation Plan

With territory goals in mind, or knowing where they want to go, salespeople will now need a territory strategy, or a plan to get there. One way to think about a strategy is as a *resource allocation plan* that is expected to lead to goal attainment. In short, a strategy is a plan. Resources are the time, information, funds, or anything else the salesperson might use to execute their strategy.

Decisions about how to use resources to reach goals are important for all executives and managers. For example, a marketing executive may need to decide how to allocate financial resources across a portfolio of products. A sales manager may need to decide how to allocate salespeople across a given geography. Similarly, as territory managers, salespeople must decide how to allocate resources in ways that will lead to the achievement of their territory goals. The next two sections look at salesperson resources in two general categories: personal resources and company resources.

Before moving to a discussion of key resources, it is worth pointing out two quotes from Professor Michael Porter about the concept of strategy:[5]

"The essence of strategy is choosing what not to do"

"Strategy requires you to make tradeoffs"

These quotes are relevant to salespeople as territory managers. That is, a salesperson's territory management strategy cannot be "do everything for everybody." As we will note, some key salesperson resources are finite. So, salespeople as territory managers must decide what will *not* be done (*not* traveling to a certain region, *not* discussing a certain product on a given sales call, *not* spending money to entertain a certain prospect). Put another way, salespeople as territory managers will always need to make trade-offs.

Managing Time

The primary personal resource that a salesperson must carefully manage is time. Time might be the scarcest resource for all of us as students or as salespeople. If time is indeed the scarcest resource, it should be spent wisely. Using time wisely is especially important for salespeople, who, compared to other employees, enjoy a relatively high level of autonomy at work.

As suggested earlier, salespeople must spend their time on various activities (attending meetings, training, and administrative tasks). So, the most important salesperson activity is actually spending time interacting with prospects and customers. In general, the salesperson will want to maximize and optimize the time spent interacting with prospects and customers. This section is related to the importance of salespeople managing their time.

Prioritizing Within the Territory

Salespeople should think carefully about which customers they spend their time with. For example, imagine a territory with 100 customers. This territory will surely have customers and prospects with varying levels of priority. Some customers and prospects in the territory should receive more of the salesperson's time than others. In general, salespeople should prioritize customers and prospects within their territory according to one broad factor: sales potential.

Bottom line: Salespeople should spend their time with customers and prospects who can potentially generate the most revenue. However, because sales potential is difficult to quantify or measure, there are several more specific criteria that salespeople can use to prioritize customers and prospects. Some of those criteria follow.

Current Spending Levels Continuing the last example (a territory with 100 customers), imagine that the top five customers in the territory spend $500,000 per year on average, and the bottom 15 customers spend just $500 per year on average. In this situation, the salesperson should probably allocate significantly more time to the top five customers than to the bottom 15 customers.

Current Spending Growth Continuing the last example, imagine that a certain customer in the territory has been growing, up from $3,000 three years ago, to $8,000 two years ago, to $25,000 last year. In this situation, the salesperson should probably be investing more time into his or her relationship with this growing customer.

Historical Spending Continuing the last example, imagine that a certain customer spent significantly in the past but no longer buys, declining from $75,000 three years ago, to $65,000 two years ago, to $0 last year and $0 this year. In this situation, the salesperson should probably still invest significant time into the relationship with this former customer, despite current spending levels and current spending growth.

Marketing Strategy Factors If the salesperson's company is prioritizing or targeting a certain buyer type, like agricultural buyers or government buyers, then the salesperson will want to allocate significant time to customers and prospects of that type. Correspondingly, if the salesperson's company is prioritizing a certain product - maybe because the product is highly profitable - then the salesperson will want to invest significant time with customers or prospects with needs related to that certain product. Similarly, if the salesperson's company is prioritizing a certain geographical region, then the salesperson will want to allocate significant time to customers or prospects in those regions.

Personal Relationship Factors To the extent that the salesperson is paid to build and maintain profitable relationships, relationship factors can also be a time management concern for salespeople. For example, a salesperson may choose to maintain very good relationships with lower priority customers (those with low spending or low growth opportunities) if these relationships might pay off in the long-term with spending or referrals. In terms of categorizing criteria, every sales organization or salesperson can take a different approach.

Common Approaches to Account Classification Potentially, a salesperson could consider each of the criteria listed above as he or she decides where and with whom to spend valuable time. Alternatively, a salesperson could base their time management decisions on just one or two of the criteria, like spending level or spending growth. Continuing our example from above, we can imagine a salesperson giving each of the customers in the territory a *priority score* ranging from 1 (lowest priority customer) to 100 (highest priority customer).

Rather than assigning individual priority scores to customers, many companies use a simpler and possibly more efficient method called the **ABC account approach** to categorizing based on priority. With this approach, customers and prospects will be given one of three labels. "A" accounts are the highest priority accounts. "B" accounts have medium levels of priority. These could be regular or reliable customers who happen to be smaller in size. These accounts could also be prospects who have not spent anything (yet), but have very high spending potential if converted. "C" accounts are the lowest priority accounts. These accounts could be prospects with low potential.

If a company or salesperson considers two criteria when prioritizing accounts (e.g., spending level and spending growth), then the salesperson can create a grid as shown in Figure 10-2.

A grid with four quadrants can be produced, allowing the salesperson to give customers and prospects one of four labels. The salesperson can think of differently important accounts:

1. High spending level and high spending growth: Accounts in this category should probably be considered the highest priority.
2. High spending level but low spending growth: moderate-to-high priority.
3. Low spending level but high spending growth: Accounts in this category should probably be considered moderate priorities.
4. Low spending level and low spending growth: Accounts in this territory should probably be considered the lowest priority.

ABC account approach
a method for categorizing accounts and prospects based on priority

Figure 10-2 Two-Criteria Territory Prioritization Grid (Example)

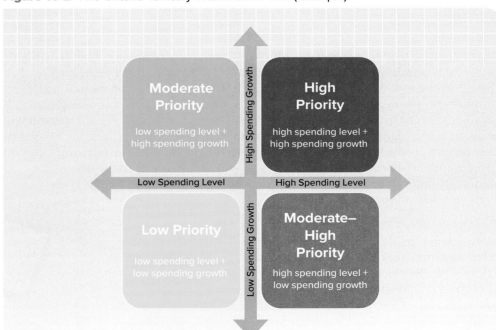

Importantly, no single approach to prioritizing customers and prospects is necessarily the best. Each approach to prioritizing - using an ABC approach based only on marketing strategy factors or a two-criteria approach based on spending potential and personal relationships - can be effective in one situation and ineffective in another. The general point is this: If the salesperson's scarce resources are to be used wisely, then customers and prospects should be prioritized based on some criteria that indicates sales potential. Salespeople should not allocate valuable resources across customers and prospects in a territory according to *gut instinct*, for example.

Two Final Account Prioritization Notes Before closing a discussion of prioritizing customers and prospects, it is important to mention two more things. First, effective salespeople are aware of the 80/20 rule, sometimes referred to as Pareto's Principle,[6] or the "law of the vital few." **The 80/20 rule** (see Figure 10-3) suggests that 80% of territory revenue comes from 20% of the territory's customers; or most business results are driven by a small number of customers. For example, imagine that you are a salesperson in a territory with 100 customers who generate $10,000,000 annually. The 80-20 rule suggests that $8,000,000 of the $10,000,000 in revenue is the result of just 20 of the 100 customers. The 20 customers in this territory could be considered the "vital few." In classifying accounts and analyzing territory potential, salespeople will often find that the 80-20 rule holds in their territory. Many effective salespeople, such as Mark Davis at Benbilt Building Systems, will attribute their success to an understanding of this principle and a choice to focus on the "vital few." According to Mark, "I attribute much of my success, especially early in my career, to understanding the importance of the 80-20 rule as a territory manager. It's important to prioritize and focus on the priorities."

> **the 80/20 rule**
> 80% of territory revenue comes from 20% of the territory's customers

Second, accounts in a territory must be reviewed and re-classified regularly, at least annually. As sales territories are always changing to some degree, with small customers growing larger and large customers going out-out-of-business or moving, salespeople should always be (re)evaluating their territory accounts in terms of sales potential. For example, what we deemed a high potential account last year may be better labeled a moderate potential account this year. Or, vice versa: What we thought was a low potential account last year may be a very high potential account this year. The bottom line: account classification is not a "set it and forget it" activity; it is an evolving or ongoing activity.

Scheduling

Salespeople should carefully develop plans to allocate their time across prioritized customers. If salespeople schedule their time without customer priority in mind,

Figure 10-3 The 80/20 Rule

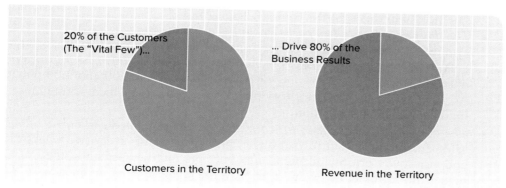

then a key resource is probably being used in a suboptimal manner. Examples of planning that incorporates territory priority could include:

- Spend 65% of time with "A" accounts, 25% of time with "B" accounts, and 10% of time with "C" accounts.
- Visit each "A" account every two weeks; visit each "B" account every month; visit each "C" account every quarter or communicate with "C" accounts mostly by phone.
- Spend 75% of time with customers classified as *high spending level* who also need a product that has been prioritized by the salesperson's company.
- Despite great personal relationships that might exist, spend *no more than* 20% of time with customers or prospects that currently spend $0.
- Spend at least two days per month prospecting potential buyers of a certain type (e.g., rural distributors)

Scheduling Across Different Calendar Horizons   As suggested in the examples above, time within the territory can be scheduled at different levels. Importantly, salespeople can engage in long-range and short-range planning. For example, salespeople often have longer-range, annual, or quarterly sales objectives (quotas) to meet. As such, and often along with their sales managers, salespeople make annual or quarterly plans. Otherwise, salespeople must also accomplish shorter-range objectives, like making eight sales calls per day or 40 calls per week. Thus, effective salespeople also make monthly and weekly plans, like spending only Wednesday afternoons on administrative tasks in the office, in addition to daily plans.

Scheduling Across Different Sales Activities   Salespeople can also schedule their time with different sales activities in mind. For example, pre-call planning activities are critical for salespeople. Therefore, daily scheduling should allocate some time to pre-call planning. We've also already established that prospecting activities are critical for salespeople. So, plans to allocate time should usually include prospecting activities.

Travel/Route Planning

For many salespeople, one important scheduling consideration is travel time. Minimizing unproductive travel time is key to optimizing the time spent interacting with customers. Travel plans within a territory or territory route plans should be made with an understanding of the following:

- *The geographic locations of all accounts.* With this understanding, salespeople can estimate travel times between accounts and the accounts that could be visited on the same days. While sophisticated mapping software does exist, free applications such as Google Maps can help most salespeople in this regard.
- *The days and times when each account is available for sales calls.* For example, a pharmaceutical salesperson might learn that one very important doctor will see sales reps only on Monday mornings. Another high priority doctor might see sales reps only on Thursdays between 2:00 and 4:00 p.m. As these examples show, territory travel/route plans must incorporate more than geographic information.
- *The desired call frequencies for each account.* As suggested earlier, a salesperson might want to visit higher priority accounts every two weeks and visit lower priority accounts only once per quarter. Generally, the higher the customer or prospect priority, the higher the call frequency should be. Considering this point, combined with geographic location and

customer availability, one can imagine the careful thinking that must be devoted to travel or route planning.

- *Minimizing waiting time.* Setting appointments as much as possible is one way for salespeople to reduce time spent wasted waiting at a customer's place of business. For example, a pharmaceutical salesperson should make plans that minimize time spent waiting in traffic or in a doctor's office waiting room.

- *Minimizing inefficient "crisscrossing" or "backtracking."* In an extreme example, imagine five customers located on the same street, in the same city, which is a one-hour drive from your home office. Of course, we would prefer to see these five customers on the same day. Continuing with this example, we would *not* want to travel one hour each way to visit each of these five customers on five different days of the week. It is often helpful for salespeople to think about breaking a large geographic territory into a number of zones, which can each be worked in a sequence.

- *A general understanding of the number of calls that can be made in a given day.* In some sales contexts, such as pharmaceutical sales, an average sales presentation maybe just a few minutes long. In other contexts, a sales call could be between a half-hour and an hour. Territory travel/route plans must incorporate this kind of information. As a reminder, calculations regarding the number of sales calls that can be made in a day should be made with *pre-call planning* in mind. Before each sales call, salespeople should spend time "studying" the customer, looking at spending history, trends, objections raised in previous calls, and rapport built in previous calls.

In terms of planning travel, one key consideration for salespeople is optimal call frequency. Salespeople must find a balance between making customers and prospects feel neglected by receiving too few calls and making customers and prospects feel uncomfortable or bothered by receiving too many calls. For example, imagine being a pharmaceutical salesperson deciding whether to visit a certain doctor every week, every two weeks, every month, etc. A salesperson wants the customers to feel appreciated, and to keep themselves and their products top of mind. At the same time, a salesperson never wants to be an annoyance who fails to bring value to each customer visit.

The nature of each individual territory will require a different travel/route plan. For example, one territory that has been segmented into four geographical zones might be best covered by a four-week plan that covers the East Zone in one week, the South Zone in the next week, the West Zone in the following week, and the North Zone in the week after that. Another territory might best be covered by spending one day in one zip code, three days in an adjacent zip code, two days in zip code adjacent to that one, etc. Another territory might be best covered by spending five days per month traveling in rural areas and ten days per month in downtown areas of bigger cities. Other territories that require more significant travel might require one week of travel per quarter to each metropolitan area. The optimal travel route plan will depend on several of the factors discussed above (desired call frequencies for each account, minimizing "crisscrossing" or "backtracking") (see Figure 10-4)

No single plan to allocate time within a territory is necessarily best. A given plan to allocate time, like spending 20% on prospecting activities, at least 50% with "A" accounts, and breaking a bigger territory into four zones covered every six weeks, can be effective in one territory and ineffective in another. The bottom line (and the important and general point of this section of the chapter): If the salesperson's time is to be used optimally, then salespeople should carefully make plans that are tied to priorities, a calendar, and a map. Many successful sales professionals, such as Mario McLean at Frito Lay agree: "To be effective as a salesperson, time management skills are key. Salespeople must think carefully about how they

Figure 10-4 Key Considerations: Territory Travel/Route Plans

Making Territory Travel/Route Plans

Must know:
- Geographic locations of all accounts
- Days and times when each account is available for sales calls
- Desired call frequencies for each account
- Number of calls that can be made in a day

To minimize:
- Waiting
- "Crisscrossing" or "backtracking"

To maximize:
- Overall time spent with the highest priority (most important) customers and prospects in the territory.

manage their territory, in terms of both traveling time and spending time with the 'right' customers." Ryan Groves, a successful Financial Advisor at Northwestern Mutual, also agrees: "As a salesperson, time may be the most critical and scarce resource. Time management is extremely important. I'm always thinking about how to make the most out of my day, week, etc."

Managing Company Resources

Just as it is important for salespeople to manage their own time, it is also important for salespeople to make good use of company resources. Accordingly, this section discusses expense management and various interdepartmental resources, followed by the use of expert colleagues in team-selling.

Expense Management

Salespeople are often supported by their company's financial resources. Specifically, many salespeople have expense accounts that they can use to help them develop profitable relationships in their territory. **Expense accounts** are arrangements in which the salesperson's company pays for certain costs that are incurred as a part of the salesperson's job. Typically, salespeople will submit an *expense report* along with receipts to their company after incurring a job-related expense. After reviewing the receipts and nature of the expense, the company then reimburses the salesperson. Reimbursable expenses usually include transportation, lodging, meals, and customer entertainment.

expense accounts
arrangements in which the salesperson's company pays for certain costs that are incurred as a part of the salesperson's job

For salespeople as territory managers, the important point about expense accounts is that these company-provided financial resources should be viewed as investments into the territory. The investments are not trivial, typically tens of thousands of dollars per year, per salesperson.[7] Ideally, the investments yield positive returns. In search of positive returns on financial investments, salespeople will want to keep at least two things in mind. First, financial investments into the territory should be made with account prioritization in mind. Second, in making decisions about territory expenses, salespeople will want to avoid both overspending and underspending with each prospect or customer in their territory.

In summary, as territory managers, salespeople should carefully determine, monitor, and analyze how expense accounts are used.

Interdepartmental Resources

To satisfy the increasingly complex—and always changing—needs of customers today, salespeople must often leverage various resources within their own company. More specifically, salespeople today often need help from various colleagues within their organization. An effective sales manager can support salespeople in this regard. However, to effectively and efficiently receive the help required, salespeople themselves must develop healthy relationships with people across various areas of the company.

Manufacturing/Production/Engineering As salespeople identify and better understand a given customer's needs, salespeople may realize that the customer needs some product(s) developed according to unique or specialized requirements. With this information, and back inside their organization, salespeople must often then become advocates for those customers. For example, if a customer needs to customize an otherwise standard product, the salesperson should advocate or "make the case" for customization to his manufacturing/production/engineering colleagues. This is an increasingly important role for salespeople, as customers today are increasingly looking for *customized solutions* to meet their unique needs instead of *off-the-shelf* designs or standard product specifications. By satisfying specialized needs with the help of manufacturing or engineering, salespeople bring unique value to customers and differentiate themselves from the competition.

Beyond creating customized solutions, it can be helpful for salespeople to have good relationships with colleagues in manufacturing, production, or engineering departments for another reason: *product knowledge*. Ultimately, the more that a salesperson knows about exactly how his or her products are designed or manufactured, the more persuasive and successful he or she will be. Indeed, research has long shown that salesperson knowledge /expertise is positively related to sales effectiveness and customer relationship quality.[8]

Sales Support/Sales Operations While organizational structure will vary from industry to industry and company to company, it is common for many sales organizations to have a *sales support* or *sales operations* department. This department may be home to two key functions for salespeople: order entry and sales analysis.

Order Entry When the salesperson closes a deal, it is often up to other employees to start the necessary order fulfillment, operationally. These employees, who may have titles such as *account coordinator* or *sales assistant*, enter new orders into systems that send instructions to other departments in the company (billing or accounting, manufacturing or shipping). To enter the required details of the purchase, salespeople may need to meet with an order entry specialist face-to-face or talk with them on the telephone. Order entry specialists can make the sales organization more efficient, as one order entry specialists could be supporting several salespeople, allowing those salespeople to spend less time on administrative tasks and more time selling.

Sales Analysis Many companies have separate *sales analysis* departments that work closely with the sales force. Analysts within these departments provide information that salespeople, sales managers, and upper management rely on.

One key function of these departments is likely to be sales forecasting. As such, salespeople may work closely with a sales analysis department to develop territory revenue forecasts required by management. Depending on the industry and company, salespeople may need to provide updated sales forecasts to management weekly. Moreover, as annual company-wide budgets are developed, salespeople may also be required to provide long-range forecasts, estimating how much revenue the territory will generate in the future and why. Information from a sales analysis department can be very useful to a salesperson looking to accurately estimate long-term territory revenue.

Another key function of a sales analysis department is likely to be reporting, in general. As such, salespeople and sales managers alike may rely on analysts from this department to better understand what business has been closed, how sales are trending toward goals, explanations of variances, product-specific reporting, and customer-specific trends.

Shipping/Installation   For at least one reason, salespeople will need good relationships with their colleagues who are responsible for shipping or installation. That reason is simple: *Keeping promises made.* Imagine a salesperson on a sales call who wins the customer over, partly owing to the following promise: "We can deliver each of those products that you need to your warehouse in New Mexico within the next ten days." Imagine another salesperson on a sales call who wins the customer over, partly because of the following promise: "We can install the new equipment that you need in your factory in Belgium by the end of the month."

Generally speaking, salespeople make promises and rely on other departments to deliver on those promises. Especially when customers need to meet special deadlines, employees responsible for shipping or installation become very important to salespeople.

Customer Service   Salespeople should maintain good working relationships with their customer service colleagues since they can provide a wealth of additional customer insight. Employees who answer help desk calls or employees in a customer service call center can help salespeople stay informed about customer problems or areas of dissatisfaction. For example, help desk employees can inform salespeople about problems a customer is experiencing and how to resolve it, allowing the salesperson to proactively, which most customers prefer, instead of reacting to the issue when the customer complains. Some customers also share different information with their customer service representative than they do with their sales representative. The better the sharing of information between the customer service department and the salesperson, the better prepared the salesperson will be to succeed.

Marketing   Various research has confirmed the importance of a close, healthy, working relationship between sales departments and marketing departments.[9] As both departments are interested in identifying and satisfying customer needs, each department can help the other.

Marketing departments can help in several ways. For example, marketing departments can provide salespeople with leads. Marketing departments can generate sales leads in various ways, including email campaigns, direct advertising, and trade shows. To the extent that salespeople should always be prospecting, salespeople need to leverage marketing department resources that can help with prospecting activities. At the same time, marketing departments can help salespeople with market research. Market research that provides information about customer preferences can help salespeople be both more effective by having the resources for more compelling sales calls, and more efficient by spending time with prospects who have the highest sales potential. Otherwise, salespeople may rely on a marketing department for sales collateral, the brochures, and other visual aids salespeople use when making presentations or demonstrations. Marketing departments may also provide salespeople with videos and PowerPoint decks to give sales presentations more impact.

Shutterstock/Africa Studio

Sales departments can help marketing departments too. For marketing departments, salespeople are a source of vital information about the marketplace. For example, salespeople can bring valuable customer insights back to their marketing department. Imagine a salesperson, having lunch with her biggest customer, learning that this customer has never used a certain product feature or does not see any benefit associated with another product feature. Imagine another salesperson, on a call with his biggest customer, learning that this customer has developed a new use or application for the product that he sells. Insights from customers such as these are useful to marketing departments responsible for developing new products, creating advertising content, working with advertising agencies, etc.

In addition to customer insights, it is helpful when salespeople bring "competitive intelligence" to their marketing department. For example, imagine a salesperson, having lunch with a prospect, and learning that her company's biggest competitor is planning to launch a new product. Or, imagine that the same salesperson learning what salespeople who work for the competition are saying to "our" customers about "our" product. Competitive intelligence of this sort is useful to marketing departments responsible for planning sales promotions, developing sales collateral, etc.

Accounting/Billing/Credit   Salespeople may need to interact with colleagues in accounting or billing departments for several reasons. Sometimes, the salesperson may need to step in and advocate for a potential new customer regarding a credit application or payment terms. Most business-to-business transactions are not paid upfront with cash. Instead, in business-to-business markets, selling organizations must often approve customers for credit, giving them 30, 60, or even 90 days to pay for the products and services that they receive. Related, not all business buyers pay their bills on time. So, salespeople may sometimes need to work with their accounting or billing department to help resolve payment disputes and collect past-due payments.

It can also be helpful for salespeople to have good relationships with colleagues in accounting or billing departments because these employees can provide salespeople with historical spending information at the customer or territory level. For example, imagine a salesperson calling an analyst in his or her accounting department asking for a report that shows how much a given customer in the territory spent last fiscal year. Depending on the company, this information may be provided by a sales analysis department or assessable from their CRM system.

Salespeople need to have good relationships with colleagues in accounting or billing because they act as gatekeepers, making decisions about customer creditworthiness and they can provide valuable information customer spending history. Accounting and billing employees also have direct contact with prospects and customers. So, these employees can affect the nature of a salesperson's relationship with a customer. Insofar as salespeople are relationship managers, it can be important for salespeople to manage relationships with their colleagues in accounting, billing, or credit departments.

To summarize, the extent to which a salesperson can build profitable relationships *externally* with customers can hinge upon the extent to which the salesperson can build healthy working relationships *internally* and leverage the resources available across departments. Many successful sales professionals, such as Matt Bollitier, President's Club Mortgage Banker at Quicken Loans, agree: "To solve customer problems and ultimately close deals, salespeople need various tools inside their organizations and access to people inside the organization who can help answer questions." See Figure 10-5.

Team Selling

Now that we've established that, to perform the sales job well, salespeople often rely on colleagues from various company departments, we can turn our attention to a related idea: Sometimes salespeople rely on colleagues from various departments to help sell.

Certain situations require a team-selling approach. A **team selling** occurs whenever two or more members of the seller's organization work together to close a sale. The successful use of the approach seeks to increase the salesperson's effectiveness by teaming them with whatever expertise is necessary. For example, imagine a salesperson accompanied on a sales call by an analyst from the finance department to talk about cash flow projections. Imagine that same salesperson also accompanied by an analyst from shipping or logistics departments to talk about

team selling
whenever two or more members of the seller's organization work together to close a sale

Figure 10-5 Interdepartmental Resources: Helping Salespeople Be More Effective and Efficient

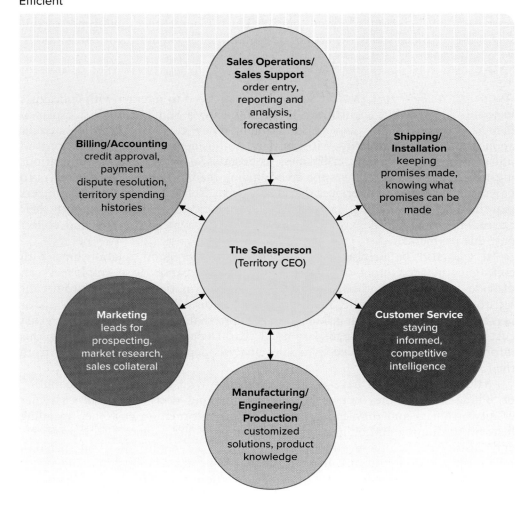

transportation possibilities. Imagine that same salesperson also accompanied by an analyst from the marketing department to talk about marketing research methodology. Imagine that same salesperson also accompanied by an engineer to talk about product design details.

With expertise from across departments, salespeople can better—and more quickly—answer technical questions that they may receive from buyers on a sales call. Bottom line: The extent to which salespeople are successful can sometimes hinge upon the extent to which salespeople can leverage a team with diverse expertise from across the company.

Self-Management in Sales

Many salespeople are given a higher than average degree of **job autonomy**, meaning they are self-directed as to how and when they perform their duties. With this greater degree of independence and less direct supervision, however, comes the responsibility for salespeople to effectively manage themselves. That is, successful salespeople do not require prodding; they drive or push themselves to get things done. Effective salespeople do not rely on prompts or reminders from their manager; they are proactive executives of their territory. Not only do they set a direction for themselves, effective salespeople then take the initiative to work hard and work smart.[10]

job autonomy
being allowed self-direction as to how and when to perform duties

Working Hard

Effective salespeople are self-motivated, hard workers. Think of **motivation** as a force that predicts the direction and intensity of effort.[11] Self-motivated salespeople give high levels of effort at work because of their own strong, personal interest in performing the job well. That said, the nature of the sales job can provide some salespeople with **intrinsic motivation**, a motivation that arises from within the individual because they find the requirements of the role naturally satisfying. Salespeople can also be driven by **extrinsic motivation**, a motivation stemming from external rewards like money, praise, or promotion. Consistently successful salespeople are motivated within themselves to achieve good results; their high effort levels at work do not depend on outside pressure from other people.

motivation
a force that predicts the direction and intensity of effort.

intrinsic motivation
motivation that arises from within the individual because they find the requirements of the role naturally satisfying

extrinsic motivation
motivation stemming from external rewards like money, praise, or promotion

The following quote is often attributed to Lee Iacocca, former Chief Executive Officer of Chrysler: "A manager's primary job is to motivate people." With this quote in mind, salespeople, as territory managers, must motivate themselves to cover their territory with a high level of effort. Many successful sales professionals, such as Sean Carter at Allstate, agree: "The harder you work, the more successful you are. Hustle beats talent when talent doesn't hustle."

Working Smart

Salespeople not only need to work hard, but they also need to work smart too. Working smarter means salespeople should constantly be reflecting, analyzing, learning, making appropriate adjustments, and generally thinking about ways to be more efficient. This final section of the chapter discusses three aspects of working smart as a territory manager: being organized, leveraging various types of information, and leveraging the power of CRM.

Being Organized   This chapter has already emphasized the importance of being efficient. In general, being organized will help salespeople be more efficient. The use of planners or calendars can help salespeople be effective as territory managers and better-organized day-to-day. Using a planner or a calendar is also important so that salespeople do not forget important activities or responsibilities such as following up with a given customer as promised or submitting a sales forecast to the sales manager when it is due.

In addition to the use of a planner or calendar, salespeople should also have a file management system, for both electronic and hard copy documents, that they are comfortable with. Salespeople typically have various documents that should be organized in a way that allows for efficient retrieval. For example, imagine a salesperson making an important presentation at a customer's office who needs to quickly access information about pricing or market research. As another example, imagine a different salesperson, traveling in an airport, on the phone with an important prospect who needs information about product specifications or available inventory as soon as possible. When salespeople waste valuable time looking for misplaced or lost documents, they are working inefficiently.

Leveraging Information   Effective territory managers handle information carefully and make use of a variety of types of information. The various types of information that salespeople, as territory managers, need to regularly record, access, and analyze include:

1. *Customer and prospect profile information.* Some of the most basic information that salespeople must record and access includes customer contact details, like their physical address, email address, phone numbers, preferred nickname, preferred times and days to be called or visited. Other information in this category can include the following: the source of the lead, names of spouses or children, personality or communication style, hobbies or shared interests, alma mater, or even birthday. For salespeople as territory managers, the information in this category is fundamental to both relationship-building and scheduling.

2. *Sales call records.* Other fundamental information that salespeople must record, access, and analyze includes notes that summarize previous sales calls. Information in this category includes:

   - Time and day of the call
   - People involved at the call
   - Notes on rapport-building
   - Uncovered needs or problems
   - Revenue potential
   - Current products/services used
   - Recent changes at the customer's organization
   - Products or solutions presented or demonstrated
   - Buyer objections raised
   - Follow-up promised or timelines discussed

   Detailed information about past sales conversations can help salespeople build credibility and customer trust. Leveraging information in this category can also help salespeople move the sales process forward in an efficient manner by sparing the need to re-identify needs or re-discover objections.

3. *Customer spending histories.* Some of the most valuable information that salespeople can regularly access and analyze as territory managers are details about historical spending figures at the customer level. Importantly, recording spending history is typically not a salesperson responsibility. Usually, there are order-entry, billing, or accounting systems that accurately track spending in the salesperson's territory over time. Also, as suggested previously, many companies have separate sales analysis departments to help salespeople analyze spending histories.

   Information about historical spending can help salespeople in several ways. For example, detailed information about how much a given customer spent in the past is important for salespeople looking to understand that customer's sales potential, and so, their territory priority. Historical spending information can also help salespeople understand their progress toward territory goals. See figure 10-6 for an example.

Leveraging information about historical spending can also give salespeople who are new to a territory some valuable perspective about territory trends. For example, they can see which accounts or account segments are growing and which are declining. Finally, accessing and analyzing spending history can help salespeople identify opportunities. For example, it may be helpful to know about former customers who have stopped buying or customers who have significantly reduced spending over time.

4. *Competitive intelligence.* Often, customers will share with a salesperson valuable information about their competitors' prices, promotions, and new products. Salespeople can also gain information in this category from other salespeople at their company, from their sales managers, or from colleagues in the marketing department at their firm. This type of information can be captured in sales call records, or it could be captured separately with other similar information. As salespeople are always interested in staying on top of the competition, salespeople and their managers are generally interested in gaining, recording and sharing this information. The information gained in this category can help salespeople differentiate themselves and their products, adapt their approaches, and be more responsive to an always-changing and competitive marketplace.

5. *Territory expense information.* Information about territory expenses is another important category of information for salespeople to regularly record, access, and analyze. Analyzing expense records can help salespeople determine whether they are allocating their resources according to their territory plans. Analyzing expense records can also help salespeople get a sense of whether they are getting a positive return on investment at the customer level. For example, have travel and entertainment expenses with a given customer started to pay off? Since the essence of territory management may boil down to making good decisions regarding the use of valuable and limited resources, salespeople need to monitor financial investments into the territory.

Figure 10-6 Tracking Progress Toward Territory Goals with Customer Spending Information: Actual vs. Goal, Mary Smith's Territory, Product A

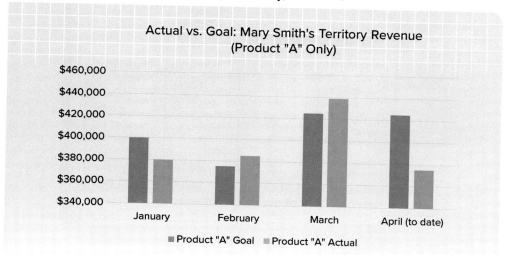

6. *Various company-related information.* Managing a territory will require salespeople to frequently access a variety of company-related information. Salespeople will often need remote and real-time access to the following, and more:

- Company marketing material
- Product information
- Pricing information
- Order forms
- Inventory and order-tracking information
- Market research

Internal company websites and apps can usually provide salespeople with the information that they need in this area. Otherwise, as suggested before, salespeople should have their own filing system that keeps information in this category at their fingertips. Leveraging information in this category can help salespeople be more efficient and effective while interacting with customers and prospects.

Working Smart with CRM Technology Tools   No tool is more powerful than CRM for helping salespeople work smarter, and better manage the relationships in their territory. As previously discussed, CRM enables salespeople to easily record, access, and analyze much of the key information described in this chapter[12]. In their simplest form, CRM can provide salespeople real-time and remote access to the information that they need. Salespeople can also quickly and directly communicate with customers through many CRMs. And a fundamental

Figure 10-7 Effective Territory Management: Summary of Key Principles

function of most CRMs enables salespeople to schedule and remind themselves about the tasks and meetings necessary to execute their territory plans.

Although mentioned in an earlier chapter, it is worth repeating that CRM can also streamline the internal communication and collaboration necessary for effective team selling. Organizations can also implement CRM to improve salesperson access to documents, marketing material, and other information to reduce the burden on the salespeople to maintain their own file management systems. And when the customer service or help desk staff use the same CRM as the sales force, a salesperson can instantly be alerted to a customer issue.

For salespeople, CRM is the ultimate organizational tool. In general, it is important for salespeople to be organized and make use of various kinds of information that can help them. Many successful sales professionals, such as Patrick Conway at DuPont agree: "As a salesperson, staying organized is key. It's also important to analyze significant information about customers. If you want to be a top performer (for both your company and your customer) you have to stay

Applying this Chapter to Salesforce

Reports and dashboards within Salesforce can tell the salesperson everything they need to know for territory management while tracking their progress to S.M.A.R.T. goals.

Once the salesperson has built their strategy, Salesforce can help with a resource allocation plan and time management. Salesforce *Report Builder* works with report fields and filters to build customized reports specific to the territory and available resources. It enables the salesperson to analyze the relationship between virtually anything related to their customers and territory.

Salesforce allows the salesperson to begin each day on their laptop or phone with a report that includes the highest priorities on the two-criteria grid. The grid clearly displays the high-spending and high-growth accounts, as well as the high-spending but low-growth accounts. Salesforce *Dashboards* show at a glance how many accounts are at each stage of the sales process and where they are located. The salesperson can *drill down* into each account to reveal additional detail, starting with the *Opportunities* and *Leads* associated with each account, and lastly, the *Contacts* for each. Salesforce makes it very easy to apply the 80/20 rule frequently, so the salesperson is always working smarter.

Dashboards in Salesforce can also inform accurate revenue forecasts, *snapshots* of the current state of the business, and a view of the salesperson's contribution to the company. Dashboards provide a variety of visual representations of data, depending on the preference for charts, tables, or graphics.

Some commonly used dashboards include: Sales Performance vs. Target, Pipeline Deals by Close Date and Opportunity Stage, Pipeline Quality Metrics, and Opportunity Conversion Rates. These dashboards show if the salesperson is on track to achieve their goal, the stage of each prospect, and when it should close, how viable the leads are, and the salesperson's close rate on past leads. Most salespeople and managers review their dashboards daily and make constant adjustments to their plans accordingly.

Chapter Summary

- No two sales territories are exactly alike. To some degree, each territory will require a unique salesperson approach.
- There are different types of sales territories such as geographic territories or territories based on customer type. Ideally, sales territories are designed with salesperson efficiency in mind.
- Goal setting is important in territory management. Territory goals motivate and guide salesperson behavior. Territory goals should be S.M.A.R.T., Specific, Measurable, Attainable (or achievable), Relevant, and Time-bound (or time-limited).

- Territory strategy should be based on territory goals. Strategy can be viewed simply as a resource allocation plan. Territory management strategy will involve finite resources and require trade-offs.
- Time is the scarcest personal resource for salespeople to manage. It should be managed carefully. Salespeople will want to spend their time with customers and prospects who can potentially generate the most revenue.
- Salespeople should manage their time not only according to customer priority, but also according to a calendar and a map.
- Just as it is important for salespeople to manage their time, it is also important for salespeople to make good use of company resources. Company resources that can help salespeople include company funds, which should be viewed as financial investments into the territory. Company resources also include employees from various departments who can help salespeople be more effective and efficient.
- Frequently given high levels of job autonomy, salespeople must often effectively manage themselves. Effective salespeople do not require prodding; they drive or push themselves to get things done. Not only do they set the direction for themselves, effective salespeople then take the initiative to work hard and work smart.

KEY TERMS

ABC account approach (p. 192)
expense accounts (p. 196)
extrinsic motivation (p. 201)
inside sales (p. 188)
intrinsic motivation (p. 201)
job autonomy (p. 201)
motivation (p. 201)

outside sales (p. 188)
S.M.A.R.T. goals (p. 189)
team selling (p. 200)
territory (p. 186)
territory goals (p. 188)
territory management (p. 186)
the 80/20 rule (p. 193)

Application 10-1

You are Jordan Smith, a newly hired sales representative for High-Tech Machinery Inc., a manufacturer of electrical components. Today is your first day on the job.

Your predecessor, Mary Johnson, took a different job within the company. On your first day, Mary emailed you a spreadsheet with the information below. Your territory has exactly 20 customers and generates more than $40 million annually. That means you have some big shoes to fill! To make things easier, Mary color-coded the spreadsheet, such that accounts who spend the most are in (dark) green and accounts who spend the least are in (dark) red.

Customer	This Year Revenue	Percent of Territory Revenue	Current Classification (Priority)
Company A	$91,369	0.21%	A
Company B	$6,181,455	14.38%	A
Company C	$72,170	0.17%	C
Company D	$454,552	1.06%	B
Company E	$44,038	0.10%	C

Company F	$2,058,453	4.79%	B
Company G	$11,822,085	27.51%	A
Company H	$76,232	0.18%	C
Company I	$670,613	1.56%	B
Company J	$4,932,226	11.48%	C
Company K	$410,589	0.96%	B
Company L	$9,297,098	21.63%	A
Company M	$572,234	1.33%	A
Company N	$60,311	0.14%	C
Company O	$1,828,564	4.25%	C
Company P	$13,739	0.03%	B
Company Q	$1,248,230	2.90%	B
Company R	$22,740	0.05%	B
Company S	$907,094	2.11%	B
Company T	$2,213,339	5.15%	C
Total Territory Revenue	**$42,977,131**		

You remember from your coursework in college that, in many sales territories, something like the 80/20 rule exists. You remember hearing about "the law of the vital few." You also remember that, in order to be an effective territory manager, you must prioritize. With this in mind, Mary's spreadsheet also contains her existing account classification. Mary used an ABC account approach to prioritizing customers within the territory.

As a new salesperson, you have several responsibilities in the coming weeks. However, you want to start thinking about prioritizing your accounts as soon as possible.

1. Thinking about the 80-20 rule, consider the four largest customers in the territory. What percentage of total territory sales comes from these four customers?
2. *Based on current revenue alone* and Mary's classification approach, which accounts should probably *not* be considered A accounts?
3. *Based on current revenue alone* and Mary's classification approach, which accounts should probably be considered an A account?

Application 10-2

You are Jordan Smith, a newly hired sales representative for High-Tech Machinery Inc., a manufacturer of electrical components. Today is your first day on the job.

Your predecessor, Alex Davis, was fired for consistently poor performance. On your first day, your new sales manager, Tina Smith, emailed you a spreadsheet with the information below. Your territory has exactly 20 customers and generates more than $40 million annually. That means you have some big shoes to fill! To make things easier, Tina color-coded the spreadsheet, such that accounts who spend the most are in (dark) green and accounts who spend the least are in (dark) red.

(Continued)

(Continued)

Customer	This Year Revenue	Percent of Territory Revenue	# of Sales Calls Made Last Quarter
Company A	$91,369	0.21%	6
Company B	$6,181,455	14.38%	5
Company C	$72,170	0.17%	10
Company D	$454,552	1.06%	13
Company E	$44,038	0.10%	5
Company F	$2,058,453	4.79%	10
Company G	$11,822,085	27.51%	44
Company H	$76,232	0.18%	29
Company I	$670,613	1.56%	10
Company J	$4,932,226	11.48%	31
Company K	$410,589	0.96%	32
Company L	$9,297,098	21.63%	26
Company M	$572,234	1.33%	18
Company N	$60,311	0.14%	6
Company O	$1,828,564	4.25%	15
Company P	$13,739	0.03%	7
Company Q	$1,248,230	2.90%	38
Company R	$22,740	0.05%	39
Company S	$907,094	2.11%	11
Company T	$2,213,339	5.15%	5
Total Territory Revenue	$42,977,131	Total Calls	360

You remember from your coursework in college that it is important for salespeople to spend their time with the most important customers. In fact, you heard that "spending time with the *wrong* customers" partially led to Alex's downfall as a salesperson at High-Tech Machinery, Inc. From the spreadsheet that Tina emailed you, you see that 360 sales calls were made across the territory last quarter (roughly 30 per week for 12 weeks).

As a new salesperson, you have several responsibilities in the coming weeks. However, you want to start thinking about planning your activities as soon as possible. You estimate that you will be able to make about the same number of calls as Alex next quarter (maybe a few more).

1. Thinking about the 80-20 rule, consider the four largest customers in the territory (i.e., the top 20%). How much of Alex's time (i.e., number of sales calls, in percentage terms) was spent with the four largest customers in the territory?

2. *Based on current revenue alone*, which of the following companies were probably neglected by Alex? That is, it probably makes sense to spend *more* time (compared to Alex) with which of the following customers?

3. *Based on current revenue alone*, which of the following companies were probably "over-serviced" by Alex? That is, it probably makes sense to spend *less* time (compared to Alex) with which of the following?

CHAPTER
11
Digital Sales

Learning Objectives

- Understand how sales technologies have transformed professional selling
- Comprehend how to apply digital selling techniques
- Recognize how the customer's journey has changed because of technology
- Identify social selling techniques and understand how to use them in professional selling
- Understand how artificial intelligence is changing professional selling
- Learn the basic uses and purpose of customer relationship management systems

dvances in technology, the internet, apps, and smartphones add complexity to the roles that salespeople play, and they will continue to affect both sellers and buyers in the future. Most salespeople use a range of digital technologies, such as customer relationship management programs, social media, and even artificial intelligence. This chapter explores popular digital sales technologies and how they are being used to enhance sales productivity. However, it is critical to recognize that technologies are constantly changing, so salespeople must adopt and adapt quickly to succeed.

Change Forces and Digital Technologies

With the constant introduction of new technologies and rapid expansion of connectivity, major change forces affect today's sales force and the salesperson's digital sales strategies. These change forces are dynamic and must constantly be monitored to ensure that salespeople are staying on top of customer expectations and optimizing success. Although this is a non-exhaustive list of change forces, many major changes fall into one of the following categories: globalization, technological changes, changes in competition, and changes in customer expectations (see Figure 11-1).[1]

globalization
the process by which organizations develop international influence through extending business, operations, or their presence into other countries

The first change force discussed, **globalization** is the process by which organizations develop international influence through extending business, operations, or their presence into other countries. Because of digital technologies, globalization has become a normal part of doing business for companies and salespeople alike. The second change force, technology is concerned with new sales technologies, such as software and hardware. Software such as Salesforce allows salespeople to track thousands of leads daily. Third, another change force, competition, must be constantly monitored by salespeople because digital technologies have leveled the playing field, allowing companies to compete in more creative and affordable ways. This parallels with the last change force, customer expectations. With the vast amount of competition in any industry, customers now expect real-time information customized to their preferences. In sum, digital technologies have and will disrupt the way both companies and salespeople work. Failing to adapt to these forces, a sales force may deliver declining performance on it's way to becoming obsolete. The following sections describe how each of these change forces influence salespeople today and their use of digital selling technologies and tools.

Figure 11-1 Change Forces

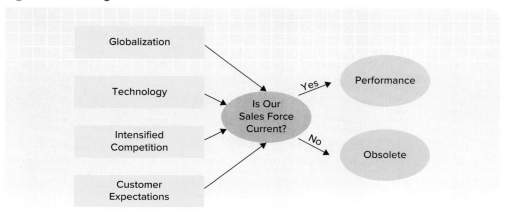

Globalization

It is almost comical to imagine now, but it wasn't that long ago that communication with people across state or country lines was not only problematic but very expensive. Services such as long-distance calling, where consumers paid a high rate per minute to talk on the phone to people in other states or countries, or faxing, where copies of documents were sent to other people using phone lines, may still be around, but they seem archaic when compared to the way digitization has changed our communication abilities. As communication became easier, with email, smartphones, and other technologies, globalization became easier for businesses and salespeople alike. The world is now more connected than ever. This connectivity allows businesses to become global influencers, start international locations, and manage an entire international workforce.

Before digitization, entering international markets or becoming a global leader in business was not only difficult but expensive. Imagine the barriers that would exist if a North American company was opening a new location in China without digital technologies such as the internet, email, and video conferencing! Today, salespeople call on prospects in France, Thailand, or Japan from the comfort of their own homes. Digitization has also provided salespeople and customers with an immense amount of available information. Learning about global businesses, prospects, and customers has become as simple as typing a few words into a browser search or scrolling across the prospect's multiple social media platforms. The rapid rise of globalization was founded on digital technologies that connect the world and provide great opportunities for salespeople today.

Technological Change

Recent technological advancements in peer-to-peer platforms, digital payment systems, and artificial intelligence have greatly changed the way the world does business. For example, social media platforms allow both sellers and consumers to share information about products and services by simply logging onto a site and sharing comments. More recently, artificial intelligence is helping businesses provide more relevant information to customers through algorithms and higher-quality service through the use of **bots**, autonomous programs on a network that interact with computer systems or users. Although these technologies are novel now, new technologies will soon be introduced that will either replace or greatly change the day-to-day activities of salespeople. Although adopting technological advancements is often critical for salespeople to stay relevant, one must keep in mind that technologies are gone as fast as they arrive. Salespeople who are willing to learn and adapt to change will reap the most benefits.

bots
autonomous programs on a network that interact with computer systems or users

Change in Competition

Globalization and technological change provide new pathways for businesses and salespeople to thrive, which leads to more entrants into the market, or more competition. Before digital technologies, it was typical that a few companies held most of the power within an industry. This was due to the often-expensive entrance costs that existed to start a business, such as having to buy a physical retail store. However, the increase in digital technologies allows all businesses and salespeople the opportunity to be directly connected to customers through online interactions. Even today, new businesses are being started daily around the globe. In some industries, such as smartphone applications, more than 6,000 new apps are released each day.[2] At this speed, it is quite a feat for salespeople to stay informed on their competition and how their product compares. Although increased competition can be difficult for businesses and salespeople, it also pushes them both to be better and do better, ultimately increasing innovations and providing customers with better products and services.

Change in Customer Expectations

The rise in product and service variety, owing to increased competition, has empowered customers and raised their expectations, leading to rapidly changing customer preferences. This rate of change in customer composition and customer preference within a market is known as **market turbulence**.[3] Market turbulence is quite a challenge for businesses and salespeople as they try to understand fast-changing customer needs and wants. Access to information has also increased customer expectations. Before the internet, customers gained most of their knowledge from word of mouth, catalogs, or salespeople. This meant that parties other than the customer controlled the flow of information regarding products and services. Today, consumers get their information from a variety of information channels that are based on digital technologies, such as social media platforms, recommendation sites, and television advertisements.

The mass amount of information available to the customers has shifted the control and power within a buying situation to the customer. For example, companies such as G2 provide sites where customers can provide reviews for business-to-business products. Although reviews have long been a standard in the business-to-consumer space, this is a game-changer for individuals who purchase goods and services for their company. Imagine buying $30,000 software that you have never used and know very little about. A customer review would certainly be helpful. Access to information across digital technologies enables the customer to not only make a more informed decision but to do so with more power and authority. Similar to increased competition, increased customer expectations also drive businesses and salespeople to innovate, ultimately providing better products and services for everyone.

In sum, digital technologies have brought and continue to bring about a lot of change for both businesses and salespeople. Specifically, globalization, technological advancements, rise in competition, and increased customer expectations have changed the business world and salespeople's roles as we know them. Salespeople must continue to research and innovate to ensure success. Next, we will explore how the customer's buying journey is different because of digital technologies.

market turbulence
the rate of change in customer composition and customer preference within a market

The Customer's Digital Buying Journey

As discussed in Chapter 2, the customer's buying journey is a critical element salespeople must understand to be successful. As customers consider purchasing a product or service, they often go through similar phases of the decision-making process. They acquire information, assess options, apply their decisions, and ensure they have received satisfactory results. These steps were explained in Chapter 2. However, it is important to understand how digital technologies influence this journey. Sixty percent of prospects or customers prefer not to interact with a salesperson as their primary source of information, and the same percent develop selection criteria and a set of vendors to choose from based completely on digital content.[4] As noted, digital technologies have brought about a change in the customer's buying journey through access to information and increased customer power. The following sections outline specific changes brought on by digital technologies. Figure 11-2 provides a detailed map of the buyer's journey.

Acquiring Information

Digital technologies increase the power of customers because of the vast amount of information available at their fingertips. Whereas before the internet customers looked to salespeople, colleagues, and advertisements for information regarding products and services, customers now have numerous ways they can access information. Considering how few customers want interaction with a salesperson for information,[5] many businesses now offer enablement or self-service tools that

Figure 11-2 The Buyer's Journey Map

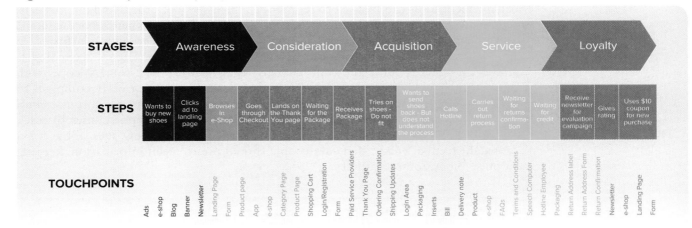

Source: https://www.brightvessel.com/customer-journey-map-2018/

allow customers to acquire information on their own. For example, some companies offer their prospects and customers websites where they can access demonstrations, product pricing, order history, and many other helpful bits of information. These websites allow prospects and customers to cut out the salesperson until they are ready to interact. Beyond information posted by the provider of the product or service, buyers also have a network of people and other media outlets that provide third-party information regarding products and services.

Long gone are the days when word of mouth only existed in face-to-face, small networks. Instead, word of mouth now travels around the whole globe, giving customers access to a larger pool of opinions and information. Digital technologies have disrupted the typical information flow, from the salesperson to the customer. Now customers are also able to attain information with little to no help from salespeople. Today, salespeople must be aware that their value no longer resides in simply being a carrier of information. Instead, salespeople must bring value to the interaction through expertise and consultation, helping the customer sift through the vast amounts of information and make an informed decision.

Assessing Options

Customers now have access to tools and software that allow them to more efficiently compare alternatives within their decision set. The rise of **crowdsourcing,** the use of platforms where many people can share their opinions on companies, businesses, and products, has completely changed the way prospects and customers evaluate their alternatives. Many companies now offer comparisons or quotes from many different vendors. Additionally, policing sites, such as TrustRadius, provide third-party reviews about business-to-business products and services. There are also digital communications technologies, such as Zoom, GoToMeeting, and online polls that allow a group of decision-makers, or the buying center, to evaluate the alternatives more efficiently and in real-time, as opposed to having to meet face-to-face or call each decision-maker individually. This is key as the average buying group size has increased. Digital technologies provide more information to help prospects and customers make buying decisions while also providing tools that make evaluating alternatives easier and more effective.

crowdsourcing
the use of platforms where many people can share their opinions on companies, businesses, and products

Achieving Satisfaction

Post-purchase, prospects and customers will evaluate their product or service, the company, and the salesperson from whom they bought the product or service. Digital tools can help the customer do this. For example, self-service and enablement tools can be used to reorder, see the history of orders and interactions, or check out new offers and products. Additionally, customer service centers, chatbots, and online reporting systems provide customers with platforms to find help, get more information, or even vent frustration. Digital technologies have brought about significant change regarding how customers cope with post-purchase dissatisfactions. A dissatisfied customer can currently complain to thousands of people on social media, review sites, and complaint forums. On a positive note, these same sites also allow salespeople ripe opportunities to track and influence customers' perceptions. Social media and review sites allow for a constant feedback loop that salespeople should use to glean information, keeping a pulse on customer attitudes.

What Is a Digital Sales Strategy?

As noted, digital technologies affect professional selling immensely, altering how salespeople and companies do business. New technologies have greatly changed available sales channels, salespeople's daily lives, and even organizational structure. For example, technologies have completely transformed sales organizations by moving many external selling jobs to the rapidly growing inside sales force segment, where digital technologies combined with the many social tools available help sales organizations expand their customer coverage without ever being physically present at the customer location. Within this environment, salespeople must have a clear and competitive digital selling strategy.

digital selling
the use of digital channels to reach out to prospects or customers, providing them with education, and ultimately offering solutions that meet their wants and needs

Digital selling involves the use of digital channels to reach out to prospects or customers, providing them with education, and ultimately offering solutions that meet their wants and needs.[6] A digital sales strategy must also consider the way customers use digital technologies. For example, a recent Forbes article suggests a rise in digital technologies has brought about an expectation that "customer service is always on."[7] Customers no longer only seek products and services from 9 a.m. to 5 p.m., but they also make decisions over dinner and on weekends. This change in cultural norms has shifted the role of the salesperson, who is now expected to always be on call for the customer. This is heightened by the newer cultural expectations of instant responses and communication that was impossible before smartphones and email. Although customer expectations have become more stringent, digital technologies provide a lot of opportunity for growth. For example, digital technologies allow salespeople to better qualify and understand their prospects and customers and provide them with personalized solutions.

Qualifying prospects is increasingly easier with digital technologies. A combination of social media platforms, news releases, company websites, and other online information helps salespeople understand the prospect's role and prioritize potential prospects much more affectionally. Additionally, using digital tools, salespeople can now reach a larger number of prospects and customers but also do so in a very individualized way. Digital sales have combined two critical parts of the traditional sales process, reaching a lot of potential buyers while personalizing each contact. These two selling aspects could not have existed in tandem without the rise of technology.

Digital Sales Strategies

Although digital sales strategies may mirror some traditional sales strategies, like educating customers, digital sales strategies should not be thought of as simply additional channels to communicate with prospects or customers with emails or social media messages, for example. Instead, digital technologies have opened a whole new resource for salespeople to use to enhance the sales process and improve customer relationships. Although not exhaustive, there are three common ways salespeople can use digital technologies to enhance each customer's experience and improve sales performance.

First, salespeople should attempt to better understand prospects and customers by using digital platforms, such as *LinkedIn*, *Twitter*, and *Instagram*. Social media platforms like these can help salespeople discover the role the prospect or customer has within the firm, their personal interests, and other individuals they may be connected to within the buying center. Salespeople should not just follow their prospects and customers, because within these social media platforms, more tools can be used to both prospect and sell. LinkedIn *Sales Navigator*, for example, assists salespeople in both targeting the right prospects and engaging with them in meaningful ways. Internal to the company, the use of data analytics software allows salespeople and companies to optimize customer data they have on hand to better understand future buying behaviors based on historical data. For example, data from a customer's buying history can be used to predict when the customer will likely need to reorder the product, allowing the salesperson to be proactive by setting a sales appointment. The effective use of data gathered through both social media platforms and customer databases provides the salesperson with critical insights regarding customer segments, the needs and wants of these segments, and how these segments behave.

Second, salespeople should be using digital content as part of their sales strategy. Anyone with a smartphone and internet access can create and share digital content. Social media allows salespeople to post about customer successes and create content relevant to their prospects and customers in just a few minutes. Other digital-based technologies, such as CRM, allow salespeople to share content both internally and with customers while also tracking who views the shared content.

Third, salespeople should be using digital channels and content to educate prospects and customers. Educating prospects and customers is a common strategy that has been used in traditional selling processes; however, the internet and social media have enriched the types of content available and increased the efficiency of doing so. For example, a medical device sales representative can become a trusted source by simply posting information on social media about the industry the salesperson is working in or by sharing personalized content based on the salesperson's prospect and customer segments. Some salespeople even hold online events such as lunch-and-learns, where the salesperson sends lunch to prospects and then uses video conferencing software to share information about her products and services while prospects eat free food.

Although there are numerous potential digital sales strategies, better understanding prospects and customers, incorporating digital content into a sales strategy, and educating prospects and customers are the foundations of many digital selling techniques. Salespeople should not think of digital sales strategies as simply other channels for sharing information. Instead, salespeople should be creating content with digital strategies in mind and using digital data to better inform sales strategy decisions. Digitization has brought about a drastic change in the traditional sales process, offering more ways to communicate, more data to better understand customers, and more content to access and create. The ultimate end game to digital sales strategies is the same as traditional sales strategies, close a sale; however, the journey there may look very different on a digital platform than it does in traditional selling situations. Often, digital sales stages end with a call to action, such as *sign up*, *discover*, *try*, or *watch*. These **calls to action**, messages designed to provoke an immediate response, are helpful in both prospecting and leading the customer through their buyer's journey efficiently. A major benefit

call to action
a message designed to provoke an immediate response

of digital strategies is that the salespeople can often track the information that the prospect or customer is being exposed to through these calls to action in the form of click-throughs, likes on social media, and video views. This allows for close monitoring of the customer buying journey and optimal assistance and intervention by the salesperson, knowing just the right time to contact them. Although opportunities abound for salespeople within the technology space, there are barriers to digital selling of which salespeople must be aware. The following section outlines one of these major hurdles, creating authenticity or a human touch.

Authenticity and the Human Touch

Digital technologies have driven down the number of face-to-face interactions salespeople have with prospects and customers. In some ways, this is a good thing, considering how much more efficient an email, text, or social media inbox message is compared to traveling to another city, state, or country to visit a prospect or customer. However, the decline of face-to-face interactions has left many salespeople asking the question, "How do we create a personal connection when we mostly communicate digitally?" Creating real, personal, human interactions with prospects and customers is difficult, regardless of the situation; however, research suggests that authenticity is a key component of life, central to most selling situations, and increases sales performance.[8] Beverland and Farrelly write in their research on consumers that, "despite the multiplicity of terms and interpretations applied to authenticity, ultimately what is consistent across the literature is that **authenticity** encapsulates what is genuine, real, or true."[9] Consumers have built-in authenticity detectors based on historical pattern recognition of the actions, appearance, and words that undermine trust.[10] Customers can detect a salesperson's lack of authenticity.[11] Salespeople already fight stereotypes of being inauthentic and self-interested. This perceived lack of authenticity is why human touch, or dealing with people in a kind and empathetic way, is so critical for salespeople.

Authenticity and the human touch are just as critical now as they were. However, moving sales interactions online makes building authentic connections more complex. Companies should be using digital technologies to optimize authenticity in both online and face-to-face interactions. A recent report suggests companies that integrate human touch into their digital sales strategies outperform their peers, creating five times more revenue and eight times more profit.[12] Although there is no "one size fits all" approach to creating human touch and authenticity online, studies suggest that a hybrid approach, using both face-to-face and digital strategies, is most often the appropriate way to increase sales performance and is usually what customers want.[13] Salespeople should research and understand where a human touch is most appropriate during the customer's buying journey. For example, customers may prefer to use self-enablement tools to learn about the salesperson's products, but they may prefer to speak to a salesperson on the phone once they have narrowed their options down. Companies and salespeople should adopt a digital sales strategy with a human touch in mind. Investing in digital technologies that make the customer's buying journey more efficient and authentic will create the biggest impact for most firms.

authenticity
what is genuine, real, or true

Digital Selling Tools

A recent study notes that 91% of business-to-business buyers use social media as a sales channel, and 84% of senior executives use social media in purchase decisions.[14] Although traditional selling and social selling are very different (see Table 11-1), they can complement each other, ultimately increasing performance. In other words, salespeople are missing out on opportunities by not including social selling in their digital sales strategies. The following sections will discuss

Table 11-1 Traditional Selling vs. Social Selling

TRADITIONAL SELLING		SOCIAL SELLING
PURCHASE LEAD LISTS	FIND	UTILIZE PROFESSIONAL NETWORKS
LIMITED PERSONAL CONTACTS		UTILIZE COMPANY SOCIAL NETWORK
NAVIGATE GATEKEEPERS		TARGET KEY DECISION-MAKERS
RANDOM CONTACTS	RELATE	CONCENTRATE ON REAL PEOPLE
LIMITED TO INTERNAL RECORDS		GATHER ONLINE INTELLIGENCE
GATHER USELESS DATA		DISCOVER SOCIAL INSIGHTS
RELY ON COLD CALLING	ENGAGE	LEVERAGE WARM INTRODUCTIONS
DEPENDENCE ON SALES SCRIPT		HAVE RELEVANT CONVERSATIONS
USE REPETITIVE PROCESS		GLIDE THROUGH BUYING PROCESS

Source: adapted from http://www.coldsalesprospecting.com/social-media-sales-prospecting

two specific types of tools salespeople can take advantage of that have completely changed and will continue to change the landscape of sales interactions: social media and artificial intelligence.

Social Selling

Salespeople and customers alike have been using the internet for decades to understand each other better and the products and services offered. However, the rise of social media offered not only another avenue to garner information, but also a new channel to allow for communications and personalization. **Social selling** is defined as the process of developing a relationship as part of the sales process through the use of social media platforms such as LinkedIn, Instagram, Facebook, etc.

Through social selling, salespeople can become authoritative figures on topics, also known as **thought leaders**, by sharing industry insights, specialized knowledge, and customer solutions through self-created or third-party content. The main goal of social selling is to build relationships and trust, so that when the time is right, the prospect or customer chooses to do business with the salesperson. Social selling is particularly important now that prospects and customers are less likely to be persuaded by traditional means of selling. Instead, prospects and customers expect personalized knowledge and customized solutions.

Social selling allows the salesperson to access very personal customer intelligence through social media platforms, where the customer chooses and shares information that is important to them. In sum, social selling is a critical tool that salespeople today should not ignore. Social selling allows salespeople to build warm, personalized leads while becoming a thought leader in their field. This builds trust with prospects and customers and ultimately increases sales performance.

Social Selling Techniques   Although each salesperson should tailor their social selling strategy to their products, services, prospects, and customers, there are a couple of techniques that tend to span all contexts.

First, salespeople must recognize that social selling takes time and patience. It is rare for a salesperson to join LinkedIn and get new business within the first week. Instead, social selling is a long-term strategy, and salespeople must build their online presence through posting and interacting regularly. Salespeople who are sharing valuable information with customers and building a personal brand online become trusted sources of information and thought leaders, making prospects and customers more trusting and willing to reach out.

social selling
the process of developing a relationship as part of the sales process through the use of social media platforms

thought leaders
authoritative figures on topics

Second, salespeople should use social selling to understand prospects and customers better, leading to the personalization of information and solutions. Social media platforms allow salespeople to access customer information that would typically not be available anywhere else. For example, if a customer is posting regularly about artificial intelligence and technology, the salesperson knows that focusing on the technological aspects of their products and services will probably be received well by this customer. Additionally, this allows the salesperson an opportunity to share information regarding artificial intelligence and technology specifically to that customer through an inbox message or by tagging them for a post. As a side note, salespeople should only share information from reputable sources. In today's world of fast responses and instant gratification, individuals are often guilty of sharing information that is not accurate or that they haven't fully read. Don't be guilty of this as a salesperson. There is no quicker way to lose the trust and respect of prospects and customers.

Lastly, salespeople should connect with other thought leaders and potential customers in their areas by joining specialized groups. Many social media sites offer online groups to connect individuals with shared interests. Specialized industry groups (e.g., medical device sales, industrial sales) are a great way to stay on top of what is current in the industry and to connect with others that may become sources of referrals. For example, there are over 1.7 million groups on LinkedIn that focus on industry topics. Salespeople can use these groups to see what challenges their customers are talking about, develop a voice, weigh in on conversations, and become a subject matter expert.

How Do Salespeople Know Social Selling Is Working?   Like traditional selling techniques, salespeople need to evaluate how well their social selling strategies are working. There are a couple of different ways to do this. First, salespeople should create a content schedule that specifies the frequency and type of content that will be shared. For example, posting three times a week on LinkedIn is a good starting point. As for the type of content that will be shared, salespeople can either share information from a third-party site (Forbes, Harvard Business Review) or create content. Creating content can be difficult and time-consuming, but when done right, it can earn the salesperson credibility. Tracking and adjusting social selling techniques is a critical part of social selling, just as it is with traditional sales strategies and metrics. Without tracking results, there is no way to know what types and frequency of content resonate with prospects and customers. In addition to self-tracking, other tools can also help evaluate the effectiveness of social selling techniques.

social selling index (SSI)
a score created by LinkedIn that assesses a salesperson's impact on their platform

The **Social Selling Index** (SSI) is a score created by LinkedIn that assesses a salesperson's impact on their platform by the use of four criteria: the salesperson's connections, engagement, ability to build relationships, and personal brand establishment. Similarly, *Klout* is a scoring system that gauges how influential a salesperson is across multiple social media platforms (Facebook, LinkedIn, Instagram, Twitter). There are many other examples online. Although these scoring systems help gauge social selling effectiveness, a high score doesn't necessarily translate to more sales. Salespeople should use these as a rule of thumb, but self-tracking is the most reliable and critical way to ensure social selling success.

Artificial Intelligence

artificial intelligence (AI)
the simulation of human intelligence by machines

Another tool that salespeople must be aware of is artificial intelligence. **Artificial intelligence** (AI) is the simulation of human intelligence by machines, and it is based on algorithmic learning. Artificial intelligence can come in many forms. Siri and Netflix both incorporate elements of artificial intelligence to determine how to respond and what to recommend to users. And bots, autonomous programs

Figure 11-3 Example of Artificial Intelligence Software—Crystal

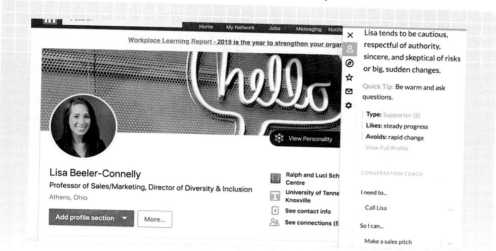

Source: Retrieved at https://www.crystalknows.com/

that interact with systems and users, are increasingly difficult to tell apart from a human response. Artificial intelligence, its complexity, and its application are expanding at an exponential rate.

There are a few notable ways artificial intelligence is being used in sales today: to profile customers based on their social media content, to help decide what to say and when to say it to prospects and customers, and to help salespeople decide which prospects or customers to prioritize. Applications such as Crystal, Node, and Seventh Sense use artificial intelligence to assist salespeople in selling smarter and more efficiently. For example, Crystal (see Figure 11-3), a web browser add-on, profiles customers based on their social media content and then provides information regarding their personality traits, guides for meetings, and even what to say in an email to that prospect or customer. Similarly, Node not only discovers potential customers and prioritizes which are most likely to close, but also tells the salesperson what to say in emails to close more sales. Seventh Sense integrates with customer relationship management programs to tell salespeople the best time to send emails to prospects or customers to increase open rates. These are only a few of the types of artificial intelligence tools available to salespeople currently, but the rise of artificial intelligence in businesses will surely bring many more. Salespeople must be aware of and willing to adopt artificial intelligence to help make the sales process more successful.

Are Salespeople Still Relevant?   The rise of technology over the last 40 years and the future of artificial intelligence has many salespeople wondering if they will still have a job in the next couple of decades. Considering that artificial intelligence can now complete many of the low-level tasks, such as sending emails, that salespeople were once expected to do, this is a fair concern. However, because a key component of salespeople's jobs is creating relationships and trust, salespeople should still have jobs available for decades to come. Although artificial intelligence is promising, it still lacks in the ability to build and understand trust or feel empathy. However, it is important to note that if a task can be automated, it probably will be, so salespeople must hone their emotional intelligence and soft skills to be relevant. Salespeople that not only welcome artificial intelligence but understand how to optimize their time by allowing the automation of menial tasks by using artificial intelligence will be most likely to succeed and thrive in this new technological era.

Customer Relationship Management Strategies

CRM has been covered in every chapter of this book because it is often the backbone of a company's approach to managing interactions with current and potential customers. These interactions might occur in different areas, such as marketing, sales, operations, customer support, customer service, or with salespeople. Because managing thousands, if not hundreds of thousands of customers at once can be an immense task, many companies have adopted CRM to enable their salespeople to keep track of their daily selling activities and analyze these activities through a dashboard of graphs, bar charts, and other visual representations. (See figure 11-4) Some companies even integrate their customer relationship management programs with their warehouse, call center, and accounting systems, so salespeople have everything about their customers in one place. A well-implemented CRM properly reflects the company's relationship management strategy by providing a 360-degree view of all the interactions with their customers. Although a whole textbook could be devoted to CRM, and each chapter of this book includes a brief description of Salesforce features that relate to each chapter, the following will provide an overview of the impact of CRM on each stage of the sales process.

Lead Generation and Prospecting

As we discussed in Chapter 4, identifying leads is the first step of prospecting. CRM is critical in this prospecting phase of the sales process since salespeople are often interacting with hundreds, if not thousands of prospects and customers at once. During this phase, CRM can be used to track phone calls, send out multi-stage email campaigns, track click-through rates on websites, or even prioritize daily activities based on the likelihood of closing specific deals. CRM enables salespeople to interact with and track relationships with many more prospects and customers than they would be able to do on their own. For example, a salesperson can send a multi-email sales campaign to 1,000 prospects with a single command or view all the interactions that have happened with a prospect over the last three years by simply selecting that prospect's name. Additionally, a simple search function can help a salesperson focus on a market segment when a topic or issue becomes relevant. For example, *60 Minutes* ran a story about the unethical handling of a hazardous product by Boston Scientific known as implantable mesh, which affected over 1 million women. Knowing that this news might cause some Boston Scientific customers to seek out an alternative, salespeople with a competing product may have searched their CRM to quickly identify Boston Scientific customers and contact them.

Planning Sales Calls

Planning sales calls and presentations is significantly easier if CRM has been used consistently during the history with the prospect or customer. Because most CRMs are cloud-based, even customer interactions with other salespeople or team members can be viewed. This allows the salesperson to access a large amount of information, including how the relationship has evolved. For example, the salesperson may learn that two years ago, the prospect wanted to buy from the salesperson's company, but wasn't able to meet the minimum financing requirements. This is critical information that would need to be incorporated into the sales call. CRM, when used properly, provides key historical insights regarding prospect and customer intelligence that can make the salesperson more likely to succeed in the present.

Figure 11-4 Salesforce Dashboard

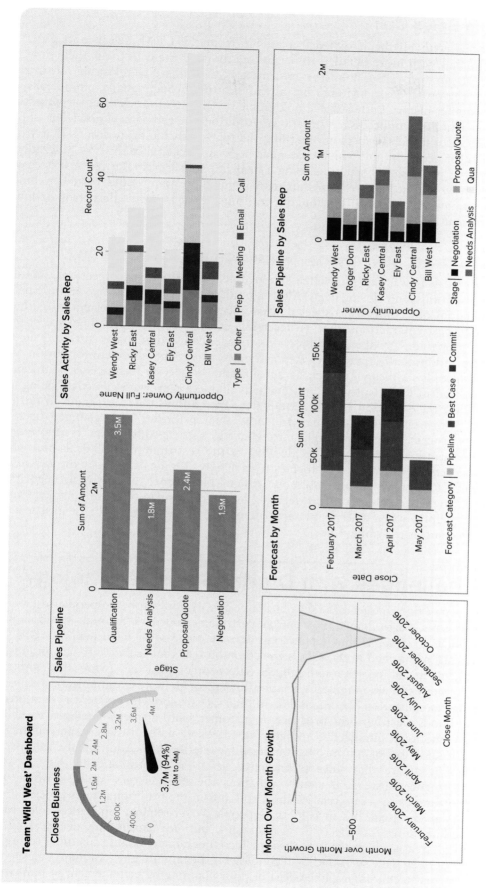

Source: https://galvintech.com/effectively-manage-sales-pipeline-using-7-powerful-salesforce-dashboards/

The Sales Call

Armed with all the knowledge available from the CRM, salespeople enter the sales call with more detailed information, allowing them to focus their time and efforts on uncovering unknown information, as opposed to revisiting information that the prospect or customer has already shared through emails, phone calls, etc. Customer history knowledge should guide the choice of needs discovery questions and eliminate unnecessary questions. Additionally, the same knowledge should help inform the salesperson regarding the types of value propositions that would be most pertinent and which ones have been unsuccessful in the past. Considering that, in professional selling, closing a deal can sometimes take years, it is easy to see how a customer relationship management program could better streamline information and make the selling process much easier for the salesperson and more efficient for the customer.

Customer Objections, Negotiations, and Closing

CRM can be very helpful when salespeople are anticipating objections, handling negotiations, and closing deals. Although salespeople should always be anticipating potential objections a prospect or customer may have, the information gathered from past interactions that is accessible with the CRM will help salespeople be prepared for specific objections or concerns that have surfaced in the past. Additionally, prospects or customers may have shared information with salespeople's colleagues, such as accountants or service technicians, that can be recorded in CRM software and made available for everyone. Further, being able to view the evolution of interactions over time allows the salesperson to tap into the priorities of the customer and how their priorities have changed over the sales process, providing insight into what key aspects to focus on in negotiations. CRM can help salespeople decide when is the best time to close deals and which prospects or customers to focus on each day. Many of the newest extensions from CRM providers are based on artificial intelligence. For example, algorithms can now assist salespeople in deciding how to prioritize their time, which can be very helpful when salespeople are attempting to serve hundreds of prospects or customers at the same time.

Challenges with Digital Sales Technology

Although this chapter has laid out many opportunities for salespeople to enhance their sales performance and enrich customer's journeys through technology, it is naïve to assume that technology doesn't come with its downfalls. One key concern mentioned previously is the common fear that technology has diminished authenticity in professional selling. Salespeople must be aware that although technology can aid in building relationships through more communication channels and personalization of content, it is still the salesperson who creates the relationship and builds trust with the prospect or customer. Until artificial intelligence exhibits high emotional intelligence and empathy, the soft skills of the salesperson are still the foundation of any professional selling relationship. Additionally, salespeople must be aware that sales technology use doesn't automatically increase sales performance. Instead, it simply enhances the salesperson's abilities, offers new opportunities to create relationships and aids in the traditional sales process.

A major issue lies in some salespeople's over-reliance on digital sales tools, spending hours prospecting on LinkedIn, but not developing deeper skills in critical areas such as needs analysis or recommending valuable customer solutions. Another key issue surrounding technology is the unwillingness of many salespeople to use new technologies, like CRM or poor planning by management to implement the use of new technology. For example, although 91% of companies with ten or more employees use CRM,[15] only 45% of companies use it to store customer data![16] In sum, although new digital sales technologies offer ripe opportunities for salespeople, these same technologies must be used with care and intention to be effective.

Applying the Chapter to Salesforce

salesforce

Digital tools like a CRM are changing the way salespeople do business, most importantly, meeting the customers where they already are, in a digital environment.

Social media monitoring through any CRM is critical for identifying important prospects. And having a strong social media presence can create a sense of trust and community between the salesperson and customers. Salesforce can automatically gather and analyze conversations from almost any social media source, allowing the salesperson to *hear* what people are saying about their products and brand. They can gather market intelligence and learn from real discussions customers are having. With that insight and intelligence, the salesperson can more effectively engage their community, providing guidance, direction, and immediate customer support. Connecting all of this social media activity to Salesforce also informs the strategy for future campaigns, messaging, and audience growth.

The artificial intelligence in Salesforce is called *Einstein*. It can increase productivity by making key predictions, intelligent recommendations, and timely automation of tasks. Previous chapters described the process of analyzing reports and dashboards for decision-making. Einstein is a bit like giving each salesperson access to their own *data scientist*. Einstein learns from the salesperson's activities and data, then helps identify the best leads, convert opportunities more efficiently, and retain customers.

Einstein can help prioritize the sales prospects most likely to close based on how other similar prospects have progressed to closure. It can also make suggestions on steps to take to improve the odds of winning. For example, Einstein may flag an opportunity that is three steps from closure and say, "Perhaps it is time to reach out to this customer on Social Media and make an introduction to (current satisfied customer's name) for a reference?" If the salesperson accepts Einstein's advice, it will provide a templated message, ready to customize. Einstein can also search and prioritize email, bringing the most important to the top, or adding a tag like "Scheduling request included" for events that can easily be added to the salesperson's calendar.

Chapter Summary

- Digital sales constantly change the face of professional selling through globalization, technological change, an increase in competition, and a change in customer expectations.
- The customer's buying journey is highly influenced by digital technologies, increasing the amount of information available.
- Digital sales strategies are an integral part of the selling process that goes beyond the traditional sales strategy.
- Authenticity and human touch are critical, especially when salespeople have access to a vast number of prospects and customers (making it easy to focus on the number of relationships over the quality of relationships), and where the traditional face-to-face channel is used less often.
- Social selling is a form of selling that involves building relationships and is often done through online social platforms.
- Artificial intelligence can augment salespeople or replace salespeople, depending on how the salesperson perceives and adopts it.

- Customer relationship management is a company's approach to managing interactions with current and potential customers, often using data analysis from CRM programs to improve relationships with customers.
- Salespeople are often resistant to customer relationship management tools when they are first implemented because they take time to learn and use.

Key Terms

artificial intelligence (AI) (p. 218)
authenticity (p. 216)
bots (p. 211)
call to action (p. 215)
crowdsourcing (p. 213)
digital selling (p. 214)

globalization (p. 210)
market turbulence (p. 212)
social selling (p. 217)
social selling index (SSI) (p. 218)
thought leader (p. 217)

Application 11-1

Sam is a salesperson for a mobile app startup called Dyanmite. Dynamite is used by businesses to streamline their employee's budget and spending. For example, employees will use this app when they return from work travel to get reimbursed for their expenses by simply taking pictures of their receipts and submitting a simple form. Since Sam is aware they are not the only providers of mobile apps with similar functions, she decides it is critical to understand the customer's digital journey and wants to map it out. The following outlines Sam's process of mapping her customer's journeys.

First, Sam starts with the customer information previously collected by other Dynamite salespeople and the marketing research department. Sam searched for current customer intelligence within Dynamite's customer relationship management (CRM) program to map out the various ways customers can encounter information regarding their mobile app. Mapping out the different types of digital journeys, or steps to purchase is critical in determining sales opportunities and purchasing barriers. Sam discovers that the marketing research team found that 80% of purchases are made on the customer's phone's app store (as opposed to Dynamite's website) and that 60% of the people that link to the download are clicking on an advertisement they saw on Twitter. Sam also uncovers that the specific link being used on Twitter is a discount product link (e.g., 20% off the first three months subscription). Now Sam has enough information to begin mapping out one of the possible digital journeys a prospect or customer takes from information seeking to purchase the Dynamite app. However, it is important to note that often many possible digital journeys exist, especially in complex buying processes that are common in professional selling situations. Sam will continue to search for more information within the CRM program that provides insight regarding the other paths of the customer's digital journey.

Second, Sam puts herself in the shoes of the customer. Sam considers the goals and values of the different types of prospects and customers that are downloading Dynamite from the Twitter link. These goals and values will often give the salesperson insight as to what types of information or touchpoints the prospect or customer may seek or encounter. For example, Sam thinks that prospects and customers that care most about the quality and service of the app may read the app store reviews or visit a rating site to attempt to understand whether other customers are having issues with the Dynamite app. Whereas, a prospect who cares most about price may go to a competitor's website to get quotes. Sam recognizes these are two very different types of touchpoints that prospects and customers encounter that are motivated by specific goals and values. Understanding customer goals and values allow Sam to better map the specific customer's buying journeys they may take based on meeting needs and wants.

Third, Sam maps out all the possible touchpoints on the digital customer's buying journey. Sam makes a list of all the possible touchpoint (interactions) a prospect or customer may encounter during their digital customer's buying journey. For example, reading one of Dynamite's blog articles, liking a LinkedIn article that highlights the mobile app, and reading a third-party review of Dynamite are all possible touchpoints a customer may experience on the search for a comparable mobile app. It is Sam's job to collect information and understand the most logical touchpoints each prospect or customer may encounter. At this point, a logical digital customer's buying journey can begin to be formed. Sam decides that in addition to linking to the website from Twitter, it is logical to assume that a segment of prospects uses a search engine such as Google to search for a general product category. Sam confirms this by exploring data the marketing research team has collected by using Google Analytics to track search engine traffic to the Dynamite's website. From there, Sam thinks prospects may visit a few different competitor's websites and then visiting review sites or even social media sites to learn more. Although Sam is unable to predict with complete accuracy the digital journey of each prospect or customer, Sam is now armed with general knowledge about the digital customer's buying journey, and ultimately how to enrich and optimize this journey.

Finally, Sam creates a graphic of the digital customer's buying journey map and validates it. Sam wanted to ensure all of her sales team was informed regarding their prospect's and customer's digital journey. Consequently, she created a simple graphic of the various journey paths from information seeking to purchase. This allowed all of her colleagues to easily understand the typical flow of the digital customer's buying journey and the likely touchpoints that the prospects or customers encounter. Sam then tested this digital customer's buying journey map for accuracy. To validate her map Sam began to track all of the proposed interactions and touchpoints and work closely with the marketing research team to integrate the information they were gathering. She recorded Interactions such as social media likes and comments, along with click-through rates of promotional links. She also analyzed potential barriers, like where prospects and customers are lost along the journey. She did this by using tracking software on Dynamite's websites. She found that customers were often placing the Dynamite app in their digital "carts" but not completing the purchase. This suggests that an issue existed at this touchpoint. To address this, Sam formed a small team of salespeople that were responsible for calling these individuals if the product sat in their cart for more than 24 hours without purchase. She found that these calls converted 65% of those prospects. Most of these prospects just had a few extra questions that needed answering before purchasing Dynamite.

1. Using Dynamite as an example, in what ways does technology change the buying journey?
2. Identify the steps in the buying journey from the Dynamite example.
3. Where should salespeople first gather information to inform the customer's buying journey map?

Application 11-2

Ally works as a salesperson at Hino, which is Toyota's division of commercial trucks. On a typical day, she calls on current customers and prospects, hoping to sell them fleets of trucks. Examples of current customers are Amazon (for shipping trucks) and Ryder (for moving trucks). Ally has worked as a salesperson for Hino for more than four years now and manages a large sales team. She has had contact with thousands of potential and current customers. Recently, Hino instituted the use of Salesforce for their salespeople, an online customer relationship management program. Although Ally is a bit frustrated that she has to take at least an hour out of each day to record her sales activities, she is starting to see the value in it. The following outlines a few different ways Ally has been using the new customer relationship management program.

Ally has been tracking her new prospects. Salesforce allows Ally to keep all her prospects and customers in one place. Although a salesperson can do the same in Microsoft Outlook, Salesforce allows salespeople to keep the history of emails and calls, and even analyzes Ally's prospect pipeline using various statistics.

Ally has been using the Salesforce dashboard to better understand her pipeline of customers and prospects and to also keep track of how her sales team is doing. Her dashboard allows her to see how much business has been closed and to keep track of which sales representatives are selling the most. Additionally, she can even track what type of sales activities she and her sales team have had over the last month.

Ally has been sending out email campaigns to current customers and prospects, letting them know that Hino will soon introduce a new truck model. Salesforce, similar to many other customer relationship programs, allows Ally to pre-plan and send emails to prospects and customers over the course of weeks or even months. Ally recently used this option to send two different email campaigns. The first campaign was to current customers who have had their Hino trucks for more than 10 years. The second campaign was to prospects who haven't owned a Hino truck, but expressed great interest in buying a fleet. Ally created these two campaigns by uploading six different emails, choosing send dates, and then choosing the contacts for them to be sent to. She attached a white paper (a report on the new truck) to the first email of the campaign. Not only did Salesforce send all six of the emails to the contacts over the course of six months, but it also tracked who opened the emails and who downloaded the white paper.

Ally has found a lot of value in the use of Salesforce to manage her pipeline of prospects and customers. Although the initial adoption of the software and time it takes to enter the data can be frustrating, she sees it now as a time investment that ultimately paid off. Plus, now that she has gotten the hang of it, she is able to record everything quickly. It may be likely that the company you end up with will also use a customer relationship management program. It may or may not be Salesforce, but it is important to understand the purpose and basic operations of a customer relationship management program.

1. Describe what CRM, such as Salesforce, allow salespeople to do.
2. Although many companies own a customer relationship management platform, many do not actively use them to track customer data. Why might that be?
3. Describe how CRM can improve a salesperson's effectiveness in each stage of the selling process.

CHAPTER

12

Selling to Strategic Accounts using Customer Business Development Strategies

Learning Objectives

- Master the concepts underlying customer business development
- Understand that some business customers are more important than others
- Apply the ways firms use strategies centered on integrative outcomes with key customer accounts
- Identify the aspects unique to team selling
- Understand the six key relationship-forging tasks that salespeople conduct to establish better business relationships when assigned to strategic account teams

C ertain customers present unique sales challenges because they are so valuable to the seller, either because of their current revenue or potential revenue. Although none of the sales principles described in previous chapters are wrong for these valuable customers, they often do require additional strategies, tactics, and resources for sales success. In this chapter, we will focus on how these customers may have different requirements, how the selling organization might deploy a team of people to sell to these customers, and how the selling process may need to be adapted for these customers.

Selling to Strategic Accounts

Not all customers are created equal. For many selling organizations, a small portion of customers generates a large portion of sales or profits.[1]

When attempting to prioritize customers, in practice, the **Pareto Principle** suggests that a firm's customer base may be represented by a *vital few* and a *trivial many*, also known as the 80/20 rule. Applying the Pareto Principle to account management, about 80% of a selling firm's profit may come from 20% of its customers. Since these customers generate so much of the firm's profits, they are strategically important to the sales organization's financial viability. For professional selling, these accounts get special attention from sales managers who allocate more resources and often assign their best salespeople to those accounts. The collection of responsibilities associated with managing the selling firm's relationships with its most strategically important accounts is referred to as **strategic account management (SAM)**.[2] As SAM jobs represent common sales openings for large manufacturers and are potentially rewarding positions for careers in professional selling, developing a general understanding of them is important for the student of professional selling.

As shown in Figure 12-1, a network of resellers may exist between a manufacturer and its ultimate targeted consumers. Each line represents a direct exchange of products between manufacturers, wholesalers, and retail customers (resellers), and consumer markets. This network is representative of industries organized like consumer-packaged goods, household goods, furniture, computer, telecommunications, and other consumer targeting industries. Resellers who reach large, economically value-targeted consumer markets, like a national chain of retail stores, are of vital strategic importance to the long-term success of a manufacturer, like Procter and Gamble. In contrast, other resellers may serve a small portion of the ultimate consumer market, and the manufacturer may not interact directly with that retail chain but only sell to it through wholesale customers.

To serve the needs of the larger, strategically important accounts, many sales organizations align their sales force to those accounts in ways that help better forge business relationships. The salespeople work in consultative sales roles, which make them valuable resources to their customer accounts as they develop, propose, and implement integrative solutions. These tailored solutions are intended to serve the mutual interests of the buyer and seller, which may center on serving the interests of the customer's customer—in the earlier example, that would be the consumer markets served by retail grocery chains. Salespeople assigned to these strategic accounts confront the more challenging, but potentially more rewarding task of forging relationships with those accounts—and some may even be *embedded* and even hold offices co-located inside the business buying account's major buying centers.[3]

A buying center, as defined previously, is the decision-making unit composed of "all those members of an organization who become involved in the buying process for a particular product or service."[4] Moreover, as the needs of these accounts

pareto principle
suggests that a firm's customer base may be represented by a "vital few" and a "trivial many" and is also known as the "80/20 rule"

strategic account management (SAM)
the collection of responsibilities associated with managing the selling firm's relationships with its most strategically important accounts

Figure 12-1 Hypothetical Network of Resellers Derving Different Consumer Markets

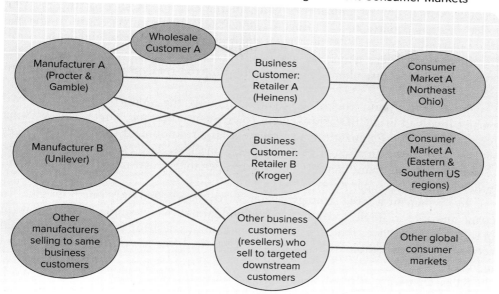

differ, so does the task of tailoring solutions to meet the customer account's needs. The recent evolution of sales roles, like category executives and category captains, are examples of these changes. In one case, salespeople assigned as members of strategic account teams don't focus on the transactional task of *pushing products* to meet a short-term sales quota. Instead, they are expected to forge better, long-term relationships with those strategic customer accounts.

The salesperson's role on each team may vary, and the salesperson may be dedicated to one account. Additionally, if an account is of substantial size, complexity, and importance, the seller may assign a team of individuals to serve the account's needs. Salespeople on these teams operate with a shared purpose focused on a collaborative effort intended to serve the mutual benefits of the seller and its strategic customer account. This adaptation of traditional sales roles involves implementing sales processes and incorporating state-of-the-art sales technology tools that are best suited to achieve the collaborative aims of vital B2B relationships.[5]

Defining Customer Business Development

Within the broader domain of strategic account management, **customer business development (CBD)** refers to one-to-one relationship marketing programs conducted between suppliers (marketers or sales organizations) and their distributors or resellers (retailers).[6] A **CBD strategy** refers to a seller's goal to manage account relationships by creating relational value through the integration of buyer and seller objectives, particularly through the effective and efficient development of the buyer's business outcomes.[7]

To implement a CBD strategy, salespeople tailor solutions by forecasting outcomes intended to meet the objectives of both the seller and the strategic account. The sales interactions and negotiations used to manage these accounts follow those associated with an integrative context. So, the focus of the buyer-seller interactions is on identifying opportunities and advancing their business relationship through *pie-expansion* agreements. As discussed in Chapter 9 on negotiation, a "pie" (or a circle, more generically) provides an analogy for visualizing how the stakes in a

customer business development (CBD)

one-to-one relationship marketing programs conducted between suppliers (marketers or sales organizations) and their distributors or resellers (retailers)

CBD strategy

a seller's goal to manage account relationships by creating relational value through the integration of buyer and seller objectives, particularly through the effective and efficient development of the buyer's business outcomes

negotiation will be divided. For *pie-sharing*, the focus is on a distributive process through which one organization's gains in the size of its slice of the pie (the seller's gains) equates to the other organization's losses in its share of the pie (the buyer's losses). Price is the typical distributive issue and the higher the price, the greater the seller's gains, and the buyer's corresponding losses. Essentially, the two organizations are slicing a pie representing the total profits gained through the exchange.

Pie-expansion, on the other hand, refers to the opportunity of the two parties involved in a CBD arrangement to create a larger pie. That is, by working together, the two organizations can create a larger amount of total profits (larger pie), which they can then divide among themselves. For example, by working together, both the manufacturer and the retailer may reach more customers than either could reach separately.

To implement a CBD strategy, a sales force may assign only one individual to cover multiple strategic accounts, one individual to cover a single account, a team of salespeople to cover multiple accounts, a team of salespeople cover an individual account or other combinations of these options with the use of *fluid* account team members.

Sales teams are formed when two or more members of a sales force work together to implement a sales strategy. Sales teams represent more than a collection of individuals—and they often have a shared identity with their team.[8] For example, a manufacturer's sales team dedicated to a customer account may use that account's name as their own sales team name—and introduce themselves to new colleagues as a member of that customer team. At P&G, for example, a salesperson might identify themselves as being on the Kroger team. Individual members of a sales team can be dedicated to a particular customer and may be actively involved with the development or implementation of the sales strategy for that customer.[9] **Account-dedicated sales team members** are individuals who serve only one account, while **fluid sales team members** are temporary or *ad hoc* members who may serve multiple accounts. Some teams result from combining dedicated and fluid members.[10] So, a CBD sales organization may consist of an individual or team of individuals, and it may vary in size and composition depending on the sales strategy and the strategic account's needs.

Sales teams often correspond with teams of individuals who serve as agents for the buyer's organization. And they often conduct complex and formalized organizational decision-making processes, also known as procurement processes.[11] To organize for these decisions, business buying organizations often co-locate all the members involved with the buying process into a **buying center**. Although we previously introduced the buying center, it merits repeating here, in the context of CBD. A large buyer with geographically dispersed operations may have multiple buying centers, often using those centers to make decisions for smaller geographic regions.

While some of the CBD salesperson tasks discussed later in this chapter apply to an individual salesperson implementing a CBD strategy without other team members, other tasks are intended to leverage the resources allocated to the team by the sales organization. Since many CBD organizations use a team-selling structure, this chapter focuses primarily on CBD team-selling contexts.

CBD Strategy, Tactics, and Leadership

In 1987, P&G dedicated a sales team to work with what was then its third-largest account, Walmart. While team selling had been used before in other ways, this

sales teams
when two or more members of a sales force work together to implement a sales strategy

account-dedicated sales team members
individuals who serve only one account

fluid sales team members
temporary or ad hoc members who may serve multiple accounts.

buying center
all the members involved with the buying process

Shutterstock/fizkes

new customer team marked a substantial change in how large manufacturers organized to serve these strategically important accounts.[12] The ensuing successes obtained through the P&G-Walmart customer team relationship helped spawn the ongoing proliferation of team selling organizations, including the sales reorganization at P&G to its current CBD account-dedicated team-selling. To help delineate the significant shift in its go-to-market strategy, during the implementation of its CBD team-selling structure in the early 1990s and for more than a decade following, P&G decided to ban using the term *sales* to refer to its sales force and replaced it with *customer business development*. The move helped establish a culture through which salespeople developed a stronger sense of identification with customer accounts, which has become an integral element across many B2B sales forces.[13] While fewer firms followed in renaming their sales organizations, many followed with adopting CBD strategies implemented through team-selling structures.

A **sales strategy** for an account represents the outcomes a sales organization seeks to achieve through its relationship with that account. **Tactics** refers to the activities or tasks that salespeople conduct to accomplish its strategy. For example, a sales approach to an account could be either transactional or relational—and it could center its interests solely on producing results, like sales and profits for the sales organization or both the buying and selling organization's interests. Sales strategy and approach may differ across accounts. For strategic accounts, and even for other key accounts that are not of utmost strategic importance, a sales strategy is often specific to an account.

A CBD team-selling structure works best when an organization has a limited number of strategic accounts that contribute substantially to the selling firm's financial viability. For these accounts, the sales organization dedicates salespeople and other employees with relevant expertise to support building the business relationship with those accounts. Additionally, a CBD team typically consists of individuals serving multiple roles—some roles are more supportive of the actual selling effort. Given the complexity and importance of its relationship forging goal, a CBD team often has operational expertise that extends beyond that found in a traditional sales team—with expertise that includes marketing (brand and category expertise), marketing research and analytics, merchandising or retail space management specialist, information technology, finance, and logistics experts.

Given the functional diversity and expertise represented on a CBD team, leading this type of sales team may be more akin to a general management role than a traditional sales management role, where the sales manager manages individual salespeople. A CBD team is often led by a sales (or CBD) manager, who usually has experience working in other salesperson or specialist roles on a CBD team. This kind of prior experience helps the sales leader understand what it is like to work as a member of a CBD team.

sales strategy
the outcomes a sales organization seeks to achieve through its relationship with that account

tactics
the activities or tasks that salespeople conduct to accomplish its strategy

CBD Team Structure and Performance Evaluation

Some marketing organizations use a sales organization to communicate relevant information supporting the marketing strategy to customer accounts. This view of the sales force constrains its purpose to essentially doing nothing more than implementing the promotion mix across aspects of the marketing program[14]. That view may not be the optimal way to deploy a sales force—and these roles are highly prone to displacement by emerging sales automation tools, including some supported by increasingly sophisticated artificial intelligence components.

relationship-forging tasks
activities performed by salespeople that help forge better business relationships with their customers

As the needs of these strategic accounts differ, the sales organization must consider how best to organize a team of salespeople specifically for the account-specific needs. The team tailors their sales proposals to reflect opportunities that deliver equitable value to both the strategic account and the sales organization.[15] Value is often co-created through interactions with the strategic account. As a bridge between sophisticated sales technology tools and key sales performance outcomes, CBD salespeople perform relationship-forging tasks.

Relationship-forging tasks are activities performed by salespeople that help forge better business relationships with their customers—and include activities like proposing integrative solutions, sharing marketing knowledge, and planning for sales calls in ways that identify mutually beneficial solutions. By co-creating solutions with their customers, the relationship can realize potential through identifying and implementing solutions that achieve results far beyond what would have been possible had both firms continued working unilaterally. In this manner, competitive intensity often leads to an escalation of expectations from the strategic account and an ensuing proliferation of CBD teams across an industry. This evolutionary mechanism partially explains why so many industries have now adopted CBD, or CBD-like, strategic partnerships between buyers and sellers. From the onset, a CBD team is designed to include members, resources, and support necessary to tailor complex pie-expansion solutions and to conduct complex negotiations necessary to improve the buyer's and the seller's outcomes. Figure 12-2 shows a common CBD structure for a consumer-packaged goods organization.

Performance Evaluation

A key difference associated with working on a sales team versus professional sales roles on non-team assignments is that the results obtained for the sales force are

Figure 12-2 Members Comprising a Customer Business Development (CBD) Team

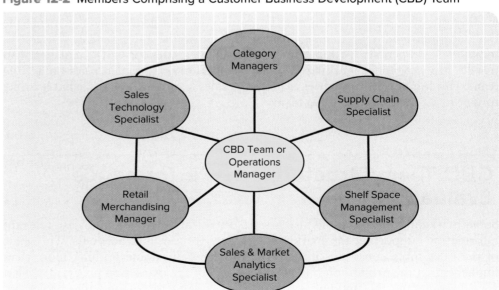

not attributable to any one individual. Instead, the results reflect the efforts of the team. Consequently, key team-level outcome measures include sales volume and profit, market share, efficiency, effectiveness, customer lifetime value, innovations, increased productivity, and improved relationship quality.

A related key point of difference involves performance evaluations at the individual salesperson level. As noted, the team's influence matters—and limiting performance assessments to easily quantifiable measures like sales volume and profit or market share may not be appropriate. In fact, given that the importance of the relationship itself is the reason the account was considered vital enough for dedicating a sales team, assessments should include contributions associated with deepening relationships with customers. Correspondingly, compensation plans are typically salary-based. When incentives are included, the entire sales team's influence on outcomes should be considered.

For individual assessments of salespeople on sales teams, a salesperson's evaluation may include both elements related to achieving business results. For example, the P&G account executive category manager for paper products may be evaluated on total sales volume and market share for Bounty towels and other paper products. But the firm may also include assessments on how well the salesperson improved the business relationship for the customer account. They may, for example, consider customer satisfaction with sales proposals or customer lifetime value enhancements through projected gains in relationship longevity for the sales organization.

Essentially, salesperson performance evaluation for a CBD team member is more complex than a simple comparison to quota. This reality may require not only a broader set of skills expected from CBD salespeople but also a more comprehensive set of leadership and management skills from CBD sales managers. So, when considering CBD sales positions, you should self-assess on whether the skills required of that position fit well with yours. Also, salesperson performance evaluations include both elements of building the business and of building the relationship or the sales organization's capacity.

For an example of how CBD salespeople could be evaluated, consider Figure 12-3, which is a version of P&G's "what counts" factors adopted for a CBD team.[16]

CBD Professional Selling Processes

This brief summary of team structure and sales performance evaluation for CBD team members helps illustrate how professional selling on a CBD or strategic account team differs substantially from professional selling in other contexts.

First, maintaining and strengthening the business relationship with the customer is the most important matter to the sales organization. Second, you will likely be dedicated to sales efforts for a single account—and that account may be too complex to be served by one person, which means this work is usually part of a sales team. Third, the salesperson's overarching goal when selling to such a strategically important account is not to *push products* by selling the account anything they will buy, but to make sure to develop and propose solutions that create mutually beneficial returns for both the buying and the selling organization.

As a result of these differences in assignments and expectations common to this professional selling context, the sales process involves the performance of tasks that leverage team and technology resources or integrate the interests of the sales organization with those of the strategic account. The CBD context requires salespeople with different skills. For many, CBD team sales roles offer career opportunities that are more attractive and rewarding than other professional selling contexts.

Figure 12-3 P&G's "What Counts" Factors Adapted for CBD Team Member

"WHAT COUNTS" FACTORS

FACTORS OF EFFECTIVE PERFORMANCE AT PROCTER & GAMBLE
The primary outcome expected from everyone has two key components:

BUILDS THE BUSINESS
- Consistently delivers high-quality results, both short and long-term.

BUILDS ORGANIZATION CAPACITY
- Develops own capabilities.
- Supports the development and full utilization of others' capabilities, and the
- recruiting, training, and retention efforts of the organization.
- Improves business processes - how the organization accomplishes its objectives.

Following are the key Factors contributing to these outcomes. The extent to which each Factor influences outcomes depends on the person's job responsibilities. Use of these Factors, therefore, should be tailored to the specific responsibilities of the individual.

PRIORITY-SETTING
- Thinks in terms of creating quality and value for consumers.
- Defines who his/her customers are; seeks to understand their needs; sets priorities with those in mind.
- Recognizes the most important issues; makes effective plans; gets resources in place to achieve key objectives.
- Works with the end-result in mind, despite obstacles.

THINKING/PROBLEM-SOLVING
- Sorts through complex data; gathers other relevant viewpoints; identifies important issues; thinks through alternatives.
- Integrates intuition and data from a variety of sources; makes well-reasoned conclusions and develops a solid plan of action.
- Learns from successes and mistakes to solve problems better.
- Recognizes developing problems and handles them well.

INITIATIVE AND FOLLOW-THROUGH
- Gets going on Important priorities; overcomes obstacles and takes appropriate risks; keeps moving toward objectives.
- Handles multiple priorities well.
- Sets specific, stretching objectives, and meets or exceeds them.
- Finds improved ways of getting results.

LEADERSHIP
- Recognizes opportunities; forms a vision of what can be achieved, then challenges self and others to get the desiredresult.
- Champions ideas and people to get breakthrough results.
- Uses a variety of resources effectively.

WORKING EFFECTIVELY WITH OTHERS
- Demonstrates integrity and high- personal standards.
- Respects and works effectively with diverse people; enables all to contribute their best work.
- Builds and maintains productive working relationships, even in difficult situations.
- Works across organizations to develop the best approaches and get the best results.

COMMUNICATION
- Seeks first to understand. then to be understood.
- Organizes and expresses thought s clearly and concisely, both in speaking and writing, so that others understand.
- Expresses ideas in ways that build commitment to them, even when unfamiliar or unpopular; involves and fully informs others in a timely way.
- Recognizes cultural differences and communicates in ways that work.

CREATIVITY AND INNOVATION
- Takes a broad view; finds meaningful connections: uses both logic and intuition to define problems and solutions.
- Goes beyond the accepted ideas; finds new improvement opportunities; generates ways to get better results.
- Searches out and reapplies proven ideas and methods to new situations.
- Translates new ideas into workable solutions; encourages others to do the same.

TECHNICAL MASTERY
- Achieves technical mastery and develops it in others.
- Converts technical skill into practical applications to better meet consumer needs.
- Integrates linkages with the business process of suppliers and customers.

CBD Tasks That Help Forge Better Business Relationships

CBD salespeople work with other team members to develop and propose solutions that help forge better business relationships with their strategic accounts. That is, the primary goal of the CBD team is not simply to sell more products, but to sell products that help the seller build a stronger relationship with the strategic account.

Several factors have important influences on how well a sales team can contribute to beneficial outcomes for the sales organization and its strategic account. These factors include aspects of organizational culture, goal congruence between the sales organization and the strategic account, interpersonal relationships between the sales team and members of the buying center, and situation-specific factors, like market turbulence and competitive actions.[17] While most of these factors were introduced previously or are self-evident, **goal congruence** is the consistency or agreement between individual goals and company goals. As an introduction, this chapter highlights a few of those factors, while centering more on the tasks that CBD salespeople perform that may differ from traditional professional selling tasks.

> **goal congruence**
> the consistency or agreement between individual goals and company goals

While some CBD tasks are common to the effectiveness of any sales team, others center on activities that salespeople conduct to improve the business relationship they have with their strategic account. The tasks can generally be considered as a set of relationship-forging tasks. Relationship-forging tasks are "activities that an individual performs to help build relationships with external constituents."[18] Here, the external constituent is the strategic account to which a CBD salesperson is dedicated.

Figure 12-4 summarizes the key relationship-forging tasks that make up a professional, CBD, team-selling based selling process. These six sales tasks represent the nucleus of key activities that CBD salespeople should perform to forge better business relationships with their strategic accounts.

Working Effectively with Others   In team-selling contexts, **working effectively with others** refers to the ability to work in constructive ways to develop solutions with team members. Working effectively with others is far more critical for team selling than is the case when working in individual professional selling contexts. Given the importance of working effectively with others, baseline expectations for reducing interpersonal conflict include the practice of ethical behaviors and accepting diversity in all forms and varieties. Additionally, being professional in all

> **working effectively with others**
> the ability to work in constructive ways in developing solutions with team members

Figure 12-4 Six Relationship-Forging Tasks Comprising the CBD Sales Process

aspects and interactions with team members helps minimize any potential conflicts with other team members.

By working effective with others, the team becomes more coherent. Coherence is a common goal for effective teams—and minimizing the conflict across team members is paramount to team coherence. Minimizing conflict may involve two key considerations: interpersonal relationships and task-related conflicts.[19] While sales managers may be more concerned than salespeople with reducing task-related conflicts, individual members of sales teams should strive to work together toward reducing interpersonal conflict with other members.

Establishing Equitable Goal Congruence   For a CBD salesperson, a starting point is a deep and thorough understanding of what their strategic account values. From there, they can better understand and discover the ways and means through which the sales organization's interests align with the customer's interests in a manner that produces equitable exchange.

In some issues, a strategic account's goals may be highly divergent from the seller's objectives, whereas those goals may perfectly align with other concerns. Recognition of the strategic account's most important issues improves the ability to prioritize and synthesize a sales proposal. However, during the sales interaction, as part of co-creating solutions, salespeople and their customers may need to compromise to synthesize their goals and achieve acceptable agreements. A clear understanding of each side's inputs into an agreement is needed to estimate and establish appropriate returns for the buying and selling organization.

Data and Market-Driven Sales Planning   In all contexts, salespeople engage in planning to work out the suitability of sales behaviors and activities. In CBD contexts, sales planning places more emphasis on customer account considerations and the development of sales proposals that improve the account's performance in its markets. Planning for sales activities should not only include consideration of possible behaviors during a sales interaction but also involve pre-sales development of proposals suitable that address the strategic account's needs. Such effective planning is required for the salesperson's provision of solutions that meet sophisticated business customer needs.

market-driven sales planning the extent to which the salesperson anticipates, collects, and evaluates information relevant to their customer's needs

Market-driven sales planning refers to the extent to which the salesperson anticipates, collects, and evaluates information relevant to their customer's needs.[20] Not only does market-driven sales planning consider how the customer can achieve its goals in the markets it serves; it is a type of customer-centric planning that seeks to improve market outcomes for the customer. The proposal should be rooted in extensive sales and market analytics whenever feasible.

Developing and Sharing Market Knowledge   Developing expertise as a salesperson is important to most sales situations, but for CBD salespeople the expertise must include extensive knowledge of their strategic account's business—and how to use the products to help the account achieve outcomes in the market they serve. **Sharing market knowledge** refers to the extent to which CBD salespeople develop relevant market expertise and share it with their team members and customers. CBD salespeople should establish themselves as knowledgeable resources for their strategic accounts—and contributors of valuable insights to peers.

sharing market knowledge the extent to which CBD salespeople develop relevant market expertise and share it with their team members and customers

This expertise involves converting data into knowledgeable insights—and those insights must be shared with customers. Ultimately, when sales proposals are successful, the customer's markets will serve as the ultimate judges of the salesperson's expertise. CBD salespeople who develop high levels of market expertise have a decisive advantage over their less experienced competitors in sharing market knowledge with customers.

Proposing Integrative Solutions   This task is vital to a successful CBD business relationship. It was discussed earlier in the chapter, but to state it more formally, **proposing integrative solutions** refers to the extent to which the CBD salesperson applies information and knowledge to construct and propose recommendations that are mutually beneficial to the seller and buyer. These recommendations require the salesperson to incorporate the objectives of the selling and buying firms in the sales proposals presented to their strategic accounts.[21]

proposing integrative solutions the extent to which the CBD salesperson applies information and knowledge to construct and propose recommendations that are mutually beneficial to the seller and buyer

Coordinating Internal Resources   CBD salespeople may serve in either, or both, dedicated and fluid strategic account management (SAM) teams. As members of sales teams, they have access to resources (e.g., other team members) intended to expand their capacity to forge better relationships with their strategic accounts. However, to leverage those resources, some level of coordinating is required.

   Coordinating internal resources refers to the CBD salesperson's efforts to coordinate the activities between people on the team with others to support objectives associated with serving the strategic account. *Coordination by plan* is proactive, where *coordination by feedback* is reactive. Ideally, coordination will be of the former type—and based on the initiative and foresight of the CBD salesperson. However, not all planned coordination activities function seamlessly.[22]

coordinating internal resources the CBD salesperson's efforts to coordinate the activities between people on the team with others to support objectives associated with serving the strategic account

Applying the Chapter to Salesforce

When an organization connects a CRM like Salesforce to their billing, accounting, warehouse, and other systems and when their salespeople consistently add information about their customers, then Salesforce can save a lot time and effort in determining which customers should be treated as strategic accounts. As described earlier, the reports in Salesforce allow the organization to filter and sort data to see correlations and trends that inform where the firm should focus its CBD efforts.

Many organizations allow the salespeople to *nominate* a customer or prospective customer within Salesforce for treatment as a strategic account. With as little as a checked box, the salesperson can trigger Salesforce to instantly route the account record for review by the individual or group responsible for determining whether a customer should be treated as a strategic account. Their approval can also be programmed to trigger a notification to members of the strategic sales team and set in motion procedures for account planning, resource allocation, and performance monitoring.

As described in earlier chapters, one of the greatest values of Salesforce is the 360-degree view it can provide of a customer for anyone from the selling organization. This is clearly beneficial for team selling, where all team members can be equally informed about a customer, their situation, and history. And the *Chatter* feature is excellent for constant sales team collaboration.

Just as Apple has the App Store, Salesforce has *Appexchange*. Appexchange is a market-place where companies that have created applications or modifications for Salesforce can sell them to any other company in the Salesforce community.

So, instead of modifying Salesforce for a specific approach to strategic accounts or CBD, a company may find that there is a ready-made solution in Appexchange. The offerings can be filtered by industry or function. And commonly-used applications are recommended for each.

Chapter Summary

- Strategic account management is the practice of managing the selling firm's relationships with its most strategically important accounts - often using the Pareto Principle to identify the small percentage of customers, often 20%, producing the bulk, often 80% of the revenue or profits.
- A customer business development (CBD) strategy refers to a seller's goal to manage account relationships by creating relational value through the integration of buyer and seller objectives, particularly through the effective and efficient development of the buyer's business outcomes.
- A sales strategy for an account represents the outcomes a sales organization seeks to achieve through its relationship with that account.
- Tactics are the activities or tasks that salespeople conduct to accomplish their strategy.
- As the needs of strategic accounts differ, the sales organization needs to consider how best to organize a team of salespeople specifically for the account-specific needs.
- Evaluating, measuring, and compensating performance for the individual sales team members is more complex than using a simple quota for the team.
- The purpose of the CBD organization is often to promote long-term relationships instead of short-term results.
- The relationship-forging tasks associated with the CBD sales process are working effectively with others, establishing equitable goal congruence, data-driven sales planning, sharing marketing knowledge, proposing integrative solutions, and coordinating internal resources.

Key Terms

account-dedicated team members (p. 230)
buying center (p. 230)
coordinating internal resources (p. 237)
customer business development (p. 229)
CBD strategy (p. 229)
fluid sales team members (p. 230)
goal congruence (p. 235)
market-driven sales planning (p. 236)

pareto principle (p. 228)
proposing integrative solutions (p. 237)
relationship-forging tasks (p. 232)
sales strategy (p. 231)
sales teams (p. 230)
sharing marketing knowledge (p. 236)
strategic account management (p. 228)
tactics (p. 231)
working effectively with others (p. 235)

Application 12-1

Having pioneered brand management as a marketing practice in the 1920s, P&G often considers itself as a "company of brands"—and thus places importance not just on building customer equity through its account relationships, but also on building brand equity through its portfolio of brands. For its strategic accounts, P&G implements a CBD, or customer development strategy, as described in this chapter. To help balance customer and brand priorities, typical account-dedicated sales teams for P&G's brands are represented by account executives and account managers, often physically located at each of a major retailer's buying centers. These account executives and account managers are those on the team whose roles are most akin to the traditional sales role as they develop and present proposals to the retailer's buying centers. Some salespeople have "dotted-line" responsibilities to P&G's brands. Dotted-line responsibilities represent formal consideration that sales managers make when evaluating the performance of these salespeople. Brands with very similar characteristics are organized into categories (e.g., Tide and Cheer are in the laundry detergent category). Categories with similar production processes and competitors are organized together to form strategic business units (e.g., laundry detergent and fabric softener are brands that are part of a strategic business unit called the "soap" unit). Generally, a grocery chain's sales organization includes three major sectors: soap, paper, and personal care.

These P&G account executives and managers not only represent the different brands for P&G, but they often have strong identifications with the customer account, as it is the only account they serve (i.e., they are account-dedicated). Some may focus on the "soap" side of the business (including fabric care brands like Tide, Cheer, and Downy and home care brands like Cascade, Dawn, and Mr. Clean); others focus on "paper" products (including family care brands like Charmin, Pampers, Puffs, and Bounty; baby care brands like Pampers and Luvs); and still others focus on "personal care" products (including oral care brands like Crest, Scope, and Oral-B; skin and personal care brands like Gillette, Ivory, and Old Spice). The retail account has different buyers across the different headquarters—and their procurement processes can be different for each buying center.

The sales team seeks to learn as much as possible about the procurement process and the people who influence the ultimate decisions for each account through its buying centers. While many of their brands compete in different categories (e.g., Bounty competes in the paper towel category, whereas Tide competes in the laundry detergent category), one goal P&G account executives have is to become the category captain for their represented categories in each of these buying centers. To be named a category captain, the salesperson and team must earn the trust of the buying headquarters. It's an important role as all major changes in product distribution, promotion, shelving, and pricing are made by the retailer, but are then communicated through the category captain to the shelf space management specialists and ultimately to the store managers. Not surprisingly, P&G would rather have this responsibility than to have the account assigned to a competing manufacturer's sales team.

In this context, sales proposals represent multimillion-dollar agreements negotiated by different team members with their counterparts comprising their retail customer's buying centers. Results often reflect decades of relationship-building efforts between the two firms. The critical expertise needed by the strategic account's procurement team and P&G's sales team includes a capacity to co-create mutually beneficial solutions that work in consumer markets served by the retailer. Sales and marketing analytics, such as understanding those consumer markets and forecasting demand based on how they will react to different efforts is a complex and involved element of sales planning. This kind of forecasting is supported by using sophisticated computer software tools—and CBD organizations consider the merits of specialized roles to aid in meeting these demands. Given this background, it's time to meet a successful CBD sales manager.

Jane Sparks is an ambitious Customer Business Development Operations Manager at Procter & Gamble. She didn't start in her current role, yet Jane is somewhat typical of the other high-performing salespeople at P&G—many who are now sales managers, sales executives, or general managers. She began her sales career after completing her undergraduate degree in marketing at the University of North Carolina at Chapel Hill, where she was the student body president and the leader of the local chapter of Delta Sigma Pi, a professional co-ed fraternity dedicated to advancing the study of business across the university while forging stronger alliances with business industries. During the summer between her junior and senior year, she learned more about P&G by working as a

(Continued)

(Continued)

summer intern for them in their CBD/Sales organization. After a successful internship, she was offered a full-time position that would begin the following year after she completed her college degree. Upon graduation from UNC with honors, Jane began her full-time sales career as an account manager, where she sold paper products to wholesalers in Georgia. After a couple of years in that role, she was promoted to Account Executive–Paper Products Division and worked for three years representing P&G's paper brands on an account team for a retail chain headquartered in Atlanta. The retail chain was an important account for P&G, but it had not been designated as a strategic account; it wasn't yet among the top revenue producers for the firm. Her outstanding performance earned her the opportunity to work as an Account Executive–Sales and Marketing Analytics on a different strategic account team, which also allowed her to stay in Atlanta while performing that role for a CBD team. While working in Atlanta, Jane completed her MBA through the online MBA program offered by UNC—and P&G even helped pay the costs associated with attaining her graduate degree. Her outstanding performance and growth, not only as a skilled salesperson but as an expert in both business practice and education, led to her promotion to her current position as an Operations Manager–Customer Business Development Team. It also earned her a formal designation as a development candidate at P&G, which makes her part of a small group of employees being groomed to become general managers at P&G. Jane is absolutely loving her professional life! In her new role, she works as second-in-command of the CBD team and is responsible for half of the team's business with the retail account. Another colleague, Alex Bordeaux, represents the other half of the CBD team's business in the other five states mostly along the eastern U.S. coastline.

Although Jane begins her workday early every morning, no two days are alike. She finds each day challenging and rewarding—and collectively, all are critical to her development as a future leader and general manager for P&G. Jane is one of two operations managers on her strategic account team, which is a major retailer as one of P&G's top five grocery retail accounts.

Jane is responsible for P&G's business with this major U.S. retail grocery chain that operates across ten states, although her part of the business represents about half of the total business P&G conducts with this major grocery retail chain. More precisely, Jane is responsible for P&G sales to this retail supermarket chain across five of the ten states in which it operates: Georgia, South Carolina, Alabama, Louisiana, and Texas. For P&G, total account sales to this retail partner exceed $1 billion annually—and Jane's half of the team sells about half of that total, or $502 million in revenues for the most recently completed fiscal year. As a reference, it may be helpful to benchmark her responsibility against the size of one of P&G's largest brand, Tide, which generated revenues of about $1.1 billion in 2014.[23] So, while a million-dollar sale may be considered substantial in some contexts, Jane's team achieves that much revenue on an annual basis by obtaining commitments from the retail chain to stock any of its 20 or so major annual new products in a majority of their retail outlets. New products are introduced on a quarterly basis, and the sales team must get ahead of the new product's release to gain commitments from retailers to stock these new products. Typically, a brand introduces only one new product each year—and those are approved only following heavy scrutiny from P&G's brand management organization.

To elaborate, Jane's retail customer account operates 342 retail outlets (supermarkets) in her assigned five states. The account makes purchase decisions for all P&G grocery products, and its competitors' products, through its three buying centers, which are in Dallas, New Orleans, and Atlanta. Products stocked and promoted in all Texas stores are represented by the Dallas buying center; all Alabama and Louisiana stores are represented by the New Orleans buying center; and all Georgia and South Carolina stores are sold to through the Atlanta buying center. Every square inch of a major grocery retailer's shelf space, including Jane's account, are subject to competitive intensity and market pressures to ensure their limited space is used optimally toward accomplishing their business objectives.

Jane's team is organized similarly to the diagram depicted earlier in Figure 12-2 of this chapter. To help manage and implement changes to the shelf space according to the agreements between Jane's account and all other manufacturers who sell products to the account, Jane's team includes salespeople who are retail store shelf specialists. These shelf space management specialists are fully embedded through co-location within each of the retailer's three buying centers. The specialists focus on changes to the store sets in the ten categories of grocery products sold by her team—and its competitors. They use a specialized software application that creates digital depictions of store shelves, called plan-o-grams, which are then provided to store managers for implementation. A plan-o-gram looks like a still picture of a category taken from a recently stocked and properly merchandised supermarket.

The retail chain has three general types of retail supermarkets: large, medium, and small store-sized formats. The large-format strives to provide a one-stop shopping experience for its consumers by including a coffee shop, dry cleaning operation, an optical shop, and a bank. The format often carries a larger range of products and has the space to sell large-count packages (e.g., those typically found at club stores like Sam's Club)—and it carries over 50,000 individual products, each having a UPC scanner code to inventory each specific stock-keeping unit (SKU) and track sales through the scanner system used at the retailer's checkout counters. The *medium* size format is the "average" grocery store that focuses primarily on stocking typical grocery items—and it carries about 25,000 to 45,000 SKUs. The *small* size format is a much smaller store with limited shelf space. The smaller stores attract more convenience-centered customers and carry fewer than 10,000 SKUs. Of course, the stores operate in different demographic conditions and the demand for grocery products varies significantly across stores. Each grocery store's market also responds differently to different types of promotional activities—indicating a need to forecast sales for each initiative across each individual retail store. The fit, revenues, and profits, among other factors, for each proposal vary. For example, forecasting sales when introducing new products is an important element of effective sales planning in developing a sales proposal. While sales forecasts have relied on sophisticated models for several years, the rise of new artificial intelligence tools may serve to improve the speed, sensitivity, and accuracy of those forecasts.

For any given initiative, all the retailer's buying centers expect forecasts for each individual store to accompany their sales proposals—and the account is notorious for holding salespeople accountable on subsequent visits for poorly estimated demands associated with previous sales proposals. At the same time, the account enjoys successful implementations of proposals, and such business success helps the team build trust with their retail counterparts. Although shelf space management specialists play a vital role on Jane's CBD team, her team includes several other important members whose roles differ.

The volume of data created by sales of products through Jane's account across geographies, stores, brands, and SKUs is substantial—presenting opportunities to gain insights through analytics. Not surprisingly, salespeople use a portfolio of sales technology tools to help them access, analyze, and communicate critical information supporting their sales proposals. Account Executives are often more experienced salespeople, while the Account Manager ranks may include entry-level salespeople who are often recent college graduates. To help the sales team with forecasting, a sales analytical specialist who is assigned to split time across all three teams selling to the account's buying centers. The work of the sales analyst may be more akin to the content of a marketing research course than to that typically covered in professional selling. In any case, the individual in this role on P&G's team may hail from prior work as either account manager or account executive, as did Jane when she was "climbing the corporate ladder". While the account executive and account managers do most of their own research using sales technology tools designed to help them access, analyze, and communicate information

(Continued)

(Continued)

about their sales proposals, they can get help from the sales and marketing analytics specialist, when needed and prioritized (e.g., at Jane's discretion). The team also includes a sales technology specialist who helps find ways for members to leverage a portfolio of information technology tools that the firm acquires and implements to stay current with advances in information technology over time. The sales technology specialist also helps to train and implement any new sales technology tools procured by the organization.

To help implement the plans sold into the retail stores, the team has a member who manages contracted labor to help the retailer re-merchandise or re-set their retail stores following any major changes in the plan-o-gram. Finally, with the volume of economic transactions and proposals that occur with this strategic account, there is a need for a financial expert—to handle accounts payments and deal compliance, which represents millions of dollars of discrepancies. There's also a supply chain or logistics specialist, who manages the related flow of products from P&G's manufacturing plants to the retailer's distribution system. Like the analytical specialists, the financial and logistics specialist split time across the three regional sales teams.

1. What types of sales tasks might Jane expect from each of her CBD team members?
2. What is most likely to be your first CBD job role following college graduation?
3. List the most likely ways you would be compensated if you took a position as a sales representative on Jane's CBD team?

Application 12-2

Refer to application 12-1 for the following.

Imagine you were just hired on Jane Sparks's team. Your new title is Account Executive—Soap Division

1. What prior experience would be useful to this role, and what would you expect your primary responsibility to be?
2. All three of your buying centers just agreed to sell a new Tide product, one of P&G's major initiatives for the year. In total, they agreed to carry the product in 300 of the account's stores.
   Write the evaluation you might expect from Jane for this sale.
3. In your new role, you represent 15 major P&G soap brands to your buying centers. All but three of the brands have a new product that they want you to sell to all of the stores your buying centers represent. Of the new products, your analysis indicates that only three of them will help your retail account achieve significant growth, although those are not the three products that P&G estimates will generate the most profit for the company, at large.
   What should you do?

Shutterstock/meanep

13 Sales Ethics

Learning Objectives

- Explain why ethics is an especially important topic for salespeople and how this has changed over time
- Describe values and how they guide ethical behavior
- Understand how different ethical frameworks affect decision making by salespeople
- Explain how trust and emotional intelligence relate to ethics
- Define key ethics laws that salespeople should know
- Identify certain actions that are legal—but still viewed to be unethical
- Describe factors that contribute to a strong ethical work climate
- Identify the benefits of a written code of ethics

T his chapter defines the elements of sales ethics and explains how they should guide the behavior of salespeople. This topic is especially important in sales because salespeople who understand ethics and behave ethically can better create long-term relationships with their customers. A key reason why this happens is that ethical salespeople are more trustworthy. Behaving ethically starts with understanding and following a variety of laws, such as those addressing bribery and price discrimination. After all, salespeople who break the law are generally viewed to be unethical. However, behaving ethically is more than just not breaking the law. That is, there are several *legal* actions by salespeople that are widely considered to be unethical. These legal but unethical actions include high-pressure sales pitches and certain business entertainment practices. Sales organizations can and should promote ethical behavior by developing a strong ethical work climate. This typically includes a written code of ethics that is widely shared with and discussed by all employees.

Ethics and Personal Selling

ethics
the moral principles that govern a person's behavior

Ethics are the moral principles that govern a person's behavior. Salespeople who act ethically are those who conform to the standards of moral behavior in our society. In other words, ethical salespeople are guided by generally held beliefs of what is right and what is wrong. These beliefs tend to vary somewhat across cultures and from person to person, yet most people in our society agree on a core set of ethical standards.

Sales ethics is an important topic to discuss because salespeople often experience situations that involve difficult choices—and they are not sure what to do. Perhaps the most frequent conflict occurs in situations where the choice is between making more money for themselves and their firm versus doing what is right for a customer. Or conversely, they might be asked to do something for the customer that violates company policy or maybe even laws. Salespeople are often tempted to make the wrong or unethical choice in these situations. We believe ethics are particularly important to salespeople because they work in relatively unsupervised settings, they tend to be evaluated against short-term objectives, they are continually presented with requests from powerful customers they do not want to disappoint, and they are under pressure to generate revenues for their firm. Together, these pressures create stressful situations that can tempt at least some salespeople to take shortcuts and engage in behavior that is unethical and perhaps even illegal. However, we maintain that this behavior goes against the salesperson's best interests. Unethical behavior is almost always not in the long-term best interests of either customers or the sales organization.

ethical dilemma
situations in which there is no possible solution that can resolve the situation in an ethically acceptable fashion

Given the complexity of the sales job, salespeople often face situations in which there is no possible solution that can resolve the situation in an ethically acceptable fashion. This is called an **ethical dilemma**. Reasonable people could expect to disagree about what to do in an ethical dilemma as there is no clear right or wrong answer. For example, suppose a customer wants to buy a product from a salesperson, but the price is too high. If the salesperson knows that a competitor sells a similar product for a lower price, should that salesperson tell the customer about this? Is it unethical to not inform the customer about this other option? Sales professionals disagree on what is right and wrong in this situation. One starting point in resolving an ethical dilemma is to focus on values.

values
specific traits, behaviors, and attitudes that a person believes are good, desirable, or worthwhile

Values are the specific traits, behaviors, and attitudes that a person believes are good, desirable, or worthwhile. Values guide behavior and determine what we see as ethical. There are hundreds of potential values for salespeople, but six common values often associated with sales ethics are shown in Figure 13-1. These are honesty, kindness, loyalty, service, trustworthiness, and commitment to excellence. The meaning of each of these values is not immediately apparent

Figure 13-1 Common Values Associated with Sales Ethics

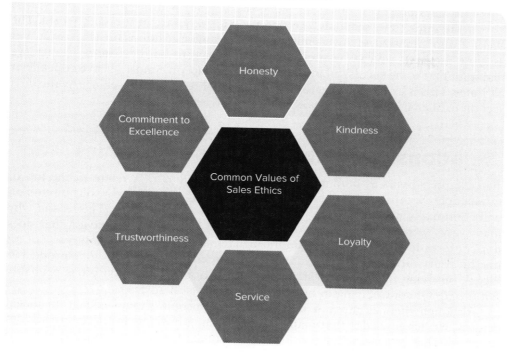

without an in-depth conversation about it, and this meaning will vary among people. For example, is loyalty more about loyalty to the customer or loyalty to the employer? This confusion explains why we say a focus on values is a *starting point* in resolving ethical dilemmas. It is critical, however, for salespeople to thoroughly understand the meaning behind their values. To ignore values is to lose sight of what is right or wrong. This carelessness can lead to unethical sales practices that turn into public relations scandals.

High-Profile Ethical Scandals Involving Salespeople

The most high-profile example of unethical behavior by salespeople is probably the Wells Fargo fake account scandal.[1] The problem started when Wells Fargo decided to encourage its salespeople to do more cross-selling. Cross-selling is a strategy where salespeople sell a complementary product, such as checking, to existing customers that already are using another product, such as credit cards. Wells Fargo provided its employees with materials and training on this strategy, which is a legitimate sales technique that many banks use. The problem arose in the way that Wells Fargo incentivized and pressured its salespeople to be successful. The unanticipated result was that many salespeople responded by creating more than two million fake accounts in the names of existing customers, who ended up paying fees for accounts they did not know that had. This scandal has resulted in the firing of more than 5,000 employees, billions of dollars in fines and settlements, and significant damage to the reputation of all involved.[2]

This scandal teaches a few lessons about ethics in sales. First, it shows how unethical behavior by salespeople can violate the law, and result in significant legal punishments as well as a public relations fiasco. This also shows how salespeople can focus on short-term goals to the detriment of what is best for their customers in the long run. The root cause of this scandal was the incentive rewards system, which is a powerful motivator of behavior that is likely to override all other efforts in creating an ethical culture. In other words, Wells Fargo was incentivizing the wrong behavior, and it resulted in a large number of salespeople engaging in unethical sales practices.

At the same time, scandals like this are relatively rare in the sales world. The Wells Fargo situation involved business-to-consumer relationships that were not as close as those typically associated with business-to-business sales. In fact, we maintain that to be successful in the long run, salespeople must behave ethically at all times. This is especially true today in the age of relationship selling. As the next section explains, however, this was not always true.

Relationship Between Laws and Ethics

This chapter discusses both ethical and legal questions that relate to the job of salespeople. Because the line between ethics and the law is murky, our discussion will continually move back and forth between the two concepts. The reason why many laws were created is to stop people from engaging in behavior that does not conform to the standards of moral behavior in our society. However, not all unethical acts are illegal. For example, lying to customers about your product is illegal, but lying to customers about how great of an athlete you are is probably not illegal. Of course, lying in both circumstances is ill-advised.

Although there is never a reason why salespeople should engage in illegal activity, we acknowledge that many laws governing business practices are seldom enforced. That is, a salesperson *could* violate some of these laws to great personal advantage, without worrying about getting caught. One such practice is for salespeople to do a bit of padding—or cheating—on their expense account. That is, salespeople might ask to be reimbursed for taking clients out for lunch when they were actually eating with friends. Although this is illegal financial fraud (or embezzlement), it is quite common in some companies because salespeople often get away with it. These companies lack a strong ethical climate, which is a concept discussed later in the chapter. That said, most salespeople do not engage in any of these questionable behaviors owing to their personal code of ethics.

Because these codes of ethics are *personal*, they can vary quite a bit from person to person. As discussed previously, this could be because different people have different values. For example, two people may value loyalty, but they have very different interpretations of what that means. Further, how people make ethical decisions with their code of ethics also varies. To better understand this process of ethical decision making, we will examine two prominent frameworks of ethics.

Ethical Frameworks and Decision Making

Experts have identified two distinct approaches—or frameworks—that affect how salespeople make decisions when faced with ethical dilemmas. The first framework focuses on *actions* or *behaviors*, and is called deontological ethics. The second framework focuses on the eventual *outcomes* of those actions or behaviors and is called teleological ethics. These two frameworks give insight into two different ways that salespeople make ethical decisions.

deontological ethics
making decisions by never deviating from certain moral rules or behaviors

In **deontological ethics**, salespeople make decisions by never deviating from certain moral rules or behaviors. These people believe, "What's right is right; what's wrong is wrong – regardless of the consequences of the actions." For example, some salespeople feel they should be honest in all situations because telling lies to customers is just plain wrong. This perspective views an action as being right or wrong because of the characteristics of the action itself ignoring any result or outcome of the action.

This approach to ethics is said to be consistent with the Golden Rule, which centers on the idea that we should interact with others in the way that we would like them to interact with us. A variation of the *golden rule* is a principle found in many religions and cultures and has been interpreted in at least these six different ways:[3]

1. Do to others as you want them to gratify you.
2. Be considerate of others' feelings as you want them to be considerate of yours.
3. Treat others as a person of rational dignity like you.
4. Extend brother or sisterly love to others, as you would want them to do to you.
5. Treat others according to moral insight, as you would have others treat you.
6. Do to others as God wants you to do to them.

All of these interpretations of the Golden Rule encourage people to place importance on the rights and needs of *other people*. Of course, two salespeople may both interact with customers in a way that *they believe* is consistent with the Golden Rule, yet behave very differently from each other because they have different values about how to treat others.

The excuse that "everybody does it" often comes into play as a rationalization for salespeople to engage in ethically-questionable activity. That is, some salespeople might see that all of their colleagues cheat on their expense accounts, and decide that this must be a perfectly ethical and moral action. Alternatively, people might come to a different conclusion about the ethics of their expense account cheating if this practice were announced to everybody in the world. In other words, salespeople might ask themselves the following question: Would I be embarrassed if everybody knew I was doing this behavior? If the answer is Yes, then it is probably an unethical act that should not be done.

Teleological ethics holds that the action or behavior itself cannot be good or bad; however, the outcome or consequence of this action on others can be positive or negative. Some argue that we should engage in behavior that generates the greatest happiness and satisfaction for most people in our society. A behavior is ethical from this perspective if it results in bad things for a few people but generates positive results for many more people. So, a salesperson might believe that misleading customers about a potential product flaw is justifiable if it ultimately results in earning enough commission to pay for a family member's medical procedures. In other words, the end justifies the means.

teleological ethics
a framework that assumes the action or behavior itself cannot be good or bad; however, the outcome or consequence of this action on others can be positive or negative

This belief that the end justifies the means should not be used as an excuse to accomplish goals through any means necessary, no matter how dishonest, illegal, or ugly the actions might be. Further, it is hard to accept the appropriateness of an action that results in a slight benefit to a huge number of people, yet does great damage to a small, marginal group. Yet there are certain circumstances when this viewpoint makes some sense. Or, at least, most people would agree that the *outcomes* of actions should be considered before pursuing a particular strategy.

Philosophers debate the relative merit of these two frameworks (i.e., deontological versus teleological ethics). We see both positive and negative aspects

Facing an Ethical Issue? Ask Yourself...

1. What would a reasonable person do?
2. Is my decision in line with my company's core values?
3. Would I be upset if a salesperson did this to me?
4. Is my decision in line with my own code of ethics?
5. What would my family members and friends think of my decision?
6. What the long-term consequences of this decision?
7. Are my actions legal?
8. How will my decision impact others?
9. Would society be worse off if everyone engaged in this behavior or activity?
10. Will I sleep soundly tonight?

of each point of view. It depends on the situation. It also depends on what the customer views as being ethical. Customers do not buy from unethical salespeople because they do not trust them. In fact, establishing trust with the customer is one of the most important reasons why a salesperson should behave ethically.

Importance of Building Trust

trust
customers believe in the reliability and integrity of salespeople who behave ethically

A key benefit of behaving ethically is that it builds **trust** with your customers. That is, customers believe in the reliability and integrity of salespeople who behave ethically. In the previous examples, the legal but unethical actions might close a deal in the short run, but eventually, customers will realize that they have been misled and might never buy from that salesperson again. Recall that we are now in an era of relationship marketing, which requires the formation of close, long-term bonds between the seller and buyer. Trust is an essential part of all good relationships.

Another reason why trust is so important today is that internet-related technology provides customers with unprecedented access to information. This leads to customers' having both the means and inclination to verify if what a salesperson says is true. When customers have discovered that salespeople are dishonest, trust is destroyed, and the relationship is likely over. A recent study reports that 79% of business buyers say that it is absolutely critical or very important to interact with a salesperson who is a *trusted* advisor that adds value to their business.[4]

Building trust can also help salespeople grow their client base through word of mouth. That is, once customers trust a salesperson, they are much more likely to recommend that person to others. Conversely, if customers do not trust a salesperson, they often share their negative experiences in a way that damages the salesperson's reputation. Social media and other online review sites are full of scathing commentary about the perceived unethical behavior of salespeople.

A review of several academic research articles concluded that customer trust in salespeople consists of three dimensions: credibility, compatibility, and expertise.[5] Salespeople who are high in credibility are honest, reliable, and highly ethical. Compatibility relates to how friendly, likable, and approachable the salesperson is. Salespeople with expertise are viewed as being competent, qualified individuals with high levels of product knowledge. To earn the trust of their customers, salespeople should strive to do well on all three of these dimensions.

Finally, salespeople tend to be better at building trust with customers when they can recognize, understand, and manage the emotions of both themselves and others[6], another way of describing emotional intelligence. Customers appreciate when salespeople understand how they are feeling. Salespeople can use this knowledge to help customers work through issues and problems that are creating stress in their work lives. Those with high levels of emotional intelligence are good listeners who are more open to feedback and ideas; so, when customers complain, they are less likely to get defensive and argumentative.[7] This results in an open, respectful dialogue that not only builds trust but also better equips salespeople with information about what customers need.

It's Not Enough to Be Merely Legal

It should be clear from this discussion that behaving ethically is more than just not breaking the law. There are several *legal* actions that salespeople could do that would be considered highly unethical by most sales professionals. For example, a salesperson might close a deal without revealing to the client that the product will be part of a big *20% off* sale in a couple of weeks. Or worse, a salesperson might *wine and dine* a client at a restaurant where a few stiff drinks are consumed, and then engage in some fancy closing technique to get the "less than sober" client to sign a contract on the spot. There is nothing necessarily illegal happening in either of these situations, but the actions are highly questionable from an ethical standpoint.

Relevant Laws

Salespeople should be aware of their legal responsibilities. This is a necessary first step toward meeting the ethical standards of society. This section outlines several legal responsibilities that are important for salespeople to know. In general, these laws exist to promote fair competition and to protect consumers.

Fraudulent Misrepresentation vs. Puffery

First, salespeople should know that it is illegal to make false, deceptive, or misleading claims about the product they are selling or about the services that accompany that product. This is **fraudulent misrepresentation**, which is a legal concept in contract law. If these dishonest claims somehow harm the customer (e.g., through misuse of the product), then the salesperson or the sales organization may be sued in a civil court. If the harm is severe enough, this could lead to criminal charges that result in significant fines and imprisonment.

Salespeople need to understand that sometimes it is what you *do not* say that can be illegal misrepresentation—like when a salesperson deliberately hides damaging facts about a product. For example, Merck & Company was accused of training its sales representatives to avoid questions about whether one of its drugs (Vioxx) had the potential to increase blood pressure. This led to litigation concerning the drug's role in causing heart attacks, and Merck eventually settled the case for several billion dollars.[8]

To minimize the probability of legal proceedings being brought against them, salespeople should make it a practice to make accurate, understandable, and verifiable statements about the product and its use. Exaggerated claims should be avoided, as it is generally better in the long run to under-promise and over-deliver. Salespeople also need to ensure that customers have the necessary knowledge and skills needed to use the product properly. Along these lines, they should carefully go through all relevant sales literature with the customer, being sure to read all warnings and labels.

At the same time, many salespeople regularly engage in **puffery**, which is making hyperbolic, exaggerated product claims that can be neither proven nor disproven. Although it may be annoying to customers, puffery is perfectly legal. These statements often use superlatives such as "best," "fastest," and "prettiest." For example, an account manager from Otis Elevator might say in a sales call, "Our elevators are hands-down the best in the world!" This statement would likely be viewed as an accepted promotional statement made to get the customer's attention, and thus be considered puffery as opposed to fraudulent misrepresentation. Alternatively, if salespeople make an objective claim that can be proved false, like, "Our coffee cures cancer," then this statement is fraudulent misrepresentation.

fraudulent misrepresentation
making false, deceptive, or misleading claims about the product they are selling or about the services that accompany that product

puffery
making hyperbolic, exaggerated product claims that can be neither proven nor disproven

business defamation
making false, deceptive, or disparaging statements about competitors or competitive products

Business Defamation

Making false, deceptive, or disparaging statements about competitors or competitive products is called **business defamation**, and is also illegal. These practices are quite common, which is surprising given that they could be a civil or criminal offense. The lies may run from falsifications about the competitor's financial stability to personal attacks on its salespeople. Defamation is a form of *slander* when a salesperson speaks to others about this information. Defamation is *libel* when the information is published in a permanent form. Salespeople should understand that passing on false information is just as illegal as being the first to make the statement. Consequently, it is unwise

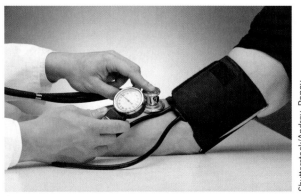

Shutterstock/Andrey_Popov

for salespeople to share defamatory online news stories with others—especially considering how often information on the internet is not true.

Bribery

It is illegal for salespeople to offer a customer money or gifts for the express purpose of winning that customer's business. This is **bribery**. Using bribes to gain information about competitors is also illegal. It is generally not bribery, however, if it is a common and open practice to provide the same gift to all equivalent customers.

Bribery in selling is an unpleasant fact of life that has existed, in varying degrees, for as long as selling has existed. Blatant bribes, payoffs, or kickbacks may be easy to spot—and they are patently wrong. Unfortunately, today much bribery is done in a sophisticated manner that is not easy to identify. Sometimes the lines are blurred between a bribe and a gift to show appreciation. We discuss acceptable gifts and entertainment in more detail in the next section.

In sales, the bribe offer may be initiated by the salesperson, or the request may come from the buyer. Usually, the buyer's request is stated in a veiled fashion, and it takes a perceptive salesperson to understand what is going on—but it is wise for salespeople to ignore these requests no matter how tempting. Certainly, salespeople should understand that "everyone else is doing it" is not a valid excuse; in fact, salespeople with integrity are not doing it. Salespeople who gain business through bribery are engaged in behavior that is both illegal and unethical. The penalties can be stiff for those found guilty of either taking or giving bribes.

Price Discrimination

The Clayton Antitrust Act (1914) and its Robinson-Patman Amendment (1936) are federal laws that generally restrict **price discrimination,** which is when the same product is sold at different prices to different buyers. This means that salespeople cannot indiscriminately grant price concessions to certain customers. Of course, it is not unusual for some customers to try to negotiate a larger discount than others are getting. These customers may even threaten to take their business elsewhere if their demands are not met. Salespeople who grant such an unusual discount might be violating this law.

In select cases, however, it may be legal for salespeople to engage in price discrimination. For example, if one customer is more costly to serve than another, then a lower price for the lower-cost customer is generally justifiable. Or also, a lower price can often be offered legally to customers that buy in bulk or to customers located closer to the seller. In general, firms can make price concessions to a customer only if those same deals are offered to all customers.

The reasoning for why price discrimination is illegal stems from the premise that consumers are better off when there are lots of companies competing with each other. If this were legal, a large and powerful firm could move into a new market and drive out all smaller competitors with especially low prices. The fear is that eventually, the firm might become an unregulated monopoly that would raise prices with no incentive to satisfy customers. Consequently, several regulatory measures protect and encourage fair competition. These are generally administered by the U.S. Federal Trade Commission (FTC).

Reciprocity

"If you buy from us, we'll buy from you. Is that a deal?" Salespeople should understand that this type of arrangement, which is known as **reciprocity** or reciprocal dealing, can be illegal if the courts decide that it unfairly reduces competition in the marketplace. Consider this hypothetical example (which would never happen): General Motors agrees to buy millions of dollars of automotive steel components from U.S. Steel for the manufacturing of its vehicles—under the condition of that U.S. Steel would buy and exclusively use GMC trucks in all of its steel mills. As a large and powerful company that is about ten times bigger than U.S. Steel, General Motors arguably has the *potential* to use its buying power to negotiate such terms. However, courts would likely view this as an unlawful agreement in that it prohibits U.S. Steel from buying Ford, Dodge, and other trucks for reasons that have nothing to do with product quality.

Shutterstock/A Lot of People

Tying Agreements

When Apple first released its iPhone in 2007, AT&T was the only option for phone service because of a contractual agreement between the two companies. In other words, iPhone customers were essentially forced into also buying AT&T phone service—and thus, could not choose Verizon, T-Mobile, Sprint, or any other competitor. This is known as a **tying agreement,** which exists when two products can only be purchased together (not separately). Sales organizations should know that, in certain cases, courts view this as an anti-competitive practice that is unlawful—especially when the two products are not naturally related to each other. In fact, the Apple and AT&T agreement ended after a few years and several lawsuits. Tying agreements often occur when a company ties a newly released product to an established, highly sought-after product. For example, Coca-Cola might consider selling Coke only to retail stores that also purchase Vanilla Coke, which is much less popular. However, this would be illegal.

tying agreement
when two products can only be purchased together (not separately)

Cooling-Off Laws

The Federal Trade Commission also has established regulatory measures known as **cooling-off laws,** which give customers a three-day right to return products that are purchased under certain circumstances. In general, these circumstances cover door-to-door sales of products primarily intended for personal, family, or household use. Under this FTC ruling, customers are not required to give a reason for why they want to return the product. That is, as long as the purchase scenario fits the FTC's criteria, customers have the right to change their mind and return the product within three days. The sales organization must refund the money within ten days (https://www.consumer.ftc.gov/articles/0176-buyers-remorse-when-ftcs-cooling-rule-may-help). These cooling-off laws were created in reaction to dishonest door-to-door salespeople that used high-pressure sales tactics to trick people into buying. Fortunately, these salespeople are much rarer today than they were many years ago.

cooling-off laws
give customers a three-day right to return products that are purchased under certain circumstances

Green River Ordinances

Another set of laws that pertain mostly to door-to-door selling are **Green River ordinances,** which are named after the Wyoming city that first banned door-to-door selling in 1931. These laws vary from city to city, but they generally establish rules and procedures that salespeople must follow when calling on residents in their homes. They require these salespeople to purchase and display a canvassing permit that can be obtained only after passing a background check. The goal of regulating this type of selling is to help protect the safety and privacy of city residents

Green River ordinances
establish rules and procedures that salespeople must follow when calling on residents in their homes

and to minimize occurrences of fraud and price-gouging from sellers who have no permanent local address. These laws typically do not relate to local, not-for-profit organizations.

Telephone Consumer Protection Act

For those salespeople who reach customers by phone, it is important to be aware of the privacy and do-not-call laws created by the Telephone Consumer Protection Act (1991). U.S. consumers can enter their names in the FTC's National Do Not Call Registry. This purportedly stops unwanted telemarketing calls, but it does not cover political calls, charitable calls, debt collection calls, informational calls, and telephone survey calls. To the frustration of many consumers, non-reputable companies (or scammers) often ignore the TCPA. Automated calls (often called robocalls) are still quite common. However, salespeople from legitimate businesses typically abide by the rules set forth in this law, and those who do not have faced significant fines. For example, Dish Network was recently found guilty of making illegal telemarketing calls, and this resulted in a $61 million verdict against the company.[9]

International Laws

Of course, laws vary from country to country; salespeople often make international sales calls. In general, these salespeople should continue to follow U.S. laws, as well as the laws of the foreign country. In fact, the Foreign Corrupt Practices Act (1977) was enacted to make it unlawful for U.S. citizens to make certain payments (i.e., bribes) to foreign government officials to assist them in obtaining business in that country.[10]

In certain foreign countries, such payments might seem to be the norm. Salespeople and their firms, however, should resist making these payments or else face significant legal punishments. For example, the U.S. firm Bio-Rad Laboratories was found guilty of bribing government officials to win business in Russia, Thailand, and Vietnam. Bio-Rad makes and sells instruments used in biomedical research. Mid-level sales managers of Bio-Rad authorized their sales representatives to make cash payments to officials at government-owned hospitals and laboratories in exchange for agreements to purchase Bio-Rad's products. In the Vietnam case, they orchestrated a scheme that paid these bribes through independent middleman distributor firms, thinking this would protect Bio-Rad from liability. Bio-Rad was eventually found guilty and agreed to pay fines exceeding $50 million.[11]

Key Areas of Concern

Behaving ethically is more than just following laws, and it extends beyond issues of right and wrong. Highly ethical salespeople are conscientious employees who strive to do their job to the best of their ability. They are proactive in helping to solve problems for their customers and colleagues. They behave professionally and do the right thing in all circumstances—even when no one is watching. This section discusses a few common areas of concern for those salespeople who fall short of these ideals.

High-Pressure Sales

The first area of concern is high-pressure sales. As discussed previously, sales training once drew heavily from the psychology of persuasion. For example, one technique was to train salespeople to engage a long monologue and continue talking in a way that makes it seems rude for a customer to interrupt. The training might be to keep the chatter going until the customer says no at least three times. This forces customers either to buy the product or to assertively stop the conversation. The tactic works because it is difficult and uncomfortable for many people to be assertive.

High-pressure salespeople often encourage potential customers to become emotional, which makes them more vulnerable to their sales pitch. That is, these salespeople might sense or provoke anxiousness in customers, and then start talking about how buying the product makes them more safe and secure. Or they might say how product availability is scarce, or how it is only available for a limited time at this price. This creates the sense that the product is more valuable, which increases the likelihood that the person will buy. Another tactic is to give customers a gift, which makes them feel obligated to reciprocate and buy out of guilt.

There is no question that high-pressure sales tactics can still work—but only in the short term. Customers usually regret the purchase soon after it is made and become annoyed (if not angry) with the salespeople that manipulated them. Salespeople who engage in these unethical practices do not form close, long-term relationships with their customers.

Gifts

The practice of giving gifts to customers, especially at the holiday season, is a time-honored practice. But today, perhaps more than ever before, the moral and ethical implications of giving gifts to customers is under scrutiny. The practice is being reviewed by both the givers and the receivers of gifts. Some firms put dollar limits on the business gifts they allow their employees to give or receive. Other companies are even more strict. In fact, some firms have stopped the practice of giving holiday gifts to customers. One of these companies is Fastenal. "We want to earn your business, we don't want to buy your business," says a Fastenal sales manager.

It is unfortunate that gift-giving to customers has become so complicated and so suspect. A reasonably priced, tastefully selected gift can express appreciation for a customer's business. Today the problem lies largely in deciding what constitutes "reasonably priced" and "tastefully selected." At some point, a gift can become an illegal bribe, and it is not always easy to identify which is which. Giving customers a $20 sleeve of golf balls with the selling company's logo on it is probably reasonable, but what about giving a customer a $500 driver? What about a $3,000 premium set of golf clubs?

The following are generally accepted guidelines that should help salespeople avoid gift-giving that is unethical or in bad taste:

- Never give a gift before a customer does business with the firm.
- Do not give gifts to customers' spouses.
- Keep the value of the gifts low to avoid the appearance of undue influence on future purchase decisions.
- Follow your company's policy on gift-giving.
- Walk away from business if the customer pushes for something that exceeds these guidelines.

Entertainment

Entertaining customers is part of many sales jobs, and a large portion of the expense money is often devoted to it. Salespeople who spend this money unwisely on accounts with little potential are wasting time and money. Their selling costs will be out of line. Indeed, a contributing factor to a salesperson's success may be their ability to know the right person to entertain and how to appropriately entertain them.

Over the years, some useful generalizations have been developed for customer entertainment:

- Entertain to develop long-term business relationships, not a single order.
- Keep the entertainment appropriate to the customer and the size of the account.
- Be sensitive to customer attitudes toward types of entertainment.
- Do not rely on entertainment as one of the foundations of the selling strategy—use it only to complement the strategy.

Confidentiality Leaks

Companies entrust many of their salespeople with confidential information about how they do business. This can include information on sales strategies with key customers, new products that are about to be launched, and other information critical to their future plans. This knowledge enables the salespeople to understand the customer's business so they can better satisfy the customer's needs. Of course, the same salesperson will often work with two customer firms that are competitors of each other. It might be tempting for a salesperson to share or leak some of this confidential information with a competitor to impress them and gain a bigger share of their business. However, it would be highly unethical for that salesperson to do that. In fact, customer firms often protect themselves from confidentiality leaks by having all salespeople sign non-compete and non-disclosure agreements. Further, most customers would never trust a salesperson who gives them information about competitors for fear that the salesperson might share their own confidential information to others.

Expense Accounts

Another area of concern is when salespeople cheat on expense account reports. Even though this unethical practice is also illegal, it is a common activity that costs U.S. businesses billions of dollars a year. There is an endless number of ways to pad expense reports, and technology has made it even easier. For example, many receipts come in a digital file form that can be opened in a word-processing program, such as Microsoft Word, to change (i.e., increase) the listed prices. There is even a website (losthotelreceipt.com) that allows people to create a fake but realistic-looking hotel, restaurant, and other receipts. One source estimates that up to 5% of travel and expense, sometimes called *T&E*, costs are fraudulent.[12]

Salespeople rationalize their expense account padding in several ways. Some believe this practice must be fine because they see it being done by their colleagues or their bosses. Certainly, when everyone sees the leaders of an organization cheat, the lower-level employees are much more likely to do the same. Others cheat because they feel that they are being cheated by company rules they view as unfair. For example, maybe the company has a rule that it does not reimburse for tips, and salespeople who feel this is unfair might pad their expense reports with fake receipts.

Salespeople should understand, however, that there is no legitimate reason for cheating on expense reports. They should also understand that if they get caught doing this, they will likely get fired. In fact, companies are placing more and more time and effort in trying to detect this fraudulent activity. Some companies are strengthening their internal controls by employing artificial intelligence software programs to analyze expense reports and catch unusual expenditures.[13] So, whereas some technology has increased the likelihood of cheating, other technology has made it easier to catch those engaging in this unethical activity. Wells Fargo recently fired over a dozen employees that falsified meal receipts in violation of its expense policy.[14]

Romantic Relationships

Romantic relationships between a salesperson and co-worker are not uncommon, and they often cause no issues of concern. However, they can lead to problems if not handled in the right way. One study found that 31% of workers who dated at work ended up getting married. However, almost a quarter of co-worker relationships (24%) were illicit affairs in which at least one of the two people was married to someone else at the time; and 6% of workers have left a job because a romantic relationship with someone at work went sour.[15]

Co-workers in a relationship are ethically bound to understand and follow any company rules for office romance. Further, it is recommended that these people communicate openly and develop a plan to stay professional in the office and keep their personal lives private. Relationships between a manager and subordinate should be avoided if at all possible.

Workplace romance can also occur between a salesperson and a customer, although many companies have policies that specifically forbid employees from dating clients or vendors. This is often a bad idea, especially when one party is in a position of power over the other. Typically, customers have power over salespeople, which creates the potential for sexual harassment. Further, the parties should consider whether or not the personal feelings they have for each other are affecting the professional interaction between the buyer and seller firms. If so, this is problematic because there may be a conflict of interest between a salesperson's personal feelings and duty to the company's success. Given this potential for conflict, salespeople who date their customers should inform their boss of the romantic relationship—even if the sales organization has no disclosure policy about this.

Working Alone and Unsupervised

Increasingly, salespeople today work out of home offices and might go many days without interacting with their sales manager. Even salespeople who work out of company headquarters typically go out every day or so to make calls and go unsupervised for several hours every week. However, these unsupervised salespeople typically report what they are doing by completing call reports. This allows their managers to see what they are up to—but only if the salespeople complete these call reports conscientiously and honestly. Unfortunately, some salespeople are notorious at finding ways to cut corners and cheat the system. In other words, their call reports might indicate that they called on customers all day long when they actually were at home, binge-watching Netflix! Of course, this is a highly unethical practice that could lead to their termination.

Increasingly, salespeople complete call reports as part of the sales organization's CRM. CRM, along with GPS technology, enables managers to more closely track their salespeople to ensure that they are doing both what they are supposed to be doing and what they say they are doing. Of course, salespeople who are tracked in this manner are more likely to be honest in completing their call reports, and some managers believe that tracking gives them the information to help the salespeople be more successful. The downside of tracking, however, is that it offends some salespeople and makes them feel like they are being micromanaged. That is, they do not feel trusted and believe that tracking equates to a spying technique that violates their right to privacy.

The best situation is when salespeople strongly identify as being a member of their sales team in a way that makes them truly committed to the company. Sales managers with strong leadership skills can make this happen by creating a situation where there is mutual respect and trust between

Shutterstock/LeonidKos

leaders and subordinates. This greatly reduces the likelihood that the salespeople will engage in these unethical actions.

Factors That Contribute to a Strong Ethical Work Climate

Salespeople are more likely to engage in ethical sales practices when working for an organization with a strong ethical work climate. An **ethical work climate** refers to the culture of an organization with respect to questions of right and wrong. This involves the moral atmosphere of the work environment and the extent to which all employees of the company adhere to the ethical standards in our society. This section points to several factors that can help ensure that such an environment is in place.

Ethical Leadership

First, ethical leadership is important for a strong ethical work climate. Ethical leadership is rooted in respect, service, justice, honesty, and community.[16] That is, the salespeople of a company are much more likely to behave ethically if they have respect for the integrity of company leaders. Not surprisingly, when high-level executives of an organization lie and cheat, then a weak ethical work climate is inevitable. For example, salespeople are much more likely to cheat on their expense accounts if they see their sales manager do it.

Servant leadership is a style of leadership that promotes ethical actions among salespeople.[17] Some might view this as an oxymoronic term that does not make sense. By definition, servants are under the control of leaders, and so it may not seem possible to be both a servant and a leader at the same time. However, leaders can be servants to their followers by placing follower needs over their self-interests. By being attentive to the concerns of the salespeople they supervise, sales managers empathize with and nurture their followers. This equates to demonstrating strong moral behavior toward salespeople, who then naturally reciprocate by exhibiting moral behavior toward their co-workers—and *their customers*. This explains why this style of leadership not only enhances the ethical work climate but also leads to greater sales performance among the salespeople.

Reward System

As demonstrated by the Wells Fargo scandal explained at the beginning of this chapter, the reward system of salespeople is a powerful motivator that can result in unethical sales practices if poorly designed. In fact, all other factors that contribute to an ethical work climate are for naught if the reward system incentivizes the wrong behavior. In general, ethical sales practices are more likely to occur under salary-based plans as opposed to straight commission plans. This is because salespeople paid on straight commission have less incentive to follow up after the sale to ensure that customers are satisfied. It also depends on what specific behaviors are being incentivized. The key is to design the reward system with both the salesperson's and customer's long-term perspectives in mind. The goal should be to create a culture that values selling as a *client-oriented service*, rather than one that emphasizes making money by pushing products.

Personal Characteristics of Honesty

The more *honest* salespeople are, the more likely they will be ethical. That is, the ethical work climate of a given organization is much more likely to be strong when all of its salespeople are honest. Honesty is considered a personality trait,

ethical work climate
the culture of an organization with respect to questions of right and wrong

servant leadership
a style of leadership that promotes ethical actions among salespeople

which means that some people have it and some people do not. So, ideally, sales organizations should hire honest people.

Although there is no foolproof way to make sure that sales applicants are honest, there are a few practices that should help with this. First, the job posting should be tailored for honest people by stressing the core values (e.g., integrity) required in the job and the type of employee that is being sought. Second, all information provided by the applicant should be checked carefully. This includes checking references and assessing the accuracy of the information on the resume. Third, the applicant should be deliberately screened for honesty during the interview process. Table 13-1 lists interview questions that screen for honesty. Finally, firms with more resources can give applicants any of several assessment tests that are designed to identify individuals who are likely to engage in unethical or illegal behavior on the job.[18]

Ethics Discussed in Training Program

Sales organizations with strong ethical work climates typically provide an ethics component to the initial training of all new salespeople. These organizations

Table 13-1 Interview Questions to Screen for Honesty

Question	Explanation of Answer
Have you seen our website?	If the answer is "yes," follow up with another question like "What did you like about it?" A vague and fumbled response could indicate a lie.
What does integrity in the workplace look like to you?	This question can help you assess your candidate's view of integrity and the value they place on it.
If you were hired, which of these three things would be the most important to you as an employee? (1) Bringing in as much money into the company as possible, (2) Being completely honest in all your work, or (3) Finishing your work quickly and on time?	All three are important and valuable, but honesty shouldn't be sacrificed at the expense of the other two.
Tell me about a time that you stood your ground against a group decision.	This doesn't necessarily have to be in the workplace. This response can help you see what value are important to your applicant.
If you were in a situation where a co-worker was doing something illegal or against company policy, what would you do?	If desired, you can adjust this question to fit the specific role the person is applying for. You can also ask the person to describe an instance of this actually happening, if you don't want to ask it hypothetically.
Describe a time in your past employment when you made a substantial mistake and you were the only one who knew about it. What did you do?	The answer to this question should reveal if this person is the type who would cover up a mistake or take ownership, even at the risk of losing his or her job.
Why did you leave your last job?	You'll soon find out the truth to this question once you contact your candidate's former employer.
Would you ever lie for me?	Obviously the answer to this question should be a definitive "No." Any other "well it depends..." sort of answer is a red flag. Assure the candidate that you would never ask them to lie, and use this opportunity to reinforce your company's core values or conduct policy.

Source: 6 Ways to Hire for Honesty (April 26, 2017). Better Business Bureau Blog https://www.bbb.org

also provide ongoing ethical training to all employees. Often, sales situations are complex, particularly in international situations. Sales professionals may want to behave ethically but may not be aware of the ethical implications of some of their decisions. Or even if they are aware of these implications, they may not know what is the most ethical action to take in a particular situation. Training—through the use of cases, role plays, and games—can simulate ethical dilemmas. This can increase ethical sensitivity and skills.

Benefits of Strong Ethical Work Climate

A strong ethical work climate benefits salespeople and their sales organizations in several ways. First of all, salespeople can feel good about themselves in that they are doing the right thing. In fact, salespeople that work in strong ethical work climates are more likely to be satisfied with their job, committed to their organization, and less likely to quit. As a group, the members of highly ethical sales forces are more likely to exhibit teamwork, which corresponds to high morale. Of course, a commitment toward ethical values lowers the likelihood of lawsuits as it helps to ensure that salespeople follow legal policies. There are also public relations benefits, as companies can build a strong public image by focusing on ethics. Finally, this all leads to an environment that lends itself to healthy, long-term relationships with customers, which leads to greater sales volume performance by salespeople.

Developing a Code of Ethics

code of ethics
the guidelines that sales organizations believe all of their salespeople should follow

Sales organizations should develop a **code of ethics**, which are the guidelines that they believe all of their salespeople should follow. Liberty Mutual, for example, requires all of its salespeople to sign the company's ethical conduct policy *every year*. In general, these guidelines are similar to the standards of conduct adopted by the National Association of Sales Professionals—and shown in Table 13-2.

Increasingly, in recent years, U.S. companies have developed a code of ethics in response to a number of revelations of bribery at home and in foreign business dealings. The code of ethics is a guideline for all employees to follow.

The code of ethics should be in writing and readily available for all salespeople to see, but it is no easy task to write one. Critics claim that such a statement usually is public relations window dressing that covers up a bad situation and corrects nothing. Nevertheless, higher levels of ethical behavior have been found in firms where codes of ethics are in place and enforced.[19] An ethical code that is part of the culture of an organization is likely to affect the decision making of that organization's employees. Such codes lessen the chance that executives will knowingly or unknowingly get into trouble, and they strengthen the company's hand in dealing with customers and government officials who invite bribes and other unethical actions. They also strengthen the position of lower-level executives in resisting pressures to compromise their personal ethics to get along in the firm.

In addition to providing guidelines for ethical decision making, a code of ethics can contribute to the general ethical work climate of an organization if it is endorsed and enforced by top management. Having a code of ethics is a concrete sign that the organization cares whether its employees behave ethically.

Reinforcing the Code of Ethics

A code of conduct must not only be written; it must be enforced. Salespeople who violate the code should be reprimanded; if they don't cease their unethical behavior, they should be fired. In other words, a code of ethics becomes an effective means of guiding behavior only if it is enforced; otherwise, it is meaningless.

Table 13-2 Standards of Conduct of the National Association of Sales Professionals (NASP)

Ethics and Professionalism:	I will act with the highest degree of professionalism, ethics, and integrity.
Representation of Facts:	I will fairly represent the benefits of my products and services.
Confidentiality Agreement:	I will keep information about my customers confidential.
Continuing Education:	I will maintain an ongoing program of professional development.
Responsibility to Clients:	I will act in the best interest of my clients, striving to present products and services that satisfy my customers' needs.
Responsibility to NASP:	I will share my lessons of experience with fellow NASP members and promote the interests of NASP.
Responsibility to Employer:	I will represent my employer in a professional manner and respect my employers' proprietary information.
Responsibility to Community:	I will serve as a model of good citizenship and be vigilant to the effects of my products and services on my community.
Conflicts of Interest:	I will disclose potential conflicts of interest to all relevant parties and, whenever possible, resolve conflicts before they become a problem.
Laws:	I will observe and obey all laws that affect my products, services, and profession.

Top managers and experienced salespeople must serve as ethical role models for employees. They must not only verbally endorse ethical behavior but also practice it. Clearly, salespeople are not going to take any code of ethics seriously if they see their senior colleagues and immediate managers behaving unethically.

Chapter Summary

- Ethics are the moral principles that govern a person's behavior. This topic is especially important in sales because salespeople are often exposed to situations that involve difficult choices—and they are not sure what to do.
- Values are the specific traits, behaviors, and attitudes that a person believes are good, desirable, or worthwhile. Values guide behavior and determine what we see as ethical. Six commons values associated with sales ethics are honesty, kindness, loyalty, service, trustworthiness, and commitment to excellence.
- There are two distinct ethical frameworks affecting how salespeople make decisions when faced with ethical dilemmas. The first framework focuses on actions or behaviors themselves and is called deontological ethics. The second framework focuses on the eventual *outcomes* of those actions or behaviors and is called teleological ethics.
- A key benefit of behaving ethically is that it builds trust with customers. Salespeople with emotional intelligence are better at building trust.

- Salespeople should be aware of their legal responsibilities, which include knowledge of the following laws: fraudulent misrepresentation, puffery, business defamation, bribery, price discrimination, reciprocity, tying agreements, cooling-off laws, Green River ordinances, Telephone Consumer Protection Act, and Foreign Corrupt Practices Act.
- Behaving in an ethical manner is more than just following laws. Salespeople should be sure to follow company protocol in the following areas: high-pressure sales, gift-giving, entertainment, confidentiality leaks, expense accounts, romantic relationships with colleagues, and filling out call reports about what they do when unsupervised.
- Factors that contribute to a strong ethical work climate include ethical leadership from executives, a culture of honesty, and a well-designed reward system and sales training program.
- Sales organizations should develop and widely share a written code of ethics, which are the guidelines that they believe all of their salespeople should follow.

Key Terms

bribery (p. 250)
business defamation (p. 249)
code of ethics (p. 258)
cooling-off laws (p. 251)
deontological ethics (p. 246)
ethical dilemma (p. 244)
ethical work climate (p. 256)
ethics (p. 244)
fraudulent misrepresentation (p. 249)

green river ordinances (p. 251)
price discrimination (p. 250)
puffery (p. 249)
reciprocity (p. 250)
servant leadership (p. 256)
teleological ethics (p. 247)
trust (p. 248)
tying agreement (p. 251)
values (p. 244)

Application 13-1

Lauren was recently hired as a sales rep for Parry Paper Company, and she was on the verge of making her first big sale to Van Buren University, a major private university in her territory. In fact, Lauren thought it was a done deal until she had the following troubling conversation with VBU's head of purchasing, Nick.

Nick: Well, Lauren, you've done an outstanding job of selling me on the benefits of Parry Paper. The only thing is, our old paper contract was with Citizen Paper, and a few of my colleagues feel like we should continue to buy from Citizen out of loyalty. I think I can convince them to switch to your company, but I'm going to need some extra incentive to make that happen—if you know what I mean.

Lauren: I'm sorry, but I'm not sure what you're saying...

Nick: Let's just say that I realize you will be making several thousand dollars in commission this year if you land this contract. It seems to me that it's not too much for me to ask you for a kickback of $500 in cash. If I receive this, then all is good. Are you with me?

1. What does Nick appear to be asking for?
2. If Lauren were to give Nick the $500, what has occurred, from an ethical standpoint?
3. If Lauren is bothered by Nick's suggestion, but concedes anyway because she desperately needs the commission money to pay for her son's tuition; what philosophy does her decision-making process demonstrate?

Application 13-2

Linda, who has been a salesperson with ABC Company for five years, is chatting in the break room with the new hire, Joseph. He has just graduated from college and was hired as an entry-level salesperson with ABC Company. Joseph finished his month-long sales training sessions a few days ago and has started calling on clients. Linda is giving him advice.

In a hushed tone, Linda tells him that a good way to make some extra money is to "get a bit creative" when he turns in his expense account reimbursement form. "At the very least, you should take your friends out to lunch at least a couple of times a month, and then turn in the receipt as a client lunch," Linda advises. She says that she has been doing that for the past two or three years, and no one cares. In fact, she says "everybody does it."

Joseph mostly just smiles and shakes his head in agreement, but he is silently not so sure about Linda's suggestion. In fact, Joseph remembers the staff trainer making a point that cheating on expense accounts is against company rules.

1. How would you judge the legality and ethics of what Linda is suggesting?
2. Linda says, "Everybody does it" —when referring to fellow salespeople cheating on their expense accounts. How should Joseph reply?
3. How has technology affected the ability for salespeople to cheat on expense reports?

Shutterstock/Quick Shot

CHAPTER

14 Role-Play

Learning Objectives

- Identify the elements of a sales role-play and its purpose
- Determine the value and importance of experiential learning and sales role-play
- Explain how sales organizations use role-play
- Understand what is necessary to prepare for and conduct effective sales role-play
- Be prepared to conduct an effective sales role-play

263

e learn and remember skills most effectively when engaged in live practice of those skills. Role-play is an important part of preparing salespeople for real sales situations without the danger of losing a sale or harming relationships with important customers. Role-play practice allows salespeople to gain and maintain skills critical to being effective. As a form of experiential learning, role-play permits salespeople to practice skills repeatedly to build the muscle memory and confidence necessary to perform intuitively during normal and difficult or stressful situations. The sales call is a complex interaction that requires the salesperson to adapt and make instantaneous decisions based upon customer actions and reactions, and the use of role-playing greatly enhances the chances of success during the sales call. Organizations use role-play to prepare new hires and help them learn their sales methodologies, their products, and their typical customers. Veteran salespeople often engage in role-play to learn new product offerings and to prepare for difficult and challenging customers.

Preparation by anyone participating as the buyer or seller should be thoughtful and planned in most instances. Veteran salespeople with experience at role-play may do impromptu role-play with others in some circumstances, but participants gain most when they have prepared and planned before role-playing. The importance of preparing both mentally and practically will become extremely evident to anyone participating in their first role-play. Similar to professional athletes who experience performance slumps by allowing a fundamental skill to get rusty, salespeople will encounter sales slumps if they fail to practice fundamental sales skills.

The Purpose of Role-Play

A role-play is a rehearsal for real life. The purpose of role-playing is to gain certain skills and habits by preparing for foreseen and unforeseen situations that occur. It also serves to build muscle memory (physical or mental) so that, in stressful or uncertain situations, responses become almost automatic or instinctive. Role-play also builds the confidence necessary to perform well in adverse situations. Participants gain confidence as they continue to practice and realize improvements in performance. Improvement most often is incremental, and perfection, though a worthy goal, is seldom achieved. John Wooden, winner of ten national championships at UCLA, and one of the most successful basketball coaches of all-time, said that the goal of learning "is to create a correct habit that can be produced instinctively under great pressure." The goal of experiential exercises and role-play in particular is to create automatic schemas or patterns of behavior that can be applied in various situations.[1]

The Value of Experiential Learning

experiential learning (EL)
when a personally responsible participant cognitively, affectively, and behaviorally processes knowledge, skills, or attitudes in a learning situation characterized by a high level of active involvement

Experiential learning (EL) occurs when a personally responsible participant cognitively, affectively, and behaviorally processes knowledge, skills, or attitudes in a learning situation characterized by a high level of active involvement.[2] In other words, EL is a holistic approach to learning and understanding. Role-play is an experiential learning tool, effective in learning personal selling skills, and one of the most effective sales training methodologies used by industry professionals.[3] The value of EL may be most obvious in sports, where athletes engage in EL in the form of practice drills that help them understand and improve their skills. Professional players practice a skill thousands of times to master it. Similarly, salespeople can only approach mastery through practice. And role-playing is practice.

If a salesperson has role-played several situations where the role-play buyer has exhibited buying signals, the salesperson will be better at noticing cues from a real prospect that indicate they are ready to make a purchasing decision. Through practice, the salesperson can learn to adapt to the buyer and move toward asking for commitment and closing the sale or making other adjustments without thinking about how or if to ask. Experiential learning is effective because it not only involves cognitive aspects of learning, but it also engages feelings, emotions, and spatial or physical components of learning that are relevant to work and other experiences in daily life.

How We Learn

What you have probably experienced in most college courses or seminars is fairly traditional learning. You read, listen to a lecture, and then demonstrate your understanding through tests and completion of assignments. In other words, most students memorize facts and repeat them on assignments and exams. Rote memorization is the foundation of learning, so it is necessary and essential, but only the starting point for understanding and developing capabilities and skills. Although Benjamin Bloom, the renowned researcher and educator, suggests there are many levels of learning, the three general domains of learning are **cognitive** (knowledge-based), **affective** (emotion-based) and **psychomotor** (physical/special action/activity-based).[4]

cognitive learning
knowledge-based learning

affective learning
emotion-based learning

psychomotor learning
learning based on physical, special action, or activity

Studies of adult learning reveal that active learning is more effective than passive learning. The more engaged one is the more likely one is to understand and retain information and improve skill development (see Figure 14-1)[5]. These experts suggest that when learning new skills individuals retain only 5% of what they hear in a lecture, 10% of what they read, 20% of what they see via audiovisual tools, 30% when observing a live demonstration, 50% when actively discussing the material or concepts, 75% when they engage in live practice of the skill, and 90% when they teach others the skill. There is some argument about the precise numbers presented by the *learning pyramid* in Figure 14-1,[6] but, regardless, there

Figure 14-1

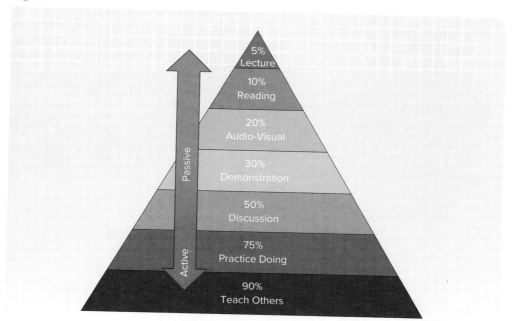

Adapted from the NTL Institute of Applied Behavioral Science Learning Pyramid. https://www.educationcorner.com/the-learning-pyramid.html

is agreement that learning and mastering skills is a progressive process and that experiential exercises result in more effective learning and skill development.

Competence, Behavior and the Need for Continuous Learning

Just as there is a *learning* process, knowledge and competence can also decay over time if it goes unused. As listed in Figure 14-2, psychologists refer to this as the four stages of competence or the hierarchy of competence: unconscious incompetence, conscious incompetence, conscious competence, and unconscious competence.[7]

A new salesperson with no training or knowledge of the sales process may have some success and also some failure, but not realize there is a more effective sales method. These salespeople are in the **unconscious incompetence** stage. They are "blissfully ignorant." They don't know what they don't know. As they see other salespeople have more success or their sales manager points out that they are falling short of expected performance levels, they may come to realize that they need to make some changes. They have now entered the **conscious incompetence** stage. They realize that they need to improve. Any person attempting to learn a new skill has come to this stage. As a reader of this textbook, you are probably at this stage.

However, as individuals practice and learn a new skill, they will become competent over time, but they have to think about the process and the mechanics as they execute the behavior(s): **conscious competence**. Like making changes to a golf swing or other athletic movements, the change feels uncomfortable, stiff, and mechanical. In most cases, people have to engage in many hours and repetitions before feeling comfortable with new skills. Learning new sales skills, and in the case of many veteran salespeople, *relearning* how to sell, can take many hours of practice and repetition before becoming comfortable to the point that they do not have to *think* about the process or behavior to perform it correctly.

When the behavior becomes a habit that feels natural and comfortable, the individual will have entered the **unconscious competence** stage. The process has become a part of who they are. It is simply what they do without having to think about it. They no longer feel mechanical when performing the skill. Unfortunately, most people do not stay in this stage. As salespeople continue in their careers, they will inevitably experience slumps in performance. Slumps occur for many reasons, but often they happen because the salesperson has gotten into bad habits without realizing it. Yes, people can cycle back to being an unconscious incompetent.

unconscious incompetence
an individual untrained and with the necessary knowledge, who isn't aware of more effective methods

conscious incompetence
an individual who recognizes their personal need for training and knowledge

conscious competence
a competent individual who still needs to think about the process and the mechanics as they execute the behavior

unconscious competence
when competent behavior becomes a habit, allowing the individual to execute effectively without thought

Figure 14-2 Hierarchy of Competence

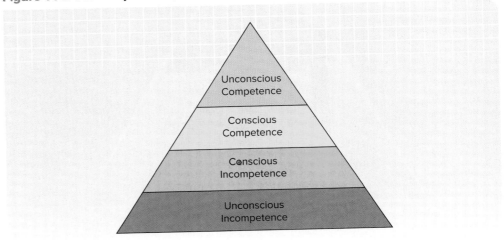

Salespeople may forget a minor detail, like forgetting to use open-ended questions, for example, or failing to ask appropriate need discovery questions.

High performers continue to practice the basic skills they have mastered. Making role-play a lifelong practice helps salespeople maintain good learning habits and reduce sales slumps. The next section introduces the value and benefits of role-playing in sales.

The Value of Role-Play for Salespeople

Role-play enhances skills and capabilities that are critical to performing well in sales.[8] Consistent, purposeful role-play practice produces habits, attitudes, and confidence that allow salespeople to perform capably in what can be difficult or stressful situations and encounters. As comfort and confidence is built, role-play also reduces the level of stress that arises in challenging situations that are inevitable in sales and life.

Role-play provides a safe environment to attempt new approaches where there is no chance of losing a sale or harming relationships with valuable customers. Organizations use role-play to prepare new sales hires and help them understand their sales process, their products, and the various situations and customer personality types they will meet. Experienced salespeople use role-play to assist them in learning new products, and to practice the most effective approaches to uncovering their customers' specific needs addressed by the new offering. Salespeople use role-play to determine the best method for presenting the value of a new product. Role-play is also used to work through methods for dealing with difficult customers and situations and to share best practices.

Preparing for Role-Play

You will not benefit from role-playing by improvising. This is true for both the person playing the role of the seller and the one playing the buyer. First and foremost, to gain the most during role-play exercises salespeople must prepare for the role-play. This includes mental attitude, as well as practical preparation. It is also true for students with no experience, new hires with little experience, and veteran salespeople with a lot of experience. The following provides a guide based on the learning pyramid scheme, industry studies of how best to prepare for sales role-play, and the authors' decades of experience in conducting sales role-play.

Mental Preparation

Role-play is pretending you are in a situation and reacting as you might if the situation were real. It is a simplified version of reality. Pretending can be uncomfortable and awkward. Veteran salespeople rarely enjoy role-playing. But, after doing a few, they realize and appreciate the benefits. And it can be a lot of fun and rewarding, regardless of the participants' experience. As with physical exercise, there may be some discomfort. But focusing on the outcomes (being a more effective salesperson and realizing higher levels of compensation) alleviates the uneasiness a participant may feel. One important fact to remember if you become nervous: There have been no reported deaths or serious injuries in the history of sales role-plays!

To be effective, role-play needs to be as realistic as possible.[9] Participants need to *get into* the role and imagine that they are *in the situation.*

The participants' engagement in the role-play learning experience is critical to gaining progressive improvement in skills they desire to learn.[10] So, how does one engage? The following are guidelines for preparing mentally for role-play.

Read the Script or Case   The setting of a role-play will be provided either through a short case, or verbal instructions regarding the setting or situation. Participants should read their roles in advance and become familiar with the situation and the characters involved. The instructor or manager may have participants conduct impromptu role-plays, or salespeople may decide to do their own role-play with fellow salespeople, in which case there would be no written case. Regardless, participants should ask questions of the instructor regarding the facts of the situation. If salespeople initiate the role-play with a fellow salesperson, they need to describe the particular facts and setting in which the role-play is conducted. Whether participants have a written case or not, they should imagine or picture how the interaction might play out. When actors get into character, they are trying to *live, breathe, and understand* their character so that the audience believes they are who they are portraying. They must do their homework. They must read through the *backstory* that is created for their character and adapt to the situations and circumstances that they create in their mind from the information about the character and setting of each scene.[11]

Write Your Script   Role-play participants should write out in *longhand* what they plan to say. Hand-writing, rather than typing, helps the individual's mind connect to the role and retain the information.[12] Role-playing is interactive by nature, and each participant (buyer and seller) must adapt to the other person or persons in the role-play, which means that, although they have a script, participants will adapt or improvise a good bit of the role-play. A good salesperson also considers all the objections that might arise. Participants should write out as many objections as they can think of for the product they are selling and possible responses. The role-play preparation worksheets at the end of this chapter will help you develop a script for a role-play.

Practical Preparation: The Seller Role

Before you begin your role-play, you will have read chapters from this book, listened to lectures, watched demonstrations, and perhaps discussed concepts and examples. Likewise, salespeople must take the time to review and study the sales process used by their organization. And they should commit to learning about the product offering. Organizations invest substantial resources and time to help their salespeople understand their product offerings. This textbook focuses on sales and the sales process rather than product knowledge, but product knowledge is essential for salespeople to succeed. Recent research by LinkedIn revealed that U.S. companies spend around $15 billion annually for sales training[13], and about 50% of the training is on product, company, and industry knowledge (see Table 14-1).[14] Thoroughly familiarizing oneself with the value proposition will help the process make sense, and, just as important, supply confidence in a sales career and in conducting role-plays. We suggest *Six Steps to Practical Preparation and Role-Play* (see Figure 14-3). This step-sequence is consistent with the way people learn.

Table 14-1 Training Spending of U.S. Companies

Training Type	% of Sales Training
Selling Skills	50%
Product Knowledge	20%
Company Information	15%
Industry Knowledge	15%

Figure 14-3 Six Steps to Practical Preparation and Role-Play

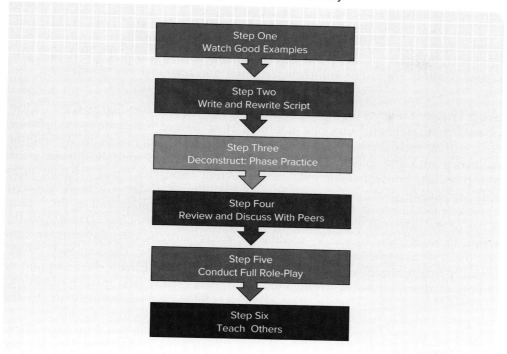

Step One: Watch Examples of Good Role-Play   Whenever practical, role-plays should be video recorded, allowing individuals to see and critique their performance. If recording equipment is not available, use a phone. Seeing others (live or recorded) conduct exemplary role-plays of the sales process to be used in this course or on the job will help participants see what is expected and present examples of how each phase of the sales call should be conducted. The basic sales process is the same across most sales approaches, but different methodologies use different wording or acronyms and include other subtle differences. Reviewing a role-play that uses the process you are learning or expected to use is more helpful than reviewing a role-play of a different process. Watching good recorded role-plays also provides insight into what might happen (both expected and unexpected) during the exercise, the strategy of the seller and how the seller responds to different situations. Watching recordings of role-plays allows the observer to stop, pause, and re-watch various aspects. The instructor may have access to recorded role-plays that are well done. Role-playing is rarely perfect. Students may identify ways the seller could have been more effective and incorporate the different approaches during their own role-play. Also, it is important to watch the individual phase of the sales call being learned. As will be suggested below, students should work on one phase of the call at a time. They should review different sales call role-play phases repeatedly until they have a firm understanding of each one.

As students watch, they should follow along with the scoring or evaluation form at the end of this chapter. They should score the seller in the role-play with the form and identify where he or she performs well and where there is room for improvement. Watching, scoring, or taking notes gives students a good mental picture of how to engage in the process correctly. Students will also take away ideas to use during their role-play (and on the job) that they had not considered when developing their script.

Step Two: Write-Rewrite Script After watching several exemplary role-plays, participants should edit the script based on the new ideas gained. Students should read the script again and make any additional edits to put the script in their own words. Again, participants should practice reading through their approach, their need identification questions, the presentation, and the close. They should also review possible objections and their responses and read them out loud.

Step Three: Deconstruct Practice Each Phase of the Sales Call How do you eat an elephant? One bite at a time. Most sales calls include several phases. And within each phase, there may be several steps and reactions. Attempting to incorporate and master complex skills constructed of multiple phases all at one time can be overwhelming. Deconstructing logical minimal learning units and sequencing them in the most logical step-by-step order is a more effective approach to mastering skills.[15] Practice each phase separately and in the logical order of the sales call with a role-play partner (buyer) until comfortable with the script. Perhaps begin by simply reading the script with the role-play partner until you are able to recite or role-play without using the script. The sequence should logically follow the chronological process of the sales call, with the exception of objections that may occur throughout a call. It is usually best to save objections until the last sequence or practice sessions. Objections add complexity to the role-play, and it is better to become competent at a skill before moving to more complex situations that require higher levels of adaptation. Build on each phase by learning and practicing and then practice the first two phases together, then the first three phases, and so on until you become comfortable with the entire process. By becoming competent and comfortable with one phase at a time, you will gain confidence in moving through a complete sales call.

During this phase, the seller should also have access to the buyer information. This time is for learning and practicing the mechanics of the skills and building confidence in being able to execute each skill. Again, there is no need to add additional complexity while learning the skill. The idea is to build the *muscle memory* or the habits needed to perform during a live situation. During live sales calls, a salesperson must have the ability to adapt to different situations without being mechanical. So, save the difficult situations, questions, and objections until you are comfortable with the rest of the process.

reflective learning
an individual intentionally thinking about and understanding what they have done during a learning experience and in turn taking corrective action

Step Four: Review and Discussion with Peers **Reflective learning** or reflective practice involves individuals' intentionally thinking about and understanding what they have done during a learning experience and in turn taking corrective action. This method of learning is facilitated through the discussion and feedback process with peers or coaches and greatly enhances improvement in learning a skill.[16] Working in groups of three is ideal when preparing for role-play. Each member of the group should participate in each of the roles: seller, buyer, and observer. The observer watches the role-play practice live and provides feedback throughout the practice. Each participant offers different perspectives on the action during the role-play. Sales role-plays can be nerve-racking. Most people do not wish to look foolish and risk ridicule, especially when attempting something they have not done or might do poorly. Therefore, the debrief and feedback process should concentrate on the role-play evaluation form and be conducted in a manner that provides honest, constructive feedback rather than ridicule.[17] Of course, there will be opportunities for laughter, because, with few exceptions, no one will conduct their first role-plays perfectly. The goal of the role-play group of coaches is to help everyone in the group improve. All discussion sessions should include both feedback on what went well and what needs improvement. The observer should use the role-play evaluation form to score the session on the specific criteria and skills being performed and record observations of the seller's performance. Providing feedback to the buyer also adds to the effectiveness of future role-play.

The following are guidelines for the role-play review, discussion, and feedback session. All discussion and feedback should be based on the evaluation criteria outlined by the role-play evaluation form. Feedback to the buyer should also be included during these sessions.

- **Start with the positive.** Attempt to focus on the positive without discussing any negative aspects of the performance until after discussing what the participant(s) did well. Allow the seller first to reflect on and discuss his or her performance of the session. Note that the person performing the seller role is often the most critical of their performance. Starting with the positive, the seller should communicate or be asked to reflect on what they felt they did well. The observer should then engage the seller in a discussion of the positives and affirming the seller's observations where possible. The buyer should also join the discussion with his or her observations regarding the positive aspects of the performance.
- **End with areas for improvement.** The seller should then be asked to communicate what areas need improvement, followed by feedback from the observer and the buyer regarding what needs improvement.
- **Focus on behaviors and techniques.** Discussion and reflection should focus on the *behavior* or *techniques* rather than on the individual. For example, "The attention-getting statement could have been focused more on benefits rather than features." The behavior or skill needs improvement, and the critique is not a personal statement about the person.
- **Suggest how to improve.** Rather than simply identifying what needs improvement, always indicate alternative ways to improve based on the sales process, and concepts and readings from the course. These are included in the evaluation form.
- **Focus on major issues.** Avoid focusing on minor concerns during the discussion. Instead, the observer should include the minor issues in notes taken on the evaluation form and provided to the seller after the discussion.
- **Identify methods.** The role-play practice and feedback session is a learning exercise for the seller but is also a vicarious learning opportunity for others in the group. Each group member should identify and discuss the specific methods and concepts learned during the course, through course readings, and used during the role-play.

Role-Play Review Discussion Example

Positive Start:

Observer: *So, I thought you did several things well. What do you think you did well?*

Seller: *Well, I thought the agenda was fairly clear and concise.*

Observer: *Yes, and the agenda also focused on the buyer rather than the salesperson and the sales organization.*

Buyer: *I agree, the agenda also positioned the meeting so that the buyer understood that the meeting would be focused on her and her organization rather than just a feature dump.*

Observer: *What else do you believe went well?*

Areas of Improvement:

Observer: *Okay, you did a number of things really well. What are some areas for improvement?*

Seller: *Well, the purpose statement really focused on features and not benefits.*

Observer: *Yes, and how could it have been stated differently?*

Seller: *It should have been, "We work with companies like yours to help them reduce their costs and improve their revenues."*

Observer: *Yes, that is a good approach.*

Buyer: *The purpose statement also might have been a little more customized to this particular buyer and her company, showing that you did your research, which would have helped build credibility.*

Review and discussion sessions should occur at the end of each phase practice session. This means that the student or salesperson potentially will have gone through up to 45 practice (one for each phase and one for each member of the three-person group), review, and discussion sessions before conducting a full role-play. While this seems daunting, the practice and discussion will put the student or salesperson in a great position to understand and internalize the process.

Step Five: Conduct Full Role-Play   The individual phases of the sales call have been practiced, discussed, reviewed, and practiced again. At this point, it is time to put all the phases together. Though this will be done toward the end of the deconstruction and practice process, conducting the full role-play as a separate practice will put the salesperson at the next level of more realistic experience. During full role-play, the seller should not have the buyer information beyond basic information about the situation and other facts that may be gathered as a part of pre-call preparation. Review, discussion, and feedback should be provided after every role-play session.

Step Six: Teach   Where practical, teach other students or salespeople, demonstrating and explaining the concepts behind the process. A class of peers is all learning at the same time, but one should assist others in the class who need help. The feedback sessions provide a good opportunity for teaching. Many universities participate in sales role-play competitions either at their respective schools or regional or national competitions. If one's school has created a sales team to compete, take advantage of the opportunities that taking part in it would afford to teach others with little or no experience.

Practical Preparation: The Buyer Role

Like the person playing the seller, the person playing the buyer must also prepare mentally and practically. The buyer should become very familiar with the setting and situation surrounding the role-play exercise and his or her role. The buyer usually has information on how the meeting was initiated, the background of the company to whom the seller is selling, a personality type (the general attitude or communication style of the buyer), a set of needs, a set of objections, and how the purchasing decision should occur. The buyer, especially, needs to become very familiar with the buying role and situation. The buyer should imagine what a real buyer would be like in the case and situation and *become* the buyer.

How well the buyer role provides a realistic context for the seller is critical in making the role-play an effective learning experience. The participant playing the buyer should also read and be very familiar with the setting of the case, the background, personality, needs, and objections of the buyer. The buyer should also write out the script or make notes of the information provided in the case. Again, writing the information related to the buyer in your own words in longhand, will help you learn and get into the role and make one more effective as the buyer. Please note that if provided a case by the instructor, the buyer should not take the printed case into the role-play exercise. If the buyer is flipping through papers to find out what his or her needs or the facts of the situation are, it distracts the seller and does not provide a realistic experience. The buyer should make the role-play a conversation and not read from a script. Knowing and realistically playing the buyer also helps one better understand buyers when one is in the seller role.

Team Selling Role-Play

Today many sales calls are conducted that include several people from the buying organization and often more than one sales team member on the call. The sales process is the same, but the dynamics are different. The salesperson must consider the needs of each of the buyers and determine the roles of each person on the sales team that is involved. Preparing mentally and practically for team sales role-play is no different from individual role-play, except that the team should rehearse or practice each of their roles before conducting a full role-play. Each of the sellers should become adept at individual role-play before engaging in a team selling role-play.

Role-play enhances selling skills and builds confidence. Sales experts and top sales organizations recommend engaging in sales role-play weekly if not daily, yet the average salesperson and sales organization rarely do it. The question is, do you want to be average? Someone who wants to be above average has to be willing to do what the average person is not willing to do. To be a high-performer and make it to the top of the field and company, practice role-playing. Learn to love role-playing. Practice, practice, practice.

Chapter Summary

- Role-play is a rehearsal for real life. It is practice. Role-play is an important part of preparing salespeople for real sales situations without the danger of losing a sale or harming relationships with important customers and it allows salespeople to gain and maintain skills critical to being effective.
- Experiential learning through role-playing creates muscle memory (physical or mental) and the confidence necessary to perform intuitively during normal and difficult sales situations and is the most effective method for salespeople to build skills and confidence.
- Sales organizations use role-play to prepare new hires and help them learn their sales methodologies, products, and about their customers. Veteran salespeople role-play to learn new products and to prepare for challenging customers.
- Salespeople go through the process of being an unconscious incompetent, a conscious incompetent, a conscious competent, and unconscious competent and may circle back to an unconscious incompetent if they do not practice their sales skills.
- Role-play participants should prepare both mentally and practically before engaging in a role-play.
- The six steps for practical preparation and role-play are: watch examples of good role-play, write and rewrite the script, deconstruct and practice each phase of the sales call, review and discuss with peers, conduct full role-play, teach others.
- The most effective learning occurs after learning a skill and then teaching others to do the skill.
- To gain the most from role-play, participants need to provide constructive feedback to both the seller and the buyer. An observer can assist during assessment of role-play.
- Use role-play worksheets to prepare for a role-play and an evaluation form to assess a role-play and to provide constructive feedback.

Key Terms

affective learning (p. 265)
cognitive learning (p. 265)
conscious competence (p. 266)
conscious incompetence (p. 266)
experiential learning (p. 264)

psychomotor learning (p. 265)
reflective learning (p. 270)
unconscious competence (p. 266)
unconscious incompetence (p. 266)

Application 14-1

Dedric sold cars at his mother's Lexus car dealership from the age of 16 through his graduation from college this year. Dedric earned a degree in psychology because he felt it would help him in a sales career. Within a month after graduating, he accepted a position as an entry-level inside salesperson at Gartner, the world's leading research and advisory company. Gartner provides research, advice, insights, and tools to business leaders at executive level management, or C-Suite. Dedric has been in Gartner's sales training program for two weeks. The initial training lasts for two months and is a mix of product and sales skills training with a substantial amount of role-play, which Dedric had no experience doing. The Gartner trainers provide video recordings of previous trainees who have done well at role-play.

Dedric was confident that he would be successful in sales because of his experience, but he has been a little nervous about the role-play. He realizes he needs to learn Gartner's products and services but does not see the need for the role-play. He knows how to sell. However, he wants to gain the confidence and respect of his sales manager, so he has decided to give the role-plays a good shot.

1. At which stage in the hierarchy of competence is Dedric?
2. What would you tell Dedric to motivate or convince him of the value of doing role-play?
3. How would you suggest Dedric prepare for doing well at the sales role-plays?

Application 14-2

Mariella is a veteran salesperson of ten years with Henry Schein Dental, the leading distributor of dental equipment, technology, supplies, and business solutions. Mariella is very successful and has been the number one salesperson in her region on several occasions.

She has been one of the top ten salespeople in her region for the past five years. However, she slumps in her sales whenever Henry Schein brings out a new product and especially technology solutions. She likes helping her clients when she feels an innovative technology will improve their practice and bottom line. Mariella reads all the training materials and participates in all the new product online learning (on technical aspects of each new product) that Henry Schein's training and product development team offers. She still finds it difficult to explain and show the value of the product when she is face-to-face with her clients; at least the first four or five times she presents the new solutions. Mariella has concluded that she is just not a technology nerd and that the slowdown in her sales is just part of a new product launch. Henry Schein is launching a new product, a dental practice management software called Easy Dental, this month and she plans to get a head start tonight reading the training materials and watching the new product webinars.

Today, Mariella has three new appointments. She mostly calls on current clients, but when new dentists open offices in her territory or her current dentists sell their practices, she calls on them to build a relationship and gain them as clients. Mariella enjoys meeting new potential clients, but it takes her several months to begin doing business with them. However, in conversations with the leading salespeople in other regions, she learned that their ramp-up time with new clients is only a few weeks. She chalks this up to "that's just the way it is" when gaining new business, and perhaps her territory is just more challenging with more competition.

1. Why do you think Mariella is having difficulty grasping and presenting the value of new technology solutions to her clients?
2. What level(s) of learning is Mariella's approach encompassing?
3. Why might role-plays with other salespeople or managers help Mariella in reducing her sales slumps when focusing on new prospects and during new product launches?

Role-Play Worksheet: Approach

Major Objectives: Establish Rapport – Gain Attention – Set Agenda	
Rapport	**Rapport**: Ideas based on known information about prospect/customer & organization 1. ______ 2. ______ 3. ______ 4. ______
Value Statement	**Gain Attention/Value Statement/Purpose**: Establish potential value for prospect/organization Script: ______ ______ ______ ______
Agenda	**Meeting Agenda:** Establish Itinerary and set up transition into needs discovery Script: ______ ______ ______ ______
Notes	**Notes:** ______ ______ ______ ______ ______ ______

Role-Play Worksheet: Discovery/Needs Identification

Major Objectives: Uncover Prospect's Concerns/Issues/Problems: Focus on pain; Develop probes that focus on strengths of your product/service	
Decision Maker	**Decision Maker:** Identify decision maker Script: _____ _____ _____ _____
Category 1 Questions	**Category 1 Questions:** Script: Develop up to 4 category 1 questions 1. _____ 2. _____ 3. _____ 4. _____
Category 1 Questions	**Category 2 Questions:** Script: Develop up to 4 category 2 questions 1. _____ 2. _____ 3. _____ 4. _____
Category 3 Questions	**Category 3 Questions:** Script: Develop up to 4 category 3 questions 1. _____ 2. _____ 3. _____ 4. _____
Category 4 Questions	**Category 4 Questions:** Script: Develop up to 4 category 3 questions 1. _____ 2. _____ 3. _____ 4. _____

Role-Play Worksheet: Presentation, Value Proposition, or Recommendation

Product:	
Major Objectives: Identify Features and Associated Value of Product/Service Prepare for potential benefits/value to present based upon current knowledge of prospect Identify potential Visual Aid(s) you might use to enhance value.	
Feature	Associated Benefit
1.	
	Visual Aid:
2.	
	Visual Aid:
3.	
	Visual Aid:
4.	
	Visual Aid:
5.	
	Visual Aid:
6.	
	Visual Aid:
7.	
	Visual Aid:
8.	
	Visual Aid:

Role-Play Worksheet: Customer Questions and Objections

List 5 key Questions/Objections you expect to encounter during your role-play.

- Write out the anticipated objection.
- Identify the technique you would use.
- Write out the actual response you will give.

Objection/Question 1	
Technique	
Response	
Objection/Question 2	
Technique	
Response	
Objection/Question 3	
Technique	
Response	

Role-Play Worksheet: Closing or Securing Commitment

Major Objectives: Gain and Confirm Customer Commitments/Share and Confirm Your Commitments

Customer Commitment: Identify up to 3 commitment approaches/techniques you might use and script what you would say

Customer Commitment

Approach 1:

Script: _____

_____

_____

_____

_____

Approach 2:

Script: _____

_____

_____

_____

_____

Approach 3:

Script: _____

_____

_____

_____

_____

Salesperson Commitments

Salesperson Commitments: Identify and script up to 3 commitments you might make to the prospect.

1. _____

2. _____

3. _____

4. _____

5. _____

6. _____

Role-Play Evaluation Criteria

Salesperson: _____ | Buyer: _____ Score: _____

Evaluator: _____ Date: _____

10 = Excellent   8 = Above Average   7 = Average   6 = Needs Improvement   3 = Vague Evidence   1 = No Evidence (260pts)

APPROACH

____ Professional introduction (firm handshake, eye contact, business card)
____ Build/Established Rapport: (raise comfort of prospect; lower barriers; build trust)
____ Salesperson gains prospect's attention
____ Set Agenda (situation appropriate) and gained commitment to continue; appropriate transition to
____ Needs ID | positioned to ask questions/uncover needs

Approach Comments

DISCOVERY/NEEDS IDENTIFICATION

____ Uncovered decision maker & process (decision criteria, people involved in decision)
____ Circumstance questions (what are facts about company and/or buyer now)
____ Challenge questions (uncover needs; current problems; goals)
____ Consequence questions (what happens to company when problems continue)
____ Value questions (uncover benefits received if challenges solved: transition to presentation)

Needs Comments

PRESENTATION

____ Benefits & needs focused vs features (e.g., what this means to you)
____ Logical, convincing presentation (display a strategy to communicate; match benefits to specific needs uncovered, customized; know where you want to go)
____ Verbiage (appropriate, clear, concise, concrete vs. abstract; no "filler" words)
____ Used appropriate/professional visual aids; multiple
____ Demonstrated product (understanding of features and value proposition)
____ Got customer to participate in a meaningful manner (entire demonstration)
____ Demonstrated active listening (clarified, probed, restated and summarized)
____ Appropriate non-verbal (eye contact, posture, vocal, no "filler" words; appropriate dress)
____ Gained agreement through trial closes (how does that sound?) (After important features/benefits)

Presentation Comments

OVERCOMING OBJECTIONS

____ Clarified (confirmed he/she understood objection; ask question)
____ Responses appropriate and helpful to the buyer; used adv. Advanced Responses
____ Confirmed the objection was no longer a concern (buyer responds)

Objections Comments

CLOSE

____ Used advance methods to close (Effective in closing; regardless of how buyer responds)
____ Presented a reason to act sooner (product value based; **not** **"discount today only."**)

Close Comments

OVERALL

____ Salesperson demonstrated enthusiasm, confidence, and a positive attitude
____ Salesperson understood facts of the role play; product knowledge
____ Conversational – non-scripted – adapted to prospect

Overall Comments

Major Strengths (What would you keep?):

_____

_____

_____

Major Weakness (What would you not keep or what would you change?)

_____

_____

Notes

Chapter 1

1. Pink, Daniel H. (2012). *To Sell Is Human: The Surprising Truth About Moving Others*. New York: Riverhead Books.
2. Manpower. (2018). Top 10 Most In-Demand Skills. *2018 Talent Shortage Survey Manpower Group*. Retrieved at https://go.manpowergroup.com/talent-shortage-2018.
3. Williams, Terri. (2018). There's a Sales Talent Crisis—But It's Solvable. *MultiBriefs*. Retrieved at exclusive.multibriefs.com/content/theres-a-sales-talent-crisis-but-its-solvable/business-management-services-riskmanagement.
4. Georgetown University Center on Education and the Workforce. (2011). *What's It Worth? The Economic Value of College Majors*. Retrieved at https://cew.georgetown.edu/cew-reports/whats-it-worth-the-economic-value-of-college-majors/.
5. Georgetown University Center of Education and the Workforce and The University of Texas System. (2017). *Major Matters Most. The Economic Value of Bachelor's Degrees from the University of Texas System*. Retrieved at https://cew.georgetown.edu/wp-content/uploads/UT-System.pdf.
6. SmartWinnr. Top 10 CEOs Who Started as Sales Reps. Retrieved at https://www.smartwinnr.com/post/top10-ceos-who-started-as-salesreps/.
7. Burg, Bob and John David Mann. (2007). *The Go-Giver: A Little Story About a Powerful Business Idea*. New York: Penguin Group.
8. Pink, Daniel H. (2012). *To Sell Is Human: The Surprising Truth About Moving Others*. New York: Riverhead Books.
9. Misra, Parth. (2018). 5 Reasons Every Entrepreneur Should Start in Sales. *Entrepreneur.com*. Retrieved at https://www.entrepreneur.com/article/315650.
10. Casserly, Meghan. (2013). The Five Sales Tactics Every Entrepreneur Must Master. *Forbes.com*. Retrieved at https://www.forbes.com/sites/meghancasserly/2013/01/30/the-five-sales-tactics-every-entrepreneur-must-master/.
11. Comer, Lucette B. and Tanya Drollinger. (1999). Active Empathetic Listening and Selling Success: A Conceptual Framework. *Journal of Personal Selling & Sales Management*, 14(1): 15–29.
12. Ramsey, Rosemary P. and Ravipreet S. Sohi. (1997). Listening to Your Customers: The Impact of Perceived Salesperson Listening Behavior on Relationship Outcomes. *Journal of the Academy of Marketing Science*, 25(2): 127–137.
13. Grant, Adam M. (2013). Rethinking the Extraverted Sales Ideal: The Ambivert Advantage. *Psychological Science*, 24(6): 1024–1030.
14. Shell, G. Richard. (2006). *Bargaining for Advantage: Negotiation Strategies for Reasonable People*, 2nd Edition. New York: Penguin Books.
15. Rickert, Bob. (2014). *Profit Heroes: Breakthrough Strategies for Winning Customers and Building Profits*. Bloomington: AuthorHouse.
16. Burg, Bob and John David Mann. (2007). *The Go-Giver: A Little Story About a Powerful Business Idea*. New York: Penguin Group.
17. Duckworth, Angela. (2016). *Grit: The Power of Passion and Perseverance*. New York: Scribner.
18. McNally, David. (2008). Fueling the Engine of Sales Success. *CRM Magazine*, 12(July): BG22.
19. Weinberg, Mike. (2013). *New Sales. Simplified*. New York: AMACOM.
20. Burg, Bob and John David Mann. (2007). *The Go-Giver: A Little Story About a Powerful Business Idea*. New York: Penguin Group.
21. Tufts, Steven D. (2017). Salesperson Personality and Sphere of Influence as Determinants of Sales Performance. Unpublished Doctoral Dissertation, University of Florida.
22. Smith, Matt. (2015). The History of Professional Selling: To Understand Where You Are Going You Need to Understand Where You Have Been. Retrieved at https://predictablerevenue.com/blog/history-professional-sales-training#disqus_thread.
23. Bradford, Kevin D., Goutam N. Challagalla, Gary K. Hunter, and William C. Moncrief, III. (2012). Strategic Account Management: Conceptualizing, Integrating, and Extending the Domain from Fluid to Dedicated Accounts. *Journal of Personal Selling & Sales Management*, 32(1): 42.
24. Pink, Daniel H. (2012). *To Sell Is Human: The Surprising Truth About Moving Others*. New York: Riverhead Books.
25. Grant, Adam M. (2013). Rethinking the Extraverted Sales Ideal: The Ambivert Advantage. *Psychological Science*, 24(6): 1024–1030.
26. Singhapakdi, Anusorn and Scott J. Vitell. (1992). Marketing Ethics: Sales Professionals vs. Other Marketing Professionals. *Journal of Personal Selling & Sales Management*, 12(2): 27–38.
27. Pettijohn, Charles E., Linda S. Pettijohn, James B. Pettijohn, and A.J. Taylor. (2007). How Do the Attitudes of Students Compare with the Attitudes of Salespeople? A Comparison of Perceptions of Business, Consumer and Employer Ethics. *The Marketing Management Journal*, 17(1): 51–64.
28. Tippett, Elizabeth C. (2016). "This Is How Wells Fargo Encouraged Employees to Commit Fraud." *The New Republic*. Retrieved at https://newrepublic.com/article/137571/wells-fargo-encouraged-employees-commit-fraud.
29. Rickert, Bob. (2014). *Profit Heroes: Breakthrough Strategies for Winning Customers and Building Profits*. Bloomington: AuthorHouse.

Chapter 2

1. Lachance, Hubert. (2016). *Confessions of a Professional Buyer: The Secrets About Selling & Purchasing Services*. Published by the author.
2. Ward, Kim D. (2016). *The New Selling IQ: Combining the Power of Buyer-Seller Intelligence to Optimize Results!* Published by the author. Copyright held by The Learning Outsource Group.
3. Institute for Supply Management. Retrieved at https://www.instituteforsupplymanagement.org/CareerCenter/content.cfm?ItemNumber=12993.
4. Konrath, Jill. (2010). *Snap Selling: Speed Up Sales and Win More Business with Today's Frazzled Customers*. New York: Penguin Group.
5. Ward, Kim D. (2010). *The New Selling IQ: Combining the Power of Buyer-Seller Intelligence to Optimize Results!* Published by the author. Copyright held by The Learning Outsource Group, pp. 80–82.
6. Curasi, Carolyn F., James Boles, and Rick Reynolds. (2018). Key Account Buying Team Members' Emotional Responses Awarding Multi-Million Dollar Sales Contracts. *Industrial Marketing Management* 75: 193–205.
7. Zeithaml, Valarie A. (1988). Consumer Perceptions of Price, Quality, and Value: A Means-End Model and Synthesis of Evidence. *Journal of Marketing*, 52(July): 2–22.
8. Srinivasan, V. (1979). Network Models for Estimating Brand-Specific Effects in Multi-Attribute Marketing Models. *Management Science*, 25(1): 11–20.

9. Wilkie, William L. and Edgar A. Pessemier. (1973). Issues in Marketing's Use of Multi-Attribute Attitude Models. *Journal of Marketing Research, 10*(November): 428–441.
10. Ward, Kim D. (2016). *The New Selling IQ: Combining the Power of Buyer-Seller Intelligence to Optimize Results!* Published by the author. Copyright held by The Learning Outsource Group.
11. Ward, Kim D. (2016). *The New Selling IQ: Combining the Power of Buyer-Seller Intelligence to Optimize Results!* Published by the author. Copyright held by The Learning Outsource Group.
12. Quelch, John. (2007). How to Avoid the Commodity Trap. *Harvard Business Review*. Retrieved at https://hbr.org/2007/12/how-to-avoid-the-commodity-tra.
13. Retrieved at https://www.chevronwithtechron.com/fuels.
14. Humphreys, Michael A. and Michael R. Williams. (1996). Exploring the Relative Effects of Salesperson Interpersonal Process Attributes and Technical Product Attributes on Customer Satisfaction. *Journal of Personal Selling & Sales Management, 16*(3): 47–57.
15. Deeter-Schmelz, Dawn R. and Rosemary Ramsey. (1995). A Conceptualization of the Functions and Roles of Formalized Selling and Buying Teams. *Journal of Personal Selling & Sales Management, 15*(2): 47–60.
16. Ward, Kim D. (2016). *The New Selling IQ: Combining the Power of Buyer-Seller Intelligence to Optimize Results!* Published by the author. Copyright held by The Learning Outsource Group.
17. Kantak, Donna Massey, Charles M. Futrell, and Jeffrey K. Sager. (1992). Job Satisfaction and Life Satisfaction in a Sales Force. *Journal of Personal Selling & Sales Management, 12*(1): 1–7.
18. Agarwal, Sanjeev and R. Kenneth Teas. (2001). Perceived Value: Mediating Role of Perceived Risk. *Journal of Marketing Theory and Practice, 9*(4): 1–14.
19. Dalal, Nemil. (2016). The Space Shuttle Challenger Explosion and the O-Ring. *Priceonomics*. Retrieved at https://priceonomics.com/the-space-shuttle-challenger-explosion-and-the-o/
20. Kelleher, Kevin. (2018). Prolonged Exposure to Heat is Making Takata Airbags Explode During a Crash, Prompting Recall. *Fortune.com*. Retrieved at http://fortune.com/2018/08/29/takata-airbags-recall-exploding-extreme-heat/
21. Agarwal, Sanjeev and R. Kenneth Teas. (2001). Perceived Value: Mediating Role of Perceived Risk. *Journal of Marketing Theory and Practice, 9*(4): 1–14.
22. Ward, Kim D. (2016). *The New Selling IQ: Combining the Power of Buyer-Seller Intelligence to Optimize Results!* Published by the author. Copyright held by The Learning Outsource Group.

Chapter 3

1. Erickson, T. J. (2008). Business Basics—Communication and the Language of Business. In T. J. Erickson, *Plugged In: The Generation Y Guide to Thriving at Work* (pp. 215–228). Boston, MA: Harvard Business School Publishing.
2. Rapp, A., D.G. Bachrach, N. Panagopoulos, and J. Ogilvie. (2014). Salespeople as Knowledge Brokers: A Review and Critique of the Challenger Sales Model. *Journal of Personal Selling and Sales Management, 34*(4): 245–259.
3. Many industry and academic studies suggest the dynamic nature of the sales environment at many levels. *See* Bush, Victoria, Alan J. Bush, Jared Oakley, and John E. Cicala. (2017). The Sales Profession as a Subculture: Implications for Ethical Decision Making. *Journal of Business Ethics, 142*(3): 549–565; Schoenfelder, Thomas (2017). How to Hire Top-Performing Salespeople in an Evolving Sales Environment. *Workforce, 96*(6), 28–29.; Hawes, Jon M., Anne K. Rich, and Scott M. Widmier. (2004). Assessing the Development of the Sales Profession. *Journal of Personal Selling & Sales Management, 24*(1): 27–37.
4. Chambers, O. (1992). *My Utmost for His Highest*. Grand Rapids: Discovery House Publishers.
5. Freidson, E. (2001). *Professionalism: The Third Logic*. Chicago: The University of Chicago Press.
6. Tanner John F., Christophe Fournier, Jorge A. Wise, Sandrine Hollet, and Juliet Poujol. (2008). Executives' Perspectives of the Changing Role of the Sales Profession: Views from France, the United States, and Mexico. *The Journal of Business & Industrial Marketing, 14*(1), 193–202.
7. Churchill, Gilbert A. Jr., Neil M. Ford, Steven W. Hartley, and Orville C. Walker. Jr. (1985). The Determinants of Salesperson Performance: A Meta-Analysis. *Journal of Marketing Research, 22*(May): 103–118.
8. Bradberry, Travis & Jean Greaves. (2009). *Emotional Intelligence 2.0*. San Diego, CA: TalentSmart.

9. Goleman, D. (2015). What Makes a Leader. In *HBR's 10 Must Reads: On Emotional Intelligence* (pp. 1–22). Boston, MA: Harvard Business School Publishing Corporation.
10. Mohapel, P. (2015). The Quick Emotional Intelligence Self-Assessment. CA, USA. Retrieved May 24, 2019, from https://msmu.campuslabs.com/engage/organization/mountsync/documents/view/943012
11. Rozell, Elizabeth J., Charles E. Pettijohn, and R. Stephen Parker. (2006). Emotional Intelligence and Dispositional Affectivity as Predictors of Performance in Salespeople. *Journal of Marketing Theory & Practice, 14*(2): 113–124.
12. Rozell, Elizabeth J., Charles E. Pettijohn, and R. Stephen Parker. (2006). Emotional Intelligence and Dispositional Affectivity as Predictors of Performance in Salespeople. *Journal of Marketing Theory & Practice, 14*(2), 113–124.
13. Bajracharya, S. (2018, January 7). Why Is Non-verbal Communication Important? *Businesstopia*. Retrieved at https://www.businesstopia.net/communication/why-non-verbal-communication-important.
14. Matsumoto, David and Hyi Sung Hwang. (2011, May). Reading Facial Experssions of Emotion. *Psychological Science Agenda, 25*(5). Retrieved at https://www.apa.org/science/about/psa/2011/05/index.
15. Coleman, Erin, R. L. (2016, October 30). *The Top 7 Health Benefits of Smiling*. Retrieved at United https://benefitsbridge.unitedconcordia.com/top-7-health-benefits-smiling/.
16. Sales experts and researchers agree on the importance of listening. A couple of examples of research that support this include Hutcheson, Susanna K. (2003). *American Salesman*. 48(2): 28–30 and Drollinger, Tanya, Lucette B. Comer. (2013). Salesperson's Listening Ability as an Antecedent to Relationship Selling. *Journal of Business & Industrial Marketing, 28*(1): 50–59.
17. Drollinger, Tanya and Lucette B. Comer. (2013). Salesperson's Listening Ability as an Antecedent to Relationship Selling. *Journal of Business & Industrial Marketing, 28*(1): 50–59. doi:10.1108/08858621311285714
18. Leimbach, M. (2016). Sales Versatility: Connecting with Customers Every Time. *American Salesman, 61*(8): 21–25.
19. Merrill, David and Roger Reid. (1981). *Personal Styles and Effective Performance*. Taylor & Francis.
20. Roman, Sergio and Rocio Rodriguez. (2015). The Influence of Sales Force Technology Use on Outcome Performance. *Journal of Business & Industrial Marketing, 30*(6): 771–783.
21. Brooks, C. (2015, June 12). 10 Distractions That Kill Workplace Productivity. *Business News Daily*. Retrieved at https://www.businessnewsdaily.com/8098-distractions-kiling-productivity.html
22. Velocify.com. (2012). Text Messaging for Better Sales Conversion. *Velocify*. Retrieved at pages.velocify.com/rs/leads360/.../Text-Messaging-for-Better-Sales-Conversion.pdf
23. Renahan, M. (2018, October 19). The Ideal Length of a Sales Email, Based on 40 Million Emails. *Hubspot*. Retrieved at https://blog.hubspot.com/sales/ideal-length-sales-email

Chapter 4

1. Patterson, Laura. (2018). Want More Customers? Get Quality Referrals from Existing Customers. *Entrepreneur*. Retrieved at http://entm.ag/ezj.
2. Reichheld, Frederick F. (2003). The One Number You Need to Grow. *Harvard Business Review. 81*(12): 46–54. Retrieved at http://search.ebscohost.com/login.aspx?direct=true&db=bth&AN=11587407&site=ehost-live&scope=site.
3. Blanco, Octavio. (2019). Mad About Robocalls? *Consumer Reports. 84*(5): 22–31. Retrieved at http://search.ebscohost.com/login.aspx?direct=true&db=bth&AN=135408463&site=ehost-live&scope=site.
4. Bernard, Tara Siegel. (2018). Yes, Those Calls You're Ignoring Are Increasing. *New York Times*: A1. Retrieved at https://www.nytimes.com/2018/05/06/your-money/robocalls-rise-illegal.html
5. Sobczak, Art. (2013). *Smart Calling: Eliminate the Fear, Failure, and Rejection from Cold Calling, 2nd Edition*. Hoboken, New Jersey: John Wiley & Sons.
6. Innovation for Marketers by Marketers. (2016). CRM Magazine, 20(6): WP21. Retrieved at http://search.ebscohost.com/login.aspx?direct=true&db=bth&AN=115880407&site=ehost-live&scope=site.
7. Innovation for Marketers by Marketers. (2016). CRM Magazine, 20(6): WP21. Retrieved at http://search.ebscohost.com/login.aspx?direct=true&db=bth&AN=115880407&site=ehost-live&scope=site.

8. Kulbyte, Toma. (2019). 10 Ways to Manage Your Sales Pipeline. *SuperOffice Blog*. Retrieved at https://www.superoffice.com/blog/sales-pipeline-management-tips; Jordan, Jason, and Robert Kelly. (2015). Companies with a Formal Sales Process Generate More Revenue. *Harvard Business Review Digital Articles*. Retrieved at http://search.ebscohost.com/login.aspx?direct=true&db=bth&AN=118648204&site=ehost-live&scope=site.

9. Infographic – The Best Day and Time to Make a Business Call. (2017). *CallHippo*. Retrieved at https://callhippo.com/seo/best-day-time-make-business-call

10. Belgray, Laura. (2019). Here's a Genius Method for Writing Emails That People Always Open. *Money* 48(5): 20–21. Retrieved at http://search.ebscohost.com/login.aspx?direct=true&db=bth&AN=136489629&site=ehost-live&scope=site; Sahni, Navdeep S., S. Christian Wheeler, and Pradeep Chintagunta. (2018). Personalization in Email Marketing: The Role of Noninformative Advertising Content. *Marketing Science* 37(2): 236–58. doi:10.1287/mksc.2017.1066; and

11. Offenberger, Brian. (2017). How to Write Sales Emails That Get Response. *SDM: Security Distributing & Marketing* 47(11): 48. Retrieved at http://search.ebscohost.com/login.aspx?direct=true&db=bth&AN=125916422&site=ehost-live&scope=site.

Chapter 5

1. Covey, S. R. (2004). *The 7 Habits of Highly Effective People: Powerful Lessons in Personal Change*. Simon and Schuster.

2. Saxe, R., & Weitz, B. A. (1982). The SOCO Scale: A Measure of the Customer Orientation of Salespeople. *Journal of Marketing Research*, 19(3), 343–351.

3. Covey, S. R., & Merrill, R. R. (2006). *The Speed of Trust: The One Thing That Changes Everything*. Simon and Schuster.

4. U.S. Securities and Exchange Commission Filings and Forms. Retrieved at www.sec.gov and www.sec.gov/edgar.shtml.

5. Cisco Systems, Inc. Form 10-Q. Retrieved at www.sec.gov/archives/edgar and https://www.sec.gov/Archives/edgar/data/858877/000085887718000015/a10qq1fy19.htm.

6. E&J Gallo Winery Announces Deal with Constellation Brands. Retrieved at http://www.gallo.com/press/2019-04-03-e-j-gallo-winery-announces-deal-with-constellation-brands

7. Marketing Technology Landscape Supergraphic (2017). Martech 5000. Retrieved at https://chiefmartec.com/2017/05/marketing-techniology-landscape-supergraphic-2017/

8. Scheibehenne, B., Greifeneder, R., & Todd, P. M. (2010). Can There Ever Be Too Many Options? A Meta-Analytic Review of Choice Overload. *Journal of Consumer Research*, 37(3): 409–425.

9. Rackham, N. (1988). *SPIN Selling Situation · Problem · Implication · Need-Payoff*. New York: McGraw-Hill.

10. Miller, R. B., Heiman, S. E., Sanchez, D., & Tuleja, T. (2004). *The New Strategic Selling: The Unique Sales System Proven Successful By the World's Best Companies*. Kogan Page Publishers.

11. Rapp, Adam, Raj Agnihotri, & Thomas L. Baker. (2011). Conceptualizing Salesperson Competitive Intelligence: An Individual-Level Perspective, *Journal of Personal Selling & Sales Management*, 31(2): 141–155.

12. Cespedes, F. V., Dougherty, J. P., & Skinner III, B. S. (2013). How to Identify the Best Customers for Your Business. *MIT Sloan Management Review*, 54(2): 53.

13. Cope, K. (2012). Seeing the Big Picture: Business Acumen To Build Your Credibility, Career, and Company. Austin, Texas: Greenleaf Book Group.

14. Palmatier, R. W., Scheer, L. K., Evans, K. R., & Arnold, T. J. (2008). Achieving Relationship Marketing Effectiveness in Business-To-Business Exchanges. *Journal of the Academy of Marketing Science*, 36(2): 174–190.

15. Miller, R. B., Heiman, S. E., & Tuleja, T. (2005). *The New Conceptual Selling: The Most Effective sand Proven Method For Face-To-Face Sales Planning*. Warner Business Books.

16. Dwyer, F. R., Schurr, P. H., & Oh, S. (1987). Developing Buyer-Seller Relationships. *Journal of Marketing*, 51(2): 11–27.

Chapter 6

1. Campbell, Kim Sydow, Lenita Davis, and Lauren Skinner. (2006). Rapport Management During the Exploration Phase of the Salesperson–Customer Relationship." *Journal of Personal Selling & Sales Management*, 26(4): 359–70. doi:10.2753/PSS0885-3134260403.

2. Orlob. (2016). Talk Less, Listen More. Do You Know the Golden Talk vs. Listening Ratio? *Saleshacker.com*. Retrieved at https://www.saleshacker.com/sales-ratio-talk-vs-listening/.

3. Witherill. (2018). Sales Discovery Process and the Power of Good Questions. Retrieved at https://liston.io/articles/sales-discovery-process/.

4. Jones, Eli, Larry Chonko, Fern Jones, and Carl Stevens. (2012). *Selling ASAP: Art, Science, Agility, Performance*. Baton Rouge: LSU Press.

5. Rackham, Neil. (1988). *SPIN Selling: Situation Problem Implication Need-Payoff*. New York: McGraw-Hill.

6. Kolowich, Lindsay. (2018). How to Write a Great Value Proposition. *Hubspot*. Retrieved from https://blog.hubspot.com/marketing/write-value-proposition.

7. Kaski, Timo, Ari Alamäki, and Ellen Bolman Pullins. (2019). Fostering Collaborative Mind-Sets Among Customers: A Transformative Learning Approach. *Journal of Personal Selling & Sales Management*, 39(1): 42–59. doi:10.1080/08853134.2018.1489727.

8. Karaman, Jason. (2017). 25 Engaging and Strategic Discovery Questions. Retrieved at https://expertcaller.com/25-engaging-and-strategic-discovery-questions.

9. Schultz, Mike. 21 Powerful, Open-Ended Sales Questions. *RAIN Group*. Retrieved at https://www.rainsalestraining.com/blog/21-powerful-open-ended-sales-questions.

10. Vision Group. How to Be Effective in Sales Using a 3 Legged Approach.

11. Retrieved at http://www.visiongroupmn.com/effective-sales.htm.

Chapter 7

1. Fisher, J. L., & Harris, M. B. (1973). Effect of Note Taking and Review on Recall. *Journal of Educational Psychology*, 65(3): 321–325.

2. Lester, M. (1998). COMMUNICATION: Communicating Technical Ideas Persuasively. *Journal of Management in Engineering*, 14(3): 17–19.

3. Aarikka-Stenroos, L., & Jaakkola, E. (2012). Value Co-Creation in Knowledge Intensive Business Services: A Dyadic Perspective on the Joint Problem-Solving Process. *Industrial Marketing Management*, 41(1): 15–26.

4. Baumann, J., & Le Meunier-FitzHugh, K. (2015). Making Value Co-Creation a Reality–Exploring the Co-Creative Value Processes in Customer–Salesperson Interaction. *Journal of Marketing Management*, 31(3–4): 289–316.

5. Panagopoulos, N. G., Rapp, A. A., & Ogilvie, J. L. (2017). Salesperson Solution Involvement and Sales Performance: The Contingent Role of Supplier Firm and Customer–Supplier Relationship Characteristics. *Journal of Marketing*, 81(4): 144–164.

6. Retrieved at https://www.salesforce.com/products/cpq/solutions/.

7. Retrieved at https://blog.hubspot.com/sales/phrases-signal-prospect-is-ready-to-buy.

8. Echchakoui, S. (2016). Relationship Between Sales Force Reputation and Customer Behavior: Role of Experiential Value Added by Sales Force. *Journal of Retailing and Consumer Services*, 28: 54–66.

9. Sherman, Stephanie G. and V. Clayton Sherman. (1996). *Make Yourself Memorable*. New York: AMACOM.

10. Verbeke, W. J., Belschak, F. D., Bakker, A. B., & Dietz, B. (2008). When Intelligence Is (Dys) Functional for Achieving Sales Performance. *Journal of Marketing*, 72(4): 44–57.

11. Lussier, B., Grégoire, Y., & Vachon, M. A. (2017). The Role of Humor Usage on Creativity, Trust and Performance in Business Relationships: An Analysis of the Salesperson-Customer Dyad. *Industrial Marketing Management*, 65:168–181.

12. Retrieved at https://www.panopto.com/panopto-for-business/.

13. Kahneman, D., Knetsch, J. L., & Thaler, R. H. (1991). Anomalies: The Endowment Effect, Loss Aversion, and Status Quo Bias. *Journal of Economic Perspectives*, 5(1): 193–206.

14. Hinterhuber, A., & Snelgrove, T. C. (Eds.). (2016). *Value First Then Price: Quantifying Value in Business to Business Markets from the Perspective of Both Buyers and Sellers*. Taylor & Francis.

Chapter 8

1. Urbaniak, Anthony "Objections: A Natural Part of the Sales Process" American Salesman 60, no.2 2015, pp 13–16

2. Reilly, Tom, "Why Do you Cut Prices?", Industrial Distribution, June 2003, pg 72

3. Sydow Campbell, Kim and Davis, Lenita, "The Sociolinguistic Basis of Managing Rapport When Overcoming Buying Objections, Journal of Business Communication, January 2006, 43–66

4. Rockwood, Mike "Desperately Seeking Objections" Electrical Wholesaling 97, no 5, 2016, pp25–26

5. Think Like a Consumer to Make Buying From You a Cinch, Selling November 2004, pg 8

6. Singh, Sunil, Marinova, Datelina, Singh, Jagdip, and Evans, Kenneth R., "Customer query handling in sales interactions." Journal of the Academy of Marketing Science 46, no. 5 (2018): 837–856.

7. Arndt, Aaron, Evans, Kenneth, Landry, Timothy D., Mady, Sarah, and Pongpatipat, Chatdanai, "The impact of salesperson credibility-building statements on later stages of the sales encounter." Journal of Personal Selling & Sales Management 34, no. 1 (2014): 19–32.

8. Zboia, James, Clark, Ronald A., and Haytko, Diana L., "An Offer You Can't Refuse: Consumer Perceptions of Sales Pressure," Journal of the Academy of Marketing Science 44, no. 6, November 2016, pp 806–21

9. Brownell, Eleanor, "How to Make Yourself Memorable" American Salesman 55, no 3 March 2010 pp 24–28

10. Anaza, Nwamaka A. and Rutherford, Brian, "Increasing Business-to-Business Buyer Word-of-Mouth and Share-of-Purchase" Journal of Business and Industrial Marketing 29, no 5, 2014, pp427–437

Chapter 9

1. Shell, Richard G. (2019). *Bargaining for Advantage: Negotiation Strategies for Reasonable People*. 3rd ed. London: Penguin Books.

2. Bls.gov. (2017). Table A-13. Employed and Unemployed Persons by Occupation, Not Seasonally Adjusted. Retrieved at https://www.bls.gov/news.release/empsit.t13.htm.

3. Pruitt, D. (1981). *Negotiation Behavior*. New York: Academic Press, p. 1.

4. Proctor & Gamble (2012). *P&G Completes Sale of Pringles to Kellogg*. Retrieved at https://news.pg.com/press-release/pg-corporate-announcements/pg-completes-sale-pringles-kellogg.

5. See the article by Terlep, Sharon and Sarah Nassauer. (2016). Wal-Mart and P&G: A $10 Billion Marriage Under Strain. *The Wall Street Journal*. Retrieved at https://www.wsj.com/articles/wal-mart-and-p-g-a-10-billion-marriage-under-strain-1465948431.

6. For an elaboration on complex pie-sharing concerns, see Jap, S. D. (2001). "Pie Sharing" in Complex Collaboration Contexts. *Journal of Marketing Research*, 38(1): 86–99.

7. For an elaboration on complex pie-expansion concerns, see Jap, S. D. (1999). Pie-Expansion Efforts: Collaboration Processes in Buyer-Supplier Relationships. *Journal of Marketing Research*, 36(4): 461–475.

8. These six foundational domains are partial adaptions of the six foundations advocated by G. Richard Shell, which include bargaining styles, goals and expectations, authoritative norms and standards, relationships, the other party's interests, and leverage. For an elaboration, see Shell, Richard G. (2019). *Bargaining for Advantage: Negotiation Strategies for Reasonable People*. 3rd ed. London: Penguin Books.

9. For more on the leadership styles derived from these two dimensions, see Blake, R., & J. Mouton. (1964). *The Managerial Grid: The Key to Leadership Excellence*. Houston: Gulf Publishing Co.

10. See Thomas, K. W. (1971). *Conflict-Handling Modes in Interdepartmental Relations*. Unpublished doctoral dissertation. Purdue University.

11. For a more recently refined version and summary of the instrument, see Xiacom. (2008). *Thomas-Kilmann Conflict Mode Instrument*. Available at: https://www.organizationimpact.com/wp-content/uploads/2016/08/TKI_Sample_Report.pdf

12. The TKI instrument is summarized in Xiacom. (2008). *Thomas-Kilmann Conflict Mode Instrument*. Available at: https://www.organizationimpact.com/wp-content/uploads/2016/08/TKI_Sample_Report.pdf

13. For an adaption of the TKI for a negotiating context, see Appendix A, pp. 204–208 in Shell, Richard G. (2019). *Bargaining for Advantage: Negotiation Strategies for Reasonable People*. 3rd ed. London: Penguin Books.

14. For a review of the literature on the five factors, see McCrae, R. & P. Costa. (2008). Empirical and Theoretical Status of the Five-Factor Model of Personality Traits. *The SAGE Handbook of Personality Theory and Assessment: Volume 1 — Personality Theories and Models* (Vol. 1, pp. 273–294). London: SAGE Publications Ltd. doi: 10.4135/9781849200462.n13

15. Research on the ambivert advantage can be found in Grant, A. (2013). Rethinking the Extraverted Sales Ideal: The Ambivert Advantage. *Psychological Science*, 24(6): 1024–1030.

16. Clark & Watson (2008) proposed using the label negative emotionality to better capture the essence of the neurotism factor. For more, see Clark, Lee Anna and David Watson. (2008). An Organizing Paradigm for Trait Psychology. *Handbook of Personality: Theory and Research*, pp. 265–86.

17. For a discussion on the importance of developing optimistic, but attainable goals and expectations. see Shell, Richard G. (2019). *Bargaining for Advantage: Negotiation Strategies for Reasonable People*. 3rd ed. London: Penguin Books.

18. Kahneman and Tversky (1979) proposed Prospect Theory, which later won the Nobel Prize in Economics in 2002. For more on Prospect Theory, see Kahneman, Daniel and Amos Tversky. (1979). Prospect Theory: An Analysis of Decision under Risk. *Econometrica*, 47(2): 263–91. Retrieved at http://www.jstor.org/stable/1914185

19. For a review of the early research on Stacy Adams's Equity Theory, see Adams, Stacy J. and Sara Freedman. (1976). Equity Theory Revisited: Comments and Annotated Bibliography. In *Advances in Experimental Social Psychology*, 43–90. Elsevier.

20. For more about the application of equity theory in B2B exchanges, see Huppertz, John W., Sidney J. Arenson, and Richard H. Evans. (1978). An Application of Equity Theory to Buyer-Seller Exchange Situations. *Journal of Marketing Research*, 15(2): 250–60.

21. For an elaboration on the importance of trust in buyer-seller relationships, see Doney, Patricia M. and Joseph P. Cannon. (1997). An Examination of the Nature of Trust in Buyer-Seller Relationships. *Journal of Marketing*, 61(2): 35–51.

22. For a research supporting the importance of proposing mutually beneficial solutions and sharing information to helping salespeople forge stronger relationship with business customers, see Hunter, Gary K. and William D. Perreault, Jr. (2007). Making Sales Technology Effective. *Journal of Marketing*, 71(1): 16–34.

23. For a more general discussion of trust in interpersonal relationships, see Lewis, J. David, and Andrew Weigert. (1985). Trust as a Social Reality. *Social Forces*, 63(4): 967–85.

24. This definition for market-driven sales planning was adapted from Hunter, Gary K. (2014). Customer Business Development: Identifying and Responding to Buyer-Implied Information Preferences. *Industrial Marketing Management*, 43(7): 1204–15.

Chapter 10

1. Doran, G. T. (1981). There's a S.M.A.R.T. Way to Write Management's Goals and Objectives. *Management Review*, 70(11): 35–36.

2. Retrieved at https://en.wikipedia.org/wiki/SMART_criteria.

3. Doran, G. T. (1981). There's a S.M.A.R.T. Way to Write Management's Goals and Objectives. *Management Review*, 70(11): 35–36.

4. Vroom, Victor Harold. (1964). *Work and Motivation*. New York: Wiley, Vol. 54.

5. Porter, Michael E. (1996). What Is Strategy? *Harvard Business Review*, 74.

6. Retrieved at https://en.wikipedia.org/wiki/Pareto_principle

7. This will, of course, will vary based on the type of sales job or industry.

8. Crosby, Lawrence A., Kenneth R. Evans, and Deborah, Cowles. (1990). Relationship Quality in Services Selling: An Interpersonal Influence Perspective. *Journal of Marketing*, 54(3): 68–81.

9. Hughes, Douglas E., Joël Le Bon, and Avinash Malshe. (2012). The Marketing–Sales Interface at the Interface: Creating Market-based Capabilities Through Organizational Synergy. *Journal of Personal Selling & Sales Management*, 32(1): 57–72.

10. Sujan, Harish, Barton A. Weitz, and Nirmalya Kumar. (1994). Learning Orientation, Working Smart, and Effective Selling. *Journal of Marketing*, 58(3): 39–52.

11. Vroom, Victor Harold. (1964) *Work and Motivation*. New York: Wiley, Vol. 54.

12. Retrieved at https://www.salesforce.com/crm/

Chapter 11

1. Jones, Eli, Steven P. Brown, Andris A. Zoltners, and Barton A. Weitz. (2005). The Changing Environment of Selling and Sales Management. *Journal of Personal Selling & Sales Management*, 25(2): 105–111.

2. Retrieved at https://www.statista.com/statistics/276703/android-app-releases-worldwide/
3. Slater, Stanley F., and John C. Narver. (1995). Market Orientation and the Learning Organization. *Journal of Marketing*, 59(3): 63–74.
4. Retrieved at https://go.forrester.com/blogs/the-ways-and-means-of-b2b-buyer-journey-maps-were-going-deep-at-forresters-b2b-forum/
5. Retrieved at https://www.forbes.com/sites/ajagrawal/2016/02/15/how-the-digital-age-has-changed-marketing-channels-forever/#184df3f8680a
6. Retrieved at https://www.market-bridge.com/2015/05/11/digital-sales-adapt-or-die/
7. Grayson, K., and R. Martinec. (2004). Consumer Perceptions of Iconicity and Indexicality and Their Influence on Assessments of Authentic Market Offerings. *Journal of Consumer Research*, 31(2): 296–312.
8. Muniz, A. M., and T. C. O'Guinn. (2001) Brand Community. *Journal of Consumer Research*, 27(4): 412–432.
9. Schaefer, A. D., and C. E. Pettijohn. (2006). The Relevance of Authenticity in Personal Selling: Is Genuineness an Asset or Liability? *Journal of Marketing Theory and Practice*, 14(1): 25–35.
10. Beverland, M. B., and F. J. Farrelly. (2009). The Quest for Authenticity in Consumption: Consumers' Purposive Choice of Authentic Cues to Shape Experienced Outcomes. *Journal of Consumer Research*, 36(5): 838–856.
11. Khalsa, M. (1999). *Let's Get Real Or Let's Not Play: The Demise of Dysfunctional Selling and the Advent of Helping Clients Succeed.* Franklin Covey Company.
12. Gross, E., and G. P. Stone. (1964). Embarrassment and the Analysis of Role Requirements. *American Journal of Sociology*, 70(1): 1–15.
13. Retrieved at https://www.mckinsey.com/business-functions/marketing-and-sales/our-insights/the-secret-to-making-it-in-the-digital-sales-world
14. Retrieved at https://www.mckinsey.com/business-functions/marketing-and-sales/our-insights/do-you-really-understand-how-your-business-customers-buy
15. Retrieved at https://www.businesswire.com/news/home/20140915006303/en/New-IDC-Study-Reveals-Senior-Influential-B2B
16. Retrieved at https://www.destinationcrm.com/Articles/Editorial/Magazine-Features/Tips-for-Maximizing-CRM-Investments-117856.aspx
17. Retrieved at https://cdn2.hubspot.net/hubfs/53/HubSpot-State-of-Inbound-Report-2016.pdf
18. Retrieved at https://www.talentcupboard.com/social-media/social-media-calendar/
19. Retrieved at https://www.crystalknows.com/
20. Bob Nadeau from CEB Corporate Executive Board, Sales Research Merrill Adamson.

Chapter 12

1. For an early discussion on organizing a key account sales structure see Stevenson, Thomas H., and Albert L. Page. (1979). The Adoption of National Account Marketing by Industrial Firms. *Industrial Marketing Management*, (8)(1): 94–100.
2. For a recent discussion on Strategic Account Management, see Bradford, Kevin, Goutam N. Challagalla, Gary K. Hunter, and William C. Moncrief. (2012). Strategic Account Management: Conceptualizing, Integrating, and Extending the Domain from Fluid to Dedicated Accounts. *Journal of Personal Selling & Sales Management, 31(1)*: 41–56.
3. For an elaboration of how sales teams serving such accounts are so committed to the mutually beneficial gains, they can be considered as serving roles "embedded" in the customer's organization, see Bradford, Kevin, Steven Brown, Shankar Ganesan, Gary Hunter, Vincent Onyemah, Robert Palmatier, Dominique Rouziès et al. (2010). The Embedded Sales Force: Connecting Buying and Selling Organizations. *Marketing Letters*, 21(3): 239–53.
4. For this definition and more discussion on buying centers see Wesley J. Johnston and Thomas V. Bonoma. The Buying Center: Structure and Interaction Patterns. *Journal of Marketing*, 45(3): 143–156.
5. To better understand how a portfolio of sales technology tools aids a salesperson in producing mutually beneficial proposals to forge better business relationships with strategic accounts, please see Hunter, Gary K., and William D. Perreault, Jr. (2007). Making Sales Technology Effective. *Journal of Marketing*, 71(1): 16–34.
6. For a categorization of customer business development within the broader domain of different types of B2B relationship marketing account management alternatives, see Parvatiyar, Atul, and Jagdish N. Sheth. (2000). The Domain and Conceptual Foundations of Relationship Marketing. In *Handbook of Relationship Marketing*, pp. 3–38. Thousand Oaks: Sage Publications.
7. For this definition and a recent research on Customer Business Development, see Hunter, Gary K. (2014). Customer Business Development: Identifying and Responding to Buyer-Implied Information Preferences. *Industrial Marketing Management*, 43(7): 1204–15.
8. For an extended discussion on differences between individual selling and team selling, see Ahearne, Michael, Scott B. MacKenzie, Philip M. Podsakoff, John E. Mathieu, and Son K. Lam. (2010). The Role of Consensus in Sales Team Performance. *Journal of Marketing Research*, 47(3): 458–69.
9. For early research noting the movement from individual to team selling, see Moon, Mark A., and Gary M. Armstrong. Selling Teams: A Conceptual Framework and Research Agenda. *Journal of Personal Selling & Sales Management*, 14(1): 17–34.
10. For elaboration and management guidance on team membership alternatives see Jones, Eli, Andrea L. Dixon, Lawrence B. Chonko, and Joseph P. Cannon. Key Accounts and Team Selling: A Review, Framework, and Research Agenda. *Journal of Personal Selling & Sales Management*, 25(2): 182–98. For a more recent account, see Bradford, Kevin, Goutam N. Challagalla, Gary K. Hunter, and William C. Moncrief. (2012). Strategic Account Management: Conceptualizing, Integrating, and Extending the Domain from Fluid to Dedicated Accounts." *Journal of Personal Selling & Sales Management*, 31(1): 41–56. The purpose here is to introduce a typical CBD sales team.
11. For an elaboration on typical business procurement process, see Gary K. Hunter, Michele D. Bunn, and William D. Perreault, Jr. (2006). Interrelations Among Key Aspects of the Organizational Procurement Process. *International Journal of Research in Marketing*, 23(2): 155–170.
12. This significant shift associated with dedicating a sales team to a serve the needs of a major customer account is the topic of the Harvard Business School case for negotiating relationships when forming strategic account teams, see James Sebenius and Ellen Knebel. (2000). Tom Muccio: Negotiating the P&G Relationship with Wal-Mart. Harvard Business School Press. At the time, P&G's business with Walmart represented about $350 million in annual revenues. Today, their relationship represents close to $10 billion in annual sales for P&G—and Walmart is its largest strategic account—with reports the current CBD team numbers almost 500 members who are located near Walmart's headquarters in Bentonville, Arkansas.
13. For a discussion on how identification with customers has evolved as a key cultural aspect of contemporary B2B sales organizations, see Donald P. St. Clair, Gary K. Hunter, Philip A. Cola, & Richard J. Boland. (2018). Systems-Savvy Selling, Interpersonal Identification with Customers, and the Sales Manager's Motivational Paradox: A Constructivist Grounded Theory Approach. *Journal of Personal Selling & Sales Management*, 38(4): 391–412.
14. The disbursement of marketing research activities as part of the CBD salesperson's role along with defining the sales roles as merely an element in the promotion mix is discussed in Hunter, Gary K., and William D. Perreault, Jr. (2007). Making Sales Technology Effective. *Journal of Marketing*, 71(1): 16–34.
15. For a discussion on the relationship-forging tasks that CBD salespeople realize from proposing mutually beneficial solutions—and how sales technology tools aid such sales activities, see Gary K. Hunter and William D. Perreault, Jr. (2007). Making Sales Technology Effective. *Journal of Marketing*, 71(1): 16–34.
16. These "what counts" factors are taken from the author's personal records—and intended as a reflection of the breadth of evaluation needed to assess salesperson performance on CBD teams.
17. For an elaboration of research on factors impacting sales team performance see Eli Jones, Andrea L. Dixon, Lawrence B. Chonko, and Joseph P. Cannon. (2005). Key Accounts and Team Selling: A Review, Framework, and Research Agenda. *Journal of Personal Selling & Sales Management*, 25(2): 182–98.
18. While Hunter and Perreault (2007) introduced the term—relationship-forging tasks—subsequent and preceding research and practice builds upon or integrates either explicitly, or implicitly, with the spirit of this concept. For the original reference see Hunter, Gary K. and William D. Perreault, Jr. (2007). Making Sales Technology Effective. *Journal of Marketing*, 71(1): 16–34.
19. For a discussion related to group conflict in team environment, although not specific to sales teams, see Jehn, Karen A. (1995). A Multimethod Examination of the Benefits and Detriments of

Intragroup Conflict. *Administrative Science Quarterly*, 40(2): 256–82. For a discussion of managing conflict ins sales contexts, see Dixon, Andrea L., Jules B. Gassenheimer, and Terri Feldman Barr. (2002). Bridging the Distance Between Us: How Initial Responses to Sales Team Conflict Help Share Core Selling Team Outcomes. *Journal of Personal Selling & Sales Management*, 22(4): 247–57.

20. For this definition and related research on market-driven sales planning, see Hunter, Gary K. (2014). Customer Business Development: Identifying and Responding to Buyer-Implied Information Preferences. *Industrial Marketing Management*, 43(7): 1204–15.

21. For elaboration on these definitions and related research on proposing integrative solutions and sharing marketing expertise, see Hunter, Gary K. and William D. Perreault, Jr. (2007). Making Sales Technology Effective. *Journal of Marketing*, 71(1): 16–34.

22. For this definition and related research on coordinating internal resources, see Hunter, Gary K. (2014). "Customer Business Development: Identifying and Responding to Buyer-Implied Information Preferences," *Industrial Marketing Management*, 43(7): 1204–15.

23. This revenue figure is based on Tide sales in the U.S. ending July 15, 2018 according to Statistica. (2019). Sales of the Leading Liquid Laundry Detergent Brands of the United States in 2018 (in Million U.S. Dollars). Retrieved at https://www.statista.com/statistics/188716/top-liquid-laundry-detergent-brands-in-the-united-states/

Chapter 13

1. Cavico, Frank J., and Bahaudin G. Mujtaba. (2017). Wells Fargo's Fake Accounts Scandal and Its Legal and Ethical Implications for Management. *SAM Advanced Management Journal*, 82(2): 4–19. Retrieved at http://search.ebscohost.com/login.aspx?direct=true&db=bth&AN=123889833&site=ehost-live&scope=site

2. Glazer, Emily. (2019). Wells Fargo Is "Working Hard" to "Rebuild Trust." *Wall Street Journal*.

3. Kubasek, Nancy K., and M. Neil Browne. (1944). Lucien J. Dhooge, Daniel J. Herron, and Linda L. Barkacs (2015). *Dynamic Business Law: The Essentials*. 3rd ed. New York: McGraw-Hill Education.

4. 26 Sales Statistics That Prove Sales Is Changing. *Salesforce.com blog*. Retrieved at https://www.salesforce.com/blog/2017/11/15-sales-statistics.html

5. Wood, John Andy, James S. Boles, Wesley Johnston, and Danny Bellenger. (2008). Buyers' Trust of the Salesperson: An Item-Level Meta-Analysis. *Journal of Personal Selling & Sales Management*, 28(3): 263–83. doi:10.2753/PSS0885-3134280304.

6. Chen, Chien-Chung and Fernando Jaramillo. (2014). The Double-Edged Effects of Emotional Intelligence on the Adaptive Selling–Salesperson-Owned Loyalty Relationship. *Journal of Personal Selling & Sales Management*, 34(1): 33–50. doi:10.1080/08853134.2013.870183.

7. Druskat, Vanessa Urch and Steven B. Wolff. (2001). Building the Emotional Intelligence of Groups. *Harvard Business Review*, 79(3): 80–90.

8. Berenson, Alex. (2007). Merck Agrees to Settle Vioxx Suits for $4.85 Billion. *New York Times*.

9. Randazzo, Sara. (2018). Don't Hang Up—This Is Not a Scam—Lawyers Who Won Marketing-Call Verdict Hit Phones. *Wall Street Journal*, New York, N.Y: A.1.

10. The United States Department of Justice. Retrieved at https://www.justice.gov/criminal-fraud/foreign-corrupt-practices-act

11. Armental, Maria. (2014). Bio-Rad to Pay $55 Million to Settle Foreign Corruption Charges. *Wall Street Journal*. Nov. 3, 2014.

12. Wieczner, Jen. (2018). AppZen Raises $35 Million to Catch Employees Cheating on Expense Reports. *Fortune*. October 30, 2018. Retrieved at http://fortune.com/2018/10/30/appzen-35-million-expense-report.

13. Pinsker, Beth. (2019). Employers Using Robots to Catch Fraud in Expense Reports. *Insurance Journal*. Retrieved at https://www.insurancejournal.com/news/national/2019/03/26/521573.htm

14. Rudegeair, Peter, Emily Glazer, and Coulter Jones. (2018). Wells Fargo Fires Bankers Amid Probe of Dinner Receipts That Were Allegedly Doctored. *Wall Street Journal*. August 30, 2018.

15. Career Builder Blog. Retrieved at http://press.careerbuilder.com/2018-02-01-Office-Romance-Hits-10-Year-Low-According-to-CareerBuilders-Annual-Valentines-Day-Survey

16. Northouse, Peter Guy. (2016). *Leadership: Theory and Practice*. 7th ed. Thousand Oaks, California: Sage.

17. Jaramillo, Fernando, Belén Bande, and Jose Varela. (2015). Servant Leadership and Ethics: A Dyadic Examination of Supervisor Behaviors

and Salesperson Perceptions. *Journal of Personal Selling & Sales Management*, 35(2): 108–24.

18. Van Iddekinge, C. H., Roth, P. L., Raymark, P. H., and Odle-Dusseau, H. N. (2012). The Criterion-Related Validity of Integrity Tests: An Updated Meta-Analysis. *Journal of Applied Psychology*, 97(3): 499–530. doi:10.1037/a0021196

19. Schwepker, Charles H. Jr. (2001). Ethical Climate's Relationship to Job Satisfaction, Organizational Commitment, and Turnover Intention in the Sales Force. *Journal of Business Research*, p. 40.

Chapter 14

1. Viosca, R. Charles and K. Chris Cox. (2014). A Process-Focused Method to Accelerate Sales Skill Development. *Atlantic Marketing Journal*, 3(2): 22–37.

2. Hoover, J. Duane and Carlton Whitehead. (1975). An Experiential-Cognitive Methodology in the First Course in Management: Some Preliminary Results. *Simulation Games and Experiential Learning in Action*. Richard H. Buskirk (ed.), 25–30. Austin: Bureau of Business Research, University of Texas at Austin.

3. Widmier, Scott M., Terry W. Loe, and Gary Selden. (2007). Using Role-Play Competition to Teach Selling Skills and Teamwork. *Marketing Education Review*, 17(1): 69–78.; Loe, Terry W. (2004). *The Instructor's Role-Play Guide*. Mason, OH: Thomason, South-Western Publishing.

4. Bloom, Benjamin, M.D. Engelhart, E.J. Furst, W.H. Hill, and D.R. Krathwohl. (1956). *Taxonomy of Educational Objectives: The Classification of Educational Goals*. Handbook I: Cognitive Doman. New York: David McKay Company.

5. The Learning Pyramid was adapted from Edgar Dale's *Cone of Experience*, which he published in his textbook *Audio-Visual Methods in Teaching* (1946), New York: The Dryden Press. The Learning Pyramid has been used by numerous teaching and consulting groups including the Education Corner. Retrieved at https://www.educationcorner.com/the-learning-pyramid.html

6. Subramony, D., M. Molenda, A. Betrus, and W. Thalheimer. (2014). The Mythical Retention Chart and the Corruption of Dale's Cone of Experience. *Educational Technology*, 54(6): 6–16; Subramony, D., Molenda, M., Betrus, A., and Thalheimer, W. (2014), "Previous Attempts to Debunk the Mythical Retention Chart and Corrupted Dale's Cone." Educational Technology, 54(6): 17–21.; Subramony, D., Molenda, M., Betrus, A., and Thalheimer, W. (2014), "The Good, the Bad, and the Ugly: A Bibliographic Essay on the Corrupted Cone." *Educational Technology*, 54(6): 22–31; Subramony, D., Molenda, M., Betrus, A., and Thalheimer, W. (2014), "Timeline of the Mythical Retention Chart and Corrupted Dale's Cone." *Educational Technology*, 54(6): 31–24.

7. *Broadwell, Martin M. (1969).* «Teaching for learning (XVI)». *wordsfitlyspoken.org. The Gospel Guardian.* Retrieved 11 May 2018.
^ *Curtiss, Paul R.; Warren, Phillip W. (1973). The dynamics of life skills coaching. Life skills series. Prince Albert, Saskatchewan: Training Research and Development Station, Dept. of Manpower and Immigration.* p. 89. OCLC 4489629.
^ *Adams, Linda.* «Learning a new skill is easier said than done». *gordontraining.com. Gordon Training International.* Retrieved 21 May 2011.
^ *Hansen, Alice (2012).* «Trainees and teachers as reflective learners». *In Hansen, Alice; et al. (eds.). Reflective learning and teaching in primary schools. London; Thousand Oaks, CA: Learning Matters; Sage Publications. pp. 32–48 (34).* doi:10.4135/9781526401977. n3. ISBN 9780857257697. OCLC 756592765.
^ Jump up to:a b c *Flower, Joe (January 1999).* «In the mush». *Physician Executive. 25 (1):* 64–66. PMID 10387273.

12. Gabler, Colin B. and Raj Agnihnotri. (2018). Take Two…Action! Using Video Capture Technology to Improve Student Performance. *Journal of the Academy of Business Education*, 19(spring): 95–105; Sellars, David. (2005). *Developing and Role Playing Effective Sales Presentations*. Canada: South Western.

13. Viosca, R. Charles and K. Chris Cox. (2014). A Process-Focused Method to Accelerate Sales Skill Development. *Atlantic Marketing Journal*, 3(2): 22–37.

14. Pascarella, E., and P. Terenzini. (1991). *How College Affects Students*. San Francisco: Jossey-Bass; Pascarella, E., and P. Terenzini. (2005). *How College Affects Students Volume 2: A Third Decade of Research*.

San Francisco:Jossey-Bass; Poitras, Jean, Arnaud Stimec, and Kevin Hill. (2013). Fostering Student Engagement in Negotiation Role Plays. *Negotiation Journal, 29*(4): 439–462.

15. Lazer, Ken. (2016). 5 Ways to Get Into Character. Retrieved at https://www.backstage.com/magazine/article/ways-get-character-7754/. Also see, Hishon, Kerry. Retrieved at https://TheatreArtLife.com and https://www.backstage.com/magazine/article/ways-get-character-7754/

16. Mueller, Pam A., and Daniel M. Oppenheimer. (2014). The Pen Is Mightier than the Keyboard: Advantages of Longhand Over Laptop Note Taking. *Psychological Science, 25*(6): 1159–1168.

17. Third Annual LinkedIn State of Sales Report. (2018). *LinkedIn.* Retrieved AT https://business.linkedin.com/sales-solutions/b2b-sales-strategy-guides/the-state-of-sales-2018/3qc

18. Infopro Learning White Paper "Investing Wisely" part 1; https://www.infoprolearning.com/blog/why-you-need-to-invest-more-on-product-knowledge-training/

19. Ferriss, Timothy. (2007, 2009). *The 4-Hour Workweek.* New York: Harmony Books; Ferris, Timothy. *The 4-Hour Chef.* New York: Houghton Mifflin Harcourt.

20. Several sources cite to the value of reflective learning in improving skills and mastering content, including: Brockbank, Anne and Ian, McGill. (2006). *Facilitating Reflective Learning Through Mentoring & Coaching.* London: Kogan Page Publishers.; Boyd, Evelyn M. and Ann W. Fales. (1983). Reflective Learning. *Journal of Humanistic Psychology, 23*(2): 99–117. doi:10.1177/0022167883232011.; Jasper, Melanie. (2003). *Beginning Reflective Practice.* Cheltenham: Nelson Thornes.; *Rivera Pelayo, Verónica. (2015). Design and Application of Quantified Self Approaches for Reflective Learning in the Workplace. KIT Scientific; Sugerman, Deborah A. (2000). Reflective Learning: Theory and Practice. Kendall Hunt.*

21. Tanner, John F. and Lawrence B. Chonko. (1992). "Avoiding the Guillotine Effect After Video-Taping Role Plays. *Marketing Education Review,* 1(3): 37–41. DOI: 10.1080/10528008.1991.11488334.

Index